Harvard Historical Monographs
LXVIII

*Published under the direction of the Department of History
from the income of the Robert Louis Stroock Fund*

The Irish Parliament and part of Trinity College, from College Green, in the 1790's

Ireland
in the Empire
1688–1770

A History of Ireland
from the Williamite Wars
to the Eve of
the American Revolution

Francis Godwin James

Harvard University Press
Cambridge, Massachusetts
1973

To Barbara

Acknowledgments

Among those who have assisted me in my research and writing I wish to thank especially two colleagues at Tulane who read the original draft and made helpful suggestions concerning both content and style: Professors Aline Taylor and Hugh Rankin. I owe an even greater debt to Professor J. C. Beckett of Queen's University, Belfast, whose thoughtful and detailed comments proved invaluable. Finally, I wish to express my thanks to the Social Science Research Council for two summer grants and to the Tulane Council on Research for a semester grant. These grants made possible the travel and research without which the study could not have been undertaken.

I wish also to thank the Trustees of the British Museum for permission to reproduce James Malton's picture of the Parliament House in Dublin and the Department of Manuscripts of the British Museum for permission to quote from the Hardwicke and Southwell Papers; the Governors of Christ Church, Oxford, for permission to quote from the Wake Manuscripts; Gill and Macmillan Ltd. for permission to quote from *The Hidden Ireland* by Daniel Corkery; the English Public Record Office for permission to quote from the State Papers, Ireland; and the Public Record Office of Ireland for permission to quote from the Calendar of Departmental Correspondence, vols. I–III, and the Calendar of Miscellaneous Papers Prior to 1760.

Contents

Tables

Maps

Ireland in the Empire, 1688–1770

Introduction

In 1688 Ireland's place in the British Empire was second only to that of England itself. Though most writers on Irish, British, and colonial history recognized this fact, implicitly if not outright, with few exceptions, historians devote only passing attention to Ireland's importance to the empire during the first two-thirds of the eighteenth century. Yet during that period Ireland had a significant share in imperial defense, Irish trade and communications with the colonies expanded rapidly, and Irish constitutional struggles paralleled and to a degree influenced those in the colonies. When George III ascended the throne Ireland still ranked second among all the political units under his dominion in population, in revenue and expenditures, and in volume of trade.

Modern estimates put the population of England and Wales in 1760 at 6,500,000 to 6,750,000, of the British American colonies at about 2,000,000, and of Ireland at approximately 3,000,000.[1] The inhabitants of Ireland accounted for nearly a quarter of all of King George's subjects, excluding the people under the control of the East India Company. Dublin, already with a population of 100,000, had attained a size no other English-speaking city except London would reach until the nineteenth century. When, in 1742, the mayor-elect of Dublin stated that he was "entering upon the office of Chief

[1] Steven Watson, *The Reign of George III, 1760–1815* (Oxford, Clarendon Press, 1960), p. 10; K. H. Connell, *The Population of Ireland* (Oxford, 1950), p. 25; Evarts B. Green and Virginia Harrington, *American Population before the Federal Census of 1790* (New York, Columbia University Press, 1932), p. 6; Frank W. Pitman, *The Development of the British West Indies* (New Haven, Yale University Press, 1917), Appendix I.

Magistrate of one of the largest cities of Europe," [2] he spoke
the truth. The public revenue of Ireland (about £700,000
p.a.) was larger than that of any single colony, in fact nearly
as large as the total revenue of the United States federal government in 1792.[3] As for overseas commerce, on the eve of the
American Revolution Ireland's exports and imports were both
roughly equal to those of all thirteen rebelling colonies combined.[4]

One reason for Ireland's importance in the age of mercantilism was its location. Before the opening up of the North
Atlantic, Ireland had lain on the periphery of the known
world; in the eighteenth century Irish ports opened onto
one of the main arteries of trade. The change had political
and military as well as economic implications. For England's
medieval rulers the conquest of Ireland represented more an
adventure than a set policy. In Stuart and Hanoverian times,
when England aspired to be a commercial and colonial power,
control of Ireland became a necessity.

Another factor contributing to Ireland's significance to the
Old Empire was that until the close of the eighteenth century

[2] *The Dublin Journal*, Oct. 2, 1742. Dublin had about 70,000 persons
in the early 1680's; there was a decline in the next decade, followed by an
increase. R. A. Butlin, "The Population of Dublin in the Late Seventeenth Century," *Irish Geography*, V (1959), 51–64. According to one
modern estimate Dublin in the eighteenth century was tied in size with
Rome and Amsterdam (each about 150,000) for fifth place among the
cities of Europe; only London, Paris, Naples, and Vienna were larger.
The Rand McNally Atlas of World History, ed. R. R. Palmer (Chicago,
Rand McNally and Company, 1957), p. 194.

[3] T. J. Kiernan, *The Financial Administration of Ireland to 1817*
(London, 1930), p. 160. The total revenue of the United States government in 1792 was $3,670,000 or under £800,000. U.S. Department of Com-
merce, Bureau of the Census, *Historical Statistics of the United States,
Colonial Times to 1957* (Washington, Government Printing Office, 1960),
p. 711.

[4] The exports of the thirteen colonies in 1769 were valued at £2,852,000,
imports at £2,623,000 (figures to nearest thousand, as are all subsequent
figures unless otherwise indicated). *Historical Statistics of the U.S.*, p. 766.
During the three-year period 1770–1772 Irish exports averaged £3,303,000
p. a. and imports £2,416,000. Thomas Newenham, *A View of the Natural,
Political and Commercial Circumstances of Ireland* (London, 1809), Appendix XII, p. 15.

the island produced an agricultural surplus. The disastrous famine of the 1840's must not be permitted to obscure Ireland's earlier role as a major exporter of salted meat and dairy products. Irish agriculture likewise provided raw materials for clothing: wool, leather, and flax. The first two were primarily consumed at home, but the last afforded the basis for a growing linen industry with large-scale exports. In short, a number of geographical considerations help to explain Ireland's importance to Britain and its empire before the American Revolution: its proximity to England, its strategic position astride the Atlantic shipping lanes, and its surplus of provisions for the colonial market.

Not until recently has the history of eighteenth-century Ireland been subjected to the kind of reexamination that began in Amercian history with the work of George Louis Beer, Herbert L. Osgood, and Charles M. Andrews.[5] Since 1940 a number of articles and monographs have treated many aspects of Irish life in the eighteenth century. The emphasis of modern scholars, as of earlier authors like James A. Froude and W. E. H. Lecky, has been principally on the latter part of the century.[6] Virtually all historians consider the Treaty of Limerick as marking an eclipse of Ireland's importance that lasted at least to the time of Henry Flood and Henry Grattan. Developments between 1688 and the 1760's have received

[5] George L. Beer, *British Colonial Policy, 1754–1765* (New York, Macmillan Co., 1907), and *The Old Colonial System, 1660–1754*, 2 vols. (New York, Macmillan Co., 1912); Herbert L. Osgood, *The American Colonies in the Eighteenth Century*, 4 vols. (New York, Columbia University Press, 1924); Charles M. Andrews, *The Colonial Period of American History*, 4 vols. (New Haven, Yale University Press, 1934–1938).

[6] James A. Froude, in *The English in Ireland in the Eighteenth Century*, 3 vols. (London, 1872–1874), devotes about a third of his work to the period before 1760. W. E. H. Lecky, in *Ireland in the Eighteenth Century*, 5 vols. (London, 1892), devotes only about a fifth. Two bibliographical essays provide a guide to recent writings on Ireland: Helen F. Mulvey, "Modern Irish History since 1940: A Bibliographical Survey (1600–1922)," in *Changing Views on British History: Essays on Historical Writing since 1939*, ed. Elizabeth Chapin Furber (Cambridge, Mass., 1966), pp. 345–378; and Herbert Butterfield, "Eighteenth-Century Ireland," *Irish Historical Studies*, XV (1966–1967), 376–390.

little study. Aside from specialized works no modern book
deals specifically with that period.[7] The lack of such a book
not only leaves a gap in Irish history, it also represents a
serious void in any comprehensive picture of the Old Empire.[8]
The present study, based on contemporary materials, but
attempting to incorporate the findings and interpretations of
recent scholars, is designed to meet this need.

[7] Three valuable but specialized studies cover most or all of the period
1688–1770: J. C. Beckett, *Protestant Dissent in Ireland, 1685–1780* (London,
1948); L. M. Cullen, *Anglo-Irish Trade 1660–1800* (Manchester, 1968);
Robert Munter, *The Irish Newspaper, 1685–1760* (Cambridge, 1967).

[8] The only extensive treatment of Ireland in any general study of the
empire before 1763 is that of Lawrence H. Gipson, *The British Empire
before the American Revolution*, 9 vols. (vols. I–III, Caldwell, Idaho, 1936,
vols. IV–IX, New York, 1939–1956), I, Chap. VII.

I

The Establishment
of the
Protestant Ascendancy

To begin a study of Ireland in 1688 is to plunge *in medias res*, for the Irish war of 1689–1691 represents the culmination of struggles that were over a century old. In one sense, the origins of the conflict may be traced back to Strongbow's invasion of Ireland in the twelfth century. Yet the Anglo-Norman penetration of medieval Ireland did not in itself inevitably mean English conquest. Under certain circumstances the Anglo-Norman invaders might have been expelled, or they might have themselves created an Ireland as independent of England as Norman England was of France. Whatever its causes, Ireland's failure to achieve unity, either under its native kings or under the Anglo-Norman lords, must be considered the primary reason for its eventual conquest. Scotland, geographically more vulnerable to English invasion and control, was able to pursue a different course. Furthermore the English conquest in itself, as it took place in late medieval and early Tudor times, did not initially preclude the possibility of a gradual amalgamation of Ireland and England in the manner that Wales and England became united.

The crucial stage of Anglo-Irish relations appears to have been the period of a little more than a century, which began with Henry VIII's creation of the kingdom of Ireland [1] and closed with Oliver Cromwell's death (1541–1658) — an era characterized by strife past forgetting and policies past undoing. The injection of religious conflict into Anglo-Irish relations must be considered as one of the paramount factors in the tragedy. Although Henry VIII's breach with Rome had only a limited effect upon the Irish, the English Reforma-

---

[1] Irish Statute, 33 Henry VIII, c. 1.

tion under Edward VI and Elizabeth created a nearly irreconcilable difference between the two peoples.[2]

Another source of Anglo-Irish dissension also dates from the mid-sixteenth century: the twin policies of confiscation and colonization, inaugurated not by a Protestant government but by that of Mary Tudor. While feudal law had long sanctioned the concept that rebels should forfeit their fiefs, there was a fundamental difference between these traditional confiscations and those begun under Mary. The earlier practice merely involved a change of landlords on great estates, the new policy provided for the wholesale expulsion of small owners and tenants from part of the forfeited land and their replacement by "English subjects born either in England or Ireland." [3] These colonists held their land by English tenure (including primogeniture), were to employ only English servants, and had to supply troops. The new system provided a means for Anglicizing Ireland by rewarding soldiers and officials with land grants, a policy that appealed to the entrepreneurial instincts of the English gentry and bourgeoisie.

The political and economic motives soon merged with the religious ones. From the close of Elizabeth's reign through the Protectorate one of the principal objectives of the English plantations in Ireland came to be the transfer of land from Catholic to Protestant owners. The combination of English religious and land policies resulted in a fateful cycle; stepped up English control, Irish resistance, suppression, confiscation, and further repression. Although the English failed either to convert or to Anglicize the native Irish, they succeeded in establishing strong Protestant minorities in many parts of the country.

By the early seventeenth century Irish society consisted of diverse and antagonistic groups. Among the native Irish were an aristocracy and a peasantry; to them before 1500 were

[2] Robert Dudley Edwards, *Church and State in Tudor Ireland: A History of the Penal Laws against Irish Catholics* (Dublin, 1935), p. 202.

[3] Edmund Curtis, *A History of Ireland*, 6th ed. (London, 1950), p. 177; William F. T. Butler, *Confiscation in Irish History* (Dublin, Talbot Press, 1917), pp. 14–17.

added the Anglo-Norman lords of the Pale and the English burghers of the port towns like Dublin, Wexford, and Waterford. When the Reformation came, most of the "English-Irish," as Fynes Moryson described them,[4] or the "Old English," as they came to be called in the seventeenth century,[5] remained loyal Catholics, but found themselves at odds with the ultramontane position of the Gaelic Irish. A few, like James Butler, the first duke of Ormond, accepted the established Church of Ireland. This initial Protestant element was soon supplemented by immigrants from Britain: officials, merchants, churchmen, soldiers, and adventurers of all types — many of them colonists on the new lands. Thus grew up a new generation of Anglo-Irish set apart from both the Old English and the Irish by religion and self-interest. Yet the Anglo-Irish themselves did not constitute a homogeneous group; they too were divided by class differences, and they adhered to various forms of Protestantism, especially after James I opened Ulster to English Puritans and Scottish Presbyterians.[6] The religious and social divisions in early Stuart Ireland soon found political expression.

The medieval Irish parliament had represented only the sections of the country with English settlements and had been dominated by a few families. Henry VIII attempted to incorporate Gaelic regions into his newly created kingdom by extending English law and administration and by making the Irish parliament more nearly a national institution. In Elizabeth's time the Irish parliament spoke for both the Catholic and Protestant landed classes. Under James I, and during the opening years of Charles I's reign, the Catholic aristocracy still possessed the richest land outside Ulster, but they had by now become a minority in parliament and feared for the

[4] *An Itinerary of Fynes Moryson*, 4 vols. (Glasgow, J. MacLehose and Sons, 1907–1908), IV, 196–198.
[5] Aidan Clarke, *The Old English in Ireland 1625–42* (Ithaca, N.Y., 1966), pp. 15–16.
[6] Edwards, *Church and State*, p. 306; T. W. Moody, *The Londonderry Plantation 1609–41: The City of London and the Plantation of Ulster* (Belfast, 1939), pp. 394–398.

future. Partly through their influence at the English court, and partly by pressure on the Irish administration, they strove to protect their religious and economic position by a set of guarantees known as the "Graces." [7] The newer Protestant landlords, meanwhile, agitated for stricter enforcement of anti-Catholic laws and an extension of the plantation system.

When Thomas Wentworth became viceroy in 1632 he set out to play these contending factions off against each other, "to govern," as he expressed it "the Native by the Planter and the Planter by the Native." [8] Once he had secured financial support from the Dublin parliament, Wentworth embarked upon a policy of increasing the power of the crown at the expense of all competing interests. Although he continued a negative toleration of the Catholics, he disregarded some of the Graces and authorized the plantation of Connacht, despite the loyalty of many of its Catholic landowners. At the same time, he alienated the Protestants, most of whom were inclined to Puritanism, by introducing Laudian reforms in the Church of Ireland. By 1640 Strafford (as he had now become) appeared to have created the most effective royal government yet established in Ireland. Actually, when his power faltered, all groups in Ireland joined in denouncing him.

The union of Strafford's enemies proved short lived. Once Strafford was removed, the longstanding rivalry between the older Catholic and the newer Protestant landlords reappeared on the surface. The conflict between the Puritan party and the crown in England also increased tension in Ireland. Agents of Charles began negotiating for Irish support. Encouraged by the crisis in England the dispossessed Catholics in Ulster rose up against the English colonists. At the time of the initial Ulster rebellion (1594–1603) most of the Old English of the Pale had opposed the rebels. Now, discouraged by their waning influence in Dublin and distrustful of the English parlia-

----

[7] For the text of the Graces, see Clarke, *Old English*, Appendix II.

[8] Wentworth to Coke, Jan. 31, 1633/34, quoted by H. F. Kearney, *Strafford in Ireland 1633–41* (Manchester, 1959), pp. 33–34.

mentary party, the majority of the Old English threw in their lot with the Ulster Catholics, though still asserting their loyalty to the crown.[9]

With the outbreak of the Ulster rebellion, in October 1641, Ireland became rent with dissension. In the ensuing struggles both Catholics and Protestants perpetrated atrocities which in turn gave rise to reprisals. The shifting fortunes of the English civil wars further confused the Irish situation. There came to be a number of factions, each striving to gain control: Irish Catholics of the Kilkenny Confederation seeking to establish an independent kingdom under Charles's nominal suzerainty; Anglo-Irish (and some Old English) who loyally supported the king; others who were pro-English first and royalists second; Puritans and Scottish Presbyterians who opposed the king, but distrusted Cromwell; Independents and sectaries who supported the Commonwealth. Cromwell's victory in England and conquest of Ireland temporarily settled the issue: the radical Protestants won out, and Ireland was forced to become part of a united Britain. Wholesale confiscation brought thousands of new colonists to central and southern Ireland, among them Cromwellian soldiers, especially officers, plus some of the London adventurers who had financed the parliamentary army in Ireland.[10]

Edmund Burke maintained that England's difficulty was Ireland's opportunity. The reverse seems closer to the truth for the sixteenth and seventeenth centuries. Between 1541 and 1658 the Irish seized almost every chance to exploit England's foreign and domestic difficulties: Mary's war with France, Elizabeth's long struggle with Spain, Charles I's dispute with Scotland, and finally the crises of the English civil wars. But at every stage, instead of achieving victory, or even winning

[9] *Ibid.*, pp. 3–4, 314–315. Kearney implies the Old English supported the rebellion with reluctance. For a different viewpoint, see Thomas L. Coonan, *The Irish Confederacy and the Puritan Revolution* (Dublin, 1954), pp. 88–121.

[10] John P. Prendergast, *The Cromwellian Settlement of Ireland* (New York, 1868), pp. 121–176; Richard Bagwell, *Ireland under the Stuarts*, 3 vols. (London, 1909–1916), II, 315–325.

concessions, the Irish ended by suffering further losses. The only favorable turn of events came not as a consequence of England's difficulties but rather because of their cessation under Charles II.

In Ireland in 1660, as in England, many of the military and civil leaders of the Protectorate cooperated in bringing about the Stuart restoration. Whatever their motives, their timely action put Charles II in their debt. It soon became apparent that no real counterrevolution would take place. In any event, the conflicts of the civil wars and interregnum had been so changeable and so many sided that few survivors had been consistent royalists. No single formula of retribution and reward could possibly be devised that would satisfy all of the king's avowed supporters. Nearly everyone rejected Cromwell's union between Ireland and England and favored the restoration of a separate monarchy under the English crown; beyond that there was little agreement.[11]

It was characteristic that Charles II should follow an ad hoc policy to compromise, balancing the equity of contending claims against the political influence of the claimants. Under the circumstances it is not surprising that possession, if not nine-tenths of the law, proved to be at least two-thirds of it.[12] Charles restored the lands of some of the Cavaliers, but protected most of the Roundhead colonists; he reestablished the Church of Ireland, but employed the royal prerogative to tolerate Catholics. He likewise dealt leniently with the Presbyterians of the north. The Catholic Irish and Old English recovered only a portion of their former property. Politically they fared even worse; after 1660 the Dublin parliament

[11] Bagwell, *Ireland under the Stuarts*, II, 362–371, III, 1–10; Thomas Carte, *Life of James, Duke of Ormond*, 2nd ed., 6 vols. (Oxford, 1851), IV, 1–13.

[12] Only a third of the confiscated land was restored to Catholic owners. J. C. Beckett, *A Short History of Ireland* (London, Hutchinson's University Library, 1952), pp. 90–91. Although the Restoration land settlement was certainly not favorable to Catholics, Protestants later alleged that its terms permitted some Catholics to gain title to land by what amounted to squatters' rights. Sir Geoffrey Gilbert, *Report of Cases in Equity . . . in Ireland* (London, 1734), pp. 236–237.

became almost totally Protestant.[13] Yet if Charles II failed
to satisfy any one group he left them all with some hope.

While politically and religiously Charles II's reign marks a
period of precarious stability, it witnessed one constitutional
development of major significance: the beginnings of legislative initiative on the part of the Dublin parliament. Many
writers have stressed the fact that, since the crown's hereditary
income in Ireland supplied a much larger proportion of the
government's needs than in England, the Irish parliament
possessed little bargaining power. This observation is strictly
valid only for the period 1667–1688. Strafford felt it necessary
to summon parliament in 1634 to vote taxes, and Charles II
needed parliamentary approval for both land and revenue
measures early in his reign. It was not until 1667, after he
had been granted new permanent taxes, such as the hearth
tax, that Charles could dispense with the Dublin legislature.
Between 1662 and 1666 the Irish Commons perfected a
method for enacting their own legislative proposals, which
had first been essayed in the reign of James I.

Poynings' Act required that all Irish bills must be approved
by the English privy council in advance of any meeting of the
Irish parliament. Under Mary the Crown introduced a modification of this procedure that permitted the Irish privy council
to draft bills while the Irish parliament was in session and to
submit them to England for approval.[14] Designed primarily
to strengthen the Irish executive, this change actually opened
the way for the Dublin parliament to participate in legislation. The Irish privy council, which always contained members of the Irish House of Lords and usually of the Irish
Commons, had close ties with parliament. In 1614 the Irish
Commons chose a select committee to "frame legislation for
transmission to the King" in conjunction with a subcommit-
tee of the Irish privy council.[15] Although the Irish Commons

[13] Bagwell, *Ireland under the Stuarts*, III, 18.
[14] Irish Statute, 3 and 4 Philip and Mary, c. 4.
[15] Kiernan, *History of the Financial Administration of Ireland to 1817*,
pp. 31–32; Edward Porritt, *The Unreformed House of Commons*, 2 vols.
(Cambridge, 1909), II, 428.

recognized the "sole power and authority" of the lord deputy and privy council to transmit proposed legislation, they obviously expected to have a share in writing bills.[16] The Commons appointed a similar committee in the reign of Charles I; but Wentworth paid little heed to their suggestions. After the Restoration the Irish parliament proceeded to formalize a method by which it could initiate legislation. It established the practice of drafting desired legislation in the form of "heads of a bill." These heads were normally drawn up by select committees. Just like regular bills in the English parliament, the heads had to pass three readings in the Commons, usually being referred to the committee of the whole house before the vote on the second reading. Upon final passage of the heads, the house named a delegation to present them to the lord lieutenant, "humbly desiring, if it may stand with his Grace and Council's pleasure, that the same may be transmitted to England, according to Poynings' Law." [17] In 1662 the first of these heads submitted was for a personal grant of £130,000 for Ormond, just after his appointment as lord lieutenant — a proposal the administration in Dublin Castle transmitted to Westminster with understandable alacrity.[18]

The English privy council could of course do as it pleased with such suggested bills: it could accept them, modify them, or simply disregard them. If the privy council decided to return a bill to the Irish parliament, that body had either to pass or reject the bill; it could not amend it. The crux of the matter was how much pressure the Dublin parliament could exert upon the government.

In the reign of Charles II Whitehall and Dublin Castle paid some heed to the Irish parliament. Although the govern-

---

[16] *Journals of the House of Commons of the Kingdom of Ireland* [hereafter cited as *Irish Commons' Journal*], 8 vols. (Dublin, 1753), 2nd ed., 23 vols. (Dublin, 1763–1786), 3rd ed., 20 vols. (Dublin, 1796–1800), May 16, 1615. Because there are three editions, all references are given to dates rather than pages.

[17] *Irish Commons' Journal*, Feb. 26, 1665/66. On Poynings' Law, see also Carte, *Life of Ormond*, IV, 25, 161.

[18] *Irish Commons' Journal*, Mar. 4, May 1, 1662.

ment was able to push through an unpopular land settlement, the Irish Commons soon sought to modify its terms by proposing a "bill of explanation." While the English privy council rejected the bill, it requested Ormond to draw up an alternative act with the advice of the Irish privy council. When members of the English privy council attempted to alter this second bill of explanation, Clarendon challenged them in words that make clear his interpretation of Poynings' Law. "To what purpose is Poynings' Act, that all acts shall be transmitted from thence hither," he demanded, "if we under pretence of mending an act shall graft new matter into it?" [19]

In 1665 the English government made a direct concession to the Irish Commons. Upon receiving from London the draft of an act of uniformity, the Irish Commons objected to the wording of several clauses. Instead of passing the bill as submitted to them, they framed a new one incorporating more desirable phrasing. This new version was then sent to the lord lieutenant in the form of heads of a bill and subsequently approved.[20] The Irish Commons also registered a partial victory over the crown when it stipulated that the revenue from the hearth tax must not be employed for pensions or royal gifts.[21] Other efforts to take the initiative appear to have failed. Several heads of bills that the Commons deemed "of great importance to this kingdom" were pigeonholed by the government.[22] By granting Charles II permanent taxes in 1667 the Irish parliament surrendered its influence. The peace following the Restoration led to economic expansion, which in turn increased customs and other revenues and eventually balanced the Irish budget. As a consequence, Charles II never again summoned the Dublin parliament.

[19] Quoted by Bagwell, *Ireland under the Stuarts*, III, 45.

[20] *Irish Commons' Journal*, Feb. 9, 26, 1665/66. Since the wording of the statute conforms to that submitted by the Irish Commons, it is evident that their version was accepted. Irish Statute, 17 and 18 Charles II, c. 6.

[21] Irish Statute, 14 and 15 Charles II, c. 17, sect. 9.

[22] *Irish Commons' Journal*, July 31, 1666. None of the three bills here mentioned appears in the Statute Books, and so clearly they were not approved.

When James II ascended the Irish throne the crown enjoyed
an economic independence that permitted him to redress the
country's political and religious balance in favor of the Catholics. As a gesture to the English Tories he appointed a strong
Anglican lord lieutenant, his brother-in-law, the second earl
of Clarendon. To his dismay, Clarendon soon discovered his
authority severely limited. James wanted to reorganize the
Irish army, which was dominated by old Cromwellian officers,
and to facilitate this plan he removed control of the army
from Clarendon and appointed a lieutenant general as commander of the Irish forces. James gave the post to Richard
Talbot, the scion of one of the Old English families of the
Pale, whom he raised to the peerage as earl of Tyrconnell.
Tyrconnell promptly commissioned a number of Catholic
officers and recommended to Clarendon a similar policy for
civilian officials. When Clarendon objected, James recalled
him and placed the civilian as well as the military government
in Tyrconnell's hands.[23] Following the tactics that Charles II
had employed in England, James revoked the charters of Irish
parliamentary boroughs and established in their place administrations strongly royalist and generally Catholic. As a
result of these changes, some of the Anglo-Irish began to leave
for England, while others plotted with James's enemies.
Nevertheless, civil war might still have been avoided in Ireland had not James II been driven from England.

As long as he remained ruler of Great Britain James II
pursued a relatively cautious policy in Ireland. Just as many
Catholic landowners had accepted the Protestant government
of his brother, it was logical to assume that a sizable portion
of the Protestant propertied classes would acquiesce in a
Catholic regime so long as it protected their estates. James
avowed his intention of respecting Protestant rights, and he
and his key minister, Sunderland, attempted to keep Tyrcon-

[23] *The State Papers of Henry Earl of Clarendon*, 2 vols. (Oxford, 1768),
I, 150–152; David Ogg, *England in the Reigns of James II and William III*
(Oxford, 1955), p. 170; John P. Kenyon, *Robert Spencer Earl of Sunderland*
(New York, Longmans, Green, 1958), pp. 101, 131, 136–137, 141–144.

nell in check. The king appointed Tyrconnell lord deputy rather than lord lieutenant, while Sunderland sought to dampen Tyrconnell's desire to attack the Settlement Act, which guaranteed Protestant lands. But the growing crisis in England in 1688 strengthened Tyrconnell's position. By the spring of that year he had persuaded the king to accept some revision of the Settlement Act.[24] When the news of William's landing reached Ireland the lord deputy quickly took steps to prevent a Protestant uprising in Ulster. In response the Protestants there, who were already organized, seized two key fortified towns, Enniskillen and Londonderry. Outside of Ulster a few Protestant Anglo-Irish remained loyal to the Stuart monarchy, but the country generally became divided along religious lines.

When James II landed at Kinsale in March 1689 he had little choice but to put himself at the head of what had become a predominantly Catholic nationalist movement. Entering Dublin on March 28 he forthwith summoned the Irish parliament to meet on May 7. Thanks to the new charters, and the strong line taken by Tyrconnell's henchmen, the ensuing elections produced a parliament nationalistic in spirit and overwhelmingly Catholic in membership.[25] Although the larger Catholic landlords hesitated to upset Charles II's land settlement, the great majority of the Catholics felt that at last the day of retribution had arrived. They had their hearts set on the repeal of the Restoration settlement, which, it will be recalled, had left most of Cromwell's colonists in possession of a large share of central and southern Ireland. In view of the composition of parliament and of his crucial need for support James felt compelled to accept their demands. Over the vigorous opposition of its Protestant minority, led by Anthony Dopping, bishop of Meath, parliament passed a sweeping statute.[26]

[24] Kenyon, *Earl of Sunderland*, pp. 162–163, 193.

[25] Thomas Davis, *The Patriot Parliament*, 3rd ed. (London, 1893), pp. 11–13, 24–33; see also J. G. Simms, *The Patriot Parliament of 1689* (Dundalk, Dublin Historical Association, 1966), pp. 5–7.

[26] Three other bishops of the Church of Ireland, all of them appointees

The law provided that, upon sufficient proof, all persons whose ancestors were "any way seized, possessed of, or entitled to any lands, tenements or hereditaments, in use, possession, reversion or remainder in this Kingdom of Ireland, on the 22nd day of October, 1641," could recover their property. Persons who had purchased any of the confiscated estates (a group that included a number of Catholics such as Tyrconnell himself) were to be recompensed, but the original Cromwellian colonists or their heirs were simply to be dispossessed. Furthermore all landowners now in rebellion against James II were to forfeit their estates. In short, the Catholics, for once identified with what appeared to be both the de jure and de facto government of Ireland, meted out to Protestant rebels the same harsh treatment they had received, at least in terms of confiscation. In dealing with religion the parliament of 1689 proved more moderate: it passed a law that gave the tithes of Catholics to Catholic clergy and those of Protestants to the Church of Ireland.[27]

Whatever its merits, the land settlement of 1689 was never put into operation; the fate of Ireland was once again to be determined on the field of battle.[28] Although in large part a religious conflict, the Irish war of 1689-1691 proved less ruthless than that of the 1640's. There were perhaps as many men engaged, but fighting was largely confined to actual combatants, and civilians suffered fewer outrages. Nevertheless, the struggle was intense and left its own bitter heritage, as

of Charles II, attended the opening of James II's parliament: Simon Digby (bishop of Limerick, 1679-1692), Thomas Otway (bishop of Ossory, 1680-1693), and Edward Wetenhall (bishop of Cork, 1679-1699). *An Exact List of Lords Spiritual and Temporal who sate in the pretended Parliament at Dublin in the Kingdom of Ireland on the 7th May 1689* (London, 1689). According to this list, seven earls, nine viscounts, and fourteen barons were also present. Dopping's speech opposing the repeal of the Act of Settlement is given in Historical Manuscripts Commission, *Ormonde Manuscripts*, n.s., 8 vols. (London, 1902-1920), VIII, 392-401.

[27] Bagwell, *Ireland under the Stuarts*, III, 232-233; Davis, *Patriot Parliament*, p. 149. The acts of the Patriot Parliament were printed in the *Hibernian Mirror* (Dublin, 1751), Pt. II.

[28] For an account of the war, see J. G. Simms, *Jacobite Ireland* (Toronto, 1969).

well as reviving the terrible memories of the 1640's. Fighting lasted for two and a half years and took place in many parts of the country.

William, even more than James, looked upon the Irish war as merely a means to an end. When, despite his victory at the Boyne, Irish resistance persisted through 1690 and into the next year he decided to negotiate. As a result his commander, Godert de Ginkel, offered generous terms to the armies still holding out in the south and the west. Waterford surrendered, and, after Ginkel's decisive victory at Aughrim in July, Galway also capitulated. On October 3 the main Irish army at Limerick accepted Ginkel's terms, thus ending the war.

One of the ironies of the Williamite War of 1689–1691 is that its immediate causes were not primarily Irish. It is far from certain that armed conflict would have broken out in Ireland had it not been for the constitutional crisis in England and the international rivalry between Louis XIV and William of Orange. Viewed from the perspective of general European history, the conflict constitutes one incident in Louis XIV's long struggle for the hegemony of Europe. Recognizing this, William invaded Ireland specifically to drive out James and thus free himself for the continental war; in return, Louis XIV supported James in order to immobilize William. To James, Ireland seems to have meant little: he hoped to use it as a stepping-stone on the road back to Westminster. In short, the Irish were pawns sacrificed in the opening moves of the War of the League of Augsburg. True, the Battle of the Boyne was an important allied victory, celebrated in Catholic Vienna as well as Protestant London. Yet it proved far from decisive as far as the general outcome was concerned. Louis XIV did not meet final defeat for another twenty years. For the Catholic Irish, on the other hand, the war of 1689–1691 meant disaster. The Treaty of Limerick marked the end of Old Ireland as completely as Appomattox meant the end of the Old South.

In evaluating the severity of a peace settlement the historian

does well to ask himself what might have happened had the
victors been the losers, and, just as Brest-Litovsk should be
remembered when considering the Treaty of Versailles, the
legislation of the Patriot Parliament should be kept in mind
when appraising both the Treaty of Limerick itself and its
modifications by Protestant parliaments. To Catholics the
original treaty represented the minimum terms on which they
would surrender; to the Protestant Anglo-Irish the treaty appeared little short of preposterous. Having won the war, were
they to lose the peace?

> Hard fate, that still attends our Irish war
> The conquerors lose, the conquered gaines are;
> Their pens the triumph of our sword's defeat:
> We fight like soldiers, but like fools we treat.
> Sure Teague has charm'd with some fatal spell
> For lest the coward should no more rebell,
> Lest he grow honest by becoming poor,
> We pardon all his bloody score
> With a new fund of our plunder'd store;
> But England doubtless in loss will share
> And, to reconquer, a new tax prepare.[29]

The military terms of the Treaty of Limerick provided for
the return of the French troops in Ireland and for the transportation of any of the Irish soldiers who desired to enter service abroad. As commander, Ginkel had the authority to carry
out these provisions without delay. Within a few months some
11,000 out of the 14,000 Irish had left for France. "Seldom in
history," writes Edmund Curtis, "have a few thousand men,
departing in exile, represented as these did almost the whole
aristocracy, the fighting force, and the hope of a nation." [30]

The civil articles of the treaty proved more complex and
controversial; their final meaning was not, in fact, clarified for
several years. Part XII of the treaty stated that the "Lords

---

[29] "Historical Songs of Ireland," ed. T. Crofton Crocker, Percy Society,
Early English Poetry, vol. I (London, 1841), 119–120. See Map I in the
Appendix for location of various places mentioned.

[30] Curtis, *History of Ireland*, p. 273.

Justices and General do undertake that their Majesties will ratify these articles, within the space of eight months or sooner, and use their utmost endeavours that the same shall be ratified and confirmed in Parliament." [31] William and Mary's ratification followed almost automatically, since the king had instigated the moderate policy in the first place. The problem was the attitude of the English and Irish parliaments toward the treaty: both bodies were strongly anti-Catholic, and both had compelling economic and political motives for objecting to Ginkel's generosity. The actual ratification would lie with the Irish parliament when it should meet; meanwhile the English parliament considered itself empowered to legislate for Ireland. In 1690 it passed a statute annulling all the proceedings of James' Patriot Parliament. The next year it enacted legislation requiring officials in Ireland to subscribe to oaths that would exclude Catholics.[32] Since such stringent oaths had not previously been required by Irish legislation, Irish Catholics naturally felt that the measure violated the treaty.

William was too dependent upon the English parliament to prevent it from enacting legislation that abrogated at least the spirit, if not the letter, of the Limerick agreement. He soon discovered that the Irish parliament could be equally difficult: the Dublin legislature did not ratify the treaty until 1697 and then insisted upon a literal and narrow interpertation of its terms.

The civil articles of the treaty dealt primarily with two interrelated subjects — land and religion. The treaty guaranteed to all of the surrendering garrisons and troops in five counties a general pardon and the retention of their lands, regardless of their religion, under the condition that they would remain in Ireland and take an oath of allegiance to

---

[31] *English Historical Documents 1660–1714*, ed. Andrew Browning (London, Eyre and Spottiswoode, 1953), p. 766; see also J. G. Simms, "The Original Draft of the Civil Articles of Limerick, 1691," *Irish Historical Studies*, VIII (1952–1953), 37–44.

[32] English Statutes, 1 William and Mary, sess. 2, c. 9, and 3 William and Mary c. 2.

the new regime. According to the wording of the original draft (which was changed by the lords justices, but restored by William) the same privilege was extended to everyone under the protection of James's army (in the same five counties). Obviously these terms represented a clear departure from the confiscation policies of the previous century, including those of the Catholic parliament of 1689. The Protestants vigorously criticized so lenient a treatment of rebel landowners. Although forced to accept the general provisions of the settlement, they succeeded in modifying them. The Irish parliament insisted upon deleting the clause protecting the dependents of the surrendering forces, thus excluding from its provisions all except soldiers actually under arms at the time of the capitulation. Although this restriction probably affected only a few,[33] it reflected the partisan spirit of the Irish Protestants.

As a consequence of the confiscation of all rebel lands not protected by the Treaty of Limerick, and because of the voluntary exodus of so many of the Irish army (who thereby forfeited their estates), William came into possession of thousands of acres. When the king gave most of this land to his advisers and favorites the English parliament successfully challenged his grants. In 1699 it passed the Act of Resumption which created a parliamentary commission empowered to reexamine the disposal of all Irish lands forfeited since 1688.[34] Even though the act contained no clauses specifically directed against Catholics, the commission, in the course of its examination of titles, did confiscate some Catholic estates on the grounds that they had illegally escaped forfeiture.

[33] J. G. Simms, *The Williamite Confiscation in Ireland 1690–1703* (London, 1956), pp. 59–62; Irish Statute, 9 William, c. 2, sect. 1. Seven Irish peers and seven Irish bishops signed a protest against ratification on the grounds that the "Act for the Confirmation of Articles made at the Surrender of the City of Limerick . . . does not agree with the Body thereof; the title being An Act for the Confirmation of the Articles etc. whereas no one of the said articles is therein, as we conceive, fully confirmed." *A Collection of the Protests of the Lords of Ireland 1634–1770* (London, 1771), p. 24.

[34] Simms, *Williamite Confiscation*, pp. 97–101.

In spite of the actions of the Irish and English parliaments, the land provisions of the treaty were honored in the main. J. G. Simms's recent study of the Williamite confiscation shows that, contrary to lower estimates by previous writers, the Catholics still retained 14 percent of all of the land in Ireland in 1703 (as opposed to 22 percent in 1688 and 59 percent in 1641). Though Protestant ownership was almost universal in the northeastern counties except for Antrim, elsewhere Catholic ownership ranged from 5 to 30 percent.[35] But the story does not stop there. Prevented by the specific commitments of the treaty from liquidating Catholic ownership, the Protestant Anglo-Irish sought by indirect means to undo Williams's liberal policy. The religious terms of the treaty offered them their opportunity. When the bill "for the confirmation of the Articles made at the Surrender of Limerick" came before the Irish Commons, they omitted any reference to the chief religious article of the treaty.[36]

The first civil article of the Limerick agreement had read as follows: "The Roman Catholics of this kingdom shall enjoy such privileges in their exercise of their religion as are consistent with the laws of Ireland, or as they did enjoy in the reign of King Charles the Second; and their Majesties, as soon as their affairs will permit them to summon a Parliament in this kingdom, will endeavour to procure the said Roman Catholics such farther security in that particular as may preserve them from any disturbance upon the account of their said religion." [37]

By refusing to clarify this article when they ratified the treaty the Irish parliament purposely left the question of Catholic rights open to varying interpretations. The laws of Ireland included a number of stringent antirecusant statutes dating back to Elizabeth. During much of Charles II's reign the government had interpreted such laws most leniently; in fact it simply failed to enforce many of them.[38] On the other

[35] *Ibid.*, pp. 195–196.
[36] J. G. Simms, *The Treaty of Limerick* (Dundalk, 1961), p. 13.
[37] *English Historical Documents 1660–1714*, ed. Browning, p. 765.
[38] In 1672 the earl of Orrery was removed from his post as lord presi-

hand, at times under Charles II, especially during the period of the Popish Plot, the statutes were more strictly enforced. Furthermore, did the Irish parliament not have the right to draw up additional religious legislation to protect the nation?

If William, and later Anne, could have dealt freely with the Dublin parliament, they might have prevented legislation deleterious to the Limerick settlement. Unfortunately the English ministers and parliament supported the Protestant party in Ireland. In 1694, for example, a special committee of the English House of Commons recommended that a parliament be called in Ireland specifically "for the passing of such laws as shall be necessary for the security" of Protestants.[39] Under such pressure the crown was forced to acquiesce in the passage of a series of penal laws against the Catholic Irish. In judging the Irish penal laws one must recognize that fear as well as greed motivated their authors. At least until 1715 a Stuart Catholic restoration remained a threat that neither the English nor especially the Irish Protestants could disregard. The Anglo-Irish viewed the Protestant ascendancy as not just a bid for wealth and power; to them it was a prerequisite for survival.[40]

The purpose of the penal laws was to ensure the Protestant ascendancy by destroying or debasing the Catholic upper classes rather than by eliminating Catholicism. The revolution of 1688 in Great Britain had established the rule of the Anglican landed and commercial oligarchy. The Anglo-Irish sought to create a similar system in Ireland. First of all they secured their monopoly of political power. Beginning by accepting an English act in 1691 that eliminated Roman Catholics from parliament and terminating with an act in 1727

---

dent of Munster because of his severity toward Catholics. Kathleen Lynch, *Roger Boyle, First Earl of Orrery* (Knoxville, University of Tennessee Press, 1965), pp. 140–141.

[39] *Journals of the House of Commons* [hereafter cited as *English Commons' Journal*], 47 vols. (London, 1742–1792), Jan. 12, 1693/94.

[40] The Papacy continued to recognize James II as king until his death in 1701 and then recognized his son as James III. Maureen Wall, *The Penal Laws 1691–1760* (Dundalk, 1961), pp. 20–21.

that deprived them of the vote,[41] the Dublin legislature successfully excluded the Papists (as they delighted in calling them) from all direct political influence. In the light of political thought and practice at the time such a policy may be defended. Established churches enjoyed similar privileges in almost every country, though in none of them did the state church represent so small a portion of the nation. Less defensible, and far more insidious in its effects, was the program by which the Protestant oligarchy endeavored to undermine the surviving remnant of the Catholic aristocracy. Since the Treaty of Limerick and royal clemency had left a portion of the land in Catholic hands, the problem was first to prevent the expansion of Catholic holdings and second to convert (or it might be better to say subvert) the Catholic landowners. A series of laws was passed that prevented Catholics from buying land or even renting large amounts on long-term leases; prohibited Protestants from marrying Catholics unless the latter renounced their faith; provided that Catholic estates should be divided among all the male heirs unless the eldest son turned Protestant, in which case primogeniture prevailed. Another law forbade all Catholics, except those specifically covered by the Treaty of Limerick, from bearing arms or owning horses worth more than £5.[42]

Accompanying this legislation were laws designed to weaken the Catholic professional and commercial classes. The armed services were naturally closed to them. Beginning in 1698 acts were passed to exclude Catholics from the legal profession.[43] Other laws prevented Catholic tradesmen from having more than two apprentices, while local regulations or custom often excluded Catholic merchants and artisans from trade associations and guilds.[44] As early as 1695 an act prohibited Cath-

[41] Irish Statute, 1 George II, c. 9, sect. 7; J. G. Simms, "Irish Catholics and the Parliamentary Franchise 1692–1718," *Irish Historical Studies*, XII (1960–1961), 28–37.

[42] Irish Statutes, 7 William III, c. 5; 9 William III, c. 3; 2 Anne, c. 6, sects. 5 and 6; 8 Anne, c. 3.

[43] Irish Statute, 10 William III, c. 5.

[44] Maureen Wall, "The Rise of a Catholic Middle Class in Eighteenth-Century Ireland," *Irish Historical Studies*, XI (1958–1959), 91–115.

olics from sending their children abroad to be educated, while Catholic schools were outlawed at home. The Dublin parliament also took steps to drive out the higher Roman Catholic clergy as well as all religious orders, thus hoping to deprive the church of leadership and cause its decline.[45]

The religion of the poorer classes caused less concern, but parliament passed legislation to suppress disorders. Following the war some of the peasants had turned to a form of outlawry, which, from the Catholic point of view, might be called a kind of national resistance movement. By an act of 1695 local communities were made responsible for the restitution of property stolen or destroyed by "tories, robbers and rapparees." Two years later an extension of this law provided that Catholic property holders must pay for the depradations done by Catholic outlaws, and Protestants for those done by Protestants — an obvious attempt to make the Catholics restrain their coreligionists.[46] Other laws were occasionally critical of the lower classes. One in 1695 alleged that "many idle persons refuse to work at their lawful calling and labour several days in the year on the pretence that the same is dedicated to some saint or pretended saint" and provided that offenders should be fined.[47] Since the law recognized twenty-two religious and three secular holidays in addition to Sundays, it seemed obviously designed more to irritate the Catholic population than to enforce industry. It omitted St. Patrick's Day, but included Guy Fawkes Day.

As has been said, however, the penal laws were aimed primarily at the upper classes. In the past one of the chief obstacles to the establishment of an effective Protestant ascendancy had been the incomplete enforcement of anti-Catholic legislation by Protestant officials and its evasion by Catholics who dissembled their religion. Social intercourse between Catholics and Protestants in regions where the former con-

[45] Irish Statutes, 7 William III, c. 4; 9 William III, c. 1; 2 Anne, c. 6; Wall, *Penal Laws 1691–1760*, pp. 13–17.

[46] Irish Statutes, 7 William III, c. 21; 9 William III, c. 9.

[47] Irish Statute, 7 William III, c. 14.

stituted an overwhelming majority frequently led to a kind of negative collusion between magistrates and violators. To prevent a repetition of such practice the new laws included many provisions that endeavored to preclude this circumvention. An officeholder or a solicitor, for example, not only had to take an oath of allegiance to the king and "swear that I do from my heart abhor, detest and abjure, as impious and heretical, that damnable doctrine and position that princes excommunicated by the pope . . . may be deposed" but also that no "foreign prince, person or prelate, state or potentate, hath or ought to have any jurisdiction, power, superiority, preeminence or authority, ecclesiastical or spiritual, within this realm." [48] Furthermore they had to take a third oath which compelled them to deny transubstantiation, to refrain from the adoration of the Virgin and the saints, and to denounce the Mass. To qualify as a bona fide Protestant for such purposes as marriage or inheritance one had to produce a certificate sworn to by two of the following: a bishop, an Anglican clergyman, or a local justice of the peace.

The long-range effects of the penal legislation will be considered below, but it is clear that the laws confronted the propertied classes of Roman Catholics with a demoralizing choice. Rebellion was no longer possible. If they did not go into exile they had three alternatives: to repudiate their faith, to resort to deception, or to accept the almost certain decline of their social and economic position. In time attrition took its toll. Many of the old Catholic aristocracy were absorbed into the Protestant Ascendancy; others sank to the level of middle-class farmers; only a relatively few retained both their religion and their positions.[49]

[48] English Statute, 4 William and Mary, c. 2.
[49] By 1749 only eight out of a total of 114 peers appear to have been Roman Catholic. In 1775 there were only four. *The Gentleman's and Citizen's Almanack* (Dublin, 1749), pp. 40–41; *Gentleman's and Citizen's Almanack* (Dublin, 1775), pp. 50–52.

II

The Structure
of Government
in 1700

The revolution of 1688 had far-reaching effects upon the relationship of England to the overseas dependencies. Up until that date the crown had been able to exercise its prerogative in such a manner that neither Ireland nor the colonies ever came under the complete control of the English parliament. To be sure, that body had asserted its right to legislate for the whole empire, including Ireland. What is more, the Irish parliament during Poynings' administration had itself declared Ireland subject to all general English statutes then in force, an action that seemed to imply a similar jurisdiction for the future. During the Tudor and Stuart period the parliament at Westminster passed several laws relating to Ireland, and the English courts had upheld the principle that the English parliament had the authority to legislate for Ireland. Regardless of all this, as long as the king controlled the enforcement of the laws and had the power to dispense with them, imperial legislation could only mean what the crown intended it to mean. Ireland, especially, as bound to England by the ties of the personal union of the two crowns, fell more in the province of royal rather than parliamentary jurisdiction. Poynings' Act gave control of Irish legislation to the king's privy council, not to parliament. The king remained, in effect, the final arbiter between the conflicting claims of the English and Irish parliaments.

The revolution of 1688 caused a significant change in the crown's position. By the Bill of Rights William and Mary renounced a number of prerogatives and recognized implicitly the dominant role of the English parliament. As far as Ireland and the colonies were concerned, this change meant that the crown could no longer set aside or disregard English legislation dealing with the empire. The gradual shift of executive control to a group of ministers responsive to parliamentary opinion also affected policy making. During the period 1688–1770 officials responsible for the administration of Ireland and the colonies became increasingly concerned with the reactions of the English parliament. At the same time, the triumph of Whig ideology manifested by the Glorious Revolution stimulated a desire for more representative government in Scotland, Ireland, and the colonies. Thus the conflict between imperial interests and the principles of self-government became a central issue in Britain's relations with its dependencies during the eighteenth century.

In Scotland the revolution led the Scottish parliament to assert greater independence of the crown.[1] In America the overthrow of James II ended the attempt to centralize and extend royal control over the northern colonies. Even though Jacob Leisler's revolt in New York met defeat and Massachusetts failed to recover its original status, New York was granted an assembly and Massachusetts received a new charter. The repudiation of the Dominion of New England meant that the separate colonial legislatures could resume their efforts to gain greater autonomy.[2] In Ireland the immediate consequences of the revolution were largely determined by the course and outcome of the civil war of 1689–1691.

If the English revolution had not led to armed conflict in Ireland the Dublin parliament, like its Scottish counterpart, might have exploited the crisis to establish itself as coequal with Westminster.[3] Fighting for survival, the Irish Protestants accepted William's leadership without condition and encouraged the support of the English parliament. They hoped that

[1] Charles Sanford Terry, *The Scottish Parliament, Its Constitution and Procedure 1603–1707* (Glasgow, J. MacLehose & Sons, 1905), pp. 149–151; George S. Pryde, *Scotland from 1603 to the Present Day* (London, Thomas Nelson & Sons, 1962), pp. 49–50.
[2] Oscar Theodore Barck and Hugh Talmadge Lefler, *Colonial America* (New York, Macmillan Co., 1958), pp. 222–228.
[3] The Irish parliament did draw up a bill of rights, but it was not approved in London. J. G. S. MacNeill, *The Constitutional and Parliamentary History of Ireland till the Union* (Dublin, 1917), p. 68.

at last the Catholic Irish would be crushed, but William's willingness to accept a negotiated peace left them embittered and insecure. One Irish correspondent wrote Robert Harley that under existing circumstances the best he could hope for was a union with Britain, as in Cromwell's day, or, failing that, the establishment of a committee by the English parliament to hear Irish grievances. He opposed the reconstitution of an Irish parliament, explaining that "It has ruined us in this kingdom from time to time to have a Parliament of our own, for it has bred jealousy of England towards us, and made us seem to have separate interests." [4] In view of the precarious plight of the Protestant Irish before William's landing and the extent and duration of the civil war, one would expect most Anglo-Irish to be ready, if not to give up their parliament, at least to cooperate fully with the English government by granting supplies and passing other legislation desired by the crown. Instead, when William's first parliament met in 1692 it proved contentious and unruly. Its hostility and independence require explanation.

Before William left Ireland in the autumn of 1690 he appointed two lords justices, Henry, Viscount Sidney, and Thomas Coningsby. The first, a brother of Algernon Sidney, had been associated with William's coming to England in 1688; Coningsby, a member of the English Commons since 1679, had likewise been one of William's consistent supporters. Coningsby accompanied William to Ireland, was wounded at the Battle of the Boyne, and was named paymaster of the troops in Ireland. In December 1690 a third lord justice was appointed, Sir Charles Porter. Although also an Englishman and member of the English Commons, Porter had seen previous service in Ireland as lord chancellor under James II. Falling out with James over Tyrconnell's policies, he joined William in 1688 and was restored as Irish chancellor in 1690. Since Sidney returned to England in 1691 to serve

---

[4] [James Bonnell] to Robert Harley, Dublin, Nov. 3, 1691, Historical Manuscripts Commission, *Portland MSS*, 10 vols. (London, 1891–1931), III, 481.

for a year as secretary of state, it was Coningsby and Porter who actually controlled the civilian administration of Ireland during the closing months of the war, and who, with General Ginkel, signed the Treaty of Limerick.

The lords justices attempted to restore order and took steps to implement William's and Ginkel's commitments to the defeated Catholics. In October 1691 they issued a proclamation, to be read by the sheriffs to all justices of the peace, charging officers and soldiers of the army and the militia and all other persons to do no injury to any of the monarchs' subjects, "whether of the British or Irish nation without distinction." They stipulated, specifically, that any person taking a simple oath of allegiance to King William and Queen Mary without any denunciation of the Pope or other religious terms, who "behaved himself according to law, shall be esteemed a subject under their Majesties' protection and equally entitled to the benefit of their Majesties' laws." [5] Those disregarding the proclamation were to be punished.

There is little doubt that the policy of the lords justices accorded with the king's intentions, but it infuriated Irish Protestants. Meanwhile the king was also meeting growing opposition to his pro-Catholic policies in England. When the lords justices sought reassurance on the oath question from London, Nottingham replied that the English parliament was discussing the issue.[6] That body left no doubt as to its sympathies: it passed a bill requiring strict anti-Papist oaths of all Irish officials including members of parliament, thus assuring that when the Dublin parliament did meet to ratify the Treaty of Limerick it would be exclusively Protestant.[7]

While the Anglo-Irish welcomed the assistance of the

---

[5] Historical Manuscripts Commission, *Finch MSS*, 4 vols. (London, 1913–1965), III, 305–306.

[6] Nottingham to lord justices, Whitehall, Nov. 6, 1691, *ibid.*, 299.

[7] English Statute, 3 William and Mary, c. 2, sect. 4. The Commons passed the bill in November, but the Lords amended it to exempt those who surrendered under the terms of the Treaty of Limerick. *English Commons' Journal*, Oct. 27, 30, Nov. 6, 10, 30, Dec. 9, 10, 1691; Historical Manuscripts Commission, *House of Lords MSS*, 4 vols. (London 1887–1894), III, 315–319.

English parliament, they did not wish to be legally dependent
upon its sanction for their privileges; their primary aim was
to have Protestant ascendancy established by acts of their own
legislature. When, in the spring of 1692, the government decided to summon an Irish parliament, the Irish privy council
sent four proposals to England for approval: a bill for recognition of William and Mary; a bill to authorize new loyalty
oaths; a bill to reverse attainders against Protestants; and a
bill to reverse the Act of Settlement passed by James II's parliament. Nottingham and other English officials felt these
proposed bills inadvisable, since the English parliament had
already dealt with the issues. The earl of Burlington (Richard
Boyle, earl of Cork in the Irish peerage) and several other
Irish lords convinced the English council that all but the second should be approved.[8] Having thus catered to Irish sensibilities, the government instructed Lord Sidney (who had been
appointed lord lieutenant in March 1692) to issue writs for an
Irish election. Neither the English ministry nor Sidney appears to have anticipated any serious difficulty with the new
parliament; Sidney reported from Dublin, on the eve of its
meeting, that he expected it to vote additional taxes to support the army in Ireland.[9]

When they assembled on October 5 in Chichester House,
the Irish Lords and Commons duly subscribed to the oaths
required by the English statute of 1691.[10] They then proceeded to pass the first of the three bills that had originated
in the Irish privy council, the Act of Recognition. Its wording
explicitly stated that the kingdom of Ireland was "annexed
and united with the imperial crown of England, and by laws
and statutes of this kingdom is declared to be justly and
rightly dependent upon, and belonging, and forever united to

[8] Nottingham to William Blathwayt, Whitehall, Apr. 1, 12, June 10,
July 8, 1692, *Finch MSS*, IV, 54-55, 68, 216, 303. English Statute, I William and Mary, sess. 2, c. 9, had annulled all the proceedings of James
II's Irish parliament.
[9] Nottingham to Blathwayt, Sept. 27, 1692, *Finch MSS*, IV, 472.
[10] *Irish Commons' Journal*, Oct. 6, 1692.

the same." [11] The act said nothing of Ireland's subordination to the English parliament.

The endorsement of the English statute on oaths, the passage of the Act of Recognition, and the election of a speaker approved by the government, the solicitor general, Richard Levinge,[12] all seemed to indicate that Lord Sidney could expect from the Irish Commons the kind of dutiful behavior he so optimistically called for in his opening speech.[13] He was quickly disabused. The parliament of 1692 behaved in so fractious a manner that the government soon prorogued and subsequently dissolved it. Aside from the Act of Recognition only three laws were passed during its heated sessions.

One of the chief causes for conflict was the Treaty of Limerick and the fashion in which the crown was administering its terms. Sensing the bitterness with which the victorious Protestants viewed the treaty, the government wisely refrained from submitting it for ratification at that time. The lord lieutenant could not, however, prevent the Irish Commons from censuring royal officials who had appropriated forfeited lands, or worse still in the eyes of the Anglo-Irish, had seen fit to return property to Roman Catholic landowners.[14] More seri-

---

[11] Irish Statute, 4 William and Mary, c. 1. The Commons received the bill from the Lords on October 12, and it passed all three readings the same day, although a resolution was then passed ordering that "hereafter no bill be read oftener than once a day." *Irish Commons' Journal*, Oct. 12, 1692. The Scottish parliament, incidentally, did not formalize the practice of three readings for bills until 1696. Robert S. Rait, *The Parliaments of Scotland* (Glasgow, MacLehose and Jackson & Co., 1924), pp. 428–429.

[12] Sir Thomas Clarges to Sir Edward Harley, Oct. 4, 1692, *Portland MSS*, III, 503. Levinge had been solicitor general since 1690. He came from Chester and represented that city in the English parliament in 1690–1692. He sat for Blessington in the Irish Commons.

[13] *Irish Commons' Journal*, Oct. 10, 1692. The Commons answer of thanks was made Oct. 12.

[14] On Oct. 11 the Commons appointed standing committees for religion, grievances, trade, justice, and for elections and privileges. The next day the Commons debated how the committee on grievances might gain access to the accounts and papers of the commissioners of revenue and other government officers. They decided to ask the lord lieutenant to direct officials to cooperate, which he subsequently did, although the Commons had to make a special request for further papers on forfeitures. Just before

ous was the fact that Sidney proved incapable of procuring
legislation to implement the peace settlement. The Commons
refused stubbornly to pass measures outlawing the actions of
James's parliament and legalizing the attainder of rebel leaders — not because they opposed the general purpose of the bills
but because they mistrusted the government.[15] Next they
threw out a mutiny act and rejected one of two revenue bills
on the grounds that it had not originated with them, although
they did pass the other with a qualifying resolution. On November 3 the lord lieutenant prorogued parliament with these
words: "I am sorry I cannot say there hath been a progress
made by you . . . towards those ends as their Majesties had
just right to expect: and I am the more troubled that you, who
have so many and so great obligations . . . should so far mistake yourselves, as to intrench upon their Majesties' prerogative and the rights of the Crown of England as you did on 27
October last, when by a declaratory vote you affirmed that it
is the sole and undoubted right of the Commons of Ireland to
prepare heads of bills for raising money." [16]

The intransigence of the Irish parliament in 1692 is surprising. As Professor J. C. Beckett remarks, the majority of its
members were newly elected, and "Ireland had no strong tradition of parliamentary activity to make up for lack of experience." [17] Their opposition seems to have arisen from several
causes. First was the example of the English parliament, in
which some Anglo-Irish had seats. The Dublin Commons rejected the mutiny bill because it was to be perpetual; in both
that instance and in the desire to initiate and limit revenue
bills one can detect English influence. A more obvious reason lies in the frustration over the limited character of the

---

parliament was prorogued Commons instructed the committee to prepare
charges against anyone suspected of diverting forfeited lands or goods.
Ibid., Oct. 11, 12, 14, 17, 22, Nov. 3, 1692.
   [15] *Ibid.*, Oct. 24, 1692.
   [16] *Ibid.*, Oct. 17, 28, 31, Nov. 1, 2, 3, 1692; Kiernan, *History of the Financial Administration of Ireland to 1817*, pp. 106–115.
   [17] J. C. Beckett, *The Making of Modern Ireland* (New York, 1966), p.
152.

Protestant victory and in the bitterness engendered by the government's leniency toward the Catholics. Although the Anglo-Irish had too much respect for William to challenge him openly, they gave vent to their feelings by attacking his lords justices, with whom Sidney himself had been associated. Indeed, it was said in London that Sidney prorogued parliament specifically to prevent the impeachment of his former colleagues.[18] The feeling against Thomas Coningsby and Charles Porter was certainly intense. The next summer Richard Coote, earl of Bellamont and member of the English Commons, appealed to the English privy council to prevent pardons for the lords justices.[19] When the English Commons met in the autumn of 1693 he instituted impeachment proceedings against the two former lords justices — who, it will be recalled, likewise sat in the Westminster Commons. In addition to allegations of arbitrary acts, fraud, and embezzlement, one of the chief charges against them was that of administering oaths of allegiance to Catholics, as described earlier in this chapter. The English Commons, after hearing evidence, dismissed some of the charges and excused the others on the grounds that they were justified by emergency conditions in Ireland.[20] The critics of the lords justices still refused to close the question; they launched a similar impeachment attempt against Lord Chancellor Porter in the Irish parliament in 1695.[21] It is obvious that, in view of Sidney's close connection with Coningsby and Porter, his choice as lord lieutenant was bound to aggravate the Irish parliament.

Whatever the reasons for the parliamentary opposition in 1692, one conclusion stands out. The Anglo-Irish, despite their internal divisions and their dependence on England, had no intention of surrendering all share in their own government. Insofar as they were able, they sought to have the crown

---

[18] Robert Harley to Sir Edward Harley, Nov. 17, 1692, *Portland MSS*, III, 507.

[19] Robert Harley to Sir Edward Harley, June 24, Aug. 3, 1693, *ibid.*, 534, 539.

[20] *English Commons' Journal*, Dec. 16, 22, 29, 1693, Jan. 2, 24, 1693/94.

[21] J. Freke to Robert Harley, Oct. 5, 1695, *Portland MSS*, III, 570.

rule Ireland exclusively in their interest. Their position seemed weak, yet they had one important advantage: if they needed the protection of the English government, it, in turn, required their full cooperation for the defense of Ireland and for raising money. Like Charles II, William expected to make Ireland pay its own way; he and his ministers hoped, in fact, to have Ireland support a substantial military establishment. Unlike the American colonists, the Anglo-Irish welcomed a standing army because of their fear of rebellion and invasion. But they were not above bargaining over its cost. In contrast to the Irish parliament of Charles II, that of 1692 clearly intended to keep control of taxation and to employ that control to ensure its own power. The one revenue act it passed was made effective for only a year.[22] Irish parliamentary leaders apparently hoped to establish a need for annual sessions. Annoyed by the uncooperative behavior of his first Irish parliament William dissolved it. An impasse had been reached.

Actually neither the English government nor the Anglo-Irish could afford to remain adamant. A tacit compromise was reached. William recalled Lord Sidney and subsequently appointed one of the new lords justices, Lord Capel, as lord deputy. In 1695 a new election produced a less recalcitrant House of Commons. Meanwhile the English privy council acted favorably on a number of heads of bills that had been submitted in 1692.[23] When the new parliament assembled in the autumn of 1695 the lord deputy treated it with firmness, but also with tact.

In his opening speech Lord Capel, omitting any reference to the recent dispute over money bills, presented a new tax bill from England (similar to the act parliament had passed in 1692) accompanying it with a polite request that Commons draw up heads of a supplementary revenue measure to meet

---

[22] Irish Statute, 4 William and Mary, c. 3.

[23] In his opening speech Lord Capel reported to parliament that "the Lord Justices of England have with great application and dispatch considered and transmitted all the bills sent to them." *Irish Commons' Journal*, Aug. 27, 1695.

the heavy financial demands of the times.[24] In other words, the government still insisted upon its power to initiate a money bill yet at the same time it recognized that the Irish Commons possessed a similar right. The Commons accepted Capel's proposals and promptly enacted the government's revenue bill; then they set to work on a supplementary measure. First, however, they successfully insisted upon examining the records of the treasury for all recent income and expenditures, including the controversial accounts of the forfeited estates.[25] Such a procedure clearly brings to mind English precedents and shows that the Irish parliament had at least achieved constitutional adolescence if not yet maturity.

The next three years, 1697–1699, demonstrated both the strength and the weakness of the Irish legislature. In deference to its wishes William, now harassed by party strife in England, acquiesced in the modifications of the Treaty of Limerick noted in Chapter I. Having won this concession the Dublin parliament duly ratified the treaty. The passage of several important penal laws at this time also seems to represent a victory for the Anglo-Irish. Furthermore, the enactment of a number of laws having their origin in heads of bills sent from Dublin shows that the English now accepted the legislative initiative of the Irish parliament as perfectly normal. On the other hand, in 1698 the Irish found themselves threatened by a bill before the English Commons that would stifle the Irish woolen trade. The prospect of such treatment from their English allies incensed the Anglo-Irish. Were they not loyal subjects and stalwart Protestants?

Is it because there is a little channel that runs between Wales and Wexford that when any English dare cross that stream, they must be divested of English privileges, as if they had transgressed some law of nature? or as if indeed

> Nequicam Deus abscidit
> Prudens Oceano dissociabili
> Terras:

---

[24] *Ibid.*, Aug. 17, 1695.
[25] *Ibid.*, Sept. 5, 7, 9, 1695.

Then 'tis the fields on the East side of that water are blest, and
those on the West are curst; but neither God, nor the king will
say so.[26]

Despite their protests, the Anglo-Irish understood the desire
of the English to limit competition with England's basic industry. The Dublin parliament voted a high export duty on
wool and woolen cloth, thus discouraging their exportation to
England.[27] They hoped by taking the initiative to forestall
English action.

The proposed English Woolens Act not only promised great
harm to the Irish economy, but it also raised the major constitutional question left unsolved by the revolution of 1688.
Now that the Westminster parliament had gained virtually
unlimited powers in England, to what degree did its authority
extend over Ireland? The exact relationship of the Irish to
the English parliament had never been explicitly defined. To
the English Dublin was clearly subordinate to Westminster.
To most Irish (Anglo-Irish as well as Gaelic) the Irish parliament was an independent body, created by the king and directly accountable to him, with its own traditions, privileges,
and jurisdiction. To the crown itself these conflicting theories
had made little difference; its chief concern was to have parliament provide taxation and enact necessary legislation. James
II was the first English king to visit Ireland since the fifteenth
century, and there is no question that all of the Tudors and
Stuarts viewed Irish affairs through English eyes. The Stuarts'
chronic difficulties with the English parliament had given
them, nonetheless, little reason to seek its assistance in governing Ireland. Normally the Irish parliament had proved a
more willing instrument and might be summoned, as it was
by both James I and Charles I, at a time when the king was
attempting to rule England without parliament. On occasion
the Irish legislature had maneuvered to increase its influence,
and several times it had objected to English statutes affecting

[26] *A Discourse on the Woollen Manufacture of Ireland and the Consequence of Prohibiting Its Exportation* (Dublin, 1698), p. 11.
[27] Irish Statute, 10 William III, c. 5.

Ireland. Until the fall of Strafford, however, no real constitutional dispute arose over the conflicting claims of the English
and Irish parliaments.[28]

In the summer of 1641, on the eve of the Irish rebellion,
there appeared a carefully developed proposal for establishing
effective parliamentary government in Ireland, entitled *An
Argument delivered by Patricke Darcy*. Darcy was a Catholic
lawyer who sat in the 1641 parliament as a member from
Galway. Three years later Darcy drew up a *Model of Civil
Government* as a guide for the Catholic Confederation of Kilkenny. In it he advocated combining the Lords (including
Roman Catholic instead of Protestant bishops) with a more
representative Commons into a unicameral body with broad
powers. The "Kilkenny Parliament" of 1644 was actually
organized according to his suggestions.[29] The subsequent defeat of the Catholic Confederation prevented the Kilkenny
Parliament from having any constitutional significance, but a
tract written in its defense did have a permanent influence on
Irish political thought: "A Declaration setting forth How, and
by what Means the Laws and Statutes of England, from time
to time, came to be of Force in Ireland." Probably Darcy was
the author of the Declaration.[30] The main purpose of the
treatise is to prove that Ireland is a separate kingdom from
England and that the English parliament had not legislated
for Ireland (and legally could not do so) except in two clearly
limited ways: its interpretations of the common law have
validity for Ireland; it may pass new laws affecting Ireland,
but these have no force until approved by the Irish parliament.

The chief critic of the Declaration was an English-born
Irish judge, Samuel Mayart. Mayart challenged the historical
accuracy of the Declaration, showing that in fact several
English statutes had been enforced in Ireland without the

[28] One writer who did deal with the question was Sir John Davies in
A Discourse of the True Causes Why Ireland was Never Entirely Subdued
(London, 1612).

[29] Coonan, *Irish Catholic Confederacy*, pp. 79, 139.

[30] Charles H. McIlwain, *The American Revolution: A Constitutional
Interpretation* (New York, Macmillan Co., 1924), pp. 34–35.

sanction of the Irish parliament. To Mayart Ireland was
clearly subordinate to England legislatively as well as judi-
cially. Its parliament might, like English corporate boroughs,
make laws concerning domestic problems, but it remained in
every respect subject to English rule.[31]

During the Restoration the issue of Irish legislative autonomy remained relatively dormant.[32] Then in 1689 the Patriot
Parliament of James II revived the claims of 1641–1644 and
proceeded to act with complete independence of England.
The Catholic defeat in 1691 did not end the argument. In
1698 the Anglo-Irish took up the cause in their own interest.[33]
They found an able exponent for their views in William Molyneux, a member of the Irish Commons for Trinity College.

Molyneux's French name serves to remind us that the so-
called Anglo-Irish included many who were not of English
background. He was descended from Sir Thomas Molyneux,
a native of Calais who migrated to Flanders where he married
the daughter of the burgomaster of Bruges. Thomas was a
Protestant and left Flanders during the duke of Alva's perse-
cutions. He lived for a while in London and finally settled
in Dublin where he eventually became chancellor of the Irish
exchequer. William's father (grandson of Thomas), who
fought on the Protestant side during the wars of the 1640's,
appears to have been a member of the landed gentry. William
was born in 1656. He attended Trinity College and, after
receiving his bachelor's degree, entered the Middle Temple

[31] Coonan, *Irish Catholic Confederacy*, p. 183. For a summary of both
Darcy's and Mayart's arguments, see Robert L. Schuyler, *Parliament and
the British Empire, Some Constitutional Controversies concerning Imperial Legislation and Jurisdiction* (New York, Columbia University Press,
1929), pp. 54–71.

[32] In 1660 Sir William Domville drew up a summary of the arguments
of both Davies and Darcy for the instruction of Ormond. Davies' book
was itself reprinted in 1664 and 1666. Caroline Robbins, *The Eighteenth-
Century Commonwealthman* (Cambridge, Mass., Harvard University Press,
1959), p. 140 and n. 6.

[33] In 1692, following the Irish Commons' dispute with Sydney, the Irish
opposition sent representatives to London to present their interpretation
of Poynings' Law. *Journals of the House of Lords* [hereafter cited as
English Lords' Journal], 31 vols. (London, 1777), XV, 261–265.

in London. Despite his legal training his chief interests lay in science and engineering. He became the king's chief engineer and royal surveyor in Ireland and in that capacity rebuilt part of Dublin Castle. In association with Sir William Petty and others he founded the Dublin Philosophical Society in 1683. Two years later he was elected to the Royal Society in London. In 1688 Lord Tyrconnell dismissed Molyneux from his government posts because of his religious and political opinions. Fearing further reprisals, Molyneux left for England where he remained until William's defeat of James II. During this time he cooperated with John Flamsteed in writing a book on optics, *Dioptrica Nova,* which became a standard work on the subject. In addition to his connection with scientists like Flamsteed, Molyneux also carried on an extensive correspondence with John Locke, whom he finally met in 1689. Upon his return to Ireland, Molyneux was elected to the 1692 parliament by Trinity College. He does not appear to have been active in the opposition in that year, but when he returned to the Irish Commons in 1695 he became a more open advocate of Irish interests.[34]

Molyneux's *Case of Ireland* in many respects seems to be a restatement of Darcy's Declaration of 1644. Although Molyneux fails to give credit to this Catholic source, he repeats many of its historical arguments, elaborating on them in order to disprove the counterclaims of Mayart's attack. The Declaration had not yet been printed, but since the Irish House of Lords had ordered copies made, one of which was in Trinity College, it is more than likely that Molyneux had read it.[35] Molyneux goes further than the author of the Declaration in justifying the historical basis for Irish autonomy. He denies that Ireland is a conquered country. Instead, he claims, the authority of the English crown over Ireland was established as a result, in part at least, of the voluntary submission of

---

[34] See the article on Molyneux by Robert Dunlop in *The Dictionary of National Biography* [hereafter cited as *DNB*], ed. Sir Leslie Stephen and Sir Sidney Lee, 63 vols. (London, 1885–1900), XXXVIII, 138–141; see also Robbins, *Eighteenth-Century Commonwealthman,* pp. 137–138.

[35] Robbins, *Eighteenth-Century Commonwealthman,* pp. 138–140.

local Irish kings, chieftains, and bishops. While some later rebelled, others remained loyal, as did also many of the Anglo-Norman barons in Ireland. Obviously these supporters of the king must have retained their liberties and immunities. In any event, the suppression of rebellion is not tantamount to conquest. Finally, even if one believes the English king holds Ireland as a conquered territory, this would give the English king, not the English parliament, the rights of conquest. Actually, Molyneux asserts, Henry II, John, and Henry III all granted the Irish the same liberties as their English subjects.

In reply to the argument that English parliaments had sometimes legislated for Ireland, Molyneux follows Darcy. He asserts that all such English laws were either declaratory in nature (that is, definitions of the common law) or were reenacted by the Irish parliament before being enforced in Ireland, except in a few instances. As regards these last, Molyneux introduces a new claim: he purports to show that these exceptions were all laws passed by English parliaments in which there were Irish representatives, and thus their acts were valid in Ireland "because they were assented to by its own representatives." [36] From these rather dubious examples Molyneux concludes that if the English parliament is to legislate for Ireland it should include Irish members. Legislative union would, he believes, be welcome but "this is a happiness we can hardly hope for." [37]

When Molyneux comes to the early events of William and Mary's reign he admits that the Irish accepted English legislation affecting Ireland. He maintains, however, that the Irish only acquiesced because of the peculiar situation existing in 1691 and in hope of having these laws reenacted in Ireland. Furthermore, he reasons with Lockean casuistry, no one can surrender fundamental rights by acquiescence or even by alienation. He concludes his treatise by disposing of several popular English arguments for Ireland's inferiority.

[36] William Molyneux, *The Case of Ireland's Being Bound by Acts of Parliament in England Stated* (Dublin, 1698), pp. 95–96.
[37] *Ibid.*, p. 98.

Though Molyneux cannot explain away the historical supremacy of the English over the Irish courts of common law, such as King's Bench, he rather weakly suggests that the right of appeal from Irish to English courts may have been authorized by an Irish statute that has since been lost. Even if that is not true, the subordination of the Irish parliament cannot be inferred from the subordination of the Irish courts. As for the allegation that England had purchased Ireland by its costly victories over Irish rebels, he dismisses this with the observation that England's financial claims may give it the right to be repaid, but nothing more. Finally, Molyneux disposes of the argument that Ireland is a colony and as such is subject to the laws of the mother country; the monarch is called king of Ireland just as he is king of England. Ireland is, therefore, as complete a kingdom as England.[38]

Whether largely borrowed from Darcy or constructed independently, Molyneux's exposition of Irish rights is a landmark. "It was," as Charles H. McIlwain wrote in 1924, "an epoch-making book, which deserved the sensation it created. From the time of its appearance until the present day, it is hardly too much to say, the constitutional problem with which it deals has been the most persistent and the most perplexing with which English statesmen have had to contend." [39] Certainly no previously published work had discussed so cogently the question of Ireland's relationship to England, and by implication the general problem of the position of local legislatures in the imperial government. The treatise won immediate acclaim in Ireland and remained one of the most influential books on its subject for over a century, not only in Ireland but later in the American colonies.[40]

The reaction to Molyneux's arguments across Saint George's Channel proved both prompt and vehement. The English Commons denounced his work as "bold and pernicious" and ordered it to be burned by the common hangman.[41] The next

[38] *Ibid.*, pp. 148–149.
[39] McIlwain, *American Revolution*, p. 46.
[40] Robbins, *Eighteenth-Century Commonwealthman*, p. 397.
[41] William Cobbett, *Parliamentary History*, 36 vols. (London, 1806–1820), V, 1181.

year the Westminster parliament passed the notorious Woolens Act. In 1671 the English attorney general, Sir Heneage Finch, had maintained that no English act could remain binding on Ireland unless the Irish parliament endorsed it, explaining that "if a statute were made in England to forbid the transportation of wool out of Ireland; yet a statute in Ireland might make it lawful again." The crown, not the English parliament, he asserted, had power over Ireland, to which Charles II reportedly replied, "I know not whether it be good law, I am sure it is very good reason." [42] It is doubtful, nonetheless, if Charles II, as king of Ireland, would ever have set aside an act he had signed as king of England; it is certain that William III never would. The Irish parliament might exploit its control over taxation to demand legislation, but it could not force concessions from Westminster when English national interests were at stake. In 1699 the English parliament further demonstrated its power by establishing a commission to dispose of the king's confiscated lands in Ireland.[43] Although it was not actually until 1719 that Westminster spelled out its full legal authority, Irish legislative equality was little more than a fiction after 1699. To paraphrase George Orwell, kingdoms might all be equal, but some were more equal than others.

The years 1697–1699 thus mark a critical point in Irish constitutional history. They witness both the fullest expression of the theory of Ireland's legislative autonomy and the defeat of that theory in actual practice. The outcome seems so clear that historians have exaggerated the totality of England's victory. W. E. H. Lecky wrote that the Protestant Irish in 1698 were "almost absolutely powerless. Divided among themselves, cut off from the great body of the nation, excluded from the highest political and judicial positions, living in a poverty-stricken, ignorant, and degraded country, they could do little but utter barren protests." [44] Most subsequent historians have

---

[42] Carte, *The Life of Ormond*, V, 123.

[43] Simms, *Williamite Confiscation*, pp. 98–99.

[44] W. E. H. Lecky, *A History of England in the Eighteenth Century*, 8 vols. (New York, 1891), II, 452.

chanted the same dirge. They are guilty of oversimplication.
The failure to win legislative independence did not send the
Anglo-Irish into full retreat. Quite the contrary. They refused
to abandon their hope for ultimate equality, either through
autonomy or possibly union, and they continued to hammer
away at Dublin Castle both to gain specific ends and to increase their influence in general.

If, in moments of crisis, Westminster might, like some *deus
ex machina*, intervene in Irish affairs, the routine task of
governing Ireland lay with the lord lieutenant. Laurence
Eachard, writing in 1691, said of that official, "Truly there is
not in all Christendom any other vice roy that comes higher
to the majesty of a king for his jurisdiction, authority, train,
furniture and provision." [45] In reality the post was somewhat
less glamorous. The Irish lord lieutenant found himself in a
position not unlike that of many eighteenth-century husbands.
The law gave him almost complete control over his fractious
spouse, but if he failed to humor her, life could prove extremely difficult. When neglected or crossed, the Irish Commons could become as petulant as a shrew; when cajoled and
bribed it could prove a willing and even a generous partner.
Most lord lieutenants chose the path of compromise and concession. During the same period that the Irish legislature suc-
cumbed to the frontal attack by the English parliament, it
made considerable gains in its relationship with the executive.

Beginning with 1695, Irish revenue bills normally granted
supplies for a period of two years, which meant that the Irish
parliament expected to have biennial sessions. This arrangement represents an example of the kind of modus vivendi that
was emerging. Some of the members of the Irish Commons
sought annual meetings, while the government would have
preferred less frequent sessions. The crown did not, for example, call the Dublin body between 1699 and 1703, and when
it assembled at the latter date Anne's first lord lieutenant (the
second duke of Ormond) tried to obtain a grant for three

[45] Laurence Eachard, *An Exact Description of Ireland* (London, 1691),
pp. 33–34.

years. He not only failed in this effort, but he had to permit the Irish Commons to examine the treasury accounts, as they had done in 1695.[46]

In 1703 the Commons also drew up an address to the queen on the state of the nation, which, among other complaints, voiced the opinion "that the want of holding frequent parliaments has been one of the principal occasions of the miseries attending this kingdom." [47] This opinion did not go unheeded; between 1703 and 1782 the Irish parliament met at least every two years with sessions normally lasting from two to six months.

The Irish parliament had not yet attained the stature of its Westminster prototype, but it was not far behind. It now met far more often than had the Westminster parliament before 1640; it also assembled more regularly than did the legislatures in many of the colonies, where the governors were sometimes able to procure revenue grants for as long as twenty-one years.[48] Some Irish legislation still came directly from the English ministry through the lord lieutenant; some originated in the Irish privy council; much began in the Irish parliament. Ultimately the actual laws that were enacted sprang from many diverse sources, and the steps involved in their passage are complex and often obscure. Far from representing only the wishes of the English government or the Irish parliament, a large part of the legislation came into being as the result of activities of various English and Irish individuals and pressure groups that succeeded by force of argument, by influence, by bribery or logrolling, or in fact by any method available, in maneuvering their proposals through the legislative maze.[49]

[46] *Ormonde MSS*, n. s. VIII, xxxviii–xxxix; *Irish Commons' Journal*, Sept. 4, 5, 7, 9, 1695.

[47] *Irish Commons' Journal*, Oct. 11, 1703.

[48] Leonard Labaree, *Royal Government in America* (New Haven, Yale University Press, 1930), pp. 275–278. That was in Jamaica. In New York the revenue bills at the opening of the eighteenth century ran for five years. *Ibid.*, pp. 283–285.

[49] As is suggested in note 8, above, standing committees played an important role in the Irish Commons at this period. They later played a similar role in colonial legislatures; see Ralf W. Harlow, *The History of*

The formal steps in the passage of legislation as recorded in the journals of the Lords and Commons frequently fail to illuminate the real forces at work. The extant correspondence between officials in Dublin and those at Westminster is more informative but seldom complete. A study of the famous (or infamous) penal statute of 1704 by J. G. Simms demonstrates how difficult it is to follow the history of a given bill.[50] Despite the impossibility of unraveling the story behind most laws, one conclusion is perfectly clear. By the opening of the eighteenth century Ireland possessed a political system that must be termed representative at least to the degree that its Anglo-Irish landholding and commercial classes had an essential share in legislation.

As a representative body the Irish parliament bore a strong resemblance to that of Westminster, with some important differences. The House of Lords in Dublin was somewhat smaller than its English counterpart. According to Sir William Petty, it contained 118 lay peers in 1672; twenty years later the number had risen to 126, but then it declined.[51] In England at the opening of the eighteenth century 168 lay peers were entitled to sit in the upper house.[52] The difference in effective membership was even greater since many of the Irish peers were absentee landlords. Because of its smaller size and because of the emphasis on religion in Irish politics, the twenty-two Irish bishops played a more influential role than

---

Legislative Methods in the Period before 1825 (New Haven, Yale University Press, 1917), pp. 1–23.

[50] J. G. Simms, "The Making of a Penal Law, 1703–04," *Irish Historical Studies,* XII (1960–1961), 105–118.

[51] Sir William Petty, *Political Anatomy of Ireland,* 3rd ed., in *A Collection of Tracts and Treatises,* 2 vols. (Dublin, 1860–1861), II, 123–124. Elizabeth I had kept the Irish Lords below thirty, but the first two Stuarts created eighty new peers, "at least thirty of whom had no connexion with Ireland." Lawrence Stone, *The Crisis of the Aristocracy 1558–1641* (Oxford, 1965), p. 104. *A True and Complete List of the Lords Spiritual and Temporal: Together with the Knights etc. of the Parliament of Ireland held at Chichester-House Dublin, 1692* (Dublin, 1692); MacNeil, *Constitutional History of Ireland Till the Union,* p. 30.

[52] A. S. Turberville, *The House of Lords in the XVIII Century* (Oxford, Clarendon Press, 1927), pp. 4–6.

did their twenty-six brethren in England.[53] Since heads of
bills originating in the Commons normally went directly to
the Irish privy council and thence to London, the Irish Lords
often had only a limited voice in important legislation. As
has been explained, when such a bill met with approval in
England it could not be amended upon its return to Ireland.
Thus the Lords had only two alternatives: to accept it without change or to reject it. Most of the legislation that actually
began in the Lords appears to have been government sponsored, and, as in England, all money bills were first considered
by the Commons. Nevertheless the Irish peers and bishops
possessed considerable political power. Many of the leaders of
the upper house sat on the privy council where they advised
the lord lieutenant (or lords justices) on both heads of bills
emanating from the Commons and on legislation that Dublin
Castle thought desirable. In addition to participating in the
works of the council, many of the lords and several of the
bishops controlled seats in the lower house, and almost all of
the lords, both lay and ecclesiastical sought to influence elections.[54] All in all, the lords enjoyed a great influence over
the Commons.

From 1682 to 1800 the Irish House of Commons contained
300 members; 234 from 117 cities and boroughs, two from
Trinity College, and sixty-four county members. The last, as
in England, were elected by forty-shilling freeholders (after
1727 only Protestant freeholders). The great landowners influenced county elections though seldom controlled them completely. The two Trinity members were chosen by the fellows
and students in a manner similar to the Oxford and Cambridge representatives. As for the citizens and burgesses, their
constituencies can be divided into four categories, three of
which resemble types found in England, freemen boroughs,
corporation boroughs, and household or "potwalloper" boroughs. The larger towns with the freemen franchise (Car-

[53] Francis G. James, *North Country Bishop* (New Haven, 1956), p. 251,
n. 14.
[54] J. L. McCracken, "Irish Parliamentary Elections 1727–68," *Irish Historical Studies*, V (1946–1947), 210.

rickfergus, Cork, Drogheda, Dublin, Londonderry, and Waterford) had a fairly numerous electorate and never came under the control of one patron. Most of the others fell under the domination of a single man or family. The corporation boroughs, largely of Stuart creation, differ from the English corporations in that in Ireland the corporation often performed no function save that of electing members of parliament. This was partly because so many of them were little more than villages and partly because some were kept inoperative by powerful patrons. Most of the potwalloper boroughs, because of their small size, did not have a large electorate and so also came under the control of patrons. The fourth and uniquely Irish type of constituency was made up of seven "manor boroughs" something like English burgage-tenure boroughs.[55]

Before the Restoration the Irish Commons had remained so unimportant that parliamentary seats had little attraction or value; the first contested election seems to have taken place in 1662.[56] After 1692 the situation changed radically. Parliamentary seats now offered both political influence and social prestige which in turn meant that they also attained a financial value. Boroughmongers appeared, patronage increased, and contested elections became common; soon, in fact, the Irish political scene displayed the same attributes that characterized the English parliamentary system of the period.[57] Edith Johnston's study of Irish elections after 1760 shows that they were then more subject to manipulation than those in England.[58] Nevertheless, judging from the size of the electorate, it seems safe to conclude that, as far as the Protestant Anglo-Irish are concerned, the Dublin House of Commons was roughly as representative (or, if one prefers, as unrepre-

[55] Porritt, *Unreformed Commons*, II, 295–98; Edith M. Johnston, *Great Britain and Ireland 1760–1800* (Edinburgh, 1963), pp. 159–178.
[56] Porritt, *Unreformed House of Commons*, II, 195. Charles II's parliament showed its sense of increased importance by fining absentee members. *Irish Commons' Journal*, Jan. 31, 1665/66.
[57] McCracken, "Irish Parliamentary Elections," pp. 211–212.
[58] Johnston, *Great Britain and Ireland*, Pt. II, pp. 120–178.

sentative) as its Westminster counterpart. There were even several Dissenters in parliament. Certainly not all Protestant property holders enjoyed the franchise in Ireland, yet probably every significant propertied group of Protestants found M.P.'s to voice its wishes. Indeed it is possible that some Catholic economic interests found indirect representation in the Dublin parliament. In fact, parliament passed a law in the 1740's to stop Catholic rent agents from influencing voters.[59]

The establishment of representative government in Ireland inevitably led to the growth of political factions and parties. Lord lieutenants might deplore the "heats and divisions" that disrupted the smooth operation of the legislative machine, but they could not prevent them. Once parliament obtained even a limited share in government it naturally became a battleground for conflicting interests.

The growth of political parties is one of the key developments of English history during the closing decades of the seventeenth century. By the reign of Queen Anne almost all politically conscious Englishmen (including many who had no vote) had become engrossed in the rivalry between Whigs and Tories. Although many of the issues that had divided the two groups had been settled by 1702, party spirit still pervaded public life. Most men identified themselves with faction, though in the language of the time they reserved the terms "faction" or "party" for their opponents, always assuming that their own particular beliefs were above partisanship. Robert Walcott has suggested that the conflict between Whig and Tory offers only a partial explanation of English politics in 1700 and that the interplay of a number of Court and Country factions proved more significant.[60] Certainly many politicians were too opportunistic to be bound by partisan principles or loyalty, while many country members prided themselves upon their independence. On the other hand, J. H. Plumb and

    [59] Porritt, *Unreformed House of Commons*, II, 224.
    [60] Robert Walcott, *English Politics in the Early Eighteenth Century* (Cambridge, Mass., Harvard University Press, 1956), pp. 156–159.

Geoffrey Holmes have demonstrated that party rivalry remained a dominant theme in the first decades of the eighteenth century.[61] As Jonathan Swift put it early in George I's reign, "there cannot properly speaking be above two Partyes in such a Government as ours, and one Side will feel themselves obliged to take in all the subaltern Denominations of those who dislike the present Establishment, in order to make themselves a Balance against the other." [62]

Writing of New York in the 1690's, Lawrence H. Leder remarks that partisan politics in the province "mirrored a reflection of developments in the mother country, although a time lag often existed." [63] Irish politics reflected English developments even more closely and quickly. Just as the Irish political structure resembled that of England, its politicians and citizens divided into Whig and Tory groups. Most Anglo-Irish leaders watched the English scene carefully and aligned themselves with whatever English party seemed to represent their interests. English officials, arriving in Ireland with a full set of party prejudices and commitments, reinforced this trend.

Both contemporary writers and historians have recognized the appearance of a Whig and Tory group in postrevolutionary Ireland, and within the Tory camp of a Hanoverian and Jacobite wing. To this degree the political divisions in England and Ireland were alike. The similarity is, however, often misleading for in Ireland there existed crosscurrents not found in England. To begin with, although religion was a political issue in both countries, the Catholic-Protestant struggle dominated the thinking of Anglo-Irish politicians far more than it did their English cousins. A more basic difference is that the relationship of Ireland to England always remained

[61] J. H. Plumb, *The Growth of Political Stability in England 1675–1725* (London, Macmillan Co., 1967, pp. 46, 132–133; Geoffrey Holmes, *English Politics in the Age of Anne* (New York, St. Martin's Press, 1967), pp. 2–6.

[62] Jonathan Swift, *An Enquiry into the Behavior of the Queen's Last Ministry*, ed. Irvin Ehrenpreis (Bloomington, Ind., Indiana University Press, 1956), p. 94.

[63] Lawrence H. Leder, *Robert Livingston 1654–1728 and the Politics of Colonial New York* (Chapel Hill, University of North Carolina Press, 1961), p. 77.

a central issue to Irish leaders, while it became only a peripheral question to the English after the defeat of James II in 1691. In Ireland the conflict between the government and opposition forces tended to crystallize along nationalistic lines — between what became known as the "English" and "Irish" (Anglo-Irish) interests.

III

Parties and Politics

1702–1714

During the reign of Queen Anne the governmental structure tentatively established under William III took definite shape along the lines that were to characterize it until the 1760's. Through its control of the Irish executive the English ministry became the ultimate decision-making body for Ireland. It did not, however, exercise absolute power. Its primary agent, the lord lieutenant, found that he could exert effective authority over the country only by winning and keeping control of the Irish parliament. To do this he required support from three sources: consistent backing from London both as regards policies and patronage, a reliable contingent of placemen in parliament, and the cooperation and votes of a sizable portion of the independent members in Commons. Since, as has been pointed out, the men who sat in Chichester House identified themselves with diverse political groups, the Dublin administration had to construct a government party or coalition in order to operate efficiently.

Although during the election of Anne's first Irish parliament in 1703 party divisions were clearly apparent, the English government's appointment of the second duke of Ormond as lord lieutenant made the prospects for harmony seem bright. Ormond was a staunch Anglican, one of William's noted generals, and the scion of a leading Anglo-Irish family, the Butlers. His grandfather had been the great leader of the Protestant Cavaliers and was lord lieutenant under Charles II. When he arrived in Dublin in June 1703 Ormond was greeted "with the greatest demonstration of joy imaginable." [1]

At the opening of the Irish parliament on September 24,

[1] Narcissus Luttrell, *A Brief Historical Relation of State Affairs*, 6 vols. (Oxford, 1857), V, 306.

1703, Ormond declared: "As my duty and gratitude oblige me to serve her Majesty with the utmost diligence and fidelity, so my inclination and interest, and the example of my ancestors are indispensable obligations upon me to improve every opportunity the most I can to the advantage and prosperity of my native country." [2] In response the Irish Commons drew up an address to the queen thanking her for choosing a governor, "whose conduct, bravery and unshaken loyalty to the crown and tender care for his native country have rendered him equally acceptable to your Majesty and to us." [3] These statements represented more than a mere exchange of compliments. Ormond's background enabled him to view Irish problems from the inside and he set out to reconcile party and national differences. The members of the Irish Commons were likewise sincere in their response for they hoped that at last they had an administration that would act as their spokesman in London. Inevitably disagreements lay ahead, yet the parliamentary session of 1703–1704 produced an impressive harvest of legislation, for most of which Ormond and his aides secured English approval. One may say, in fact, that Ormond's dealings with parliament during his first term of office (1703–1707) became something of a model for the operation of the Irish legislative machinery during the first half of the eighteenth century. Relations between parliament and Dublin Castle had not, as we have seen, been too satisfactory during William's reign. Ormond's relative success, both from the point of view of the government and the Anglo-Irish, did much to prove that the existing system could be made to work.

Ormond's first significant concession to the opposition forces was to accept the election of a Whig, Alan Brodrick, as Speaker of the House of Commons. The Brodrick family had acquired its initial holdings in Ireland during the Cromwellian period, and Alan himself owed his office, as solicitor general, to William of Orange.[4] Although, like Brodrick, many of the

---

[2] *Irish Commons' Journal*, Sept. 24, 1703.
[3] *Ibid.*, Sept. 29, 1703.
[4] Brodrick had been solicitor general since 1695. His life is in the *DNB*, VI, 383–384.

Irish Whigs were more recent arrivals than their Tory adversaries and had closer ties with England, they were suspicious of Anne's first ministry with its Tory leadership. Ormond's predecessor, the earl of Rochester, had favored the High Church Tories and alienated the Whigs. Because of William's policy of working with leaders from both parties (he chose, for example, about an equal number of Whig and Tory judges), the conflicts of his reign between the executive and parliament had not been primarily party conflicts.[5] Under Rochester, the Whigs found themselves excluded from favor. They were now prepared to refurbish the traditional Whig arguments against the crown and apply them to the Irish scene, to become the defenders of the Irish Commons against Dublin Castle. Though a minority themselves, the Brodericians (as their enemies liked to call them) thus became for the moment the leaders of the "Irish" as opposed to the "English" interest. Brodrick's election as Speaker demonstrated the strength of the opposition.

Instead of meeting this challenge head on, Ormond chose to accept the situation that confronted him and to pursue what appeared at least to be a nonpartisan policy: to play the role, so to speak, of a "patriot" lord lieutenant who placed national welfare above party interest. Whether this was his real objective or merely a pose to permit him to divide the opposition is not clear. The point is that in cooperation with parliament Ormond succeeded in shaping and enacting a broad legislative program. He did not eliminate the opposition but he avoided stalemate, and he won the support of most of what may be called the Irish country party, that is, the independent members.

First among Ormond's aims, of course, was to get a satisfactory money bill. He hoped to increase the revenue sufficiently to reduce the debt, and, as is mentioned in the last chapter, he also hoped to win approval for a three-year tax bill. Brodrick and his followers, by contrast, sought to limit

---

[5] F. E. Ball, *The Judges in Ireland, 1221–1921*, 3 vols. (Dublin, 1926), II, 9.

taxes to one year. As regards the debt, they alleged that the
government greatly exaggerated its size. Early in October the
House revived the committee for accounts.[6] After "having sat
de die in diem, early and late, both mornings and afternoons,"
the committee accused the deputy vice-treasurer of Ireland,
Sir William Robinson, of falsifying his report on the debt. Although Robinson was saved from expulsion from the Commons by six votes, a resolution did passs that declared him
unfit for government service and ordered that he be imprisoned during "the pleasure of this House."[7] The committee then took up the question of royal pensions charged
to the Irish establishment. When they made their report to
Commons on October 25, the committee of the whole house
severely criticized a number of the pensions, especially those
to absentees. Since the government paid the pensions out of
the crown's hereditary income, Commons could not actually
stop them. They did succeed, however, in including in the
money bill a 20 percent tax on pensions paid to absentees.[8]
As for the main terms of the heads of proposals for the revenue
bill, the government won adequate taxes to meet current needs
but was compelled to accept a compromise on the question of
the act's duration. Dublin Castle had to be satisfied with a
grant of taxes for two years instead of three. In fact, the government only defeated a Whig attempt to limit taxes to one
year by the narrow margin of three votes.[9]

The struggle over the passage of the revenue bill illuminates
considerably Ormond's position and policies during his first
year as lord lieutenant. Ormond seems to have recognized that
the members of the Irish Commons needed to vent some of
their pent-up animosity and that they required assurances of
better treatment in the future. The Anglo-Irish in 1703 felt
a strong sense of grievance over a number of recent English
policies, particularly the English Woolens Act of 1699 and the
administration of the Irish forfeited estates. They understood,

[6] *Irish Commons' Journal,* Oct. 7, 1703.
[7] *Ibid.,* Oct. 12, 1703.
[8] *Ibid.,* Nov. 10, 1703; Irish Statute, 2 Anne c. 4, sect. 3.
[9] *Ormonde MSS,* n.s., VIII, xxxix.

at the same time, their fundamental dependence on English power, even if they disliked admitting it. Furthermore, with memories of 1690–1691 still fresh, the Anglo-Irish were willing to contribute their share to the war against Louis XIV. It must have exasperated Ormond to let the Brodericians attack Tories like Robinson and Francis Annesley (whom they evicted from Commons on the grounds he had defamed the Irish Protestants);[10] to permit them to denounce royal pensions; and to accept their changes in the money bill. Still, as long as parliament came through with a decent revenue measure the lord lieutenant could feel he had achieved his immediate goal. Meanwhile he could lay the groundwork for a stronger position in the future.

In addition to compromising over the money bill, Ormond took other steps to placate or circumvent opposition forces. During the summer months preceding the convening of parliament he had brought pressure to bear on the English privy council to approve several pending heads of bills left over from the last session of the Irish legislature as well as getting them to consider proposals of the Irish privy council for new bills. In October he was able to submit to the Dublin parliament three bills that they promptly enacted into law.[11] Ormond also received with tact recommendations from the Commons concerning patronage and certain administrative actions, such as a request for more naval protection in the Irish Sea.[12] When the Irish parliament asked for a change in the English Navigation Acts to permit the direct shipment of Irish linen to the colonies he seconded their efforts and obtained a promise from the English ministry that the Queen would "be graciously pleased to interpose with the Parliament in England" on their behalf.[13] Most important of all, Ormond

----

[10] *Ibid.* Annesley was one of the commissioners appointed by the English parliament to supervise the Irish forfeited estates. The hostility of the Irish Commons arose from his activities in this capacity. Simms, *Williamite Confiscation*, pp. 99–100, 156.

[11] *Irish Commons' Journal*, Oct. 16, 1703.

[12] *Ibid.*, Oct. 7, 8, 1703, Mar. 2, 3, 1703/04.

[13] *Ibid.*, Nov. 20, 1703.

worked for unity in the Irish parliament by encouraging it to draw up a new bill against the Roman Catholics.

During the autumn of 1703 the Irish Commons devoted much of its time and energies to forging what was probably the most comprehensive of the Irish penal laws: the act of 1704 (discussed in Chapter I), which among other provisions struck at Catholic inheritance rights. Though disagreement arose over details, most Tories and Whigs joined with enthusiasm in the work at hand and looked to Dublin Castle for support and approval. The dismayed Catholics' only chance of modifying the proposed legislation was to exert influence in London. The English government, sensitive to the reaction of its Catholic allies (Austria and Savoy), seems to have considered softening the bill on the grounds that some of its provisions violated the Treaty of Limerick.[14] The Irish Catholics employed eminent lawyers to plead their case and had the assistance of some influential noblemen.[15] Their associates in London also published pamphlets in an effort to win support.[16] For a number of weeks the English privy council postponed reaching a decision — much to the alarm of the waiting Commons in Dublin. Throughout much of the winter Ormond's agents in London, like William Wogan and Lord Coningsby, worked tirelessly to secure the bill's approval.[17]

In the end Ormond's friends were successful. The bill came back as strong as it went over, but with one significant change. Included in the bill as amended by the English privy council was a provision to exclude Protestant Dissenters from office in Ireland, which made it, in other words, an Irish version of the English Test Act. Gilbert Burnet asserts that the ministry

[14] W. Wogan to E. Southwell, London, July 6, 1703, British Museum, Additional Manuscripts [hereafter cited as BM Add. MSS.], 37.673, fol. 3 (printed by permission of the Department of Manuscripts of the British Museum).

[15] Wogan to Southwell, Dec. 14, 1703, ibid., fol. 23.

[16] Wogan to Southwell, Dec. 18, 1703, Jan. 20, 1703/04, ibid., fols. 25–26, 47.

[17] Wogan to Southwell, Jan. 29, 1703/04, ibid., fol. 53. There is a life of Wogan in the DNB, LXII, 288–289; on Coningsby, see note 39, below. Coningsby's life is also in the DNB, XII, 11–13.

added this provision with the hope that it would kill the whole measure (something like the American Tariff of Abominations in 1828).[18] A recent study of the act concludes that Nottingham, acting for the High Church party, inserted the Irish test.[19] Whatever the truth of the matter, there is no denying that the inclusion of the test alienated many of the Irish Whigs. They argued against the measure as one that would divide the Protestants when the main purpose of the act was to unite them. Speaker Brodrick reportedly called the test "poison," adding that "Whatever comes from England has poison in it." [20] Nonetheless, the Irish Commons passed the amended bill with a comfortable majority. The test may have estranged the Whig leaders, but it apparently did not disturb the less partisan country members, who were almost to a man Anglicans. As Richard Cox, Ormond's lord chancellor, once put it, there might be some need for Dissenters to be saints, but there was none that they should be justices of the peace.[21] Froude quotes a contemporary opinion that out of 300 members in the Commons less than ten would ever be Dissenters.[22] Even in Ulster most of the landed gentry belonged to the Church of Ireland. Although there is no evidence that Ormond and the Irish Tories were responsible for the test, they benefited from it, since it divided the Whigs from their non-partisan supporters. Ormond's administration emerged at the end of the session, in March 1704, far stronger than it had been the previous autumn.

Besides the successful shepherding of the popery bill through the English privy council, Ormond and his associates won English approval for a number of other Irish heads of bills dealing with a variety of subjects such as naturalization

[18] Gilbert Burnet, *History of His Own Times*, 4 vols. (London, 1818), IV, 24.

[19] J. G. Simms, "The Making of a Penal Law," *Irish Historical Studies*, XII (1960–1961), 105–118.

[20] Lt. Gen. Stewart to Robert Harley, May 30, 1704, *Portland MSS*, VIII, 121–122.

[21] Ball, *Judges in Ireland*, II, 25.

[22] Henry Maxwell to Lord Molesworth, Apr. 9, 1716, quoted in Froude, *English in Ireland*, I, 430.

of aliens, a Dublin workhouse, and judicial reform. According to Wogan's complaints from London the attorney general and particularly the solicitor general had looked with disfavor on several Irish bills.[23] Since Irish legislation was referred to their offices before being acted upon by the privy council, their criticism much disturbed Wogan. The fact that, despite the two law officers, most of the Irish legislation was accepted indicates that Nottingham, Godolphin, and other ministers must have been strongly inclined to back Ormond's administration. There is a possibility, too, that Sir Edward Northey and Sir Simon Harcourt's objections may have been motivated by something besides questions of policy. Annesley, writing from London in late January 1704, reported that the "Attorney and Solicitor think £200 too little for the trouble and loss they have been at about Irish bills." He suggested that instead £200 each would be "but a modest compensation" for their pains.[24]

By February most of the Irish bills had returned safely from London to come before the Irish parliament for final action. The Irish Commons summoned the lord lieutenant's clerk to present them with a full list, with text, of all the heads of bills actually submitted to London so that they could check on the exact changes made by either the Irish or English privy council.[25] Each bill again went through three readings. About some, like the popery bill, there was conisderable debate. One, dealing with tolls, was rejected because of an amendment, though in order to implement its other terms a resolution was passed declaring that the exacting of certain tolls "is against law and an high misdemeanor."[26] Although the Irish Commons voted their "hearty acknowledgments" to Ormond for "the many good bills which have been transmited to us this

[23] Wogan to Southwell, Jan. 8, 11, 15, 1703/04, BM, Add. MSS. 37.673, fols. 38, 39, 44.
[24] Annesley to Ormond, Jan. 29, 1703/04, *Ormonde MSS*, n.s., VIII, 56–57.
[25] *Irish Commons' Journal*, Feb. 24, 1703/04.
[26] *Ibid.*, Feb. 29, 1703/04. The vote to reject the bill was forty-four to thirty-nine.

present session of Parliament," [27] they continued to display their independence.

In October 1703 the Commons had drawn up a representation to the crown which, while protesting their loyalty, had expressed their concern over the economic plight of Ireland and the recent threats to "the constitution of this kingdom." The representation called on the queen to save Ireland from ruin either by changing English regulations or by providing for a union between the two nations.[28] The queen's reply proved evasive. With difficulty Ormond's henchmen delayed the official publication of the representation, but nothing could suppress the Commons' disappointment over the failure of the English government to take steps to help Irish trade. On March 1, three days before the end of the session, the Commons resolved, *nemine contradicente*:

> That by reason of the great decay of trade and discouragement of exportation of the manufactures of this Kingdom, many poor tradesmen are reduced to extreme want and beggary.
> That it will greatly conduce to the relief of the said poor, and to the good of this Kingdom that inhabitants thereof should use none others than the manufacturing of this Kingdom in their apparel, and the furniture of their houses.[29]

The members then unanimously pledged themselves to conform to the resolution.

The events of the parliamentary session of 1703–1704 tell much about the Irish legislative process in general and Or-

[27] *Ibid.*, Mar. 2, 1703/04.

[28] *Ibid.*, Oct. 20, 1703; *Ormonde MSS*, n.s., VIII, xli. For the queen's reply, see *Irish Commons' Journal*, Feb. 11, 1703/04. The anonymous author of a contemporary pamphlet warned that "The unkindness of England is the cause of the present uneasiness of both nations, . . . no free monarchy can ever govern its provinces in pure subjection, for a Province Governed in pure subjection, must either be governed with force or lost. And the force that keeps its obedience will sometime destroy the Liberty of the superior state." *An Essay upon an Union of Ireland with England* (Dublin, 1704). On the arguments for union, see Robbins, *Eighteenth-Century Commonwealthman*, pp. 148–149.

[29] *Irish Commons' Journal*, Mar. 1, 1703/04.

mond's administration in particular. For one thing, they show
how the Irish Commons made constant and effective use of
both standing and special committees and of the committee
of the whole house.[30] Their practices closely resemble those
of seventeenth-century English parliaments and were well in
advance of the procedures in contemporary colonial legislatures. At this time most of the active members of the Irish
privy council sat in either the Commons or the Lords so that
the government managed to have spokesmen on all important
committees. By retaining, for the time being, Brodrick and
a few of his associates on the privy council, Ormond gave the
opposition leaders a voice in the deliberations of the executive.
The result, if not responsible government in the accepted
sense, was a rough sort of harmony. Ormond apparently
understood how to play the legislative game.

In many respects an Irish lord lieutenant faced a more difficult task than that confronting an English ministry. To please
the Irish parliament he had to allow some changes in government bills as well as accept new bills originating in the Irish
legislature. On the other hand, he must be careful to see that
the legislative menu he recommended to London would be
palatable to the English ministry. Having submitted the bills
to England he must employ his influence to secure their approval with a minimum of changes lest the Irish parliament
refuse final passage. The lord lieutenant needed to keep the
Irish parliament in session until the whole process was completed, merely having parliament recess for several weeks while
the Irish bills, like suitors, awaited their fate before the English privy council. Like suitors, too, the bills were much in
need of a friend in court. Their enemies, such as the Irish
Catholics in the case of the popery bill, made every effort to
block or delay the council's approval. Furthermore there was
always the possibility that the English parliament might intervene. In January 1704, for example, William Wogan was not

[30] The committee of the whole house, for example, cooperated with the
special committee for accounts to limit supply and criticize government
expenditures. *Irish Commons' Journal*, Oct. 14, 19, 25, 26, Nov. 1, 2, 10,
1703. On standing committees, see Chapter II, note 14.

only busy trying to discredit the Roman Catholic attack on the popery bill, but he was also occupied with visiting English parliamentary leaders to persuade them to support an Irish duty on calicoes, strongly opposed by the East India Company.[31] Wogan's chief ally in such ventures was Lord Coningsby, a former lord justice of Ireland and M.P. for Leominister. Without the assistance of an active representative in London and the support of several key men in the ministry, a lord lieutenant could scarcely hope to command influence in Dublin. Similarly, a lord lieutenant incapable of managing the Irish parliament could expect his opinions to carry little weight in London. He must, in short, succeed simultaneously both as Ireland's advocate in England and England's governor in Ireland; if he failed in the one he would almost certainly fail in the other.

Burnet, with Whiggish optimism, wrote that the Irish parliament ended its session of 1703–1704 "in so much heat that it was thought that parliament would meet no more if the Duke of Ormond was continued in government." [32] The duke took a different view. In the first place, despite the activities of the opposition, the session had been far more successful than Burnet implies. In the second place, Ormond intended that, when next it met, the Irish parliament would prove far more amenable to control from Dublin Castle. Ormond now abandoned his efforts at nonpartisanship and openly created a Tory administration. Immediately after the closing meeting of parliament he left for London, appointing as lords justices Sir Richard Cox, Major General Thomas Erle, and Hugh Montgomery, earl of Mount Alexander. From London, where he could arrange patronage matters in consultation with the ministry, Ormond promptly sent the lords justices what they describe "as a pleasing account of her Majesty's gracious sense of the service of those gentlemen who were zealous in her interest in the last session of parliament." [33] Though in nam-

[31] Wogan to Southwell, Jan. 1, 4, 1703/04, BM, Add. MSS. 37.673, fols. 29, 31.
[32] Burnet, *History of His Own Times,* IV, 24.
[33] Lords justices of Ireland to Ormond, Apr. 11, 1704, *Ormonde MSS,* n.s., VIII, 64.

ing Mount Alexander, and by some other appointments, Ormond took steps for "keeping the Dissenters in the North in
a good temper," [34] most government patronage now went to
avowed Tories. Sir Richard Levinge replaced Brodrick as
solicitor general. The opposition was to be taught the price
of independence. As Robert Johnson (a Tory, recently made
a baron of the Exchequer) gleefully wrote to Ormond, "the
late though but few signal instances of your Grace's high
resentments to some, and your Grace's great favours conferred
on others, have both of them given so convincing an evidence
of your power and readiness in both, that nobody in this
Kingdom can doubt either." [35]

In addition to consolidating Tory control of the Irish parliament, Ormond continued to work for Irish concessions from
the English government. Nothing would strengthen his position in Dublin more than tangible proof of the English ministry's concern for Irish welfare. Ormond had, it will be
recalled, backed the appeal of the Irish parliament for a
change in the English Navigation Acts to permit the direct
exportation of Irish linen to the colonies. Between January
and March 1704 the government recommended the Irish appeal to both the English Lords and Commons. In the Commons, despite Wogan's efforts to muster support for it, the
measure was tabled.[36] The Lords proved more attentive.
After hearing the judges' interpretation of existing laws, they
created a committee to evaluate the Irish request.[37] During its
investigations this committee received reports from the commissioners for trade and plantations and from the commissioners for the customs. Both bodies strongly opposed granting
any concessions to Ireland, as did two private groups, the
Hamburg Company and a group of London drapers. On the

[34] Earl of Mount Alexander to Ormond, Mar. 25, 1704, *ibid.*, 61.

[35] Robert Johnson to Ormond, Apr. 29, 1704, *ibid.*, 67.

[36] Wogan to Southwell, London, Jan. 8, 15, 1703/04, BM, Add. MSS.
37.673, fols. 28, 44. The English Commons postponed three times consideration of the Irish proposal, apparently without ever debating it.
English Commons' Journal, Jan. 15, 20, 25, 1703/04.

[37] *English Lords' Journal*, Jan. 20, 1703/04.

other side, the committee heard the testimony of "several gentlemen of Ireland,"[38] among them Brodrick, who apparently went to London during the recess of the Irish parliament. Despite the disapproval of the two government boards and other English interests, the Lords' committee reported favorably on the Irish proposals. On March 23, 1704, the House unanimously passed an address asking the queen to recommend favorable legislation to the English parliament "at the proper time."

The recommendation of the English Lords came after the close of the Irish parliament and only a week before the end of the parliamentary session in Westminster. Thus no action was taken in 1704. The next January, however, the English Commons appointed a committee to draw up a bill incorporating the Irish demands. The chairman of the committee was a justice of the Irish Court of Common Pleas, Sir Gilbert Dolben, M.P. for Peterborough. With him on the committee (it had thirteen members) were two other men close to the Irish administration, Lord Coningsby and Major General Erle.[39] Again there was opposition, this time from Lancashire linen manufacturers, but the Commons approved the bill in February.[40] A fortnight later it passed the Lords. The act received the royal assent on March 14 and became operative on June 24, 1705.

The Irish parliament of 1703–1704 had voted a money grant for two years, yet Ormond decided to reconvene it in February 1705, only eleven months after its last meeting. Apparently he and the ministry wanted to exploit Dublin Castle's new

[38] Historical Manuscripts Commission, *House of Lords MSS.*, n.s., 8 vols. (London, 1908–1923), V, 348–349; *English Lords' Journal*, Mar. 17, 1703/04.

[39] *English Commons' Journal*, Jan. 11, 1704/05. Thomas Coningsby, created baron Coningsby of Clanbrassil in Ireland by William III, had served as vice-treasurer of Ireland and sat in Westminster for Leominster. Major General Thomas Erle, commander of the forces in Ireland in 1702–1706, sat for Portsmouth in the English Commons.

[40] *Ibid.*, Jan. 27, Feb. 13, 1704/05. The bill became English Statute, 3 and 4 Anne, c. 8.

position of strength.[41] Certainly the English government
proved cooperative, not only by supporting the linen act, but
also by giving rapid approval to a number of proposed bills
that Ormond submitted to them. In January 1705, when
Wogan delivered the bills to Sir Edward Northey, the attorney general, much to Wogan's obvious surprise and pleasure,
expressed his "affection for Ireland and a sense of the hardships it labours under." [42] Four days later Wogan jubilantly
reported that the bills had already been approved by a meeting of the cabinet council, "something unprecedented and
more than I expected." [43]

Despite his precautions to ensure Tory preponderance in
the Irish parliament, Ormond discovered that the opposition
could still be troublesome. In the Commons Brodrick and his
associates made an effective bid for the support of the independent members by pushing through heads of a bill to protect parliamentary privileges. The opposition members also
did their best to postpone the passage of a revenue bill until
Dublin Castle would meet a number of their demands. News
of the English Linen Act defeated their efforts. When the Irish
Commons learned that the English act had passed, they voted
the new money bill by the overwhelming majority of 142 to
67.[44] Early in April Wogan hurried back to London with
fifteen public bills that he immediately referred to the attorney and solicitor general. The queen and the lord treasurer
were, unfortunately, away at Newmarket, and the attorney
general was off for Epsom; the next meeting of the council,
Wogan ruefully observed, "will hardly be this fortnight." [45]
Actually the Irish Commons were kept waiting until late May
before they could vote on the returned bills. The bill defining
parliamentary privileges had been so drastically altered that

[41] *Ormonde MSS*, n.s., VIII, xliii.
[42] Wogan to [E. Southwell], London, Jan. 16, 1704/05, BM, Add. MSS.
37.673, fol. 57.
[43] Wogan to Southwell, Jan. 20, 1704/05, *ibid.*, fol. 61.
[44] *Ormonde MSS*, n.s., VIII, xliii.
[45] Wogan to [E. Southwell], London, Apr. 5, 1705, BM, Add. MSS.
37.673, fol. 67.

the Commons refused to accept it. On that score, however, Ormond found a way to placate the lower house. Following the advice of Coningsby, he permitted the Commons to salve their pride by passing a sweeping resolution. As Coningsby had put it, such a step would be preferable to dissolving parliament, "since whilst you can keep this House of Commons it is well known here in England you can manage them," adding that, even though Ormond had the backing of the ministry, "yet it is not amiss to have it known that you have a parliament in being that by your own personal interest you can be sure on all occasions to influence for the Queen's service." [46]

By the summer of 1705 it indeed appeared that Ormond and his Tory lieutenants had established nearly complete control over the Irish parliament. Yet party rule had its risks, among which was the influence of English politics upon Irish parties. Between 1702 and 1705 the High Church wing of the Tory group in England had become increasingly disenchanted with the Godolphin minister. They may have succeeded in introducing the Irish test against the Dissenters, but at home they had three times witnessed the defeat of the occasional conformity bill. Although the ministry had outwardly supported the measure, they had good reason to suspect its enthusiasm for High Church policies. Moderate Tories and Whigs were replacing Highflyers in office. To rally the High Church forces, Rochester and Nottingham introduced in the English Lords, in November 1705, a resolution declaring the Church to be in grave danger because of the growth of nonconformity and atheism. Though Rochester's resolution met defeat, "the Church in Danger" became the battle cry of the Tories until they were finally victorious in 1710.

Many of the Irish Tories shared the same opinions as the English Highflyers, especially recent arrivals, among whom were a number of civil and ecclesiastical appointees — "a body

---

[46] Lord Coningsby to Ormond, June 7, 1705, *Ormonde MSS*, n.s., VIII, 159–160.

of hot clergymen sent from England," as Burnet called them.[47]
The Dublin High Church leaders formed the Swan Tripe
Club, ostensibly a social group, actually a center of propaganda. The Whigs, who controlled the Dublin city government, struck back. In November 1705 a Dublin grand jury
indicted the leading members of the club for sedition.[48] Writing to Ormond in December, Thomas Keightly (Tory M.P.
and a member of the Irish privy council) bitterly accused
Brodrick of "taking upon himself, by creating in his mouth
only, a High and Low Church in this Kingdom, to set up one
gentleman and one neighbor against another, and to make a
show of taking more care of the Kingdom . . . than the government is inclined to do." [49] That same month Brodrick
went to Limerick where he successfully helped his candidate,
George Evans, win a by-election for knight of the shire against
the concentrated efforts of the Castle party.[50] Obviously the
opposition had found a new issue on which to attack Ormond's
government.

During 1706, though there was no meeting of the Irish
parliament, party feeling did not abate. Most influential
Anglo-Irish received letters and journals from England, and
Irish newspapers themselves were full of English news. If, as
Jonathan Swift observed during an election at Leicester, "there
is not a chambermaid, prentice, or schoolboy in this whole
town, but what is warmly engaged on one side or the other," [51]
it is not surprising that some of the same partisanship found
an echo in Ireland. In June 1706 Swift complained from Dublin that "Whig and Tory have spoiled all that was tolerable
here, by mixing with private friendships and conversation,
and mining both; though it seems to me full as pertinent to
quarrel about Copernicus and Ptolemy, as about my Lord

[47] Burnet, *History of His Own Times*, IV, 102.

[48] *Ormonde MSS*, n.s., VIII, xlvi.

[49] Keightley to Ormond, Dec. 10, 1705, *ibid.*, 198.

[50] Sir Richard Cox to Ormond, Dec. 22, 1705, *ibid.*, 200-201.

[51] Swift to Abp. William King, Leicester, Dec. 6, 1707, in *Correspondence of Jonathan Swift*, ed. F. E. Ball, 6 vols. (London, 1910-1914), I, 62.

Treasurer and Lord Rochester, at least for any private man, and especially in our remote scene." [52]

The administration rode out the storm, using its patronage to increase its power and to win by-elections, while it checkmated the Dublin Whigs by quashing the indictment against the Swan Tripe men. But Ormond's position was being slowly undermined by the changing character of the English ministry. Instead of appointing his attorney general to a vacancy on the Irish Court of Exchequer, as Ormond requested, they gave the post to an English Whig, Richard Freeman.[53] By the spring of 1707 the English government clearly felt the need for a different kind of leadership in Ireland. Though as late as March 22 Ormond was writing to the lords justices to prepare legislation for the meeting of the Irish parliament, he was not destined to direct affairs during its next session.[54] In April the queen announced that the earl of Pembroke would succeed him as lord lieutenant.

Thomas Herbert, eighth earl of Pembroke, may be classified as a Court Tory with friends in both parties.[55] Still, there was no question as to the change in party orientation that accompanied his appointment. His choice to replace Edward Southwell as chief secretary was George Dodington, an outspoken critic of the High Church interest. Soon afterward he named Brodrick attorney general. In his opening speech to parliament in September 1707 Pembroke expressed the hope that steps could be taken to draw all the Protestants of Ireland closer together, implying that the government wished to see the repeal of the test clause in the Popery Act of 1704.[56] A little later Pembroke held conferences with parliamentary leaders to canvass their attitude toward repeal. When he dis-

[52] Swift to John Temple, Dublin, June 15, 1706, *ibid.*, 57–58.
[53] *Ormonde MSS.* n.s., VIII, xlv, 212.
[54] Ormond to lords justices, London, Mar. 22, 1706/07, Irish Public Record Office, Calendar of Departmental Correspondence, I, 77 (printed by permission of the Irish Public Record Office).
[55] On Pembroke's appointment, see Luttrell, *Brief Relation*, VI, 159–160, 179, 181, 187, 242. Herbert's life is in the *DNB*, XXVI, 217. See also Walcott, *English Politics in the Early Eighteenth Century*, p. 120, n. 4.
[56] *Irish Commons' Journal*, July 1, 1707.

covered that his proposal had small chance of success he abandoned his efforts for the time being. Ormond had built too strong a Tory parliament to permit such a radical change in policy. Dodington reported in disgust to London that the measure could never succeed in the existing parliament since it was "made up of two-thirds of as High Churchmen as any in England. You would hardly believe there should be such a creature as an Irish Protestant Jacobite, and yet 'tis most certain there are a great many such monsters." [57]

Tory strength in the Irish Commons does not alone explain Pembroke's defeat over the test. Although Froude accepts Dodington's statement at face value it is doubtful if most of the defenders of the Irish test were thoroughgoing High Churchmen, let alone Jacobites. In Ireland, as in England, the majority of the landed classes, including many with Whig affiliations, supported the political monopoly of the Anglican Church as the only safe method of ensuring the status quo. Even among the clergy, as Lecky so well points out, support of the test was not synonymous with High Church beliefs.[58] To modern eyes the issue may be simply toleration versus bigotry; to Queen Anne's contemporaries the political disabilities placed on the Dissenters appeared essential for the security of the state. They honestly believed that the religious groups that had overthrown the monarchy and established the Puritan Commonwealth could not be permitted to wield political power. The concentration of Dissenters in one particular part of Ireland — Ulster — reinforced rather than lessened their concern for the establishment. The intolerance of the Presbyterian regime in Scotland seemed to offer ample proof that the Ulster Scots could not be trusted. Both Brodrick and the Whig leaders in England were to find out that if they wished to consolidate their influence in the Irish Commons they would have to stomach the test. In 1707 they had not yet recognized this fact.

During the winter of 1707–1708 the ministry in England

---

[57] Quoted by Froude, *English in Ireland*, I, 358, n. 1.
[58] Lecky, *History of England in the Eighteenth Century*, II, 442–445.

seems to have hoped to gain support for the repeal of the test
by offering in return a reward for Irish churchmen.[59] Archbishop King of Dublin and a number of other Irish clergy
were then engaged in an attempt to have the crown remit the
twentieths and firstfruits of the Church of Ireland and contribute them to a fund for aiding the poorer Irish clergy. Since
Queen Anne had just taken a similar step in England, the
time seemed auspicious. Among those working for the project
was Jonathan Swift, who at this time acted as a kind of London lobbyist for the Church of Ireland. Pembroke appeared
in favor of the plan as did a number of other ministers, but
not Godolphin. After consulting with King, Swift approached
the Lord Treasurer. He met with a cool reception. Godolphin
hinted that the government would be unlikely to sponsor the
project unless it could be assured that the Irish clergy would
accept a repeal of the test.[60] At least such was Swift's interpretation, and events tend to bear him out. Despite his avowed
expectations to the contrary, Pembroke failed to win final
endorsement for the firstfruits project before his resignation
late in 1708.

Pembroke's resignation as lord lieutenant, to become lord
high admiral, constituted part of a shake-up that marked the
final transformation of the Godolphin ministry into virtually
a Whig administration. Among the government's new Whig
allies few stood out more clearly as a champion of the Dissenters than Lord Wharton. It was he who now became lord
lieutenant of Ireland. Dublin Castle, it appeared, had finally
fallen to the Brodericians. At Chichester House, on the other
hand, the same divided Commons must soon assemble, unless
a new election was called. Apparently the ministry did consider that alternative, rejecting it because it feared that the
Church party might make further gains.[61] Wharton and his
new secretary, Joseph Addison, arrived in Dublin on April 21,

[59] Swift to King, London, Jan. 1, 1707/08, in *Swift Correspondence,*
ed. Ball, I, 67 and n. 1.

[60] Swift to King, June 10, 1708, *ibid.,* 93–94.

[61] *Ibid.,* 129, n. 1.

1709, a fortnight before the opening of parliament. Thomas, viscount Wharton, who was one of the best political managers of his age, set out at once to line up support for the Castle, but with few illusions. He wrote to Charles Spencer, earl of Sunderland, that parliament would undertake its business "as amicably and quietly, as could be expected, from a number of men, that hate one another as heartily as 'tis possible to imagine, and yet are pretty equally divided." [62]

Wharton had clearly demonstrated his sentiments toward the test, not only by his activities in Westminster but also by appointing as his chaplain Ralph Lambert, who had recently preached a sermon favoring the Dissenters. [63] When it met, the lord lieutenant asked parliament to take measures to strengthen the Protestant interest in Ireland by tightening the restrictions on Catholics and removing those on Dissenters. [64] One recent event added urgency to his appeal: a threatened French invasion in 1708. On the other hand, the latest Whig efforts on behalf of the Nonconformists had stirred up resentment in Ireland. During the past year Brodrick and his allies had attempted to have the English parliament set aside the Irish test, which, as Swift wrote from London, would be "of terrible consequence, both as to the thing and the manner by the Parliament here interfering in things purely of Ireland." [65] True, Swift detested Brodrick, but when he wrote those words he still considered himself a Whig. It is probable that his point of view was shared by many who sat in the Irish parliament, certainly by the episcopal bench.

In 1703 the Brodericians had been the champions of the "Irish Interest"; now they were identified with the English party, the Tories with the Irish party. In opposition the Tories proved they could defend the test almost as effectively as when they had been in power. Recognizing their strength,

[62] Quoted by Peter Smither, *The Life of Joseph Addison* (Oxford, 1954), p. 154.

[63] *Swift Correspondence*, ed. Ball, I, 124, n. 3.

[64] *Irish Commons' Journal*, May 5, 1709.

[65] Swift to Dean John Stearne, Apr. 15, 1708, in *Swift Correspondence*, ed. Ball, I, 84.

Wharton, like Pembroke, dropped the issue. In truth he needed to, for he had trouble enough engineering more necessary measures through the volatile Commons. After some maneuvering the Castle party pushed through a money bill and a new bill to curtail Catholic inheritance rights. Unfortunately both contained provisions that annoyed the English ministry. The government gave Wharton to understand it was highly displeased with his disregard for the queen's interest. When the bills returned from London they had been amended in ways that aroused considerable opposition in Dublin. Nevertheless Dublin Castle marshaled its forces, and the Commons finally accepted the revenue act by a vote of 147 to 57 and the Popery Act by a similar margin.[66] In 1709 Wharton also won parliamentary approval of a plan to settle several thousand Palatine refugees in Ireland. Everything considered, Wharton and Addison could feel pleased with the outcome of the session. Nevertheless, the parliament of 1709 had done nothing for the Dissenters, and it had not completed its legislative agenda. Wharton decided to call another session in May 1710 instead of waiting until 1711. When May came, however, the chances for removing the test had all but disappeared.

Once again the political scene had changed in London. Since Henry Sacheverell's impeachment late in 1709 a strong Tory wind had arisen in Westminster. In Dublin the weather vanes were quick to respond. There was talk of a new ministry, and there were rumors that Wharton might be impeached. Like Ormond four years previously, Wharton discovered that a lord lieutenant without prospects of strong ministerial support cut a poor figure in Dublin. He managed the 1710 parliament better than might have been expected, but before the session had finished word came of Sidney Godolphin's replacement by Robert Harley and of a new election in England. Wharton himself was dismissed in October.

On first appearances the shift of government in England,

[66] There is an account of the passage of the money bill, dated Aug. 13, 1709, in the Southwell Papers, BM, Add. MSS. 34.777, fol. 65.

followed by the reappointment of Ormond as lord lieutenant, promised to restore a better rapport among the Irish parliament, Dublin Castle, and London. Except for the changes owing to a few by-elections the Irish Commons still contained the same members as it had in 1703. As for the administration, Ormond soon replaced a number of Whigs with Tories. Southwell came back in place of Addison, Levinge became attorney general and two Whig judges, Brodrick (whom Wharton had named to Queen's Bench) and James Macartney, were turned out so that Tory preponderance was restored in the courts. The death of Freeman also permitted Ormond to appoint as lord chancellor (and speaker of the Lords) an English Highflyer, Constantine Phipps, who had served as counsel for Sacheverell during his famous trial.[67] Thomas Keightly likened Ormond's return to the coming of William of Orange in 1691: "One delivery was from popery and the arbitrary power of a king, . . . and the other is from Presbytery and the insults of a Dissenting faction just going to devour us and all kingly government together."[68] Yet too much Tory partisanship might alienate independents. A number of current controversies — over alleged Jacobite activities at Trinity College, censorship of the press, and favoritism to Presbyterians — had aroused the High Tories against Wharton and his supporters. The extremists of the Church party clamored for vengeance. Archbishop King told Swift: "the greatest danger I apprehend, and which terrifies me more than perhaps you will be able to imagine, is the fury and indiscretion of some of our own people."[69] It is unlikely that Swift paid much

[67] Ball, *Judges in Ireland*, II, 34. Levinge had apparently been behind the move to impeach Wharton. Swift to King, Dec. 30, 1710, in *Swift Correspondence*, ed. Ball, I, 227. In addition to reshuffling the bench Ormond removed Brodrick and another Whig leader from the privy council. Wogan to [E. Southwell], London, June 14, 1711, BM, Add. MSS. 37.673, fol. 120. Ormond also urged the lords justices, on June 27, 1711, to do their best to influence by-elections in Ireland. Calendar of Departmental Correspondence, I, 221.

[68] Keightley to Ormond, Oct. 28, 1710, *Ormonde MSS*, n.s., VIII, 321.

[69] King to Swift, Dec. 16, 1710, in *Swift Correspondence*, ed. Ball, I, 223–224.

heed to King's warning; now firmly in the Tory camp, Swift himself had just published a withering attack on Wharton.[70] This course of events before Ormond's arrival to meet parliament in July 1711 tended to substantiate the archbishop's fears. The Highflyers pushed their advantage and were soon denouncing moderates like King as no better than Whigs. Ormond aided their efforts by naming the new lord chancellor as one of the two lords justices in January 1711. Phipps knew little of Ireland, but this did not deter him from throwing his full weight on the side of the High Tories. In May he and his associates espoused the cause of a rejected candidate for mayor of Dublin, Alderman Constantine, who had met defeat in 1709. Although Constantine's appeal to the privy council had been dismissed by Wharton, the change at Dublin Castle gave him new hope. As an avowed Tory he expected and received a sympathetic hearing. Soon the council and the city government were embroiled in a long and bitter struggle.[71]

Ormond meanwhile prepared for his return to Ireland, apparently unaware of the intensity of party rivalry in Dublin. He would bring with him one welcome gift to the Church: the Tory ministry had finally come through with the queen's long-awaited grant of twentieths and firstfruits.[72] Ormond could also expect thanks in Ireland for having assisted in

[70] King to Swift, Jan. 9, 1710/11, *ibid.*, 233–234. King did not share Swift's extreme hostility to Wharton. Having just read Swift's new (but anonymous) *Character of the Earl of Wharton* he wrote that he condemned all such diatribes. "If a governor behave himself ill, let him be complained of and punished; but to wound any man thus in the dark, to appeal to the mob, that can neither inquire nor judge, is a proceeding that I think the common sense of mankind should condemn."

[71] For King's summary of the Dublin dispute, see his letter to Swift written in May 1711. *Swift Correspondence*, ed. Ball, I, 259–261. See also *ibid.*, I, 295, n. 2; II, 72, n. 1. Southwell was especially upset that the Dublin affair had not been settled before Shrewsbury met parliament in 1713. "We who know Ireland pretty well are sensible of the pleasure country gentlemen have to run riot at that time upon the government and council." Southwell to Joshua Dawson, Oct. 17, 1713, Calendar of British Departmental Correspondence, I, 306.

[72] Wogan to [E. Southwell], June 30, July 12, 17, 1711, BM, Add. MSS. 37.673, fols. 131, 135, 139.

stopping an English duty on Irish yarn. When the proposal came before the English Commons in April 1711 Ormond called a meeting at Southwell's lodgings. Swift describes what took place: "All the Irish in town were there to consult upon preventing a bill for levying a duty on Irish yarn; so we talked a while, and then all went to the lobby of the House of Commons, to solicit our friends, and the Duke came among the rest; and Lord Anglesea solicited admirably, and I did wonders." [73]

Ormond's warm reception in Dublin and parliament's favorable response to his opening speech pointed to a harmonious session. When the Whigs tried to rephrase parliament's address of thanks in order to delete implied criticism of Wharton they could muster little support.[74] The Commons voted supplies for two years and approved other government proposals. Furthermore, the English Tories (unlike the last Whig ministry) cooperated by accepting the Irish legislation without significant changes. In October Ormond wrote Oxford that "the money bills returning without alteration have given great satisfaction; and will make the session much easier than it would have been." [75] Despite all these achievements the session nearly foundered on local issues.

By autumn the Castle's disagreement with the Dublin aldermen and citizens had reached serious proportions. The Whigs made the most of the Castle's interference with local government (in other towns as well as Dublin) and chided it for its support of the Tories in a number of other disputes. The Lords and the Commons had fallen into a quarrel over their respective prerogatives. On October 27 the Whigs attempted to bring the Dublin controversy before the Commons; they were defeated by only two votes. They also threw out a corn bill because it gave administrative powers to the lord lieutenant and privy council.[76] The legislature and the executive

[73] Jonathan Swift, *Journal to Stella*, ed. George A. Aitken (London, Methuen and Co., 1901), p. 187.

[74] Ormond to Oxford, Dublin, July 15, 1711, *Portland MSS.* V, 49.

[75] Ormond to [Oxford], Oct. 17, 1711, *ibid.*, 102.

[76] King to Swift, Oct. 27, 1711, in *Swift Correspondence*, ed. Ball, I, 293; *Irish Commons' Journal*, Oct. 25, 27, 1711.

had virtually come to an impasse. Early in November Ormond prorogued parliament and packed up for England. He had succeeded in obtaining a satisfactory revenue act and some other pressing legislation. He also finally imposed a settlement of the Dublin contest. His close dependence on the Tory leaders had, on the other hand, acerbated rather than diminished party feeling. The lords justices, Sir Constantine Phipps and Lieutenant General Richard Ingoldsby, who now took over the government, faced a growing opposition.

The winter of 1711–1712 saw Tory power reach new heights in England. To ensure approval of the peace negotiations Anne created a dozen new peers and thus deprived the Whigs of their hold on the English Lords. In view of the situation in England neither the ministry nor the Irish lords justices saw any need for compromise or retreat in Ireland. Conditions became difficult for the Dissenters. Following the request of the last Irish parliament, London had stopped the royal grant (*Regium Donum*) which had been allowed Presbyterian ministers in Ulster annually since the time of William III.[77] In a number of dioceses church officials took action against Dissenting congregations.[78] Thanks to the determined partisanship of Phipps, Ormond's solution of the Dublin dispute proved short lived; soon the privy council and the city were fighting again. Meanwhile the government dispensed patronage in both church and state to adherents of the High Church party.

Froude, like the Whigs of the time, assumes the government's ultimate aim was to prepare the way for the Pretender. It is true that some Tories, like Ormond and Phipps, eventually turned Jacobite, but there is little evidence they harbored such designs before 1714. Furthermore, the absence of any Irish revolt in 1715 discredits Froude's allegations. What the Tories were aiming at was to entrench themselves so thoroughly they could not be dislodged when Anne should die.

[77] Froude, *English in Ireland*, I, 385–386. The *Regium Donum* was first given in 1672.

[78] *Ibid.*, 380–381; Francis Iredell to [Oxford], Sept. 23, 1713, *Portland MSS.* V, 339–340.

Ormond, who was created supreme commander in place of
Marlborough in the spring of 1712, left Irish affairs largely to
Phipps and his subordinates. Given a few years in control of
Dublin Castle, the Irish Tories could hope to ensure their
hold on local government and parliament. What was later
called the spoils system in America already thrived in eighteenth-century England and Ireland. An administration felt
no compunction about exercising what might be called a
political right of eminent domain: placemen were given the
choice of joining the government party or being evicted. To
bolster their power the Tories decided to call a new election
in Ireland in the autumn of 1713, following the triennial election in England. The ministry had just ended the war; everything pointed to a sweeping victory.

The Castle did not, however, leave the outcome to fate. In
the Southwell Papers there are several lists of boroughs with
candidates for the 1713 election, clearly classified as desirable
or "bad." [79] Comments following the names show that the
government was busy lining up its forces. In some counties
and boroughs, for example in most of Cork where the Brodricks held sway, Southwell and his henchmen recognized defeat
as inevitable. In other constituencies "good men" had the
election sewed up. Elsewhere steps needed to be taken to
assure victory. All in all prospects appeared promising. When
the Tories estimated the results they were jubilant. In England William Stratford congratulated Harley: "Your Lordship without doubt has an account of the new spirit which
has risen up in Ireland, by which the Tories, beyond all expectations are three to two in that Parliament." [80] From
Dublin the earl of Anglesey, just four days before the opening
of the Irish parliament, reported optimistically: "I hope we
shall be able to give a good account of the parliament here,
we having exerted a better spirit and met with greater success
in our election than the most sanguine did expect; and I may
affirm with truth that this island by your countenance and

[79] BM, Add. MSS. 34.777, fols. 20–27.
[80] Stratford to Oxford, Nov. 19, 1713, *Portland MSS.* VII, 172.

encouragement will in a short time be brought to as good a temper toward her Majesty's present administration as that of Great Britain." [81] False prophecy is a prerogative of politicians.

When the Commons assembled on November 25, 1713, Tory complacency quickly turned to dismay. Instead of electing Levinge Speaker, the Commons chose Alan Brodrick by a vote of 131 to 127.[82] Next they picked an ardent Whig (former speaker John Forster) as chairman of the committee on elections, which meant, of course, the Whigs would increase their majority when the House acted on disputed contests. There was consternation at Dublin Castle and amazement in London. "We are astounded at your strange choice of a speaker," wrote Wogan.[83] Swift wanted to know how it was that "the other party should be a majority?" He had looked over a list of members, and at worst the Tories should have had a margin of one, which "would easily rise to a great majority, by the influence of the government, if that had been thought fit . . . for the government there has more influence than the Court here, and yet our Court carried it for many years against a natural majority, and a much greater one." [84]

The arithmetic of elections is not an exact science despite its fascination for political managers and historians. The explanation for the Whig success cannot be determined by

[81] Earl of Anglesey to [Oxford], Nov. 21, 1713, *ibid.*, V, 361. Phipps wrote Swift (Nov. 7, 1713) "Our elections . . . prove beyond expectation, for by the newest calculations that can be made we shall have a majority of three to two." *Swift Correspondence*, ed. Ball, II, 86.

[82] J. G. Simms, "The Irish Parliament of 1713," *Historical Studies*, IV, ed. G. A. Hayes-McCoy (London, 1963), p. 87.

[83] Wogan to Dawson (n.d. but probably late Nov. 1713), Calendar of British Departmental Correspondence, I, 308.

[84] Swift to King, London, Dec. 31, 1713, in *Swift Correspondence*, ed. Ball, II, 110–111. On October 20, 1713, Swift had bluntly warned King that "If your House of Commons runs into any violences disagreeable to us here; it will be the worst consequences imaginable . . . for I know of no maxim more strongly maintained at present in our Court, than that her Majesty ought to exert her power to the utmost, upon any uneasiness given on your side to herself or her servants." *Ibid.*, 79. It is clear that at this stage of his career Swift identified himself with the English Tory ministry rather than with Ireland.

merely adding up the votes controlled by recognizable factions
or "interests." As the archbishop of Dublin remarked, it was
strange the Tories should fail to win a majority since "the
Government, Privy Council, benches, custom house, army pensioners, officers of all sorts, dependents and expectants were
all for them." [85] It was strange, but not inexplicable. King
attributed their defeat primarily to the Dublin mayoralty
fracas. Other reasons were a personal antipathy toward Phipps
and a jealousy of English influence. All of these factors helped
to give the opposition wide popular support. Even some who
voted with the government seemed content with Brodrick's
victory: "I never saw men better pleased by being worsted," [86]
commented King to Swift, and one suspects the archbishop
himself derived some satisfaction from Phipps's embarrass-
ment — since the chancellor had refused to take his advice.

In hopes of placating the Irish Whigs, the ministry named
the moderate Charles Talbot, duke of Shrewsbury, as lord
lieutenant. Edmund Curtis quotes Shrewsbury as describing
the office of lord lieutenant as "a place where a man had business enough to prevent him falling asleep but not enough to
keep him awake." [87] He must have soon changed his mind.
Upon his arrival in Dublin at the end of October, Shrewsbury
had attempted, in accordance with his instructions, to termi-
nate the festering problem between Dublin Castle and the Dublin corporation. Chancellor Phipps, who dominated the privy
council, disregarded the duke's advice.[88] Phipps obviously distrusted Shrewsbury's loyalty to the Tory cause and felt confident that the English ministry would back him against the
lord lieutenant. When Shrewsbury found he could not effect
a settlement of the Dublin quarrel he warned Oxford of an
impending storm in the Commons: "I want words to describe
the uneasiness of my condition, exposed to the censure of
everybody if the business in Parliament miscarry and yet with-

[85] King to Swift, Dublin, Dec. 15, 1713, ibid., 100.
[86] King to Swift, Jan. 13, 1713/14, ibid., 117.
[87] Curtis, History of Ireland, p. 279.
[88] Shrewsbury to [Oxford], Dublin, Nov. 3, 1713, Historical Manuscripts
Commission, Bath MSS. 3 vols. (London, 1904–1908), I, 242.

out authority (unless in conjunction with the Council) to make those steps that would have prevented it." [89]

Three weeks after opening parliament, Shrewsbury was even more dismayed: "things have been driven to such an extremity of heat and disorder that the methods of getting out of them surpass my comprehension." [90] The Commons has presented an address to the queen asking for the dismissal of Chancellor Phipps as necessary "for the peace and safety of her Protestant subjects." [91] The House of Lords and the Irish Convocation, both of which bodies had High Church majorities, sent representations to the crown defending Phipps and denouncing his enemies. Although the Whigs assured Shrewsbury of their "zeal in dispatching the public business, their duty to her Majesty, and their good will," [92] they remained adamant in their determination to eliminate Phipps — even if it required impeachment proceedings in the English Lords. The Commons only voted supplies for three months. Then on Christmas Eve, they adjourned for three weeks with an intimation (made explicit by some members) that the government could expect no further legislation until the lord chancellor had been removed. Archbishop Thomas Lindsay of Armagh likened the times to those existing in England in 1641. The opposition, he explained, maintained that "it is a duty incumbent on the Crown, to turn out that minister, how innocent soever he be, whom the Commons have addressed against." [93]

Actually the impasse in Ireland had scarcely reached a point comparable to the English crisis of 1641; it resembled more the situation in England in 1614 at the dissolution of the "Addled Parliament." The crown's ministers did not have to make concessions; they could carry on without parliament

[88] Carteret to Newcastle, Sept. 27, Oct. 15, 1729, Boulter to Newcastle,
[90] Shrewsbury to [Oxford], Chapelizod, Dec. 14, 1713, *Portland MSS.* V, 372.
[91] Swift to King, London, Dec. 31, 1713, in *Swift Correspondence*, ed. Ball, II, 110.
[92] Shrewsbury to [Oxford], Chapelizod, Dec. 14, 1713, *Portland MSS.* V, 372.
[93] Lindsay to Swift, Dec. 26, 1713, in *Swift Correspondence*, ed. Ball, II, 109.

since there was a surplus in the treasury and the end of the war reduced the urgency of military expenditures. The question was whether to reconvene parliament in the hope of recapturing the initiative or to manage the government without new taxes. In January 1714 Shrewsbury approached the Whig leaders with the intent of working out some agreement, but without success.[94] In England Bolingbroke advised against recalling the Dublin parliament, while Swift talked of a new election.[95] After proroguing parliament for a month the government concluded that it could not regain control of the Irish Commons and ended the session without a further meeting. Upon leaving for England in April Shrewsbury did not reappoint Phipps as one of his deputies, but in June the lord chancellor once again became a lord justice. The High Church party was still pushing every advantage. In 1707 when Brodrick had failed to repeal the Irish test, he had sought to gain his ends by an act in the English parliament. The Tories now repaid him. In June 1714 the Highflyers in the English Lords amended the Schism Act to include Ireland, much to the dismay not only of Whigs and Dissenters but of all who were jealous of Irish rights.[96] The Schism Act proved to be the Tories' parting shot. In less than two months their whole regime collapsed with the death of Queen Anne.

Probably at no time between 1692 and 1770 did English party rivalry so closely affect Irish politics as during Anne's reign. The polarization of English political life had a profound effect upon Ireland, producing an environment in which nearly everyone felt compelled to affiliate with either the Whig or Tory camp.

On many issues Irish Whigs and Tories shared the prejudices of their English counterparts. But there were differences. Few if any native-born Anglo-Irish Tories (as opposed to some recent arrivals from England) could tolerate the prospect of a Jacobite victory for their lands and political monop-

[94] Lindsay to Swift, Jan. 5, 1713/14, *ibid.*, pp. 115–116.
[95] Bolingbroke to [Oxford], Whiehall (undated but endorsed Dec. 17, 1713), and Windsor Castle, Dec. 31, 1713, *Portland MSS.* V, 373, 377; Swift to King, Dec. 31, 1713, in *Swift Correspondence*, ed. Ball, II, 111.
[96] *English Lords' Journal*, June 4, 9, 14, 1714.

oly depended on the Protestant succession.[97] At the other end of the spectrum, only a minority of Irish Whigs favored concessions to Protestant Dissenters whom they identified with Ulster Scots. English partisan conflicts became deflected when projected into Ireland, making it difficult for English politicians to comprehend or direct Irish politics. When parties changed in London the Irish administration shifted with them. But, in contrast, the complexion of the Irish parliament was much less susceptible to party shifts in England. As a result, Anne's lord lieutenants had difficulty in keeping the support of the Irish parliament. The opposition leaders in Ireland usually cast themselves in the role of defenders of Irish interests. The lord lieutenant represented, by the very nature of his office, Irish subordination to English rule. The Castle party was thus almost inevitably the "English party." The independent Anglo-Irish gentry and merchants in the Commons, who resented English interference except when they sought it, were more than ready to join the opposition on many issues. The coalition required by Dublin Castle to enact legislation was not easy to maintain.

Normally the Castle could control, through patronage and pension, something approaching a third of the 300 men who composed the Irish Commons. Judging from available evidence, the opposition could count definitely on some fifty to seventy. With a majority of the independent votes, they had a chance to defeat the government; otherwise they did not. In other words, the country members held the balance of power. In practice poor attendance and lack of interest restricted their influence to issues of major concern, such as the penal laws and the Test Act. They appear to have had approximately the same proportional strength and political importance as did the country members at Westminster.[98] Their aims too were similar. Writing of the English parliament in 1700, the Prussian envoy remarked on the importance of the country group who voted "according to their own light." He

[97] Simms, "Irish Parliament of 1713," p. 90.
[98] Archibald S. Foord, *His Majesty's Opposition, 1714–1830* (Oxford, Clarendon Press, 1964), p. 23.

stated that their guiding principles were the preservation of the established religion and individual liberty and the promotion of manufacturing and "the profitable cultivation of the land," adding that, "whichever party rules and however eloquent it may be, it will never win if it attacks one of these."[99] The same comment might have been made of the Irish Commons, with special emphasis on the defense of the established church and the landed interest. On money bills the Castle could usually depend on economic pressure to carry the day, for many members of the House were half-pay officers on inactive duty. Only in 1713 had the government actually failed to push through a supply bill. Still, Dublin Castle had to bargain for taxes, and on other issues it often ran into difficulties. The opposition forces, for example, elected the Speaker in 1703, 1705, 1711, and 1713.[100]

It was clear at the close of Anne's reign that the system by which the English ministry managed Ireland left much to be desired. Bolingbroke seems to have recognized this. If, after Harley's dismissal in August 1714, Bolingbroke had held power for a few years instead of a few days it is possible he would have drastically altered the Irish constitution. The accession of George I removed the threat: Ireland continued to be governed much as it had been. The Whig ascendancy brought party stability to England, and to a degree to Ireland, but it did not remove the fundamental causes for friction between Dublin Castle and Chichester House.

[99] Quoted by Clayton Roberts, *The Growth of Responsible Government in Stuart England* (Cambridge, Cambridge University Press, 1966), p. 290, n. 3.

[100] The Whigs were able to select the Speaker throughout Anne's reign, choosing Brodrick every time except 1711, when they picked John Forster. *Swift's Correspondence*, ed. Ball, II, 75, n. 1. Ormond seems to have considered refusing to pay Brodrick's stipend as Speaker in 1704, but Sir Richard Cox dissuaded him on the grounds that it would establish a harmful precedent. Cox to Ormond, June 4, 1704, *Ormonde MSS.* n. s., VIII, 82–83. Colonial governors in Massachusetts and New Jersey, like Ormond, found it impractical to reject Speakers chosen by the assembly. Evarts Boutell Greene, *The Provincial Governor in the English Colonies of North America* (New York, 1898), p. 150.

IV

The Origins
of a
Patriot Party

The parliamentary crisis in Dublin in 1713 revealed that the English did not yet exercise full control of the Irish government. To achieve complete power the English ministry must pursue one of two divergent policies, each of which in turn offered two possible alternatives. One solution was to disregard the Dublin parliament, either by collecting taxes without its authorization or by having the English parliament levy taxes on Ireland, as it later did on the American colonies. The second general policy was to maintain the existing system but to take steps to assure control of the Irish parliament. Again this might be done in two ways, by modifying Irish borough charters to enable Dublin Castle to nominate burgesses (as Charles II had tried in England and James II in Ireland), or by careful political management to construct a strong and durable Castle party that could dominate the Dublin parliament. All of these methods except the last required an open break with Irish and English constitutional tradition and threatened to arouse violent opposition. Out of both a respect for constitutional principles and a desire to avoid conflict, the Whig ministers of George I chose the last alternative. They set out to entrench their regime in Ireland, as well as in England and Scotland, by building what in the United States is described as a political machine. In the end Walpole's ministry achieved this goal, but not until it had aroused so much resistance that it had created a vigorous opposition.

Events during Anne's reign had shown that the creation of an efficient Castle party was not simply a matter of buying votes through patronage and favors. First, there must be some degree of consistency on the part of the English ministry:

dilatory or vacillating policies in London seriously weakened
a lord lieutenant's position in Dublin. Second, the Irish administration must woo the independent members of both
houses by respecting their prejudices, it must at least appear
to defend Irish interests in London, and its leaders must be
tactful and astute in handling everyday business. The lord
lieutenant needed either to know Ireland well or to depend
upon the advice of men who did. The Castle, for example,
should avoid becoming embroiled in merely local or personal
disputes, such as the Dublin mayoralty fight in 1711.

This last problem was of greater significance than is generally recognized. One is inclined to think of party management in both eighteenth-century England and Ireland as
largely an affair of a clique of politicians who maintained
power by manipulating "interests." Given the existing electoral system and the universal acceptance of the patron-client
relationship, it seems safe to assume that initiative always lay
with the leaders of the oligarchy. The familiar picture is such
as that described by one of Harley's faithfuls: "I went down
frankly and freely upon my own expenses to Nottingham upon
the election of members and voted according to Lord Middle-
ton's dictate . . . As I have endeavoured to serve the Crown
and you to the best of my power, I hope that it may please
you to warrant me a tidesman in fee." [1] It all sounds so efficiently corrupt, but there was another side to the story. Just as
a weak ally may sometimes involve a great power in war, so
scheming or fanatical subordinates may succeed in inflating
their petty squabbles into national issues. "A bold opinion is
a short way to merit, and very necessary for those who have
no other," [2] wrote Swift. As Archbishop King commented,
"this is an inconveniency in parties, that whoever has a private quarrel, and finds himself too weak, he immediately becomes a zealous partisan, and makes his private a public
quarrel." [3]

---

[1] John Barker to (earl of Oxford), Sept. 18, 1713, *Portland MSS*, V, 339.
[2] Swift to King, Mar. 26, 1709, in *Correspondence of Jonathan Swift*, ed.
Ball, I, 150.
[3] King to Swift, Dublin, May 15, 1711, *ibid.*, p. 261.

The situation in Ireland at the end of 1714 appeared very favorable to the Whigs. The policies of the Highflyers had alienated moderates like Archbishop King. The Jacobites found few active followers even among the Roman Catholics. The moment was propitious for the establishment of an alliance between Whigs and Hanoverian Tories that could work closely with the Castle. If the new ministry proved willing to heed the lessons of Anne's reign it could hope to govern Ireland without serious difficulty. Unfortunately the Whig leaders in London were too preoccupied with English politics, Scottish rebellion, and continental diplomacy to devote much time to Ireland. To begin with, the ministry appointed Sunderland lord lieutenant, a man whose interests lay almost exclusively in London and who resigned the position in less than a year without ever visiting Ireland.[4] Sunderland did, however, have the good judgment to name Addison his secretary.

Addison had learned much about Irish affairs during his term as secretary under Wharton; although Addison also remained in London he undertook his duties seriously. With the full support of Sunderland, and in close cooperation with the lords justices, Addison set out to remove the stalwarts of the last administration in order to replace them with Whigs. He even expelled Joseph Dawson who had served as secretary to the lords justices throughout Anne's reign, giving the post to his own cousin Eustace Budgell.[5] A Whig majority was rapidly created on the Irish privy council and on the Irish bench. Unlike many Englishmen, Addison saw the value of rewarding Anglo-Irish politicians who could wield influence in the Irish parliament.[6] As a result of Addison's efforts, the

[4] Charles Spencer, third earl of Sunderland, was appointed lord lieutenant on Oct. 4, 1714, and resigned on Aug. 23, 1715.

[5] Addison to King, Oct. 8, 1714, in *Letters of Joseph Addison*, ed. Walter Graham (Oxford, 1941), p. 300; see also *ibid.*, p. 140, n. 2.

[6] See Addison's letters to King, Nov. 23, 1714, Mar. 12, 29, Apr. 12, May 5, 1715, *ibid.*, pp. 304, 314–315, 316, 318. The ministry decided to replace almost the entire Irish bench because of its partisanship; the following new appointments were given to Anglo-Irishmen: Alan Brodrick, raised to peerage as Viscount Midleton, became lord chancellor; William Whit-

groundwork was laid for a broad-based Castle party. Then a further change in administration interrupted Addison's work: in August 1715 Sunderland resigned.

Instead of choosing a new lord lieutenant immediately, the ministry replaced the Irish lords justices (Archbishop King, Archbishop John Vesey, and the earl of Kildare) with two men sent from England. One of the two, Henri de Ruvigny, earl of Galway, was a Huguenot general who had served in Ireland under William some twenty years before. The other was Charles Fitzroy, duke of Grafton, whose only connection with Ireland was that his father had been a hero in the Williamite Wars.[7] Other appointments went to Englishmen, suggesting that the English ministry would now pay little heed to the claims of Anglo-Irish Whigs. Probably the Whig administration felt that with the Tories discredited it would have little difficulty managing the Dublin parliament. The election of 1715 in Ireland had resulted in a Whig victory, and the new Commons chose William Conolly, a long-time associate of Brodrick's, as Speaker. Sunderland had already had Brodrick raised to the peerage (as Viscount Midleton) and made lord chancellor. With Midleton to direct the Lords and Conolly

shed became chief justice of King's Bench; William Caulfield was appointed to King's Bench; Godfrey Boate was also appointed as the third member of King's Bench; John Forster became chief justice of Common Pleas; James Macartney, removed from the bench by the Tories, was appointed to Common Pleas; Joseph Deane became chief baron of the Exchequer. Two Englishmen were named barons of the Exchequer, John Pocklington and John St. Leger, and upon Deane's death in 1715 Jeffrey Gilbert, another Englishman, was appointed chief baron; thus the Exchequer court was entirely composed of English-born judges. Ball, *Judges in Ireland*, II, 78–85.

[7] Henri Massue de Ruvigny (1648–1720), whose brother died fighting for William in Ireland, took part in the siege of Limerick and the negotiations for peace. He served as a lord justice in 1697–1701. A description of his life is in the *DNB*, XXXVI, 17–22. Charles Fitzroy (1683–1757), second duke of Grafton, was the son of Henry Fitzroy, second son of Barbara Villiers and Charles II. Henry was killed in the siege of Cork in 1690. Charles's mother was Isabelle, daughter of Henry Bennet, first earl of Arlington. Charles served in Flanders in 1703, was lord lieutenant of Suffolk, and became a lord of the bedchamber and a privy councillor under George I.

to preside over the Commons, the stage seemed set for a harmonious session.

Ireland's first Hanoverian parliament assembled at Chichester House on November 12, 1715, at the very moment that Jacobite troops were invading northwest England. In their opening speech the lords justices, after pledging to protect the Irish "constitution in church and state," appealed for immediate supplies "to defray such expenses as you may think proper for your own security." The justices promised a "frugal application of the money given," and they further assured their listeners that "we have his Majesty's orders to acquaint you, that he will readily consent to such good laws as may conduce to make you an easy and happy people." [8]

Parliament responded to this appeal by promptly passing a temporary six-month revenue bill, thus meeting the needs of the emergency without in any way curtailing a careful deliberation of the regular two-year budget. It then turned its attention to attacking Irish Jacobites. Heads of a bill to disgrace the duke of Ormond were authorized on November 15, and the following day, in their address of thanks to the crown, the Commons avowed that it was "with the utmost concern we find this country has been so unfortunate as to give birth to James Butler, the late Duke of Ormond." [9] Although the Pretender had few active supporters in Ireland, the disaffection of Ormond and his former lord chancellor, Phipps, gave the Whigs an opportunity to attack all High Tories. In a series of moves they ordered the arrest of Tory demonstrators in the recent Dublin elections, demanded apologies from M.P.'s who in 1713 had signed addresses in favor of Phipps, and censured judges, like Sir Richard Cox, who had displayed Tory prejudices.[10] The Whig majority did its best to discredit the Tories as the party of treason. Disputed elections that came before the Commons were, naturally, decided in favor of Whig candidates.

[8] *Irish Commons' Journal,* Nov. 12, 1715.
[9] *Ibid.,* Nov. 15, 16, 1715.
[10] *Ibid.,* Nov. 16, 26, 30, Dec. 1, 5, 7, 15, 1715; Ball, *Judges in Ireland,* II, 86–87.

Perhaps the most colorful election contest was that of Kilkenny City between two former Tory incumbents, Sir Richard Levinge and Darby Egan, and their Whig opponents, Colonel Edward Warren and Maurice Cuffe. Levinge, who had served as Ormond's attorney general and had been the unsuccessful Tory candidate for Speaker in 1713, had met clear defeat in the Whig victory of 1715, but his henchman, Egan, had been certified by the sheriff as elected, after a "scrutiny" of the returns demanded by Levinge. According to Egan's allegations, Cuffe (with Warren's aid) had created thirty-eight spurious freemen. The method employed was ingenious: Cuffe's father granted them temporary leases to some freehold land. Anticipating an investigation, the senior Cuffe had taken the precaution to pass around among the thirty-eight a glove stuffed with forty shillings so that they could all "swear to having livery and seisin of their freehold." Cuffe in reply stated that eleven of Egan's voters were under age. Needless to say, Egan, who had openly admitted admiration for Ormond, was unseated by the Whig Commons. In addition, because of the strength of Jacobite sympathizers in Kilkenny, the Commons drew up a bill changing the city's charter.[11]

Having met the immediate fiscal needs of the government, chastised the Highflyers, and passed a security measure to prevent Papists from serving as high or petty constables, parliament turned its attention to more normal business. In considering the regular supply bill the Commons proved mindful of the Castle's needs but watchful of extravagance, criticizing the size of the pension list. As had become customary since 1695, the Commons required a full accounting of the state of the debt, the income of the past two years, and a firm estimate for the next two years. Furthermore, lest the passage of the temporary money bill in November should prove a harmful precedent, the Commons unanimously subscribed to the following resolution:

[11] *Irish Commons' Journal*, Dec. 14, 1715. The act changing the Kilkenny charter (Irish Statute, 4 George I, c. 16) was not passed until 1717.

That no money bill be read in the House until the report from the committee of accounts be first made. . .

That the said resolution be declared a standing order of the House.[12]

Grafton and Galway tactfully expressed satisfaction with the revenue bill and, in general, supported the other legislation passed during the session of 1715–1716. The Whig government wished to demonstrate that it could do as well by Irish interests as had the Tories. When the English Linen Act of 1705 (permitting the Irish to ship linens to the colonies) came up for renewal in 1716, the ministry, urged on by a resolution from the Irish Commons, extended the act for a year. The next year, despite considerable English opposition, the English parliament renewed the Linen Act for its full period of ten years.[13] Yet, regardless of its efforts to consolidate its position by catering to Irish wishes and by patronage, the Whig administration discovered that it could not dictate to Chichester House when it came to questions of religion.

One of the chief aims of both King George I and his Whig ministers was the extension of full civil and political rights to Protestant Nonconformists. In view of the strength of the Church Whigs in Westminster, the government seems to have felt it wisest to breach first the Anglican monopoly in Ireland and thereby clear the way for reform in England. Certainly the times appeared favorable for success in Ireland. The High Church party had antagonized most moderates by their intransigence toward Dissenters, especially by such actions as suspending the royal subsidy to Presbyterians in 1714 and the unpopular extension of the Schism Act to Ireland. The en-

[12] *Ibid.*, May 17, 1716. On Aug. 5, 1707, the Commons had made it a standing order that no "petition, motion, address, bill or vote of credit, for granting any money" should be acted upon without being considered by the committee of the whole house.

[13] English Statutes, 1 George I, Stat. 2, c. 26, 3 George I, c. 21; *Proceedings and Debates of the British Parliaments Respecting North America*, ed. Leo Francis Stock, 5 vols. (Washington, 1924–1941), III, 383–384; Conrad Gill, *The Rise of the Irish Linen Industry* (Oxford, 1925), pp. 66–67.

thusiastic loyalty of the Ulster Dissenters during the 1715 rebellion proved their great value to the Protestant establishment. The moment to repeal the test of 1704 seemed to have arrived. As a start, the administration proposed a bill to indemnify Dissenters who had volunteered to serve as army officers during the rebellion (in technical violation of the test) and to allow them to continue to serve as officers in both the militia and regular army. In the Commons the Castle barely mustered sufficient support to pass the bill; in the Lords Archbishop King offered a substitute measure that would restrict the indemnity to the present only. In the privy council the bishops finally agreed to open the militia to Dissenters but not the regular army. The duke of Grafton wrote to London recommending this compromise as the only one that could hope to pass both houses.[14] Instead of accepting it, the ministry decided to drop the proposed legislation, apparently preferring to wait until the Castle party could gain more strength in the Irish Lords.

After a period of three years during which no lord lieutenant had set foot in Ireland, Charles Paulet, second duke of Bolton, arrived in Dublin in August 1717. Although Bolton did not know Ireland well, he had served there as lord justice under William, and his appointment indicates that the Whig government had finally recognized the need for having an active viceroy rather than employing the office of lord lieutenant as a convenient sinecure for idle ministers like Sunderland or Townshend. What is more, during the first months of his term of office Bolton had in London a secretary who understood Irish affairs, Joseph Addison.[15] The new administration was guided by a desire to handle the Irish parliament cautiously rather than force through any particular policies.

[14] Beckett, *Protestant Dissent in Ireland*, pp. 71–74; Froude, *English in Ireland*, I, 416–428.

[15] Between December 1716 and April 1717 Charles, second Viscount Townshend (1674–1738), had been lord lieutenant but he never went to Ireland. Paulet, second duke of Bolton (1661–1722), was appointed lord lieutenant in April 1717, sworn in in August 1717 and served until June 1720. Addison was secretary of state for the southern department from April 1717 to March 1718.

In his opening speech at Chichester House Bolton omitted any reference to the need for easing the lot of the Dissenters, such as Grafton had hinted at in 1715.[16] During the ensuing session Bolton strove to avoid controversy and to placate the opposition. On advice from London he omitted summoning the convocation of the Irish Church when he called parliament.[17] Convocation, which had not met since 1714, had proved a center for High Church criticism; it was well to dispense with its services.[18] The government dissolved the English Convocation in 1717 for similar reasons. To please the Church interest, however, the administration arranged for a royal grant of £5,000 for the completion of the library at Trinity College, with the hope, as Addison put it, that "this mark of royal favour" would encourage "those honest and loyal principles which . . . begin to revive there." [19] Addison also did much to expedite the approval of Irish legislation by the government in London. Before the end of December the last bill had been returned from England, and Bolton was able to prorogue parliament. When he departed for London, the lord lieutenant left as lords justices Chancellor Midleton, Speaker Conolly, and Archbishop King, a solid Hanoverian triumvirate of influential Anglo-Irishmen.

By the time of the next meeting of parliament in 1719 the ministry felt strong enough to venture once more in the cause of the Dissenters. The appointment of five English bishops to the Irish episcopate gave new strength in the Lords while the threat of another Jacobite invasion in the summer of 1719 served to remind the Anglo-Irish of their continuing need for the support of the Ulster Scots.[20] Bolton returned to Dublin

[16] *Irish Commons' Journal*, Aug. 27, 1717.

[17] Addison to Bolton, Whitehall, Aug. 3, 1717, in *Letters of Addison*, ed. Graham, p. 369.

[18] *History of the Church of Ireland from the Earliest Times to the Present Day*, ed. Walter Alison Phillips, 3 vols. (London, 1933), III, 188–192.

[19] Addison to Bolton, Hampton Court, Sept. 19, 1717, and Whitehall, Oct. 12, 1717, in *Letters of Addison*, ed. Graham, pp. 375–376, 381–382.

[20] The five bishops were: Henry Downes of Killala, John Evans of Meath, Timothy Goodwin of Kilmore, John Lambert of Dromore, and

with a bill ready to submit to parliament, but, after consulting
with the Irish bishops and Speaker Conolly, he accepted in
its stead heads of a bill from the Irish Commons. Although
this bill did not meet the full demands of the Dissenters it
would have a better chance of success. The Commons' bill
offered the same kind of official recognition to Irish Dissenters
as did the Toleration Act of 1689 to their English brethren.
Since in practice the Irish Nonconformists were already permitted to have their own meetinghouses and schools, the bill
seemed modest enough. As a result, the measure elicited little
enthusiasm among the Ulster Presbyterians. Yet its passage
would clarify the status of Dissenting congregations and clergy
and might, as Archbishop King ruefully predicted in opposing
it, open the door to further concessions.[21] The bill passed the
Commons with relative ease and was accepted by the Lords.
In London the government added only one amendment, exempting from the penalties of the Test Act anyone then under
prosecution.[22] Even this modest revision aroused strong opposition in the Irish Lords where the amended bill passed by
one vote, thanks to the support of five "presbyterian prelates." [23]

William Nicolson of Derry. On January 18, 1717, Archbishop King wrote
to Archbishop Wake of Canterbury complaining that of six Irish bishops
created by George I four had been English and advising that Derry not
be given to an Englishman. *A Great Archbishop of Dublin, William King
D.D. His Autobiography, Family and a Selection from His Correspondence,*
ed. Sir Charles Simon King (London, 1906), p. 202. Nicolson became,
nevertheless, bishop of Derry. As a result he received a cool reception
from King and most of the Irish episcopate. See James, *North Country
Bishop,* pp. 249–250. On the invasion threat, see Basil Williams, *Whig
Supremacy,* 2nd ed. (Oxford, Clarendon Press, 1962), p. 173.

[21] Froude, *English in Ireland,* I, 434.

[22] Beckett, *Protestant Dissent in Ireland,* pp. 73–80.

[23] The Commons sent the bill to the Lords on October 16; the bill
passed the Lords on October 22. According to the *Lords' Journal* there
were thirty-two peers and thirteen bishops present. Sixteen lords pro-
tested, including nine bishops (all except the five English bishops listed
in note 20, above). It should be noted that the English bishops who accepted the act would not, however, support the repeal of the Test Act.
In June, before the opening of parliament, Nicolson and Evans told Bolton
that the whole bench of bishops would oppose repeal of the test. Nicolson

Despite the clamor of conservative churchmen, the law of 1719 did little more than legalize existing conditions. It was, however, accompanied by an indemnity act that gave office-holders who had not yet taken the test until March 1720 to do so.[24] Although a similar indemnity act was not passed again until 1725, the Irish act of 1719 pointed the way to a practical method for circumventing the Test Act, which was subsequently followed not only in Ireland but in England as well.[25] Thus, the events of 1719 did in a sense constitute the first breach in the Anglican monopoly.

To Froude, "the resolute obstinacy, three parts disloyal and one part bigotry, of the Irish hierarchy" in defending the Test Act was beyond rational explanation.[26] Nonetheless, in 1716–1719, as earlier during Wharton's efforts for toleration, a majority of the laity as well as the clergy of the Church of Ireland refused to see the need for sharing political power with Dissenters. Beckett astutely comments that "the best way to interpret this struggle is as one between the established church and the presbyterians over the spoils secured by the revolution — the established church in possession, the presbyterians discontented with the conduct of their former allies. The whole thing was really treated by both sides on the basis of expediency and not of principle." [27] Since the Presbyterians could be counted upon to support the government against the Roman Catholics, there was no necessity to grant them concessions. In short, the Anglo-Irish intended to run Ireland for their own benefit with as little interference, from either the English or the Ulster Scots, as circumstances permitted.

---

to Wake, Dublin, June 27, 1719, Christ Church College, Oxford, Wake Manuscripts, Vol. XIII (no folio numbers). Printed by permission of the Governing Body of Christ Church, Oxford.

[24] *Irish Commons' Journal*, Oct. 24, 1719; *Journals of the House of Lords of the Kingdom of Ireland, 1634–1800* [hereafter cited as *Irish Lords' Journal*], 8 vols. (Dublin, 1779–1800), Oct. 28, 1719; Irish Statute, 6 George I, c. 9.

[25] Beckett, *Protestant Dissent in Ireland*, pp. 80–84; Irish Statute, 12 George I, c. 6.

[26] Froude, *English in Ireland*, I, 428.

[27] Beckett, *Protestant Dissent in Ireland*, p. 16.

From the point of view of the growth of either modern nationalism or liberalism the parochial exclusiveness of the Anglo-Irish appears reactionary. They sometimes spoke of the welfare of the Irish "nation" or "people" rather than always in terms of their own class or church, but in view of their actions such terms sound specious. Yet this narrow oligarchy would soon give birth to men of broader visions — Charles Lucas, Edmund Burke, and Henry Grattan. Already it had produced champions of Ireland like Molyneux, King, and Swift. How can one explain this paradox?

If nineteenth-century writers too fequently read into the past their own liberal interpretation of history, perhaps those of the twentieth century have swung too far in the opposite direction. It is the fashion today to emphasize the selfish conservatism of men who opposed absolutism in the seventeenth and early eighteenth centuries: groups such as those who participated in the Fronde, resisted the House of Orange in the Netherlands, or sought to defend the Prussian or Hungarian diets against their rulers. Even the struggle of the English parliamentary party against the Stuarts appears in part reactionary. By similar standards the leaders of the Irish parliament in the early eighteenth century can scarcely be classified as harbingers of liberalism or nationalism. Like the Frondeurs or the Prussian Junkers, they appear far more concerned with preserving their own "liberties" than in protecting abstract "liberty." Yet in the process of defending their own peculiar interests the Anglo-Irish, like the English and later the American Whigs, came to advocate constitutional practices and ideological principles that could be, and were, gradually extended. Within fifty years the Irish parliament would become a potential instrument for the establishment of a self-governing Irish nation. Indeed, perhaps the very homogeneity of the Irish legislature that resulted from the Anglo-Irish ascendancy contributed to the cause of future reform. If the ruling classes in Ireland had not enjoyed control of the Irish parliament they might never have presumed to challenge English rule. To be sure, the challenge proved hesitant and incomplete; nevertheless ever since 1692 Chichester House had endeavored to check the power of the English administration, and with considerable success. The defeat of the Whig effort to repeal the Test Act was in itself evidence of the strength of the "Irish party." During the sessions of 1717 and 1719 another issue revealed even more clearly the latent nationalism in the intense if contradictory ethnocentrism of the Anglo-Irish: the question of the appellate jurisdiction of the Irish House of Lords.

The upper house of the Irish parliament closely resembled its English prototype in composition, procedure, jurisdiction, and in its relationship with the Commons. It was far more important than a colonial council, not only because of its longer tradition and large size, but because of the prestige enjoyed by the titled nobility, the episcopal bench, and the royal judges who constituted its membership. What is more, colonial councils were composed of the governors' nominees, men who might and often did serve for years but who did not have permanent tenure. Aside from the judges, all laymen who sat in the upper chamber in Chichester House were hereditary peers while the bishops served for life. A further factor enhancing the importance of the Irish Lords was that, as with the English Lords, its leaders controlled outright a number of seats in the Commons and exerted influence over many more.

There existed, of course, significant differences between the Irish and the English upper houses. The Irish body had fewer members. In 1713 the House contained ninety-nine lay peers.[28] Because of the greater subordination of Ireland to the crown a larger proportion of the Irish than the English peerage were clients of the court. Another important difference arose from the greater relative size of the episcopal bench; with twenty-two dioceses Ireland had almost as many bishops as England and Wales with twenty-six. The bishops

[28] MacNeil, *Constitutional and Parliamentary History of Ireland*, p. 30; printed lists of the Lords for 1713 and 1725 are in BM, Add. MS. 34.777, fol. 147. There were 126 lay peers in 1725.

all owed their positions to the crown, and many looked to the government for promotion. The Irish sees varied in their income, and, even more than in England, episcopal translation (from poor to wealthier sees) had become a major form of ministerial patronage. Different administrations naturally sought to strengthen their position by suitable appointments and advancements. It 1714 Archbishop Thomas Lindsay of Armagh wrote to Swift in London urging the Tory ministry to translate William Lloyd of Killala to the bishopric of Meath when it fell vacant. "I believe it would be an acceptable post, and the truth is, he has always in the worst of times, voted honestly and behaved himself as a true son of the church." [29] From the Tory standpoint the worst of times were yet to come. When the Whigs came into power a few months later they filled five of the first seven vacancies with English Whigs.

Ecclesiastical influence in the Irish Lords was even more pronounced than the size of the episcopate suggests. Unfettered by the burden of large dioceses, the Irish bishops attended parliament with greater regularity than the English bishops, and their attendance record was far superior to that of the lay peers. For example, during the four sessions of 1719, 1721, 1723, and 1725 there was an average of twelve bishops at each meeting out of total average attendance of twenty-eight; thus the bishops accounted for over 40 percent of the active membership.[30] The ecclesiastical bias of the Irish Lords resulted in its emphasizing religious problems, and it originated most legislation concerning church affairs. When united, the episcopal bench proved virtually irresistible. On such matters as tithe collection, raising curates' salaries, or protecting episcopal properties the bishops could initiate and push bills through the House of Lords almost at will, though of course they often met with opposition and sometimes defeat in the Commons.[31] On the big questions concerning the treatment

[29] Lindsay to Swift, Jan. 5, 1713/14, in *Swift Correspondence*, ed. Ball, II, 115.

[30] James, *North Country Bishop*, p. 251, n. 14.

[31] In 1719 the Commons rejected a tithes bill from the Lords, but passed

of Dissenters and Roman Catholics, however, the episcopate
could seldom unite. It will be recalled that five Whig bishops
voted against the rest of the episcopal bench to pass the
Toleration Act of 1719. Two years later enough conservative
bishops voted against a popery bill to defeat it.[32] Yet, even
if partisan divisions prevented the episcopal bench from ever
dominating the Irish government, the leaders of the Church
of Ireland, whose communicants numbered only about a sixth
of the population, wielded far greater political power than
did the Anglican bishops of England.

In dealing with both ecclesiastical and secular patronage
the government faced a dilemma. Appointing Englishmen to
Irish offices served several useful purposes: it gave an opportunity to pay off political debts; it afforded a means of removing embarrassing supporters from the English scene; and
it swelled the ranks of the Castle party in Dublin. At the
same time, nothing more obviously aroused Anglo-Irish jealousy. The rewards of honor and office had to be dispensed
judiciously — or at least profitably. "Under the rose," wrote
Sir William Robinson to the lords justices' secretary, "if [you]
know any desirous to be a viscount in your country and would
come up to £3,000; it should be done and not a word said
thereof but betwixt ourselves."[33] Both the duke of Bolton
and Lord Carteret requested the raising of several men to
the peerage whom they wished to place on the privy council.[34]
As a result of the diverse motives influencing Irish patronage
it is not surprising that, although nearly half of the bishops
were replaced during the first decade of the Hanoverian rule

three other laws concerning the church. *Irish Commons' Journal*, Oct. 29,
30, 31, 1719.
   [32] *Irish Lords' Journal*, Nov. 2, 1719; Nicolson to Wake, Derry, Nov. 30,
1719, Wake MSS, XIII.
   [33] Robinson to Joshua Dawson, London, Aug. 30, 1708, Calendar of
Departmental Correspondence, I, 115.
   [34] Addison to Bolton, Hampton Court, Sept. 12, 1717, in *Letters of
Addison*, ed. Graham, p. 374; Carteret to Newcastle, Dublin Castle, Aug.
9, 1725, English Public Record Office, State Papers [hereafter cited as Eng.
P.R.O., S.P.], 63/386, fol. 24 (reprinted by permission of the English Public
Record Office).

and the number of lay peers increased by twenty-seven, the Irish House of Lords still remained free from complete Castle control. In fact, in George I's reign the "Irish party" in the upper house proved more troublesome to the government than in the Commons.

One characteristic of the Irish Lords helps to explain its strong esprit de corps and jealous concern for Irish interests. The minority of the lay lords who actually attended parliament consisted largely of peers resident in Ireland; the majority, who seldom if ever crossed the threshold of Chichester House, were absentees who lived abroad. For example a count for the parliament of 1727 shows that although a total of thirty-three different peers put in an appearance only seventeen were present for a third or more of its sixty-five meetings. The fathers of sixteen of these men seem to have been Irish born, and most of them represented families established in Ireland for several generations, some stemming from Old English and even Gaelic stock. Eleven of them had Irish-born mothers, ten of them wives from Ireland. Four had attended Trinity College, seven had served in the Irish Commons, and a like number were members of the Irish privy council.[35] It is true that the Irish House of Lords, like the English, permitted proxies but their use was restricted to persons officially excused, and no peer in attendance could vote more than two

[35] The above statistics are based on information found in G. E. Cokayne, *The Complete Peerage of England, Scotland, Ireland, Great Britain and the United Kingdom*, rev. Vicary Gibbs, Geoffrey White, and R. S. Lea, 12 vols. (London, Saint Catherine Press, 1910–1959). The peers, with their record of attendance, are: John Dillon, seventh earl of Roscommon (54 meetings); James Caulfield, third viscount Charlemont (51); Thomas Bermingham, fifteenth baron Athenry (50); Henry Tichborne, first baron Ferrard (47); George St. George, first baron St. George (46); Marcus Beresford, first viscount Tyrone (42); Joshua Allen, second viscount Allen (41); Richard Annesley, fifth baron Altham (39); Robert Fitzgerald, nineteenth earl of Kildare (34); Edward Moore, fifth earl of Drogheda (33); Thomas Southwell, second baron Southwell (33); Richard Lambart, fourth earl of Cavan (32); Henry Barry, third baron Santry (29); Richard Parson, second viscount and first earl of Rosse (27); James Hamilton, first viscount Strabane and sixth earl of Abercorn in the Scottish peerage (27); Theobold Bourke, sixth viscount Mayo (25); Trevor Hill, first viscount Hillsborough (24).

proxies. Furthermore, lay peers could only accept proxies from lay peers, bishops from bishops. Seldom did proxies constitute more than a fifth of the votes cast.[36]

Of all the functions of the Irish House of Lords none was more exalted than its role as the kingdom's highest court. The crown had a clear right to override legislation with a royal veto, and by Poynings' Law the English ministry as well as the king controlled Irish legislation. In contrast, the Irish judiciary seemed to enjoy greater independence. On a number of occasions cases from the Irish courts had been appealed to English courts, usually King's Bench, but these instances dated chiefly from the period before 1688 when the Irish Lords was rarely in session. When the Irish parliament began to meet regularly, there was an increasing precedent for appeals going instead to the Irish House of Lords. Colonial appeals went, of course, to the English privy council following the pattern established for appellate jurisdiction from regions like the Channel Islands and the Isle of Man. As a separate kingdom with its own parliament, Ireland was in a different category; the only logical rival to the supreme jurisdiction of the Irish House of Lords was its English counterpart. The relationship between the two houses had never yet been clearly determined.

The English revolution of 1688 and the Irish civil war of 1689–1691 quickly resulted in a clarification of the subordinate position of the Irish legislature, but the events of that period, despite their long-range constitutional importance, caused no immediate redefinition of the status of the Irish judiciary. Late in William III's reign a dispute between the Ulster Society and William King, bishop of Derry (later archbishop of Dublin), forced an apparent showdown between the Irish and the English Lords. The society and the bishop both claimed a block of land outside Londonderry. The society successfully sought an injunction against the bishop in the

---

[36] *Irish Lords' Journal*, Oct. 27, 28, 1719, Apr. 17, 1727; *Rules and Orders to be Observed in the Upper House of Parliament of Ireland* (Dublin, 1778), pp. 7, 38–40.

Irish Chancery; Bishop King retaliated by appealing to the Irish Lords, who ordered Chancery to withdraw the injunction. Defeated in Ireland, the society petitioned the English Lords. After hearing arguments from both sides the English Lords decided that the bishop's appeal from Irish Chancery to the Irish Lords should be disregarded since the Irish upper house was *coram non judice*. They held that the Chancery in Ireland should proceed, notwithstanding the order of the Dublin Lords, as if there had been no appeal. If either party still felt aggrieved, recourse lay in an appeal to the English not the Irish Lords. Although this opinion was forwarded to the lords justices in Dublin, the society received little immediate satisfaction. When the sheriffs of Derry were arrested for carrying out the Chancery order against Bishop King, the lords justices apparently hesitated to interfere. Hearing of these events, the English Lords renewed their investigation of the case, collecting, among other information, a list of precedents concerning earlier appeals both to London and to Dublin. In the end the English Lords stood by their first decision, and finally by November 1699 the society gained possession of the disputed property.[37]

The bishop of Derry's case did not settle the question of the Irish Lord's appellate jurisdiction. Instead of accepting the outcome, the Irish Lords continued to act as if they constituted the supreme court of Ireland. In 1703, when the English Lords upheld an injunction of the palatine court of Tipperary against the earl of Meath, the Dublin peers issued an explicit statement of their position. Early in 1704 they passed a series of resolutions, *nemine contradicente*, the substance of which is as follows:

1. That by the ancient laws of the kingdom the queen "hath undoubted jurisdiction and Prerogative of judging in this her High Court of Parliament in all Appeals and Causes within her Majesty's Realm of Ireland."

[37] *House of Lords MSS*, n.s. III 16–56; *English Lords' Journal*, May 24, 1698.

2. That anyone in Ireland who presumed to "remove any Cause determined in the High Court of Parliament to any other court" should be deemed a betrayer of the privileges of parliament and of the "rights and liberties of the Subjects of this Kingdom."

3. That any person who carried out "any order from any other court, contrary to the final Judgment" of the Irish Lords, should be deemed the same.

4. That any sheriff or other official who should refuse to execute an order of the High Court of Parliament "shall incur the utmost Displeasure of the House."

5. That the sheriff of Tipperary forthwith put the earl of Meath in possession of the disputed property.[38]

Ten days later the earl of Meath reported to the Lords that he had recovered his lands and thanked the House for its assistance.[39] Apparently the case ended there. Ormond's influence in London may explain why the English government raised no objections to the Irish Lords' pretensions. In any event, the troublesome issue of rival jurisdictions remained quiescent until the reign of George I.

In 1716 the Irish House of Lords reversed two decrees of the Irish Exchequer in a long drawn out suit between Hester Sherlock and Maurice Annesley. Hester Sherlock was the sister of Christopher Sherlock, whose estate had been forfeited after the Williamite War. The estate had been charged to provide portions for his sisters Hester and Mary and for his younger brothers. The widowed mother of the children allegedly requested Annesley to lease the estate from the trustees of the forfeited estates (he was the receiver for the trustees in County Kildare) and to act as the guardian of the minor children. Annesley claimed that he spent more than the estate was worth on the children, and, as a result, the trustees gave him the entire property to defray his expenses.[40] When Hester

---

[38] *Irish Lords' Journal*, Feb. 11, 1703/04.

[39] *Ibid.*, Feb. 21, 1703/04.

[40] Simms, *Williamite Confiscation*, p. 145; *Irish Lords' Journal*, June 19, 1716.

sued to recover some of the estate, she lost in the Exchequer
Court and so appealed to the Irish Lords. When Hester won
her suit in the Lords, Annesley took the case to the English
House of Lords on the grounds that the Irish peers had no
appellate jurisdiction from the Irish Exchequer. On her part,
Hester petitioned the Irish Lords to protect her property; they
responded to her plea, ordering first the reading of her petition and next the reading of the resolutions passed in the
Meath case in February 1704. The temper of the Lords became clear when they voted down a court motion to refer
the question to the judges for advice and instead resolved to
uphold the "Honour, Jurisdiction, and Privileges" of the
House by granting relief to Hester Sherlock. The judicial
committee of the House was instructed to determine what
steps should be taken to implement this resolution.[41] Recognizing the seriousness of the situation Lord Lieutenant Bolton
wrote to London for advice.

Because of the ultimate outcome of the Annesley case one
would assume that the English government welcomed the
opportunity it offered to humble the Irish parliament. That
was certainly *not* the intention of the Whig ministry in 1717.
Addison first told Bolton to do his best to avoid involvement
in the dispute.[42] To this advice he added a specific suggestion
for ending the cause célèbre without either side losing face:

> as His Majesty is sensible of the ill consequences which may
> arise from a rupture between the House of Lords in this King-
> dom and that in Ireland, as the sum of money which gives
> occasion to this dispute is too inconsiderable to be put in
> balance with the good understanding that ought to be kept
> up between the two kingdoms, H.M. had rather allow it out
> of the public revenue of Ireland than that the peace and tran-
> quility of the kingdom should be endangered. If therefore
> your Grace can by this means procure the petition to be with-
> drawn, or, by another private application to the parties con-
> tending, moderate the proceedings in this case, it is H.M.'s

[41] *Irish Lords' Journal*, Sept. 23, 1717.
[42] Addison to Bolton, Sept. 5, 1717, in *Letters of Addison*, ed. Graham,
pp. 373–374.

pleasure that such a sum should be employed for so good an end. And whatever assurance your Grace shall give on this occasion will be made good here by an order from H.M. on the Treasury.[43]

Before Bolton had the opportunity to follow the ministry's plan the Irish Lords voted an award of £1,508 to Hester Sherlock, charging the sheriff of Kildare to seize certain lands of Annesley's to guarantee payment.[44] Although both Bolton and parliament appear to have dropped the matter for the rest of the 1717 session, the dispute was far from over.

In 1718, following an order from the English Lords, the Irish Exchequer Court instructed the sheriff of Kildare, Alexander Burrows, to carry out its judgment denying Hester's claims on the estate. Upon his refusal the barons of the Exchequer fined Burrows £1,200. The sheriff appealed to the Irish Lords for protection. When the Irish Lords next assembled in July 1719 they promptly referred Burrows' petition to the judicial committee. Apparently the original case had now been settled by the method London has proposed, for the committee discovered that a member of the Castle party in the Commons, a Captain John Pratt, had purchased Hester Sherlock's decree for £1,860. The Commons waived privilege and permitted Pratt to testify before the Lords. The captain explained that he had acted solely on the advice of certain private gentlemen and with no advance promise of repayment, though he admitted that he did hope to be recompensed by the government.[45] Faced with this *fait accompli*, the Lords voted against a resolution to put Hester Sherlock again in possession of the disputed lands; nothing more could be done about her part in the affair. The Irish party,

---

[43] Addison to Bolton, Sept. 19, 1717, *ibid.*, p. 376.

[44] *Irish Lords' Journal*, Oct. 3, 4, 1717.

[45] Lecky, *History of England in the Eighteenth Century*, I, 456; *Irish Lords' Journal*, July 10, 28, 29, 1719. Pratt was deputy vice-treasurer of Ireland. Annesley's daughter petitioned the English Lords to compel either Pratt or Hester Sherlock to account for the rents and profits collected during the time Hester Sherlock held the disputed lands. *English Lords' Journal*, Jan. 29, 1719/20.

however, was fully aroused and determined to vindicate Burrows and to clarify, once and for all, the supreme jurisdiction
of the Irish House of Lords.

The Lords' judicial committee now formally examined the
barons of the Irish Exchequer. When these three judges asserted that they had merely defended the royal prerogative,
Archbishop King demanded: "Do you think the overthrow
of the jurisdiction of this House a support of the king's prerogative?" Lord Chief Justice Gilbert refused to answer. The
archbishop then inquired: "Did you acquaint the Government here with the Injunction you had from the Lords in
Great Britain, before you executed it?" [46] The chief baron
replied that he had not. After further questioning the barons
were instructed to withdraw. On July 29 the Lords passed a
series of resolutions applying the principles expressed in the
Meath case of 1704 to the present situation. They condemned
the judges of the Exchequer for executing "a pretended order
from another court contrary to the final judgment of this High
Court of Parliament." Pronouncing the three barons to be
"betrayers of His Majesty's prerogative and the undoubted
ancient rights and privileges of this House and of the rights
of the subjects of this Kingdom," the Lords solemnly ordered
that the offenders should be taken into the custody of the
gentleman usher of the black rod and imprisoned during the
pleasure of the House. [47] Shocked by the behavior of the
Lords, Bishop Nicolson of Derry moved for a division on the
question. To his dismay he discovered that only ten out of
the thirty-eight present would vote to reject the resolution
and that only six, besides himself, were willing to enter a
protest against it. [48] It is significant that four of the others
signing the protest were, like Nicolson, recent English ap-

[46] Nicolson to Wake, Aug. 6, 1719, Wake MSS, XIII. Among Archbishop
King's supporters was Robert Molesworth, who had just been raised to the
Irish peerage as viscount Molesworth. The *Irish Lords' Journal* reports
him attending regularly throughout the session. On Molesworth and King,
see Robbins, *Eighteenth-Century Commonwealthman*, pp. 145–147.

[47] *Irish Lords' Journal*, July 29, 1719.

[48] Nicolson to Wake, Aug. 6, 1719, Wake MSS, XIII.

pointees to the episcopal bench; the other two signers were Viscount Doneraile (brother of one of the judges) and Lord Chancellor Midleton.[49] In 1713, as leader of the Whig opposition in the Commons, Alan Brodrick had led the Irish party to victory over a Tory administration; now, as a peer and lord chancellor, he could command only a handful of English bishops and one lay peer. For the moment at least, Irish politics appeared to be a struggle between the English and the Irish parties, rather than a question of Whig against Tory.

Since the three barons of the Exchequer quite naturally refused to ask for pardon from the Irish Lords, Ireland now witnessed the strange sight of three royal judges being kept in prison at a time when they were scheduled to go on circuit. An open confrontation between the Irish and the English peers could no longer be avoided. In September the Irish Lords decided to draft an address to the crown justifying their position. The English party vainly tried to delay the address or at least to soften its wording, but they met with little success. On October 2 Nicolson wrote disgustedly to Archbishop Wake of Canterbury describing the success of Archbishop King and the Irish party: "After a long squabble about the two imperial Crowns of England and Ireland, the supreme judicature of this Kingdome was asserted in such a strain as will hardly be allowable on your side of the water. I was called to order for saying that one of the paragraphs was *seditiously* express'd: But happily rescu'd by a greater man's telling them that such language had a harder name given it, in the Law Books, than that by which I had called it. His Lordship (Midleton) wished them to consider the precipice they were upon: and to look before they made the fatal leap." [50]

The Irish peers paid little heed to Midleton's warning. In November they sent the address to King George. Although some of its stronger clauses had been modified, the document

[49] *Irish Lords' Journal*, July 29, 1719. The bishops were John Evans of Meath, Henry Downes of Killala, Timothy Godwin of Kilmore, and Welborn Ellis of Kildare.
[50] Nicolson to Wake, Oct. 2, 1719, Wake MSS, XIII.

contained no basic concessions to the English party.[51] Furthermore, when, after a month, no reply was received, the Lords
took the unprecedented step of ordering their address to be
published without the king's answer, should none arrive before January 1. The Irish party had no desire to compromise;
"never," reported Nicolson, "where more pains taken to irritate a giddy populace into barefaced rebellion." [52]

In the final analysis the question of the jurisdiction of the
Irish parliament was, as Lecky says, one of power not of
argument.[53] Archbishop King might boldly declare that acts
of the British parliament signified no more than the bylaws
of a piepowder court until confirmed by both houses in Dublin;[54] in actual fact, the Anglo-Irish were compelled to bend
to the will of Westminster. They could resist British rule by
argument, maneuver, and evasion; they could not afford to
do so by force. The Protestant ascendancy rested on British
arms.

In January 1720 the English House of Lords voted a com-
mendation of the three barons of the Irish Exchequer and
asked the king to confer upon the judges some mark of royal
favor. The English Lords then devoted themselves to the
congenial task of writing a law that would not only strip the
Irish Lords of all appellate jurisdiction but that would state
in unmistakable terms the subordination of the Irish nation
to the British parliament. Anglo-Irishmen in Westminster
attempted to tone down the proposed legislation without success, though they did delay its passage for several months.[55]

---

[51] *Irish Lords' Journal*, Oct. 17, 1719.

[52] Nicolson to Wake, Nov. 30, Dec. 18, 1719, Wake MSS, XIII.

[53] Lecky, *England in the Eighteenth Century*, I, 456.

[54] Nicolson to Wake, Oct. 6, 1719, Wake MSS, XIII.

[55] On January 25, 1719/20, the English Lords examined true copies of
the section in the *Irish Lords' Journal* on the Annesley case. On January
28 they passed the resolution in favor of the barons of the Exchequer and
ordered that a bill be drawn up dealing with Irish appellate jurisdiction.
The bill was first read on February 8 and after a few amendments was
passed February 22. Two Irish peers who also sat in the English Lords
signed a protest: the erratic young duke of Wharton (marquess of Cather-
lough, earl of Rathfarham, and baron Trim in the Irish peerage) and

The progress of the bill was followed in Ireland with increasing dismay. Feeling ran so high that the English party in Dublin found themselves virtually ostracized. "We are all treated," complained Nicolson, "by Friends and Foes, Whigs and Tories, as Enemies of the public interests of this Kingdome: notwithstanding that we are thoroughly persuaded in our consciences, that the cry of Independency (which universally prevails) leads to misery and confusion." In April, when Dublin learned that the Declaratory Act had passed the English Commons with only minor amendments, the Anglo-Irish were filled with impotent anger. Nicolson wrote Wake that "the Rage of our Gentlemen (whose fathers or grandfathers were trueborn English or Scotch) . . . is not to be described. Here's an End, says one of the wisest of them in my hearing, of all the liberties and properties of Ireland." [56]

To men like Nicolson, who had recently come from England, Irish nationalism made no sense. To the great majority

---

viscount Tadcaster (Henry O'Brien, earl of Thomond and baron Ibackan in the Irish peerage). On March 4 the Commons defeated a motion to postpone consideration of the bill by a vote of 140 to 88. The Commons did accept, on March 11, an amendment to delete the following sentence from the introduction: "Attempts have lately been made to shake off the subjection of Ireland unto and its dependence upon the imperial crown of this Realm; which would be of dangerous consequence both to Great Britain, and Ireland." On the other hand, an amendment to validate previous appellate decisions of the Irish Lords was defeated on March 26, and the bill passed its final reading that same day, 119 to 44. Among those who opposed the bill in the English Commons were the following: John Brownlow (viscount Tyrconnel in the Irish peerage). Trevor Hill (viscount Hillsborough in the Irish peerage), and a Mr. Molyneux (probably Samuel, son of William, who sat for Bossiney). *English Lords' Journal* Jan. 25, 28, Feb. 8, 22, 1719/20, and *English Commons, Journal* Mar. 4, 11, 26, 1720. Robert Molesworth, who sat for St. Michaels in the English Commons and in the Irish Lords as viscount Molesworth, also strongly opposed the bill. O. W. Ferguson, *Jonathan Swift and Ireland* (Urbana, Ill., 1962), pp. 52–53. Regarding the Annesley dispute it is worth noting that during the 1719–1720 session the English Lords were considering three other Irish appeals: *Ludlow v. Macartney* from the Irish Chancery (dismissed), *Bermingham v. Lord Shelburn* from the Irish Exchequer (reversed), and *John Burke v. William Butler* from the Irish Chancery (dismissed). *English Lords' Journal*, Jan. 13, 20, 23, Feb. 6, 1719/20.

[56] Nicolson to Wake, Feb. 19, 1719/20, April 3, 1720, Wake MSS, XIII.

of the Anglo-Irish, on the contrary, the defense of Irish rights had become a patriotic cause. Molyneux's *The Case of Ireland* was now reprinted, and along with it appeared several new tracts arguing for Irish autonomy. Poor economic conditions increased popular discontent and engendered bitterness against English regulations like the Woolens Act of 1699. The English ministry further aggravated Irish resentment by refusing to approve an Irish tillage bill to encourage grain cultivation, on the grounds that the measure would endanger English interests.[57] In May 1720 the dean of St. Patrick's joined in the attack on England with his *Proposal for the Universal Use of Irish Manufacture in Cloaths and Furniture of Houses, etc. Utterly Rejecting and Renouncing Every Thing that comes from England.* Though primarily concerned with a remedy for Irish economic ills, Swift's pamphlet was calculated to arouse anti-English feeling.

Confronted with so much outspoken criticism, the government felt compelled to take action. Since Swift's authorship of the *Proposal* could not easily be proved, the Castle moved against the printer of the tract, Edward Waters. Under the guidance of Lord Chancellor Midleton the Dublin grand jury indicted Waters for seditious libel, and he was brought to trial in the Court of King's Bench before Chief Justice Whitshed. When the trial jury refused to convict the printer, Whitshed demanded that they withdraw and reconsider their verdict. Nine times the jury refused to accede to the judge's instructions until finally they rendered a special verdict leaving the decision of the case up to the judge himself. Whitshed wisely refrained from immediate action, and the next year the Castle dropped the charges against Waters.[58] The trial had only served to demonstrate the strength of the Irish party.

Events in Ireland during 1719–1720 marked the beginning of a new national movement. Although the different political and religious groups in the country disagreed violently among themselves on many issues, the Irish response to the Declaratory Act showed that the nation might unite in the cause of

---

[57] Ferguson, *Swift and Ireland*, pp. 47–48, 64.
[58] *Ibid.*, pp. 49–56.

Irish autonomy. Already before 1719 men of different party affiliations had sought to identify themselves with Irish national interests. In 1703 the Irish Commons had passed resolutions anticipating the nonimportation agreement advocated by Swift in his *Proposal*.[59] The most vocal advocates of Irish rights were Whigs, such as Robert Molesworth and Henry Maxwell.[60] But even High Tories took up the theme. Attacking the Hanoverian succession in 1711 a Catholic Jacobite declared that the English Act of Settlement did not bind Ireland, "a distinct realm, a different nation," with its own laws, parliament, and officials. "Ireland," he wrote, "hath never acknowledged her king to be chosen by the people, but to succeed by birth . . . She knows more righteous things and scorns to make heretical England her pattern."[61] In 1714 a Whig pamphleteer, arguing against the government's efforts to control sheriffs and juries, proclaimed that, "Liberty which has deserted most parts of Europe, seems to have chosen Ireland for its seat."[62] In 1718 the Irish bishops objected to distributing Bibles sent over by the archbishop of Canterbury, preferring to use only those printed in Ireland.[63]

Obviously the movement for Irish autonomy appealed to various groups for different if not contradictory reasons. Yet a common sense of grievance against English rule could offer a basis for united action. By 1720 the nucleus of an Irish party, embracing men of all shades of opinion, had come into existence. While in England during the first decade of Hanoverian rule the Tories and dissident Whigs lacked a unifying cause and could only form a disorganized, if stubborn, opposition,[64] the Tory opposition in Ireland had the potential of becoming a patriot party.

[59] See Chap. III, above.

[60] Robbins, *Eighteenth-Century Commonwealthman*, pp. 147–149.

[61] *A Jacobite Narrative of the War in Ireland 1688–1691*, ed. John T. Gilbert (Dublin, 1892), p. 183.

[62] *A Defense of the Constitution or an Answer to an Argument in the Case of Mr. Moor* (Dublin, 1714), p. 4.

[63] Nicolson to Wake, Feb. 9, 1718/19, Wake MSS, XIII. In 1721 the Irish bishops objected to using a prayer because it had been written in England. Nicolson to Wake, Nov. 21, 1721, *ibid.*

[64] Foord, *His Majesty's Opposition*, pp. 108–109.

V

The Limits
of
English Power

The crisis of 1719–1720 clarified Ireland's constitutional status; it did not alter the practical problems of Irish politics. The Declaratory Act removed all doubts regarding England's complete supremacy over Ireland. The theory, expounded by men like Darcy and Molyneux, that Ireland was a parallel kingdom under the English crown but not the English nation had proved untenable. Yet the English did not wish to control Ireland by force; they expected to govern peacefully through the Irish administration and parliament. The practical limits of English power were thus not determined by royal proclamations or English statutes, but depended upon the attitude of the ruling classes in Ireland. In 1720 the Whig ministry was aware of considerable opposition in Ireland to the Declaratory Act, but was confident that a little patience combined with a firm hand would soon restore harmony in Dublin. The government grievously underestimated the extent of Irish disaffection.

In August 1720 Bolton was replaced by the duke of Grafton, who had already demonstrated his ability to deal with the Irish parliament during his tenure as a lord justice. Grafton faced a difficult situation. The crash of the South Sea Company in the late summer precipitated a recession in England that soon spread to Ireland, causing popular discontent. The crash also disrupted British politics and caused a change in the ministry. Sir Robert Walpole, who seized leadership early in 1721, had little understanding of Ireland. Still, by the time of the next session of the Irish parliament in September 1721 both kingdoms had quieted down.

In addition to the customary platitudes, Grafton's opening speech contained an appeal for unity that betrayed his concern over Irish opposition. "Whatever hopes the disaffected may conceive from unhappy divisions among ourselves," he declared, "I doubt not, but you will frustrate and defeat them by your prudent conduct and perfect unanimity, which cannot but contribute to the security of our most excellent church as by law established and to the strengthening of the Protestant interest." [1] Parliament's reply to Grafton showed their confidence in him. The lords specifically thanked him for his "so good, so easy, so endearing" conduct since his return to Ireland and for having "interposed your Credit and Interest for our good and Advantage." [2] The only dissident voice came from King. The outspoken archbishop approved of the thanks to Grafton but not the wording of the address to the king. He had, he explained tersely, "always been against addresses of mere compliment between the crown and Parliament, believing they may be of ill consequence." [3]

Notwithstanding his popularity, Grafton had difficulty handling the Irish parliament in 1721. The English party in the Commons could not count on a majority, and, as might be expected, opposition in the Lords was even stronger. On one important policy the government met clear defeat. On the recommendation of lords justices Midleton and Conolly the ministry had endorsed a proposal to establish a bank in Ireland. A group of Anglo-Irish entrepreneurs, headed by Lord Abercorn, proposed the creation of a Dublin bank closely resembling in character the Bank of England.[4] The idea of the bank dated back to 1695, and the plan seemed well designed both to solve one of Ireland's economic problems and to appease wounded national pride. When Grafton requested action on the project in his opening speech to parliament, both houses had voted to consider the matter. The temper of

---

[1] *Irish Commons' Journal*, Sept. 12, 1721.

[2] *Irish Lords' Journal*, Sept. 14, 1721; see also *Irish Commons' Journal*, Sept. 14, 1721.

[3] *Irish Lords' Journal*, Sept. 14, 1721.

[4] Malcolm Dillon, *The History and Development of Banking in Ireland from the Earliest Times to the Present Day* (London and Dublin, 1889), pp. 37-39.

Irish opinion in the autumn of 1721 was scarcely hospitable
to the establishment of a government-sponsored bank. The
South Sea Bubble had made members of parliament wary of
all high finance; the English Declaratory Act had made them
suspicious of any proposal advocated by the English ministry.
Midleton's and Conolly's support probably also damaged
chances for the bank, since both had become identified with
the English interest. As for Lord Abercorn, he was considered
as an absentee courtier; in Anne's reign parliament had successfully attacked his monopoly of Irish lighthouses.[5] On
November 7 the Castle party in the Commons managed to
push through a report favorable to the bank by a vote of 76
to 63. The next day the Lords countered with a resolution
that "the erecting of a Bank in this Kingdom or incorporating
any number of persons into a Body Politick for the management and government of such a Bank, may, in the present
circumstance, be prejudicial and of extreme ill consequences
to this Kingdom." [6]

During the next month the opposition, aided by numerous
pamphlets (some of which were probably by Swift), mobilized
the country members.[7] On December 9 the lower house reversed itself and denounced the bank by a crushing vote of 157
to 80. A disappointed defender of the project, who published
a satirical rejoinder, *The Last Speech and Dying Words of
the Bank of Ireland which was executed on College Green on
Saturday, the 9th instant*, was summarily punished by the
Commons for his impertinence.[8] Whatever its merits, the
bank had become in popular minds another English scheme
to exploit Ireland. Grafton hastened to forward the Commons' address to London. When the House thanked him for

[5] R. V. Clarendon, *A Sketch of the Revenue and Finances of Ireland*
(London, 1791), pp. 19–20. Abercorn was viscount Strabane in the Irish
peerage.
[6] *Irish Lords' Journal*, Nov. 8, 1721; see also *Irish Commons' Journal*,
Nov. 7, 1721.
[7] Ferguson, *Jonathan Swift and Ireland*, pp. 64–75.
[8] *Irish Commons' Journal*, Dec. 9, 1721; Dillon, *History of Banking in
Ireland*, p. 40; see also *Irish Lords' Journal*, Dec. 9, 1721.

his cooperation, he assured them, "I am very glad that my conduct has been acceptable to the House of Commons; I shall always endeavour to the utmost of my power to promote the true Interests of this Kingdom." [9]

The Irish parliament in 1721–1722 displayed an independent spirit in other matters besides the bank question. The Commons passed a tillage bill similar to the one rejected by the English in 1719. To impress Dublin Castle with the importance of the measure, the whole House visited the lord lieutenant to present the heads of the bill instead of sending it by the usual committee. Grafton promised to recommend the measure to Westminster.[10] By his responsive attitude on this and the bank issue he won sufficient support to enable him to engineer the passage of the new revenue act well before the end of the session. The Commons normally withheld its final approval of supplies until all other bills had been returned from London, but "as a peculiar mark of confidence, which the Commons repose in his Grace," they passed it in December.[11] Their confidence in the lord lieutenant proved well placed as far as the bank was concerned; the government withdrew the proposal.[12] The tillage bill, however, was again quashed in England, and three other Irish bills were apparently amended in ways unacceptable to the Irish Commons for it threw them out upon their return in February.[13] Though Grafton had done his best to smooth ruffled feelings, complete harmony obviously had not been restored between the government and Chichester House. Before the next meeting of parliament in 1723 a new storm was to arise that would prove even more violent than that over the Annesley case.

Probably no event in Irish history during the first half of

[9] *Irish Commons' Journal*, Dec. 13, 1721.
[10] *Ibid.*, Oct. 16, 1721.
[11] *Ibid.*, Dec. 21, 1721.
[12] *Ibid.*, Jan. 16, 1721/22.
[13] As was customary, the Commons appointed a committee to "examine what alterations have been made in the heads of bills sent from this House this session of Parliament." *Ibid.*, Jan. 3, 9, 1721/22. Nicolson specifically stated that the three bills were rejected because they had been altered by the privy council. Nicolson to Wake, June 13, 1721, Wake MSS, XIII.

the eighteenth century is better known than the dispute over Wood's halfpence. In 1722 George I granted a patent to his mistress, the duchess of Kendall, to supply £100,800 worth of copper coins for use in Ireland. The duchess sold the patent to an ironmaster, William Wood, who planned to realize a handsome profit from the venture. Ireland possessed no mint although the Irish privy council and lords justices had frequently requested one. Instead, the nation had been supplied with money like Wood's, much of it of debased value. Since Wood's coins were supposed to be of relatively good quality their introduction into Ireland might have proved beneficial, at least in limited amounts. But to the Irish the whole project represented a scheme to defraud the country for the advantage of a foreign grafter, a scheme far worse than the bank. In the summer of 1722 when news of Wood's patent reached Dublin, Lord Justice King and the commissioners of revenue wrote to London opposing the proposal.[14] The government disregarded their warnings, and Wood quietly went ahead with his plans. His agents began introducing the coins in the summer of 1723.

Upon Grafton's return to Ireland to convene parliament he found men of all parties vehemently hostile to the patent. On September 13, two weeks after the opening of the session, the Commons went into committee of the whole house to consider the state of the nation "particularly in relation to the importing and uttering of copper halfpence and farthings into this Kingdom." They requested the lord lieutenant to lay before the House Wood's patent and all other available papers relating to the coinage. When Grafton disclaimed having any such documents, Commons demanded that the commissioners of revenue provide them. On Grafton's orders the commissioners promptly complied with the request. The House likewise asked the deputy clerk of the rolls and the deputy clerk of the paper office to supply information concerning previous patents for coinage. Having completed their

[14] A. Goodwin, "Wood's Halfpence," *English Historical Review*, LI (1936), 657, n. 3.

investigations, the House passed, on September 25, six resolutions denouncing Wood's patent as "highly prejudicial to his Majesty's revenue, destructive of the trade and commerce of this nation and of most dangerous consequences to the rights and prerogatives of the subjects." They accused Wood "and his accomplices" of both misrepresentation in applying for the patent and of sending to Ireland coins of less value than that required by the terms of the patent. (The House had questioned several of Wood's agents in Dublin and examined sample coins.[15]) On September 27 they incorporated the substance of these resolutions in an address to the crown. The Lords prepared a similar address the next day.[16] The lord lieutenant forwarded these messages to London. He had already told Walpole that he could not find a single member of the Irish parliament who would support the government on the question of the patent.[17]

The ministry remained unimpressed. Walpole's response to Grafton's complaints was devastating:

I will not enter into the merits of the question, I write merely as a friend. Parliament, under your administration, is attacking a patent already passed *in favour of whom and for whose sake you know very well* . . . The patent was passed by those that you have hitherto looked upon as pretty nearly engaged with you in your public capacity. Are they no longer worth your trouble? . . .

The objections to the patent now come over, I venture to pronounce, are frivolous, and such as a very common understanding with a willing mind may easily refute. I never knew more care taken than in passing this patent. I am still satisfied it is very well to be supported. What remedy the wisdom of

[15] *Irish Commons' Journal*, Sept. 9, 13, 14, 16, 17, 19, 1723.

[16] In their address the Commons explained that their inquiry had proceeded "entirely from our love to our country." *Ibid.*, Sept. 27, 1723. The Lords' address took a similar line: "We . . . are under the utmost concern to find that our Duty to Your Majesty and our Country, indispensibly calls upon us to acquaint your Majesty with the ill consequences which will inevitably follow from a Patent for coining Halfpence and Farthings, to be uttered in this Kingdom." *Irish Lords' Journal*, Sept. 28, 1723.

[17] Froude, *English in Ireland*, I, 584.

Ireland will find out for this supposed grievance I am at a loss to guess, and upon whom the consequences of this Irish storm will fall most heavily, I will not say. I shall have my share, but, if I am not mistaken, there are others that will not escape.[18]

Sir Robert plainly saw the whole affair in terms of English politics. He was then engaged in a power struggle with Lord Carteret, who as secretary of state for the southern department handled Irish business. He knew that Lord Chancellor Midleton and his son, St. John Brodrick, were his enemies; he suspected that Grafton was scheming with Carteret to discredit the administration by means of the Irish crisis. Walpole's interpretation may have contained some truth, but it was woefully inadequate. To the Irish parliament the fight over Wood's patent was no sideshow to London politics; it was a national issue of first importance.

Despite his limited approach to the crisis, Walpole recognized the need to avoid antagonizing the Irish parliament any further until it had voted supplies for the next two years. The government framed an evasive reply to the Irish addresses to the crown. "His Majesty is very concerned," it ran, to learn that his granting the patent for coining halfpence had caused so much uneasiness in the Irish parliament. "If there has been any abuse committed by the Patentee, his Majesty will give the necessary order for inquiry into and punishing these abuses and will do everything that is in his power, for the satisfaction of his People." The Irish Commons, with perhaps more hope than conviction, thanked the king for his generous answer and assured the crown that they relied on "his Majesty's goodness" to take the most effective means for stopping the new coinage.[19] The thanks of the Irish Lords was even more pointed: "As it has been the distinguished Glory of your Majesty's life, to be universally eminent for your steadfast Adherence to your Word and your paternal care of your People, so neither we nor any of your Majesty's subjects . . . can remain under appre-

---

[18] Walpole to Grafton, Sept. 24, 1723, quoted in *ibid.*, I, 585–587.
[19] *Irish Commons' Journal*, Dec. 12, 17, 1723.

hension of suffering from the great evils that, without your Majesty's interposition, would undoubtedly arise from the said Patent." [20]

Having thus clearly expressed its expectation that the government would soon revoke Wood's patent, parliament returned to its regular business. The Castle succeeded once again in having a satisfactory revenue act passed before the end of the session.[21] Apparently leaders in the Commons thought that by giving Grafton supplies early they would strengthen his position in London. Other legislation went less smoothly; as is so often the case, religious issues proved divisive. A bill exempting Quakers from taking oaths passed both houses but the Church interest in the Lords killed a bill legalizing marriages performed by Dissenting ministers.[22] Probably in retaliation, the Commons threw out a bill from the Lords for increasing the salaries of curates of the established church.[23] A new popery bill, begun in the Commons, to restrict the rights of converts from Catholicism and persons married to Catholics met resistance in the Lords and was pulled to pieces in the privy council. "The Popery Bill, where on the Commons appear to set their hearts," wrote Nicolson, "has gone through a fiery ordeal (as hot as Purgatory itself)

[20] *Irish Lords' Journal*, Dec. 17, 1723.

[21] In his speech upon the presentation of the revenue bill to the lord lieutenant, Speaker Conolly made clear the connection between the granting of supplies and anticipated revocation of Wood's patent: "The many proofs of his Majesty's paternal care and tenderness, but particularly his most gracious answer to the address of the Commons, relating to the coining of copper halfpence and farthings, that he will do everything in his power for the satisfaction of his faithful People, cannot fail to attach the hearts of his faithful Subjects of Ireland and excite them to greater degrees, if possible, of zeal for his Majesty's service and interest. The kind part your Grace has taken in this transaction and everything in which the interest of this Nation is concerned, gives the Commons just grounds to hope, they shall soon be freed from the late coinage, and that your Grace will represent them to his Majesty as dutiful and loyal Subjects." *Irish Commons' Journal*, Dec. 24, 1723.

[22] Only four out of sixteen bishops present in the Lords voted against the Quaker bill. Nicolson to Wake, Dublin, Jan. 27, 1723/24, Wake MSS, XIV.

[23] The vote was 60 to 56. *Irish Commons' Journal*, Dec. 24, 1723.

before our Lords of the Council. They have made Amendments, Additions, Subtractions, heard council, etc., and at last cook'd the whole in such a manner that the Lord Lieutenant was hard put for a Quorum to subscribe. Many of us seem to be exceedingly afraid of provoking our Roman neighbours." [24] Another proposal of the Commons, a bill to reform legal procedure, came back from London so amended that the lower house rejected it.[25] In short, except on the question of Wood's "brass farthings" there was little harmony in Chichester House. Grafton must have welcomed the close of the session with relief. At one point he had written in despair to Walpole that the situation in Dublin was "above my reach." [26]

In the eyes of many, Grafton's timidity and poor judgment were responsible for much of the government's trouble in dealing with the Irish crisis of 1723–1724. Walpole chided him, Swift pilloried him, and Walpole's first biographer, Archdeacon William Coxe, depicted him as devious and incompetent. Following Coxe, one of the most recent writers on the period flatly states: "If ever the wrong man was in the wrong job at the wrong time, it was the Duke of Grafton in 1723–24." [27] His contemporary, Lord Hervey, remarked that "the natural cloud of his understanding . . . made his meaning always as unintelligible as his conversation was unentertaining." [28] Yet perhaps the duke of Manchester came nearer the truth when he called Grafton "shrewd, witty, and only seem-

[24] Nicolson to Wake, Dublin, Dec. 14, 1723, Wake MSS. XIV.
[25] The bill was rejected 89 to 76. *Irish Commons' Journal*, Feb. 1, 1723/24.
[26] William Coxe, *Memoirs of the Life and Administration of Sir Robert Walpole, Earl of Orford*, 2 vols. (London, 1798), I, 223. The votes given in notes 23 and 25 show how evenly divided the Commons were. In a vote on a disputed election for West Meath, the House approved the seating of Sir Richard Levinge by a vote of 89 to 88. *Irish Commons' Journal*, Oct. 19, 1723.
[27] Ferguson, *Swift and Ireland*, p. 92. Goodwin is also critical of Grafton ("Wood's Halfpence," p. 657 and n. 5).
[28] John Lord Hervey, *Memoirs of the Reign of George II*, 3 vols. (London, 1884), I, 315. Hervey did go on to admit that Grafton's early training at court had given him "that style of conversation which is a sort of gold-leaf that is a great embellishment."

ingly simple." [29] The fact is that Grafton placated the Irish parliament, kept it in session, and induced it to vote supplies — which was more than Shrewsbury had been able to do in 1713. More than that, Grafton seems to have kept its confidence. At the close of the session the Lords thanked the lord lieutenant with more than customary courtesy: "We cannot but think ourselves safe and happy under the government of a Lord Lieutenant who has no views but that of his Majesty's service, inseparably united to the Interests of his Subjects. Grafton responded with an assurance that it would be his "constant care to preserve your good Opinion, by my further services to this Kingdom." [30]

The Irish parliament seems honestly to have believed that Grafton could persuade the ministry to revoke Wood's patent when he returned to London. But Grafton's days as viceroy of the "dependent kingdom," as the English called it, were nearly over. A few days later Charles Fitzroy, grandson of Charles II and the countess of Castlemaine, set out for England to confront the ire of his Hanoverian chieftains — the last of the Stuart rulers, one might say, to be humbled by imperious commoners.

Grafton's removal, two months later, bore witness to the fact that Walpole's ministry had no intention of surrendering to Irish demands. To fulfill the promise contained in the King's message of the previous November, a committee of the English privy council investigated Wood's activities. The committee's report proved a disappointment to the Irish: Wood was cleared of all charges of fraud.[31] He could now continue with his coinage, though the government did reduce the amount to £40,000. In May 1724 Lord Carteret was named the new lord lieutenant by Walpole, who thus at one stroke removed a rival from the ministry and provided a strong ruler

[29] Quoted in Cokayne, *The Complete Peerage*, VI, 46.
[30] *Irish Lords' Journal*, Feb. 6, 7, 1723/24.
[31] Grafton had been unable (or unwilling) to convince Irish witnesses to go to London to testify before the English committee. Goodwin, "Wood's Halfpence," pp. 658–659.

for Ireland.[32] Instead of waiting until time for the next meeting of parliament in the summer of 1725, Carteret left for
Dublin in October 1724. Both he and the ministry expected
his presence to put an end to Irish resistance to the new coinage. It was a vain hope. Within a few hours of his landing
Carteret discovered the state of Irish opinion. The day he
arrived the fourth and most inflammatory of Swift's *Drapier's
Letters* was being hawked on the streets of Dublin. In this
pamphlet the Drapier no longer concentrated his attack primarily on Wood (as he had in the first three letters); he sharply criticized the government and called on his compatriots to
defend their rights: "Were not the People of *Ireland* born as
Free as those of *England*? How have they forfeited their Freedom? Is not their *Parliament* as fair a *Representative* of the
People as that of *England*? And hath not their Privy Council
as great a share in the Administration of Publick Affairs? Are
they not Subjects of the same King? Does not the same *Sun*
shine on them? And have they not the same *God* for their
Protector? Am I a *Free-Man* in England, and do I become a
Slave in six hours by crossing the Channel?" [33]

Although Swift's wording betrays his identification with the
Anglo-Irish, he voiced a patriotism that could appeal to anyone who called Ireland home. Even many who had recently
come over from England, but who now held office and property in Ireland, might well respond to his arguments. Within
a few weeks the Drapier became a national hero.

Carteret had once hoped to see the Irish crisis ruin Walpole;
instead he now found himself in a position where he must
either solve the Irish problem or jeopardize his whole political
career. The new lord lieutenant rose to the challenge. He
immediately summoned the privy council and demanded that
steps be taken against the author of *The Drapier's Letters*.
Carteret was a friend and admirer of the dean of St. Patrick's,

[32] Basil Williams, *Carteret and Newcastle* (Cambridge, Cambridge University Press, 1943), pp. 70–71.
[33] Jonathan Swift, *The Drapier's Letters*, ed. Herbert Davis (Oxford,
1935), pp. 39–40. The fourth Letter was significantly entitled *Letter to the
Whole People of Ireland*.

but he had no intention of permitting Irish resistance to threaten English supremacy. Somewhat reluctantly the privy council agreed to condemn certain passages in the fourth letter as seditious and to offer a reward of £300 for the identification of the author. They also ordered the arrest of John Harding, the printer of the letters.[34] Three royal judges, led by Chief Justice Whitshed, summoned a grand jury to indict Harding. Before it assembled, Swift's *Seasonable Advice* appeared, urging the grand jury to refuse to bring a true bill against Harding; if they did indict him they would be sanctioning the hated halfpence. Carteret thereupon ordered the judges to seek a presentment against the anonymous author and printer of the *Seasonable Advice* before taking up the matter of *The Drapier's Letters.* The redoubtable Whitshed was no more fortunate on this occasion than he had been in Waters' trial in 1720. The grand jury refused to indict even though Whitshed polled the members separately. Stubbornly, and probably illegally, Whitshed then summoned a second grand jury. This body proved even more recalcitrant than the first: they not only declined the indictment; they took the occasion to present, instead, anyone who had "attempted or shall endeavour by fraud or otherwise" to introduce Wood's coin into Ireland, expressing their gratitude to "all such Patriots, as have been eminently zealous . . . in detecting the Fraudulent Impositions of . . . Wood."[35]

[34] Ferguson, *Swift and Ireland*, pp. 114–115. Bishop Henry Downes reported that "Our Lord Lieutenant is a prodigious man, and an excellent and ready speaker. He assured us that his Majesty never thought of using compulsory methods to oblige anybody to receive the halfpence; so that we need not receive them if we do not like them: but to provoke England to that degree as some have endeavoured to do, is not the true way to keep them out. The prosecution of a certain Author, and the reward of three hundred pounds for the discovery of him, . . . must not be construed as doing anything in favour of the halfpence, but as a discouragement to sedition." Downes to Nicolson, Oct. 25, 1724, in *Letters on Various Subjects, Literary, Political and Ecclesiastical to and from William Nicolson D.D.*, ed. John Nichols, 2 vols. (London, 1809), II, 587–588.

[35] Quoted by Ferguson, *Swift and Ireland*, pp. 127–128. Ferguson (p. 126) suggests that Carteret may have deliberately postponed Harding's case in order to protect Swift.

The defection of the two successive Dublin grand juries represented a tremendous blow to the government's prestige. The independence of the trial jury in the Waters case in 1720 had been serious enough; the rebellion of a grand jury was far worse. Under the political system prevailing in the early eighteenth century, grand juries were carefully chosen bodies that could normally be counted upon to carry out the wishes of the administration in power. When they revolted, it was a sign that Dublin Castle was losing control of local government. And revolt they did. In a number of Irish counties grand juries drew up memorials condemning the introduction of Wood's coins.[36] The boycott of Wood's coppers, so strongly advocated by *The Drapier's Letters* and other pamphlets, became a national cause that few dared to disregard. The Irish commissioners of the revenue had themselves refused to accept the new coins for use in paying the army. Since copper money was not legal tender by either English or Irish law, Dublin Castle had no grounds for action against the boycott. If the civilian officials of the country would not assist in introducing the new coinage the only method by which the government could effect its avowed policy was by the threat of military force. Carteret faced a nasty dilemma.

By January 1725 the lord lieutenant had come to recognize the intensity of Irish opposition. He wrote to Townshend explaining that he felt it his duty "not to conceal from the King the true temper of his People of Ireland." Even though the government had explicitly announced that the crown had no intention of forcing Wood's coins on the public, "the ferment is but part allayed and will, I fear, show itself on any occasion that ill intentioned persons may lay hold of." [37] Archbishop Hugh Boulter of Armagh, newly arrived from England, quickly came to the same conclusion. Everyone, he assured Newcastle, opposed Wood's halfpence, and the whole business had had "a very unhappy influence on the state of

[36] Nicolson to Wake, Derry, Aug. 21, Oct. 20, 1723, Wake MSS. XIV.
[37] Carteret to Townshend, Dublin, Jan. 9, 1724/25, Eng. P.R.O., S.P. 63/385, fols. 9–10.

affairs here, by bringing on familiarities and intimacies between the papists and Jacobites and the Whigs who before
had not the least correspondence with them." [38] Despite
Carteret's and Boulter's advice the ministry remained adamant. By August, Carteret felt compelled to warn bluntly
that action must be taken on Wood's patent before parliament
met. He asked that he be authorized to assure parliament at
its first meeting that the king "had or would take such means
as would put an Entire End to this affair." He added that he
had consulted with the crown's leading supporters in Dublin
"who have all concurred to give it as their opinion to me,
that what I now mention to your Grace in this letter is the
only Expedient that can procure the desired success to His
Majesty's affairs in the ensuing session." [39] In other words,
either the government must retreat or the Irish parliament
would refuse supplies. Grafton had been right after all. A
few days later London sent word that the patent had finally
been revoked.[40]

When the lord lieutenant spoke at Chichester House on
September 21, 1725, he announced the welcome news:

I have his Majesty's Command, at the opening of this session, to acquaint you that an Entire End is put to the Patent,
formerly granted Mr. Wood . . . by a full and effectual surrender thereof to his Majesty, an exemplification of which,
under the great seal of Great Britain, shall be laid before you.
So remarkable an Instance of his Majesty's royal favour and
condesention must fill the Hearts of a loyal and obedient
People with the highest sense of Duty and Gratitude: And I
doubt not but you will make such sensible Returns as may
convince the World, that you are truly sensible of the Happiness you have enjoyed under his Majesty's most mild and
gracious Government.[41]

The lord lieutenant then appealed specifically for a revenue

[38] Boulter to Newcastle, Dublin, Jan. 19, 1724, *ibid.*, fol. 15.
[39] Carteret to Newcastle, Dublin Castle, Aug. 6, 1725, Eng. P.R.O., S.P. 63/386, fols. 6–7.
[40] Charles Delafaye to Carteret, Whitehall, Aug. 19, 1725, *ibid.*, fol. 30.
[41] *Irish Lords' Journal*, Sept. 21, 1725.

bill sufficient to provide funds to reduce the debt, and he asked also for more effective legislation to control the assize of bread and to provide for the employment of the poor.

The Commons responded, at least for the moment, with an appropriate display of "duty and gratitude," but in the Lords the intrepid archbishop of Dublin sounded a discordant note. King and his followers insisted that the words "great wisdom" should be added to a clause thanking his Majesty for his "grace and condesention." They clearly intended to imply that, if the king showed wisdom in revoking Wood's patent, he had demonstrated quite the opposite in first granting it. Boulter and the English party defeated this move, and for the moment peace prevailed at Chichester House.[42] The animosity built up during the past two years could not, nevertheless, be dispelled by an exchange of compliments between the crown and parliament. The minister's long delay in rescinding Wood's patent had given the Irish party time to consolidate. There was now, as Chancellor West put it, "a set of men in this Kingdom" who discounted the crown's generosity and represented "the surrender of the Patent as the pure effect of their vigorous opposition." He added that recent events had given them much greater strength than otherwise would have been possible; "they have in fact taken possession of the House of Commons."[43] The occasion for Chancellor West's comment was the Commons' attitude regarding the budget.

In considering supplies the Commons normally reviewed reports from the government on the expenditures and revenues of the past two years together with estimates of the anticipated revenue and expenses for the next two. The procedure followed was to have the House request these figures from the lord lieutenant, who then instructed the proper officials to supply them to the Commons. On October 6 Carteret's chief secretary, Thomas Clutterbuck, informed the House that the Castle had commanded that the budget be laid before

<hr/>

[42] Boulter to Newcastle, Sept. 21, 23, 1725, Eng. P.R.O., S.P., 63/386, fols. 80 and 136.

[43] Chancellor West to [Newcastle], Dublin, Oct. 26, 1725, *ibid.*, fol. 214.

them. The accountant general (who had the equally felicitous name of Matthew Penefather) presented the accounts and estimates. The Commons referred Colonel Penefather's report to a committee of the whole house to consider a motion for supply. The next day the House voted unanimously "that a supply be granted to his Majesty" and appointed the customary committee to inspect public accounts. So far all seemed to be clear sailing for Dublin Castle, but trouble lay ahead. Since his arrival in October 1724 Carteret had exposed considerable corruption in the Irish treasury and had reformed its practices. Although parliament complimented the lord lieutenant on his reforms, they apparently still mistrusted the treasury officials. The Irish party was, furthermore, in a contentious mood.[44] On October 14 the chairman of the committee on accounts, Richard Warburton, informed the House that he had been directed to move for a humble address asking the lord lieutenant to provide an account of government expenditures, receipts, and borrowing since 1709. The fact of the matter was that the committee on accounts refused to accept the Castle's figure for the total government debt. Carteret complied with this request, and two days later Penefather produced an abstract of all accounts for the years 1709–1725.

Having gone over the abstract, the committee on accounts reported on the budget on October 25. According to its figuring, the charge for the civil and military establishment for 1725–1727 would come to £886,000. The hereditary revenue of the crown (which included the customs duties and hearth tax voted at the time of Charles II) would supply £698,000, and the existing additional duties if renewed would provide £292,000.[45] Such a budget would afford over £100,000 above expenditures for debt retirement. Two questions were involved in providing for the debt: whether or not there would be that large a surplus, and whether £100,000 would reduce the debt sufficiently. The Castle answered both these ques-

[44] Williams, *Carteret and Newcastle*, p. 73.
[45] *Irish Commons' Journal*, Oct. 25, 1725. The figures given here and elsewhere in the chapter are to the nearest thousand.

tions negatively and therefore sought new taxes. The opposition maintained that the surplus had been accurately estimated and that it was quite adequate to pay off most of the debt. Further taxes were thus unnecessary.

A test of strength between the two viewpoints came on October 26. After the House had voted to consider ways and means for raising revenue on the following day, the Castle party moved for adjournment. The opposition, led by Midleton's son, St. John Brodrick, defeated the motion 98 to 78 and then pushed through a resolution that the total government debt did not exceed £122,000, a sum well below that claimed by Dublin Castle.[46] During the next fortnight both sides sought to gain support. On November 15 the House reconsidered the question of the debt. This time the opposition beat down a move to postpone action by a vote of 114 to 93. It then triumphantly passed a resolution declaring the total debt to be only £119,000 (the vote was 122 to 71). The Castle party now proposed adjournment in the hope that, as one commentator put it, "they might have time by proper means to bring them [the members] to a better temper." [47] The House rejected the adjournment motion by 111 to 83. Next the House passed a resolution "that the hereditary revenue and the present additional duties continued from Christmas 1725 to Christmas 1727 will support the necessary branches of the establishment for the said period and be a sufficient provision for the debt of the nation until 1727." [48]

Carteret, who felt that the opposition had juggled the estimates, explained to Newcastle that the court might have pre-

<hr/>

[46] Ibid., Oct. 26, 1725; on the debt, see Clarendon, Finances of Ireland, Appendix 4. On October 26 the House voted stipends for the clerk of the House and several other officials, including £300 for Matthew Penefather for his expenses and trouble in preparing the accounts.

[47] William Stratford to Oxford, Nov. 30, 1725, Portland MSS, VII, 405.

[48] Irish Commons' Journal, Nov. 15, 1725. The Commons committee alleged that at one point the government put the debt at £140,000, at another time at £187,000. Ibid., Nov. 23, 1725. Whatever the discrepancy between the government and the committee, the Commons still wanted to make sure that interest payments would be maintained at agreed rates. Ibid., Oct. 28, 1725.

vailed had not the Irish party won over the "gentry" by its slogan of "NO NEW TAXES." [49] Boulter put it more bluntly: "I am very sorry that I must send your Grace word that the Discontented carryed everything before them." [50] Under the circumstances the government had to abandon its original budget. Carteret, however, had no intention of losing control of the Irish parliament. He played along with Chichester House and as tactfully as possible awaited the opportunity to reestablish Castle leadership. His chance soon came.

During the closing months of 1725 an international crisis developed that threatened war between Spain and England. War would obviously bring the danger of renewed Jacobite plots, a prospect always alarming to both the Anglo-Irish and the Ulster Scots. Parliament, during this session, passed the second Indemnity Act, mentioned above, as a gesture of friendship to the Dissenters. The foreign danger also caused parliament to have second thoughts concerning the financial difficulties of the government. Late in January 1726 the Lords and Commons sent loyal addresses to King George upon his return from Hanover, the Commons assuring him that they were anxious to take the most effectual means "to discourage all attempts of his Enemies." [51] When Carteret forwarded these resolutions to London he accompanied them with a suggestion that the king's reply be gracious and that it arrive before parliament reassembled the middle of February.[52] The ministry, though hardly in a friendly mood toward Ireland, heeded Carteret's advice. "I hope you like the Answers," wrote Newcastle, "I thought it was right that they should be as civil

[49] Carteret to Newcastle, Dublin Castle, Nov. 16, 1725, Eng. P.R.O., S.P. 63/386, fols. 292–293; see also Carteret to Newcastle, Oct. 28, 1725, *ibid.*, fols. 224–225.

[50] Boulter to Newcastle, Dublin, Nov. 16, 1725, *ibid.*, fol. 312.

[51] *Irish Commons' Journal*, Jan. 27, 1725/26. St. John Brodrick and Thomas Carter attempted to amend the resolution in a manner designed to reflect on the crown's previous mistakes in much the same way Archbishop King and the senior Brodrick had tried to do in the Lords back in September. They were defeated by a vote of 103 to 8.

[52] Carteret to Newcastle, Jan. 28, 1725/26, Eng. P.R.O., S.P. 63/387, fols. 17–18.

as possible." [53] The results justified Carteret's predictions. Despite efforts of the opposition, the Commons voted, on February 24, to provide an immediate advance of £10,000 to pay the army. It assured the king "if the funds already granted this session of parliament shall not prove sufficient to make good this sum, that your faithful Commons will provide the same out of such aids as shall be granted to your Majesty the next session of parliament." [54] In his closing speech at Chichester House two weeks later, Carteret conveyed the crown's thanks "for the supplies you have so cheerfully given to the Establishment," particularly "the late instance of your invincible attachment to his Majesty's interest and service." [55]

Although Carteret's patience thus restored outward harmony between Dublin Castle and parliament, there was no denying that the government's position remained shaky. In every session since 1717 some issue had arisen to cause strong Irish resistance to English policy: the Annesley case in 1719, the bank project in 1721, Wood's halfpence in 1723, and the debt payment in 1725. The government had not yet learned how to manage Irish politics.

The only peaceable way to assure English control of Ireland was to create a broad-based Castle party that could maintain a majority in both the Irish Lords and Commons. The English ministry and the Irish administration recognized this need: the problem lay not in determining ends but in discovering the proper means. One obvious method of strengthening the English interest was to increase the number of English office-holders in Ireland. In 1724 the ministry had virtually forced Viscount Midleton to resign the chancellorship because of his opposition to Wood's halfpence.[56] That same year Archbishop Thomas Lindsay of Armagh had died. The ministry took the opportunity to fill the two posts, respectively, with an English jurist, Richard West, and the bishop of Bristol, Hugh Boulter. Thus both the chancellor and the primate now became En-

---

[53] Newcastle to Carteret, Whitehall, Feb. 3, 1725/26, *ibid.*, fol. 34.
[54] *Irish Commons' Journal*, Feb. 25, 1725/26.
[55] *Ibid.*, Mar. 8, 1725/26.
[56] Ball, *Judges in Ireland*, II, 100.

glishmen. How much further should the government go in restricting appointments to Englishmen? Boulter, who was close to Walpole and Newcastle, believed in giving every possible place to Englishmen; Carteret, a friend of Swift's and other Dubliners, believed in using the Castle's patronage to win supporters among the Anglo-Irish.

Boulter advocated his policy very convincingly. "I must request your Grace," he told Newcastle, to employ your influence "to have none but Englishmen put into the great places for the future: that by degrees things may be put into such a way as may be most useful for his Majesty's service and for the ease of the ministry." [57] When Chancellor West died in December 1726 Boulter wrote: "I take it for granted that his successor will be a native of England, who besides his being duly qualified as a lawyer must be one of an undoubted Whiggish character, or it will cause great uneasiness in this country." He then recommended either of two English judges then in Ireland, Chief Justice Thomas Wyndham or Chief Baron Thomas Dalton, adding that he hoped that "some person of worth" from England could be induced to fill the vacancy created by the advancement of Wyndham or Dalton.[58] The ministry followed part of Boulter's advice: it picked Wyndham for chancellor, whom Carteret also approved, but made an Anglo-Irishman, William Whitshed, lord chief justice of Common Pleas. When Whitshed died in August 1727 Boulter again reiterated his conviction that it was "of utmost consequence" that the vacancy be filled from England.

We have found by experience since the Lord Chief Baron Dalton has been the only Englishman among the three chief judges, things have run heavy in the privy council here. When anything is transacting in the council, that can be thought to be for the advantage of England more than of Ireland, or when any person of consideration here may be offended, the best we can hope from a native of this place is that he will stay away . . . There are so many Irish in the council and

[57] Boulter to Newcastle, Apr. 29, 1725, Eng. P.R.O., S.P. 63/385, fol. 94.
[58] Boulter to Newcastle, Dec. 3, 1726, Eng. P.R.O., S.P. 63/388, fol. 99.

many of them more opposite to England than anyone ought to be, that it is of the last importance to us, to have two of the Judges who shall always be in the interest of England.[59]

Carteret, though he too backed some Englishmen like Wyndham, favored a number of Anglo-Irish with preferment. He seemed especially concerned with maintaining a privy council representative of Irish interests. In 1725 the ministry discouraged his appointing new members to the council on the grounds it was already too large, but in 1726 he successfully recommended that five Irish peers be added to that body. Boulter, much irritated, informed Newcastle that "the new list of privy-councillors has very much offended several who are best affected to his Majesty here"; the archbishop warned that the influence of those of "the English Nation" had been seriously reduced.[60] Carteret likewise used his influence over military patronage to advance Anglo-Irishmen and, to Boulter's great annoyance, even over ecclesiastical appointments. Among others the lord lieutenant preferred several of Swift's friends who undoubtedly had Tory sympathies.[61] Boulter's arguments convinced the ministry of the need of depriving Carteret of his power to grant military commissions or to fill deaneries in the gift of the crown.[62] Carteret continued, nevertheless, to have his way with some nominations. It was left to London to reconcile the conflicting advice of the primate and the lord lieutenant.

Walpole's own inclinations agreed with Boulter's. J. H. Plumb maintains that after the incident of Wood's halfpence Walpole felt little sympathy for the sensibilities of the Anglo-Irish; "from Walpole's day onwards," he remarked, "the Irish administration, as with the Church of Ireland, wore an increasingly alien air," with the result that the Anglo-Irish upper

[59] Boulter to Newcastle, Aug. 26, 1727, Eng. P.R.O., S.P. 63/389, fol. 58.
[60] Newcastle to Carteret, Whitehall, Mar. 13, 1724/25; Carteret to Newcastle, Arlington St. Mary, May 1726; Boulter to Newcastle, May 19, 1726, Eng. P.R.O., S.P. 63/385, fol. 64, and S.P. 63/387, fols. 184, 197.
[61] Williams, *Carteret and Newcastle*, p. 75.
[62] Eng. P.R.O., S.P. 63/388, fols. 282–283.

and middle classes became frustrated and hostile.[63] Yet despite Walpole's attitude and his position of leadership in the ministry, the actual record shows an increase, not a decrease, in the proportion of Anglo-Irish named to the Irish bench while the Irish episcopate remained equally divided. During the reigns of Anne and George I (1702–1727) twelve judicial appointees came from England and only eleven from Ireland; during George II's reign (1727–1760) fourteen Irish-born appointees became judges as compared with nine of English birth.[64] When George II ascended the throne there were eleven bishops of Irish birth and eleven from England; the numbers were the same at his death in 1760.[65] This apparent contradiction requires explanation.

Between 1721 and 1725 the Whig ministry under Walpole had concentrated on securing its position in Westminister. At the same time it had neglected Irish affairs, apparently assuming that they were determined largely by English party politics and would settle themselves automatically once the ministry had consolidated its strength at home. This assumption had proved fallacious: by 1725 it was clear that the time had come to reconsider Irish policy. In the next few years, with the assistance of Archbishop Boulter and two successive lord lieutenants, Carteret and Dorset, Walpole's ministry devised a method for handling the fractious Irish parliament. Contradictory as Boulter's and Carteret's viewpoints on patronage may appear, they were in the end combined to form a general scheme for increasing the government's influence in the Irish parliament. Top positions were now normally given to Englishmen but at the same time a share of patronage went to key Anglo-Irish churchmen, lawyers, and landlords, par-

---

[63] Plumb, *Growth of Political Stability in England*, pp. 183–184.

[64] Ball, *Judges in Ireland*, II, 67–72, 189–211.

[65] These statistics are based on information from the *DNB*; Henry Cotton, *Fasti Ecclesiae Hiberniae*, 5 vols. (Dublin, 1845–1860); and *Alumni Dubliensis*, ed. G. D. Burtchaell and T. U. Sadleir (London, 1924). There were eleven Irish and eleven English bishops in 1727 (of whom two each were archbishops). In 1760 the ratio was the same, but only one of the archbishops was Irish.

ticularly those who controlled parliamentary boroughs. This policy is known in Irish history as the system of "undertakers," a term referring to the Anglo-Irish leaders who provided the votes necessary to sustain the government's majority.

The idea of parliamentary undertakers enjoyed considerable currency in seventeenth-century England. In 1612 Sir Henry Neville proposed to James I that he would undertake to secure parliamentary support for the crown in return for high office.[66] As late as William III's reign Sunderland seems to have envisaged playing a similar role, failing to see the difference "between the minister's use of royal patronage to influence the proceedings of Parliament and the politician's use of parliamentary support to wrest office from the King." [67] With the tentative formation of cabinet government in England, parliamentary undertakers were becoming obsolete. This was not so in Ireland, or for that matter in the colonies, where there existed as yet nothing comparable to the English ministry. The lord lieutenant and the colonial governor stood, so to speak, *in loco regis*, not in the place of chief minister. They and their administrative staff were not responsible to the legislature, while neither the Irish parliament nor the colonial assembly looked upon the executive as representing them. As we have seen, the use of patronage alone could not guarantee Castle control.[68] Subcontracting the job to influential leaders in parliament might prove more effective.

The traditional interpretation of the undertaking system is well expressed by Edmund Curtis when he writes: "This irresponsible government ruling in English interests, and this shackeled and spiritless legislature, were to last almost unquestioned till 1760." [69] A closer look at events following 1725 reveals a different picture. The English administration did not maintain its position simply by dispensing patronage to

---

[66] Roberts, *Growth of Responsible Government in Stuart England*, p. 18.

[67] *Ibid.*, p. 269.

[68] The power of patronage proved even less effective in the American colonies. See Bernard Bailyn, *The Origins of American Politics* (New York, Alfred A. Knopf, 1968), pp. 72–80.

[69] Curtis, *History of Ireland*, p. 296.

the undertakers; it took pains to avoid offending Irish pressure groups, and it made a number of tangible concessions to Irish interests. Judging from his letters, one must conclude that this was especially true of the duke of Newcastle, Walpole's secretary of state for the southern department, who handled Irish affairs. The administration in Ireland was neither completely irresponsible nor exclusively subordinate to English interests. Furthermore, throughout the period 1725–1760 an active opposition stood ready to challenge the Castle's control. The Irish parliament of these years can scarcely be described as fully "shackled"; it certainly cannot be called "spiritless." It had been, as J. L. McCracken states, "the extent and the vehemence of the opposition experienced by the administration in 1723–25 which led to the evolution of the undertakers." [70] The government's decision to work through parliamentary undertakers is not evidence of the decline but of the growing power of the Irish legislature.

[70] J. L. McCracken, "The Conflict between the Irish Administration and Parliament 1753–56," *Irish Historical Studies*, III (1942–1943), 159.

VI

The Beginning
of a
New Reign

The sudden death of George I in June 1727 put the Hanoverian succession to the test. On hearing the news the Pretender hastened from Italy to Lorraine, the Spanish court revived its hopes of recovering Gibraltar, and Jacobites in Britain and Ireland enjoyed a few weeks of eager anticipation. But the immediate danger of a Jacobite coup passed. It became quickly apparent that England was committed to the House of Hanover. It is more surprising that the new king decided not to change the ministry. In view of the coolness that had existed between George I and his heir the opposition forces had every reason to expect that they might capitalize on the change of rulers, especially as they had cultivated the former prince and princess of Wales. So also, in a quieter way, had Sir Robert Walpole. After a brief attempt to hand the government over to Spencer Compton, George II turned to Sir Robert as the only minister who could manage parliament and thus supply the court with ample money and support. In brief, George I's passing did little to alter either the domestic or international scene. The flurry of excitement it caused proved but a passing squall.

The reign of George II, which lasted for thirty-three years, witnessed two long wars, the first of which precipitated a bloody rebellion in Scotland. Yet for England the period was one of remarkable stability and increasing wealth. For the British Empire overseas the reign of George II marked an age of comparable stability and even greater economic development, despite the dangers inherent in the wars of the forties and the fifties. Ireland, which partook of the nature of both a dependent part of the metropolis and of the overseas colony, likewise experienced an era of relative calm and accelerating, if intermittent, prosperity. In many respects the decades between the death of George I and the accession of George III in 1760, the time that American historians often designate as the age of "salutary neglect," represent the high point of the Old Empire.

The political peace and economic activity of this era were closely interrelated. The ruling Whig oligarchy consistently devoted its energies to fostering trade and colonial expansion, at first cautiously under Walpole, later with vigor and imagination under Pitt. Government, not only at the center but throughout the empire, was largely in the hands of men who, jealous of their special interests, directed their efforts to encouraging commerce and agriculture. The empire was ruled by a kind of hierarchy of pressure groups in which the vested classes of England dominated, but in which all major propertied groups aspired to and received a share of power. The legislative machinery at almost all levels was representative. "Never during the eighteenth century," writes Leonard Labaree, "did the British government authorize a governor by his commission to legislate without the assistance of an elective assembly in any province containing a substantial number of English inhabitants." [1]

The prevailing concept of representation was, of course, narrow. First it was restricted by nationality. Although in theory all free subjects of the British crown enjoyed the legal rights of Englishmen, the privilege of a voice in legislation was principally confined to English colonists. Indeed, if Ireland had possessed a parliament since the Middle Ages, its survival after 1691 may well be attributed to the fact that its Anglo-Irish members were considered essentially as transplanted Englishmen. The franchise and the right to hold office in the different parts of the empire were also restricted by property and often by religious qualifications. The constituencies represented in the various legislatures, particularly in Ireland, were inequitable and irrational. Finally, the authority of all provincial legislative bodies was clearly subordi-

[1] Labaree, *Royal Government*, p. 176.

nated to Westminster. The sovereign power of the British
parliament had been explicitly stated in the Irish Declaratory
Act of 1720; it would be repeated in almost identical words
in the colonial Declaratory Act of 1766. Yet normally the
government did not vaunt its power; it avoided the threat
of compulsion. With all their limitations the legislatures of
Ireland and America reflected the will of the electorate, that
is, of the propertied groups.

Determined to rule by persuasion rather than by force, the
British ministry sought continuously to placate the diverse interests of the empire by compromise or procrastination, even
by inconsistency. Overseas, through the colonial governors and
the Irish lord lieutenant, London attempted to direct the
activities of the local representative bodies; both at home and
overseas it strove to control local administration through patronage. On their part, the different interest groups throughout the empire gained concessions by agitation in the local
assemblies, by pressure on the royal governor, by sending
agents to plead before such administrative bodies as the Board
of Trade, and by seeking friends in the British parliament.[2]
The resulting scheme of official and unofficial representation,
directed by a politically minded executive, gave to British
mercantilism its flexible and pragmatic quality, attuned to
the manifold economic needs of the far-flung empire. Dissident groups could hope to achieve at least some measure of
their objectives within the existing imperial structure. The
guiding principle of the system was well expressed by the
Anglo-Irish writer Sir John Browne in 1728. "Governments
that have depending upon them many lesser states ought so
to model their affairs, that each may have its particular oc-
cupation, and labour jointly with the rest for one great end:
for the wealth and grandeur of the whole, without encroach-
ing upon the business of each other, or impairing that of the
superior kingdom."[3]

[2] Ella Lonn, *The Colonial Agents of the Southern Colonies* (Chapel Hill, University of North Carolina Press, 1945), pp. 151–163.
[3] *Seasonable Remarks on Trade* (Dublin, 1729), p. 7.

Events during the opening years of George II's reign reveal the similarities of governmental problems and practices in different sections of the empire. In 1728 William Burnet arrived in Massachusetts as the new governor. After being received with a display of loyalty to the new king and himself, he opened the General Court with a speech that, with few modifications, might have served almost any colonial governor or the lord lieutenant of Ireland.[4] The formalities over, the Massachusetts assembly and Governor Burnet fell to arguing over a proposal for permanent salaries for the governor and other officials. Burnet received a generous grant for the year, but failed in his efforts to achieve fixed stipends. Burnet served simultaneously as governor of New Hampshire and he met with a similar defeat there the same year. The year before Governor John Montgomerie of New York had likewise tried unsuccessfully to have the assembly provide a permanent grant for administrative salaries. In Jamaica in 1728, on the other hand, Governor Robert Hunter persuaded the assembly to pass a permanent revenue act to cover all regular expenses of the colony. Actually the sum provided proved, as had the Irish grants to Charles II, to be inadequate, and so subsequent assemblies regained considerable control over the budget.[5] These disputes represent colonial versions of the age-old parliamentary struggle over the financial independence of the executive. Even in England the question could still cause disagreement. In the opening session of George II's first parliament at Westminster, in January 1728, the opposition tried to curtail the size of the secret service fund.[6] Fiscal poker, indeed, was the favorite game of all the imperial legislatures.

[4] Thomas Hutchinson, *The History of the Colony and Province of Massachusetts Bay*, ed. Lawrence S. Mayo, 3 vols. (Cambridge, Mass., Harvard University Press, 1936), II, 252–253.

[5] Labaree, *Royal Government*, pp. 282, 338, 347–348, 360–362. A somewhat similar sequence of events took place in Virginia, where the legislature granted a "permanent" revenue act in 1681. Jack P. Greene, *The Quest for Power: The Lower Houses of the Assembly in the Southern Royal Colonies, 1689–1776* (Chapel Hill, University of North Carolina Press, 1963), p. 28.

[6] *English Commons' Journal*, Feb. 29, 1727/28.

Other issues besides money that occupied most of the legislatures were land grants, the position of established churches
and religious minorities, the parliamentary privileges of legis-
lators, defense, and control of the military. Naturally the
specific form these problems took and the methods by which
they were resolved varied tremendously; the legislative bodies
were at different stages of evolution, and each region possessed
its own peculiarities. But the general legislative and administrative processes had much in common. Sooner or later, too,
some sort of partisan division emerged. In the American colonies as in Ireland party rivalry sometimes reflected a mixture
of local and English conflicts. Such appears to have been the
case in New York at the close of the seventeenth century.[7]
Perhaps, as Katherine and Robert Brown contend, historians
like Carl Becker have exaggerated the cleavage between vested
and popular factions in the American colonies,[8] but one line
of conflict was virtually endemic, that between what might be
called (to use an Irish term) the "English Interest" and a party
dedicated to local interests. The governor usually drew his
chief support from those most closely identified with Britain:
crown officials, Anglican clergy, conservative lawyers, and recent arrivals who retained family or business ties with the
mother country.[9] In Pennsylvania, for instance, there was a
continuous struggle, from at least 1740, between a proprietary
group of officials and merchants allied with the Penn family
and an antiproprietary party eventually led by Joseph Gallo-
way and Benjamin Franklin.[10] In this instance, as in others,

---

[7] Leder, *Robert Livingston*, p. 129.

[8] Robert E. and Katherine Brown, *Virginia 1705–1786, Democracy or
Aristocracy?* (East Lansing, Mich., Michigan State University Press, 1964),
pp. 129, 165.

[9] For possible seventeenth-century origins of an official party in the
colonies, see Bernard Bailyn, "Communication and Trade: The Atlantic
in the Seventeenth Century," *Journal of Economic History*, XIII (1953),
384–386.

[10] G. B. Warden, "The Proprietary Group in Pennsylvania, 1754–1764,"
William and Mary Quarterly, 3rd ser., XXI (July 1964), 371. Though
Greene tends to minimize the idea that the royal governors had a political
faction, he emphasizes the opposition of colonial legislatures to having

governors set out to build up an administration party. Even when they did not consciously pursue such a policy, colonial issues often created pro-English and anti-English groups. Writing from Jamaica in 1703 Governor Thomas Handasyd remarked that he found that the "Creolians are at great variance with those born in England as if they themselves were not descended from English parents." [11]

It is clear, then, that by the accession of George II the administrative and legislative structure of the empire had become reasonably uniform. Governing Massachusetts, Virginia, Jamaica, or Ireland presented many of the same difficulties. In meeting them Walpole's ministry, though inconsistent in detail, followed similar general policies. The ultimate aim seems to have been to tighten central control, but not at the expense of open conflict. Since local legislative bodies were becoming increasingly aggressive and seldom retreated before executive pressure, the British government rather than extending its power had actually to concentrate upon preserving the status quo. And slowly it lost ground. In the southern colonies, for example, the assemblies increased their control over finances, established the rights and privileges of their members, and began to interfere with the governors' power over appointments and with executive policies.[12] Although legally the position of the central government remained as strong at the end of George II's reign as at the beginning, the fact is that between 1727 and 1760 the local legislatures grew in prestige, in experience, and in independence. The Irish parliament was no exception.

The position of the Irish parliament in the early eighteenth century is not easy to define. To Molyneux Ireland had possessed far more rights than any mere colony, while Swift once indignantly accused the English of looking down "upon this

---

officeholders among their members. Obviously they feared the threat of a gubernatorial faction. *Quest for Power*, pp. 28–29, 44–45, 188.

[11] Handasyd to Board of Trade, Aug. 27, 1703, quoted by Labaree, *Royal Government*, p. 277.

[12] Greene, *Quest for Power*, pp. 7–8.

kingdom as if it had been one of the colonies of outcasts in America." [13] Colonials, on the other hand, felt that they enjoyed greater autonomy than Ireland. Labaree, in remarking on the resistance of the Jamaican assembly to the revenue bill of 1726, notes that "When the draft bill arrived in the island the assembly would have none of it. The preparation of a bill in England and its transmission to the colony for enactment there, smacked too much of the hated Poynings' Act system which the island had successfully resisted nearly fifty years before." [14] Yet, in fact, the Jamaican assembly did accept the government bill with only a few changes while that same year the Irish parliament refused to vote taxes for debt retirement despite heavy pressure from London. In 1713 the legislature in Dublin had even refused to vote any supplies. In practice Poynings' Act had come to mean something very different under George I than it had under Charles II. By 1727 the Irish parliament had secured a large measure of legislative initiative and exercised much control over the budget.

In truth the Irish parliament was, at one and the same time, both more and less independent than a colonial assembly. Because of Ireland's larger population, its strategic importance, and, above all, its proximity to England, London was far more concerned with Irish affairs than with those in any single colony. Thus, although the English recognized the Irish legislature as a genuine parliament (a status they would never concede to a colonial assembly), they insisted on its subordination to the English parliament and watched over its activities with a close attention never given any colonial legislature. The lord lieutenancy of Ireland may have been treated as a ministerial post of secondary rank but it was filled with men of far greater prestige and public stature than those sent overseas as colonial governors. When the Anglo-Irishman Richard Coote was named governor of Massachusetts in 1699 the General Court voted him £1,000 to show their apprecia-

[13] *The Prose Works of Jonathan Swift,* ed. Herbert Davis, 14 vols. (Oxford, 1939–1968), IX, 21.
[14] Labaree, *Royal Government,* p. 281.

tion for having a peer (he was earl of Bellamont in the Irish peerage) made governor of the province.[15] In contrast, the Irish lord lieutenant was, almost as a matter of course, a prominent nobleman. If lord lieutenants spent less time in residence than did colonial executives, the lords justices who served as their deputies were men of the first rank in the Irish church and state. At the same time, because of the importance of Irish business and the ease of communications between London and Dublin (letters took only a week or less except during very bad weather), the British ministry exerted far more consistent supervision over the Irish administration than over that in the colonies.[16] The ministry's contacts with the leaders of the English party in Dublin were, furthermore, direct and continuous so that there almost always existed a government faction in the Irish parliament. Possessing a full-fledged House of Commons and House of Lords, with traditions reaching back into medieval times, the Irish parliament could assert its rights and privileges more confidently than could a colonial assembly. But, since every move it made was known immediately in London, the parliament in Dublin had to defend each step it took. Distance and relative obscurity often permitted colonial assemblies to circumvent the wishes of London or at least to delay their implementation; not so the Irish parliament. Until the time of the crisis leading up to the American Revolution, the contest between central authority and local authority, though characteristic of nearly the entire empire, was more explicit and open in Ireland than in any overseas colony. The study of Anglo-Irish relations under George II thus constitutes an essential chapter in imperial history.

The meeting of the Irish parliament in 1727–1728 proved to be one of the most harmonious in many years. Walpole kept Carteret as lord lieutenant; thus the new reign brought no change at Dublin Castle. The election following the accession

[15] *Ibid.*, p. 353. American historians usually spell Coote's title as "Bellomont," but "Bellamont" is the correct Irish spelling.

[16] On the Irish postal system, see Howard Robinson, *The British Post Office* (Princeton, Princeton University Press, 1948), pp. 19–20, 90–92.

of George II resulted in some eighty new members at Chichester House, but did little to alter the political complexion of the Commons, which unanimously reelected Conolly as speaker. With Wyndham rather than Midleton now chancellor, the government had reliable leaders in both houses. On November 30, two days after parliament convened, Carteret wrote Newcastle that there was a "general good inclination in the Parliament for dispatching the publick business." He anticipated trouble over disputed elections, but otherwise "it is the opinion of those who are best able to judge of the disposition of the House, that there is no reason to apprehend difficulties." [17] Certainly the Commons' response to Carteret's opening speech was cordial; in it they thanked him for having "omitted no opportunity to promote the safety, honour and Interest of this Nation." [18] Within a month parliament had passed a new Indemnity Act and two other bills sent from England and "after a faint opposition" had provided for new supplies including a renewal of the advance made to the army in 1725.[19] Other measures desired by the government that passed during the session included an extension of the Quaker Act and a law to prevent the abuse of parliamentary privilege. The latter met with determined opposition in the upper house from a group of peers, who jealously guarded parliamentary immunity from arrest because, according to Archbishop Boulter, they "are very much in debt and value themselves upon paying nobody." The bill only passed with the support of the bishops by a vote of 25 to 19.[20] Viscount Midleton led the opposition in the Lords on the privilege bill while in the Commons his two sons, St. John and Thomas Brodrick, along with a handful of others such as Thomas Carter, kept opposition alive, but their only successes came on votes concerning disputed elections. They won at least two or three of these contests and lost two others only when Speaker Conolly broke

[17] Carteret to Newcastle, Nov. 30, 1727, Eng. P.R.O., S.P. 63/389, fol. 95.

[18] *Irish Commons' Journal*, Nov. 30, 1727.

[19] *Ibid.*, Dec. 12, 23, 1727; Carteret to Newcastle, Dec. 12, 23, 1727, Eng. P.R.O., S.P. 63/389, fols. 115, 123.

[20] Boulter to Newcastle, Apr. 30, 1728, Eng. P.R.O., S.P. 63/390, fol. 72.

a tie vote.[21] The larger size of the vote on the occasion of the opposition's victories suggests that many country members were still hostile to Dublin Castle. Still, there was little question that the government held the initiative during the session, which, as Boulter happily remarked, passed more useful bills than had been approved "for many sessions put together." [22]

One reason for the government's success arose from Carteret's popularity; equally if not more important was the ministry's willingness to accept the heads of bills presented by Chichester House. After a half dozen previous refusals or evasions the English privy council finally approved a tillage bill to encourage Irish grain production despite the opposition of the English landed interests.[23] Both Boulter and Carteret urged Walpole to accede to this and other Irish proposals; economic distress in Ireland added weight to their arguments. Probably, too, Walpole's concern for his political position at home made him anxious to avoid friction in Ireland. In any event, the ministry endorsed every bill submitted by the Irish parliament. In his closing speech on May 6, 1728 Carteret could justly boast: "It gives me great satisfaction at my coming to put an end to this session of Parliament that I can observe to you that all publick bills transmitted from hence have been returned under the great seal of Great Britain." [24] In addition to those already mentioned, the measures passed included an act to reduce the crown's hereditary revenue "for the ease of the subject and the encouragement of trade," an act to establish a Dublin workhouse, an act for relief of debtors, and an act to regulate elections.[25]

The electoral reform act is significant in that it represented the last of the major penal laws: the statute that deprived the Roman Catholics of the franchise. In view of the restric-

---

[21] *Irish Commons' Journal*, Dec. 20, 21, 1727, Feb. 2, 15, 1727/28.

[22] Boulter to Newcastle, Apr. 30, 1728, Eng. P.R.O., S.P. 63/390, fol. 72.

[23] Irish Statute, 1 George I, c. 10, sect. 7; F. G. James, "The Irish Lobby in the Early 18th Century," *English Historical Review*, LXXXI (1966), 552.

[24] *Irish Commons' Journal*, May 6, 1728.

[25] Irish Statute, 1 George II, cc. 9, 14, 16, 27.

tions already limiting voters, the number affected by this legislation must have been small. The act constituted more a
display of Protestant power than any real innovation, but its
passage marks the high point of the Protestant ascendancy.[26]
Political tides have an ebb as well as a flow. At last assured
of a complete monopoly of political power, the Anglo-Irish
became less fearful. Slowly their distrust of Roman Catholics
diminished. Eventually after 1745, when the last Jacobite uprising evoked almost no response from Irish Catholics, the
Protestant rulers of Ireland began to reconsider the whole
Catholic question. The year 1727, thus, in a sense, ushers in
a new era in Irish history — one during which the old ani-
mosities of the civil war of 1689–1691 gradually faded and the
concept of a united Ireland began to take form.

The session of 1727–1728 also prepared the way for a new
period in Irish parliamentary history in yet another way: it
provided for the building of a new Parliament House. Chichester House had originally been the residence of two lord
deputies of Ireland. The first, Sir George Cary, built it toward
the end of the sixteenth century and then sold it to his successor, Sir Arthur Chichester.[27] Later the government rented
the building to house the law courts. Parliament first met
there in 1661, and during the late 1670's Chichester House
was leased for ninety-nine years specifically for the use of
parliament at an annual rent of £180. According to contemporary descriptions, it then contained a large room upstairs
for the Lords along with two committee rooms for the upper
house and two more for the Commons. Downstairs the Commons itself occupied a large conference chamber. The ground
floor also contained a room for the speaker and another for
the sergeant at arms. In 1677 William Robinson, general
superintendent of fortifications and buildings, was appointed

[26] Some Catholics did vote before the passage of this act. See J. G.
Simms, "Irish Catholics and the Parliamentary Franchise, 1692–1728," *Irish
Historical Studies*, XII (1960–1961), 28–37.
[27] Sir Thomas Gilbert, *An Account of the Parliament House, Dublin*
with Notices of the Parliaments Held There 1661–1800 (Dublin, 1896), pp.
1–6.

official keeper of the building. The Irish parliament was thus well housed before the opening of the eighteenth century, but in time Chichester House proved inadequate to suit its demands, despite the expenditure of considerable sums for repairs. In 1727, upon the recommendation of a special committee, parliament decided to raze Chichester House and replace it with an entirely new structure.

The cornerstone of the new Parliament House was laid in 1728 by the three lords justices, Boulter, Conolly, and Wyndham; the building was ready for occupancy by the session of 1731. The cost of the initial construction ran to over £30,000, while later eighteenth-century improvements and additions raised the final figure to over three times that amount.[28] The architect, Sir Edward Lovet, surveyor general of Ireland, had visited Italy where he had made drawings of numerous public buildings. He designed the Parliament House in what can be called an Italian classical style, with a facade of lofty Ionic columns. Inside the edifice contained, in addition to the necessary smaller rooms and offices, an impressive circular chamber (fifty-five feet in diameter) for the Commons and a smaller but elegant rectangular hall for the Lords. Diagonally across College Green, facing the Parliament House, stood Trinity College, then still housed in its original Elizabethan buildings. Behind the college proper rose the majestic form of its new library which, begun in Queen Anne's reign, was completed in 1732. Georgian Dublin with its array of gracious classical buildings was beginning to take shape. Within half a century the Irish capital would come, as James Malton described it in 1799, to rank with "the very finest cities in Europe for extent, magnificence and commerce." [29]

In fact, by the 1730's, Dublin was already the second largest city of the British Empire and had acquired the character of a small metropolis. Charles Brooking's map of 1728 shows

[28] *Irish Commons' Journal*, Nov. 19, 1737 (ten-page report on the building accounts).
[29] Quoted by Constantia Maxwell, *Dublin under the Georges 1714–1830* (London, 1936), p. 56.

that the area between the older city (around Christ Church Cathedral and the Castle) and College Green was completely built up, while across the Liffey new streets reached northward for half a mile to the new Linen Hall.[30] This last, constructed in 1728, had been financed by a grant from parliament. Modeled after London's Blackwell Hall, the Linen Hall served as an exchange where drapers and factors could arrange sales, a storage depot, and an office for the government-sponsored Linen Board, which met weekly to encourage and supervise the linen trade. Most Dublin streets were now paved, and a statute passed during William III's reign had provided street lights to "the several liberties adjoining" the city. A new act stipulated that lamps on all thoroughfares should be not more than twenty-two yards apart, on smaller streets not more than thirty-three yards. Another law the same year dealt with improving the city's water system.[31] A new customshouse (which would soon have to be replaced as inadequate) had recently been erected on the north bank of the Liffey to serve the river's lengthening quays.

Social and intellectual life as well as business was expanding. Trinity College (which would be entirely rebuilt within a few decades) had just added a laboratory, an anatomy theater, and a printing house, in addition to its new library. The Dublin Philosophical Society, founded in the late seventeenth century by Sir William Petty and others, had become a center of experimentation and discussion. A decade before theaters were apparently established in Philadelphia and New York, Dublin boasted four or five theaters as well as other places of entertainment, such as Madame Violante's amusement booth in Fownes' Court.[32] Between late October 1735 and

---

[30] *Ibid.*, pp. 57–58, 257. Dublin had begun to extend beyond its walls after the Restoration in 1660. C. L. Falkiner, *Essays Relating to Ireland* (London, 1909), pp. 154–157.

[31] Irish Statutes, 9 William III, c. 7, 3 George II, cc. 13, 22. In 1735 there were 1,640 lamps maintained chiefly by a fee on 5,538 houses for a cost of about £1,000 per annum. *Irish Commons' Journal*, Dec. 3, 1735.

[32] Maxwell, *Dublin under the Georges*, p. 213; Dublin *Evening Post*, June 14, July 22, 1735; Carl Bridenbaugh, *Cities in Revolt, Urban Life in America 1743–1776* (New York, Alfred A. Knopf, 1955), pp. 168–169.

early April 1736 the Dublin *Evening Post* (published twice weekly) reported or advertised over thirty different plays, six operas, and four or five concerts. During a week in July the players of the Aungier Street Theatre trekked out to Carlow "to divert the ladies and gentlemen who may resort to the races." [33] Social and political life found a combined outlet in such groups as the Protestant Society of Truck Street, which celebrated the anniversary of the Battle of the Boyne, and the Hanover Society with its regular dinner meetings.[34] If Protestant Whiggery was much in evidence, so too was a deepening sense of Irish nationality. As a result of the Dublin mayoralty dispute of Anne's day, the Annesley case and the Declaratory Act, and the fight over Wood's coinage, Dubliners had developed a strong feeling of Irish patriotism. Dean Swift, as the recognized champion of Irish interests, had become almost a symbolic figure. At word of his growing deafness in 1735 the *Evening Post* published this epigram:

> What though the Dean hears not the knell
> Of the next church's passing bell.
> What though the thunder from a cloud
> Or that from female tongue more loud
> Alarm not! At the Drapier's Ear
> Click but Wood's halfpence, and He'll hear.[35]

A decade after the revocation of Wood's patent the issue was still a rallying cry; the tradition of opposition would not die. Even with skillful leadership and the help of the undertakers, it was difficult to keep Dublin quiet and to rule Ireland in peace.

At first glance the methods employed by the British ministry and Dublin Castle to run Ireland under George II appear to constitute a definite and effective system. When their methods are examined more closely, they seem less orderly, their actions as often determined by ad hoc decisions as by long-range ob-

[33] Dublin *Evening Post*, July 5, 1735. On the Dublin stage before 1720, see William Smith Clark, *The Early Irish Stage* (Oxford, 1955).

[34] Dublin *Evening Post*, July 29, Nov. 1, 1735, July 3, 1736.

[35] *Ibid.*, May 13, 1735.

jectives. Although by now the Whig ministry had devised
what may justly be called a political machine in Ireland, it
could never achieve unchallenged control of the Irish parliament. In fact, though the term "machine" has the value of
customary usage it is not altogether the proper metaphor.
Managing the Irish legislature far more resembled riding a
skittish horse than operating a mechanical vehicle. Carteret's
experience in 1729 well illustrates the unpredictable nature
of the task.

For one thing, the power of patronage alone could not
guarantee reliable followers. It was possible, of course, to
build up the Castle party by this means. A good example
appears to be the career of Thomas Carter. In 1725 Carter
had been such an outspoken critic of the government that
Boulter had strongly recommended that he be imprisoned.
Carter was, nevertheless, reelected in 1727 and led the fight
to unseat Castle candidates in several disputed elections. Then
in 1729 Carter was appointed to a government post and two
years later received further preferment; in 1732 he was placed
on the privy council.[36] Carter had, clearly, been won over to
the government faction. But matters did not always work out
that way. A man like Alan Brodrick felt free to oppose Dublin
Castle on vital issues even after receiving the highest judicial
position in the country. On a number of questions placemen
simply refused to stand with the Castle. Boulter pointed out
to Newcastle that only ten out of fifty officeholders in parliament had followed the wishes of the duke of Bolton and supported the repeal of the test in 1719.[37] Much the same thing
happened again in 1731.

Another factor contributing to the precariousness of the
government's position was even more unavoidable. At any
moment sickness or death might remove their most depend-
able leaders. In the autumn of 1729, only a few days after

[36] Dorset to Newcastle, Sept. 29, 1731, Newcastle to Dorset, Oct. 30,
1731, Eng. P.R.O., S.P. 63/394, fols. 75, 103; Dorset to Newcastle, May 24,
1732, *ibid.*, 63/395, fol. 124.
[37] Boulton to Newcastle, Jan. 15, 1731/32, *ibid.*, fol. 3.

the opening of parliament, Speaker Conolly fell victim to a fatal illness. Conolly had served as the Castle's chief advocate in the Commons for a decade, and his removal immediately strengthened the opposition, even though the Castle succeeded in having its candidate, Sir Ralph Gore, replace him.[38] Fortunately for the government, death had also recently taken two of its ablest critics, Archbishop King and Viscount Midleton. Yet the fact remains that the loss of key officials, such as judges, bishops, and Commons' leaders, constantly required a reshuffling of administration forces.

A further cause for the Castle's difficulty in maintaining a reliable majority arose from the jealous pride of the Irish parliament. Like the parliaments of early Stuart England, the Irish legislature contained its share of independent-minded members who harbored a negative attitude toward the executive.[39] Since they distrusted the British government they were inherently suspicious of any move by Dublin Castle. As early as 1712 Archbishop King wrote that the best that could be expected of a lord lieutenant was "that he will do us no more hurt than he must — that he will not out of malice or ignorance willfully injure us." [40] In other words, even when a lord lieutenant was himself friendly, the Irish parliament must be on guard lest London exploit his popularity. In 1729 Carteret discovered the persistence of this underlying suspicion. His proposed budget of that year included provisions for floating a new loan to reorganize the debt and reduce the rate of interest. After some opposition a bill was drawn up in Commons that met most of his demands, though not in the exact form recommended by the administration. When the supply bills were sent to London for approval the ministry saw fit to

[38] Carteret to Newcastle, Sept. 27, Oct. 15, 1729, Boulter to Newcastle, Oct. 30, 1729, Newcastle to Boulter, Nov. 11, 1729, Eng. P.R.O., S.P. 63/391, fols. 146, 166, 188–190, 200.

[39] Foord, *His Majesty's Opposition*, pp. 117–126. By comparison Walpole's opposition in England appears to have been more sophisticated and largely led by men seeking office rather than opponents of the power of the executive.

[40] King to Swift, Mar. 27, 1712, *Correspondence of Swift*, ed. Ball, I, 321.

revise one of them in a manner more closely conforming with
their initial plans. Their revision proved a serious tactical
mistake.

Although the Irish Commons had in general responded
favorably to the Castle's budget, it was evident that the opposition had gained strength since 1727, partly because Gore
could not wield the influence of Conolly. Boulter had reported early in the session that "there is a very bad spirit, I
fear artfully, spread among all degrees of men amongst us, to
the utmost grumbling against England." [41] When the money
bill returned from London with the changes made by the
English privy council, the opposition seized the opportunity
to attack the government. "The alterations in the New Money
Bills," Carteret told Townshend, "have put people so much
out of humour that I shall have a great deal of difficulty to
bring them into temper again, and tho' I cannot bring myself to believe that they will be so rash and inconsiderate as
to throw out the Bills, . . . yet I may possibly be mistaken." [42]
London hastened to inform Carteret that had the council
known the several steps by which the bill passed Commons,
"the Lords of the Council would have advised sending it back
as it came rather than hazarding its being lost in Ireland." [43]
It was gratifying to know that London was learning to respect
Irish sensibilities but the damage had already been done.
What the crisis meant to a government spokesman in the Irish
Commons is well expressed in a letter of Thomas Clutterbuck:

Whatever His Majesty is pleased to do in Councill, is beyond
dispute perfectly right: the ministers have their reasons for
advising it, it is our duty to support it here; nor can there be
the least doubt that the bill is much more accurately drawn
now than it was when it went from here: but still the bill as
it went would have raised the money, for the subscription to
the new loan was full. I don't apprehend it will do more now.
It seems concessions have been made which it were wished

41 Boulter to [Newcastle?], Oct. 23, 1729, Eng. P.R.O., S.P. 63/391, fol.
184.
42 Carteret to Townshend, Dec. 14, 1729, *ibid.*, fol. 254.
43 [Newcastle or Townshend?] to Carteret, Dec. 25, 1729, *ibid.*, fol. 280.

could have been avoided . . . I must tell you freely 'tis a very indifferent situation to serve under a govt that has neither power, nor party, to support it, but is left at the mercy of a Parliament. I hope everything will turn out right at last.[44]

In the end it did turn out right. Carteret listened to Commons' objections and then patiently persuaded a majority to accept the revised bills rather than scuttle the budget. But if it acceded to Carteret's appeals, the House first made clear its disapproval of any change being made in money bills by the English privy council.[45] During this same session it also spelled out its opposition to accepting any bill whatsoever that had not been first introduced into the Irish parliament. By a vote of 93 to 54 it rejected a bill to prevent rioting in Dublin on the grounds it had originated in the privy council. "It is very common in debates in Commons," reported Boulter in alarm, "to abuse the privy council, but this is the first time since my coming hither, that a bill has been in plain defyance of our constitution thrown out for taking its rise in the council." [46] Carteret was less upset; he had learned to take the Irish Commons in his stride. In April he closed the session with the usual thanks, particularly complimenting parliament for having raised new funds and at the same time reducing the interest on the old debt. The Commons replied with more than usual eloquence. "The many good laws which passed in the two preceding sessions, and those which are now ready for Royal Assent will be so many monuments to Posterity of your wise administration and we shall ever remember that you held that parliament wherein His Majesty was graciously pleased to consent to the appropriation of a fund for Encouraging the Tillage, Employing the Poor — and improving the Trade of this Kingdom."[47] Carteret's administration had, in truth, been one of the most successful in many years. It is fortunate that

[44] Clutterbuck to Delafaye, Dec. 14, 1729, *ibid.*, fols. 260–261.
[45] Boulter to Newcastle, Dec. 16, 20, 1729, *ibid.*, fols. 264, 268.
[46] Boulter to Newcastle, Mar. 19, 1729/30, Eng. P.R.O., S.P. 63/392, fol. 76.
[47] *Ibid.*, fol. 104; *Irish Commons' Journal*, Apr. 15, 1730.

his successor, Lionel Cranfield Sackville, first duke of Dorset, was to prove as adept as Carteret in pleasing the Irish.

Dorset's relations with the Irish parliament in 1731 showed that he had benefited from Carteret's experiences. Carteret had spent more time in Ireland than the minimum required to hold parliament, and he had associated himself with some of Dublin's leading social and intellectual figures. Dorset followed a similar course, becoming especially noted as a patron of the theater.[48] To start with, he arrived a month before the opening of parliament and devoted himself to cultivating Irish leaders.[49] His secretary, William Cary, gives us an account of Dorset's first days in Dublin. "We are in this Honeymoon of government (as you probably call it) so full of ceremony, noise and feasting, that I can scarce get a minute to myself. My back is almost broke with bowing, and my belly with eating, and what is to become of my head I can't tell; But what is most vexatious amongst all this crowd, there are but few members of Parl. come, as yet, to Dublin, so that we can do but little business in our cups. However we are making the best disposition we can for the approaching campaign which opens Tuesday senight, the 5th of October. God send us good deliverance." [50]

In dealing with patronage Dorset devised a new tactic: he recommended that several vacancies occurring at this time should not be filled until the end of the session; competition for royal favor, he felt, would provide a strong motive for obedience among the "king's servants." [51] Even so, he too discovered that the reward of office would not alone assure a government majority. The ordinary members of parliament were not only proud of their rights and privileges; they were also men of strong convictions. Walpole now believed that the time had finally arrived when the Irish parliament could

[48] Maxwell, *Dublin under the Georges*, pp. 221–222.
[49] Dorset to Newcastle, Sept. 15, 1731, Eng. P.R.O., S.P. 63/394, fol. 70.
[50] Cary to ?, Sept. 26, 1731, *ibid.*, fol. 73.
[51] Dorset to [Newcastle ?], Oct. 27, 1731; Dorset to Newcastle, Feb. 12, 1731/32; Dorset to Newcastle May 30, 1732, Dec. 14, 1733, *ibid.*, fol. 101; 63/395, fols. 52, 126 and 63/396, fol. 112.

be coaxed into repealing the test. He was mistaken. The threat to the Church of Ireland's political monopoly brought country members to Dublin, and as Cary put it, "when they are together, they are apt to give themselves and the government more trouble than could be wished." [52] Boulter reported that it was estimated that the Dissenters had between fifty and a hundred friends in the Commons, and thus Dublin Castle's influence ought to provide a majority — "but this I very much doubt: since in this and the last session many who have places under the crown have voted wrong, where the crown was directly concerned." [53] Cary's and Boulter's fears were well grounded: once again the Whig hope of repealing the test evaporated in the face of stubborn opposition. Dorset piloted an adequate supply bill through parliament and found support for several other government measures, but he was forced to drop the question of toleration. In another area, too, that of legislation to curb smuggling, Dorset met with little success.

From the administrative point of view the prevalence of smuggling in early eighteenth-century Ireland was a cause for alarm on two counts: it represented a loss of potential revenue, and it constituted a threat to the whole mercantilist system of trade regulations.[54] The Irish parliament scarcely shared the government's concern, since British regulations were looked upon as unreasonable and oppressive, particularly the Woolens Act. Irish landlords and farmers considered the exportation of both Irish wool and woolen cloth to the Continent as a natural and beneficial trade wrongly denied them by the arbitrary action of the English parliament. Ever since the passage of the Woolens Act in 1699 numerous Irish pamphleteers and politicians had denounced its terms and sought its repeal or revision. The continued Irish objections to the Woolens Act and to other English restrictions such as

[52] Cary to Delafaye, Feb. 22, 1731/32, *ibid.* 63/395, fol. 64.

[53] Boulter to Newcastle, Jan. 15, 1731/32, *ibid.*, fol. 3.

[54] Dorset well expressed the dilemma facing the government when he wrote that any additional duty on spirits would "certainly encourage" more smuggling and thus reduce the yield on existing duties. Dorset to [Newcastle ?], Oct. 8, 1731, *ibid.*, fol. 93.

the Navigation Acts resulted in lengthy, if unofficial, negotiations between Irish leaders and the government. In return for modification of British regulations the Irish offered to support more effective measures for the enforcement of the trade laws. These negotiations reveal an aspect of Anglo-Irish relations that has so far only been touched upon: the importance of what may be called the Irish lobby in London.

In the preceding chapters much has been said of the ways in which the Irish parliament strove to influence government policy by bargaining over supplies and other legislation desired by the Castle. In addition to this parliamentary maneuvering, Irish leaders employed whatever means they could muster to plead their special interests in London. Individual pressure groups seldom commanded sufficient strength to achieve their objectives. The Roman Catholics' efforts to have London veto the Irish penal law of 1704 had failed, as had the attempts of the Ulster Presbyterians to convince the British parliament to pass an act repealing the Irish test. In these instances, however, opposing Irish parties had likewise lobbied in London. When it came to economic matters the diverse Irish parties often worked together with the result that they sometimes met with success. In explaining the passage of the Woolens Act of 1699 Hugh Kearney states that at that time no Irish lobby existed in London.[55] Although there was some opposition to the measure on the part of Anglo-Irish in Westminster there appears to have been no organized effort to stop the bill. Within a decade after that, however, an effective Irish lobby had appeared in Westminster. It will be recalled, for example, that in 1705 Irish pressure had led to the passage of an English act permitting the exportation of Irish linens to the English colonies. Similar Irish lobbying defeated a bill to increase British duties on Irish yarn, and Irishmen in England were later active in the attack upon Wood's halfpence.

Historians of the British Empire in the eighteenth century

[55] Hugh F. Kearney, "The Political Background to English Mercantilism 1695–1700," *Economic History Review*, 2nd ser., XI (1959), 485.

have long recognized the political importance of pressure groups representing such interests as the East India Company, the West Indian planters, and the American continental colonies.[56] A number of monographs have appeared on the role of the colonial agents in Britain. Yet in dealing with Ireland most writers have assumed that Ireland had no one to defend its interests in the British capital except an occasional lord lieutenant or softhearted minister with Irish friends or connections. In actual fact perhaps no other overseas group was as well represented in London as the Anglo-Irish, and even the Catholic Irish as well as the Ulster Scots had their spokesmen in the capital.[57]

It is true that no single person could do more for Ireland than the lord lieutenant; we have seen how Ormond and Carteret especially succeeded in furthering Irish interests. But the lord lieutenant was never Ireland's sole advocate in London. His chief secretary often exerted great effort in behalf of Irish objectives; certainly this can be said of both Southwell and Addison. A third official came even closer to being a kind of regular Irish agent in London, the resident secretary of the chief secretary, such as William Wogan who served for many years under Southwell or Edward Young under Addison. In the late 1720's Charles Delafaye held this position successively during the term of two chief secretaries.

Since both the chief secretary and the lord lieutenant normally went to Dublin for the sessions of the Irish parliament, the resident secretary in London had the task of shepherding

[56] Lillian M. Penson, "The London West India Interest in the Eighteenth Century," *English Historical Review*, XXXVI (1921), 373–392, and *The Colonial Agents of the British West Indies* (London, University of London Press, 1924); Mabel Pauline Wolff, *The Colonial Agency of Pennsylvania* (Philadelphia, Bryn Mawr College, 1933); James Joseph Burns, *The Colonial Agents of New England* (Washington, Catholic University of America Press, 1935); Lonn, *The Colonial Agents of the Southern Colonies*; Lucy S. Sutherland, *The East India Company in Eighteenth-Century Politics* (Oxford, Clarendon Press, 1952).

[57] The following paragraphs are based on F. G. James, "The Irish Lobby in the Early Eighteenth Century," *English Historical Review*, LXXXI (1966), 543–557.

Irish bills through the offices of the attorney general and solicitor general and finally through the English privy council. Because these men received their appointments from the Irish administration one might have expected them to be subservient to the ministry in power. Ultimately they were dependent upon the government, and yet they definitely acted as Irish agents. The Irish Commons approved the funds from which came both their salaries and the money they required for fees and gifts for English officials. It is clear from the correspondence of Wogan and his successors that these London secretaries looked upon themselves as responsible to the Irish parliament as well as to Dublin Castle.

The lord lieutenant, his chief secretary, and their under-secretary in London were all government officials, and they alone can scarcely be considered as constituting an Irish lobby. The term can more accurately be applied to unofficial groups with whom they normally cooperated: the Anglo-Irish members of the English Lords and Commons, plus various influential Irish peers, churchmen, and politicians who happened to be in London, and who often had come specifically to advocate or oppose some British policy or legislation. In addition to these Anglo-Irishmen there also existed a number of Englishmen who had property or family connections in Ireland and who thus sometimes supported Irish interests. When an issue united all of these different groups the Irish lobby could exert real pressure on the government. During the decade of the 1720's they sought a series of changes in British trade laws affecting Ireland. The Irish asked specifically for a revision of the Navigation Acts to permit direct imports of unenumerated goods from the colonies to Ireland, the removal of all British duties on Irish wool and yarn, and, if possible, a revision of the Woolens Act to allow Irish friezes free entry into Britain.[58]

The leader of the Irish group in the British parliament at this time was Viscount Percival, an ally of the ministry. Per-

[58] To pave the way for English concessions, Irish Statute 3 George II, c. 3, sect. 45, removed Irish export duties on wool and woolen yarn shipped to England.

cival worked closely with a half dozen other Anglo-Irish in the Westminster Commons. Walpole appeared sympathetic to the Irish proposals, but insisted that the removal of the yarn and frieze duties must be contingent upon the Irish parliament's taking stringent measures to curtail wool smuggling to foreign countries. In reply the Irish maintained that the smuggling would become negligible if the British market were opened to Irish yarn and friezes; Walpole refused to believe this supposition and insisted that the Irish must accept a plan requiring English and Irish dealers to register their wool with the government, thus guaranteeing that none of it would be shipped illegally. In April 1731 Percival and his colleagues called a meeting of all the members of the Irish parliament then in London to consider Walpole's terms. The Irish members drew up resolutions promising to work for new laws to prevent wool smuggling but vehemently opposing the registry plan.

The next day Walpole made it clear to Percival that the Irish members in the British parliament must support the wool registry if they hoped to have Irish yarn put on the free list. Caught between both sides, Percival and his friends decided to split their vote so that neither side would "take it ill of us." [59] Walpole, apparently, was not pleased. He did endorse the yarn bill in the Commons but the measure was defeated in the Lords by three votes. A year later Horace Walpole admitted to Percival that the ministry could have pushed through the bill had they really desired its passage.

The Irish thus lost their chance for free yarn; the question of friezes was dropped as well. On the other hand, they won a signal success as regards the Navigation Acts.[60] After some

[59] Historical Manuscripts Commission, Egmont MSS, *Diary of the First Earl of Egmont* (Viscount Percival), 3 vols. (London, 1920–23), I, 173 [hereafter cited as *Diary of Viscount Percival*].

[60] J. H. Plumb discounts the influence of the Anglo-Irish lobby at Westminster, quoting Percival (later earl of Egmont) to show how discouraged he was by Walpole's lack of interest in the bill to permit Irish trade in unenumerated articles with the colonies, but Plumb misses the fact that the bill was passed only a month later. *Growth of Political Stability in England*, p. 182.

stalling Walpole, prompted by Dorset's advice, threw his weight behind a bill to allow the importation of the unenumerated articles into Ireland. Within a month the bill had passed both houses. Its passage ushered in a new era in Irish-colonial trade and represents an impressive victory for the Irish lobby.

VII

Hibernia Non Movere
1733–1753

In American history 1733 is chiefly remembered for the passage of the Molasses Act. In Irish history that year may be said to mark the government's recognition of the undertakers on a more or less regular basis. Both events are characteristic of the period. As written, the Molasses Act represented mercantilist principles as well as a concession to the powerful West Indian interest; in practice the government refrained from effective enforcement of the act to avoid antagonizing the continental colonies. Officially imperial policy was thus rigidly controlled while actually it was administered loosely to minimize friction. In dealing with the transatlantic colonies the main problem was that of reconciling the divergent interests of the different colonies with those of the British commercial groups concerned with imperial trade. In administering Ireland the primary task consisted in managing the Dublin parliament. Although for several decades the lord lieutenants had been striving to gain reliable control of the Irish parliament they had so far met only with intermittent success. During the parliamentary session of 1733–1734 the duke of Dorset finally established such control, but only after a period of considerable conflict during which it seemed that Irish affairs might again reach the kind of impasse that had existed in 1713 and at the time of Wood's halfpence.

From the government's point of view the year began inauspiciously with the death of Speaker Gore in February 1733, a half year before the scheduled meeting of parliament. During the next six months competing groups in the Irish Commons maneuvered to line up his successor. To the ministry the most acceptable candidates were Henry Singleton, Marmaduke Coghill (both veteran supporters of the administration in the Commons), or possibly Thomas Carter (a more recent but ambitious convert to the Castle party).[1] Unfortunately for the government its adherents had become divided on the death of Speaker Conolly in 1729 and had not yet been reunited. Among independent candidates the most influential proved to be Henry Boyle. Scion of one of the most prominent Anglo-Irish families, Boyle had been identified with the country party in the Commons and enjoyed the backing of opposition leaders. The government faced a dilemma: if it insisted upon backing its own candidate, it risked a contest that would harden existing divisions without any assurance of success. By the end of the summer Boyle's position was so strong that the administration acquiesced in his unanimous election as Speaker at the opening of parliament on October 6.[2] Although in his acceptance speech Boyle stressed his consistent loyalty to the House of Hanover he attributed his election to the Commons' recognition of his "love to my country."[3] Later he reputedly told the lord lieutenant's secretary, Walter Cary, that he felt no obligation to the government for his position, since the administration had not supported him until they saw that his interest would carry the election without them.[4] Obviously Dorset would only be able to manage parliament if he could come to terms with the new Speaker.

During the first months of the session opposition forces caused Dublin Castle much difficulty. First of all there was trouble over the budget. The Commons demanded a review of accounts dating all the way back to 1700, apparently in part because they wished to reassert their authority to determine the correct size of the public debt and in part because the money intended for debt reduction had not been promptly

[1] *Diary of Viscount Percival*, I, 339–340; J. L. McCracken, "The Undertakers in Ireland and their Relations with the Lord Lieutenant, 1724–71," unpub. M.A. thesis, Queen's University, Belfast, 1941, pp. 77–81.

[2] *Irish Commons' Journal*, Oct. 4, 1733.

[3] *Ibid.*, Oct. 5, 1733.

[4] *Diary of Viscount Percival*, I, 462–463.

applied to that purpose.[5] The Commons went over the records carefully and ordered that the accounts be printed in order to give them full publicity.[6] The flurry of criticism over finances did not prevent the passage of a satisfactory supply bill in November, but it was symptomatic of a growing spirit of opposition. One cause for this was the suspicion that the government planned a new attempt to repeal the test. Fear of such a move kept the Commons full, "which, you know," wrote Cary to London, "is an ugly circumstance here." [7] The secretary attributed the delays over the budget to the belief in Commons that the government would not try to repeal the test until supplies had been voted. Once the budget had been approved, the Commons forestalled government action by voting by a "majority that was little short of unanimous" not to entertain any heads of bills to repeal the test unless they were presented immediately.[8] Walpole had instructed Dorset to sound out the Irish leaders on the test and, if possible, to push for its repeal.[9] In view, not only of the opposition of Boyle, but even of men like Carter, Dorset realized he had little chance of carrying out the ministry's wishes. After a conference with his lieutenants in December he decided to abandon the project, though not until much damage had been done to the Castle's position in parliament.[10]

Next the opposition raised a question of parliamentary procedure with serious constitutional implications. In 1716 the House of Commons had passed a resolution recommending that heads of bills passed in the lower house should be submitted to the Lords for consideration before being sent to the

---

[5] The deputy vice-treasurer, Luke Gardiner, had allegedly not paid out the money collected for debt retirement as fast as he received it. Gardiner blamed the accountant general, Penefather, for not providing the money; Penefather in turn blamed the commissioners of the revenue. *Ibid.*, 450.

[6] *Irish Commons' Journal,* Oct. 12, 15, 17, 19, Nov. 13, 14, 1733.

[7] Cary to Delafaye, Nov. 20, 1733, Eng. P.R.O., S.P. 63/396, fol. 19.

[8] John Wainwright to [Newcastle ?], Jan. 16, 1733/34, S.P. 63/397, fol. 19.

[9] *Diary of Viscount Percival,* I, 439.

[10] *Ibid.*, 470; Dorset to Newcastle, Dec. 14, 1733, Eng. P.R.O., S.P. 63/396, fols. 121–122.

lord lieutenant.[11] Though the proposal had not been put into
effect, the idea persisted; it was now revived. The Commons
were still upset over the government's efforts to repeal the
test and blamed the lord lieutenant for the high-handed
fashion in which Secretary Cary had attempted to browbeat
members into accepting it. The Lords, who shared similar
sentiments toward the test, also appear to have become alienated from the government because of a recent slight on the
part of the court to the Irish peers resident in London.[12] In
December both houses passed resolutions calling for a regular
practice of exchanging heads of bills between the houses
before their submittal to the Castle.[13] The nature of the
reform was clear. If it were carried out, the process of legislation in the Irish parliament would become virtually identical
with that followed at Westminster. In other words, although
the two houses would still only pass heads of bills, subject to
executive approval and revision, their mutual consultation
and cooperation would invest their joint heads of bills with
the same kind of authority as bills submitted by the British
parliament to the crown.

Word of the two resolutions caused concern in London.
The ministry unanimously opposed the proposal, some government leaders even advocating that steps be taken to reduce
the existing powers of the Irish legislature.[14] The strength of
the reaction in London had a sobering effect in Dublin. Faced
with the possibility of a showdown with the British government, the leaders of the Commons pretended to have a falling-
out with the Lords and in January rescinded their earlier
resolution by a new one completely reversing it.[15] If the exact

[11] *Irish Commons' Journal*, Dec. 7, 1733; see also *Irish Lords' Journal*,
June 9, 14, 1716.
[12] *Diary of Viscount Percival*, II, 2. The slight to the Irish peers involved their order in the procession at a royal wedding. Viscount Percival
was himself deeply involved in this dispute. See *ibid.*, I, 409–422, 426–432,
436–437, 440, 448, 458.
[13] *Irish Commons' Journal*, Dec. 7, 1733; *Irish Lords' Journal*, Dec. 5,
1733.
[14] *Diary of Viscount Percival*, II, 19.
[15] Wainwright to [Newcastle ?], Jan. 16, 1733/34, Eng. P.R.O., S.P.
63/397, fols. 19–20.

causes for this about-face remain obscure, the general reasons appear obvious. Secretary Cary might complain to Delafaye that the ministry greatly exaggerated the extent of the suggested change,[16] but the fact remained that the adoption of the proposed procedure would have made explicit the power of the Irish parliament to initiate legislation. Walpole's administration could not officially accept such an interpretation of the Irish constitution; the British parliament would almost certainly have rejected it totally. The result would no doubt have been a new declaratory act redefining the relationship between the two kingdoms in terms that would have greatly diminished the importance of the Irish parliament. Confronted with the possibility of British retaliation the Irish leaders retreated.

It was a wise decision. The system under which the Irish parliament already operated permitted that body a significant degree of initiative with considerable practical if little theoretical power. Almost all Irish legislation now started in one of the two houses even if, as in England, much of it was government sponsored. In the Irish State Papers in London there is a list of seventeen Irish bills enacted during the session of 1731–1732 with a note on where they originated: ten came from the Irish Commons, six from the Lords, and only one from the Dublin privy council.[17] The plan to effect official consultation between the Lords and Commons in drafting heads of bills would undoubtedly have given greater opportunity to exert pressure on the administration, yet unofficial cooperation already existed. When united, the Anglo-Irish peers and Commoners could, with the assistance of the Irish lobby in London, hope to win extensive concessions from Britain, such as approval of the Irish Tillage Act or the passage of the British act to open colonial trade in unenumerated articles. The existing constitutional machinery offered them ample chance to make their wishes known. The limits of their power were set not by the prevailing forms of government; they resulted from the dependence of the Anglo-Irish upon

[16] Cary to Delafaye, Jan. 10, 1733/34, *ibid.*, fol. 17.
[17] Eng. P.R.O., S.P. 63/395, fol. 11.

the British to maintain their predominant position in Ireland. In short, given the social and political state of Ireland in the 1730's, the Irish parliament was probably as effective an instrument for independent action as could then have been made to work.

If the abandonment of the proposal for procedural reform in 1734 represented a check on the pretensions of the Irish opposition, it did not constitute a retreat from the gains already made by the Irish parliament. The best evidence of this is Dorset's acceptance of Boyle and his henchmen as what amounted to parliamentary managers. Although the beginnings of the system of undertakers can be traced back to the mid-twenties, it may be said that until 1733–1734 the lord lieutenants had sought primarily to create a court or castle party under their direct control, a kind of earlier Irish version of the "King's Friends." For a score of years after 1733 the policy of government, as J. L. McCracken has shown, took a different tack.[18] Instead of attempting to govern primarily through such a clique, the Castle subcontracted this function, so to speak, to parliamentary entrepreneurs, who provided for the cooperation of the Commons in return for government support. This change in tactics is reflected in Dorset's decision in February 1734 to make Henry Boyle one of the three lords justices before leaving for London. During the time of Conolly's term of office as Speaker the administration had consistently appointed him a lord justice, and Speaker Gore had served in the same capacity. But by 1733 the government had become alarmed lest the practice harden into precedent; furthermore Boyle was far more independent than Conolly or Gore. Nevertheless Dorset came to the conclusion that he really had no practical alternative: "I have look'd around here and considered, as well as I am able, ever since my arrival whether it would be more for His Majesty's service to appoint any other person to that office. But I can truly assure your Grace, that I can find no one to whom there are not stronger objections, than to the present Speaker, Mr. Boyle, and the

[18] McCracken, "Undertakers," pp. 82–88.

chief of His Majesty's servants, whom I have consulted on this occasion, are of the same opinion." [19]

Dorset took other steps to placate what he referred to as the Whig majority in Commons. Despite its strong aversion to aiding the Dissenters by repealing the Test Act, the Irish parliament was staunchly Protestant. In 1733 it held solemn religious services on both October 23, "the anniversary thanksgiving day for the deliverance from the horrid rebellion which broke out in this Kingdom the 23 October 1641," and November 5, "the anniversary thanksgiving day for the happy deliverance of King James . . . and also for the happy arrival of his late majesty King William for the deliverance of this church and nation." [20] In 1731–1732 several heads of bills to strengthen the penal laws had been transmitted to England: a bill to disarm Catholics, a bill to outlaw mixed marriages performed by Catholic priests, and one to prohibit "popish" solicitors from practicing any type of law.[21] In London anti-Catholicism was giving way to tolerance; diplomatically speaking, it had become distinctly embarrassing since it damaged relations with Catholic countries. The English council therefore amended the anti-Catholic bills so radically that the Irish parliament refused to pass them. In 1733–1734 when the Dublin Commons again drew up a bill proscribing Catholic solicitors Dorset wrote to London urging its approval.[22] This time the government returned the measure for final enactment. Other legislation desired in Dublin also met with success in 1734. The most important act from the Irish point of view was one for compensating the creditors of Burton's Bank, whose failure came close to becoming a kind of Irish South Sea Bubble. The bill in question provided for the payment of creditors by the sale of lands held by the heirs of the bank's partners. These heirs sought unsuccessfully to block approval

[19] Dorset to Newcastle, Feb. 22, 1733/34, Eng. P.R.O., S.P. 63/397, fol. 53.
[20] See resolutions in *Irish Commons' Journal*, Oct. 6, 1733.
[21] "List of Irish Bills," Feb. 3, 1731/32, Eng. P.R.O., S.P. 63/395, fol. 44; Newcastle to Dorset, Feb. 5, 24, 1731/32, *ibid.*, fols. 7–8, 66.
[22] Dorset to Newcastle, Jan. 17, 1733/34, Eng. P.R.O., S.P. 63/397, fols. 24–25; Irish Statute, 7 George II, c. 5.

of the measure both in the Dublin and in the London privy council.[23] The passage of the act restored confidence and strengthened the government's popularity. When Dorset closed the session in May he could point with satisfaction to its accomplishments.[24]

In addition to pleasing the Irish parliament by supporting its legislation, Dorset sought to improve his position by distribution of patronage. Naturally he desired to hand out some plums to his own henchmen: he named his son clerk of the council and made his chaplain, George Stone, a dean.[25] That kind of nepotism caused little difficulty for it was accepted practice. Dorset also dealt fairly successfully with ecclesiastical appointments by working more closely than had Carteret with Archbishop Boulter. The primate was highly regarded in London, and, although Boulter continued to advocate English candidates for many posts, he had now become more sensitive to Irish needs and prejudices. In conjunction with Archbishop John Hoadly of Dublin and the lord lieutenant he recommended a number of Irishmen for ecclesiastical preferment,[26] a step that enhanced the government's prestige with the episcopal bench. When it came to secular appointments, Dorset found himself caught in the middle between English and Irish pressures.

One of the chief obstacles preventing both colonial governors and Irish lord lieutenants from consolidating their influence was their limited control of patronage. The London government sought to utilize colonial and Irish patronage for its own political purposes while local interests attempted to fill as many offices as possible with their representatives.[27]

[23] Cary to Delafaye, Jan. 26, 1733/34; Cary to [Delafaye ?], Apr. 19, 1734; Newcastle to Dorset, Apr. 3, 1734, Eng. P.R.O., S.P. 63/397, fols. 34–35, 90, 118; Diary of Viscount Percival, II, 19, 69.

[24] Irish Commons' Journal, Apr. 29, 1734.

[25] The Weekly Miscellany (Dublin), May 2, 1732, p. 4; Dorset to Newcastle, Jan. 5, 1733/34, Eng. P.R.O., S.P. 63/397, fol. 1.

[26] Dorset to Newcastle, Jan. 5, 1733/34, Eng. P.R.O., S.P. 63/397, fol. 1, and Dorset to [Newcastle ?], Oct. 4, 1735, S.P. 63/398, fol. 50; McCracken, "Undertakers," p. 54.

[27] Bailyn, Origins of American Politics, pp. 72–76.

Upon Dorset's becoming lord lieutenant, George II had informed him that the crown intended to have an important hand in dispensing Irish patronage, and Queen Caroline appears to have been instrumental in raising George Berkeley to the Irish episcopate.[28] Normally, of course, "crown" influence meant that of the Walpole ministry. Since the ministers counted on the lord lieutenant to manage Ireland effectively, they should have allowed him the largest say in patronage, but that was too much to expect from men like Walpole. When Dorset reached his understanding with Boyle the ministry proved willing to make the speaker chancellor of the Irish Exchequer; when Dorset took upon himself to appoint one of Boyle's men, named Dickson, to a customs post Walpole had reserved for another, that proved a different matter. On his return to London Dorset attempted to explain to Walpole that "there is no doing the King's business if members of Parliament, who usually side with the Court are not provided for." Walpole replied that all places of revenue were in the gift of the treasury.[29] Disregarding Dorset's pleas, he sent his appointee to take up the post in question. When the man arrived in Ireland Boyle was furious. He wrote to George Dodington in terms that demonstrate the Speaker's relations with the Castle.

If it is to be understood that Dickson is to be laid aside to make way for him [Walpole's appointee], where's my credit, where's my influence, or what business have I here, when I can no longer be of use or service to His Majesty's affairs? . . . You, Sir, very well know the difficulties I laboured under at my first setting out, and the pains I was frequently obliged to be at from four in the afternoon to five or six in the morning to persuade my troops to fight in a cause foreign to their principles or natural inclination, and now, just as they have been brought into good discipline, I can expect no less than a revolt, if they find their endeavours to support me have proved altogether ineffectual. [30]

[28] *Diary of Viscount Percival*, I, 193; II, 9.
[29] *Ibid.*, II, 109.
[30] Boyle to Dodington, May 21, 1734, Historical Manuscripts Commission, *Various Collections*, 8 vols. (London, 1901–1914), VI, 60–61.

Although it is not known whether Dickson received the post in question, he must have been compensated in some fashion for Boyle was fully reconciled to the administration before the opening of parliament in 1735. It soon became a recognized need on the part of the viceroy to share patronage with the undertakers. In a letter to Newcastle in 1739 Dorset's successor, Devonshire, noted that the king had given him leave to reserve an army commission for Boyle to fill.[31] The responsibility of satisfying the undertakers led the lord lieutenants to require more independence of London in handling patronage. Recognizing this need, Lord Chesterfield refused to become viceroy in 1745 unless he was given full control of Irish appointments.[32]

The results of Dorset's rapprochement with Boyle and his associates proved encouraging. During the next few years relations between the government and the Irish parliament remained fairly smooth. The undertakers normally kept the Commons in line, while on its part the Castle attempted to prevent trouble by persuading the ministry to respect the wishes of the Dublin legislature. Nevertheless there remained an opposition group in parliament even in the calmest of sessions. One reason for this resulted, as J. G. Beckett remarks, from the system of undertakers itself: by granting favors to one set of men, others were inevitably alienated.[33] Another reason, at least as important, was that for forty years opposition to Dublin Castle had been identified with the defense of Irish interests. Still another factor contributing to a spirit of independence arose from the Commons' esprit de corps.

At the opening of the session of 1735 the lower house passed a series of resolutions condemning the interference of the

[31] Devonshire to [Newcastle ?], Sept. 29, 1739, Eng. P.R.O., S.P. 63/402, fol. 25.
[32] Chesterfield to the Reverend Dr. Richard Chenevix, Apr. 27 (N.S.), 1745, *The Letters of Philip Dormer Stanhope 4th Earl of Chesterfield*, ed. Bonamy Dobrée, 6 vols. (London, 1932), III, 603. Still Chesterfield was careful to grant patronage so as to please the undertakers. Chesterfield to Harrington, June 28, 1745, *ibid.*, 638.
[33] Beckett, *Making of Modern Ireland*, p. 192.

Lords, and of the lord lieutenant, in parliamentary elections.[34] A month later the Commons rejected a petition against customs officials for illegal seizure by a majority of only 107 to 87.[35] The court party proved, furthermore, unable to prevent the creation of a committee to investigate customs collections. Dorset had specifically requested the Commons to formulate a more effective act against smuggling; [36] instead they appeared more anxious to criticize officials for unfair enforcement. In the end all Dorset could get out of parliament was a renewal of the existing law which the government deemed inadequate. On the whole, though, the 1735–1736 session went well. Most of the legislation submitted reflected parliament's concern with certain domestic improvements. One act established a four-man board (drawn from the members of the "King and Queen's College of Physicians in Ireland") to stop the sale of fraudulent drugs,[37] two acts dealt with improving church properties, ten acts provided for turnpike corporations to repair roads, and one set up a corporation to rebuild Cork cathedral. London could approve such bills without qualms but in one area the ministry felt compelled to restrain the Irish parliament.

Fear of popery still prompted the Anglo-Irish to seek further extension of the penal laws. A petition in the British parliament by Lord Clancarty to recover property forfeited by his family after the revolution of 1688 aroused anti-Catholic feeling and led to an Irish parliamentary address to the crown calling for a guarantee of all Protestant holdings.[38] The Dublin parliament also made a move to prevent Catholics from enlisting in foreign armies, a practice long illegal but now condoned by the government. Heads of a bill were drawn up to prohibit Irish subjects from emigrating to foreign countries. This bill was summarily quashed by the English

[34] *Irish Commons' Journal*, Oct. 7, 1735.

[35] *Ibid.*, Nov. 25, 1735.

[36] *Ibid.*, Oct. 7, 1735.

[37] Irish Statute, 9 George II, c. 10.

[38] Dorset to Newcastle, Dec. 7, 20, 1735, Eng. P.R.O., S.P. 63/398, fols. 92–93, 97.

council.[39] On the other hand, Dorset succeeded in persuading the government to issue a strong pronouncement to the effect that it would protect the rights of Protestants who possessed forfeited estates in Ireland.[40]

In 1737 William Cavendish, third duke of Devonshire, replaced Dorset as lord lieutenant. During his tenure of office, which lasted until 1745, Devonshire carried on Dorset's line of policy with perhaps less energy but with equal success. One factor that undoubtedly smoothed his task during his first years as viceroy was that he chose as his chief secretary Walpole's second son, Edward. By working with the undertakers he minimized friction in Dublin, while with the help of "Ned" Walpole he obtained the cooperation of the British ministry. Though new to the job, Devonshire displayed an appreciation of the sensitivity of the Irish legislature that seemed to reflect a more understanding attitude toward Ireland on the part of the Walpole ministry. In his opening speech the lord lieutenant explicitly recognized the Dublin parliament's role in initiating legislation. "It is," he asserted, "the peculiar distinction of His Majesty's subjects that they have frequent opportunities of preparing and offering such laws as they think for the general good of their country." [41] That Devonshire did not consider this an empty phrase was illustrated later in the session. Hearing that the English council had revised two Irish bills he had Edward Walpole write urgently to Newcastle that the bills "should not be returned as they now stand, as it is evident that the Alterations made by the council will admit of very great Difficulties in passing the Houses of Parliament in Ireland . . . my Lord Lieutenant therefore hopes that Your Grace will please to bring them before the Council to be restored to the Form they came over in from Ireland." [42]

---

[39] *Diary of Viscount Percival*, II, 258.

[40] Dorset to Newcastle, Feb. 18, 27, 1735/36, Eng. P.R.O., S.P. 63/399, fols. 39, 42.

[41] *Irish Commons' Journal*, Oct. 4, 1737.

[42] E. Walpole to [Newcastle ?], Feb. 21, 1737/38, Eng. P.R.O., S.P. 63/401, fols. 125–126.

Newcastle did just that.[43] The incident illustrates how drastically Poynings' Law had become modified in practice.

Two problems that perennially caused disagreement between Dublin and London — the position of the Irish Catholics and Irish wool smuggling — moved closer to solution during Devonshire's administration. Agitation against Catholics increased as war with Spain became first imminent and then a reality. Irish leaders urged Devonshire to make recommendations for tightening the penal laws in 1739. Following instructions from London, he declined, saying it would be better for parliament to take the initiative.[44] When they did, the British government once again stopped their efforts in the privy council. As the war expanded to include France, the threat of a Jacobite invasion appeared more threatening. Devonshire seems to have shared the Anglo-Irish distrust of the Catholic Irish but the British government refused to resort to extreme measures. Though rumors of Catholic plots abounded, there was little real evidence of Irish Catholic sympathy with the Bourbon powers or with Jacobite aspirations.[45]

In dealing with the Catholic question the government pursued a policy of postponement; on the wool question it worked for mutual concessions. In spite of the defeat of the yarn bill in the English Lords in 1731, the Irish lobby kept up their efforts to modify the Woolens Act of 1699. Anglo-Irishmen like Viscount Percival and Lord Limerick seem to have felt that aid to Irish wool producers should have priority over most other considerations. They determined, for example, not to raise objections to provisions in the Molasses Act of 1733 that prohibited the direct shipment of West Indian sugar to Ireland, on the grounds that the trade affected was too small to warrant dissipation of their influence in efforts to stop it.[46]

[43] Newcastle to the Lord President of the Council, Feb. 22, 1737/38, *ibid.*, fol. 127.

[44] Devonshire to [Newcastle ?], Sept. 21, Oct. ?, 1739; Newcastle to Devonshire, Nov. 8, 1739, *ibid.*, S.P. 63/402, fols. 14–15, 52, 90.

[45] Catholics petitioned the king assuring him of their loyalty and implying that if their disabilities were not lifted they might be forced to emigrate. *Ibid.*, fols. 28–29.

[46] *Diary of Viscount Percival*, I, 221, 329.

It is true that Lord Limerick kept a careful watch on a bill to regulate printing lest English interests should seek to interfere with the right of the Irish to reprint English books, but in general the Anglo-Irish in London concentrated on the wool issue.[47] For its part, the ministry also directed its attention to the same question, from the opposite point of view. The government maintained that if the Irish parliament would devise an effective method of stopping the illegal exportation of Irish wool and woolen cloth (the former chiefly to France, the latter to Portugal), then Britain would make concessions in return. Each side strove to convince the other to make the first move; in the end the government took the initiative. Early in 1739 the Westminster parliament passed an act that placed Irish wool yarn on the free list and likewise opened up several new English ports to Irish wool.[48] In addressing the Irish parliament the next autumn Devonshire requested that, in view of British generosity, the Irish legislature should tighten up antismuggling laws.[49] The 1740 Irish customs enforcement act, however, introduced no new provisions.[50]

Most of the legislation proposed during Devonshire's term as viceroy did not give rise to controversy. Aside from the agitation over Catholic policy, probably the most disputed government action of the period was a proclamation of 1737 that changed the official ratio of gold to silver coins. Ireland had no mint and like the American colonies suffered from a chronic shortage of specie, although bills of exchange, drafts, debentures, and similar instruments of credit provided a form of paper money for larger transactions. The only coins produced in England for Ireland were copper pence, halfpence, and farthings. Much of the silver and gold in circulation was foreign. To avoid counterfeiting and to reduce confusion,

[47] *Ibid.*, II, 374; see also *ibid.*, 19, 26–29, 69, 162, 171–172, 407–408.
[48] English Statute, 13 George II, c. 3; see also James, "Irish Lobby," p. 555.
[49] *Irish Commons' Journal*, Oct. 29, 1739; Devonshire to [Newcastle ?], Sept. 29, Oct. 12, 1739, Eng. P.R.O., S.P. 63/402, fols. 25, 50.
[50] Irish Statute, 13 George II, c. 3.

foreign coins in common use, such as Portuguese guineas and moidores, were assigned an official value by proclamation. During the first three decades of the eighteenth century many of these coins, chiefly the silver ones, were overrated. As a result silver tended to drain out of Ireland to England and elsewhere. Since there was only an insufficient supply of poor copper coins to meet demands, everyday business transactions suffered greatly. According to one traveler in 1732 many of the Irish halfpence, or raps, were of such a bad metal that they "will not go, except at coffee houses, where they who give 'em take 'em again." [51] That same year another visitor remarked that "the want of silver and small change is such . . . the Publicans often refuse to draw liquor to Strangers, until they are sensible they can make change, and often quarrels arise and sometimes blows on this account." [52] The exodus of silver debased the value of the Irish pound, the official money of account. In the middle of the seventeenth century the Irish pound had been equivalent to the English. During the Restoration it dropped, apparently because of the adverse trade balance resulting from the Cattle Act and similar legislation. Following 1688 the ratio had been established at £100 English to £108/6/8 (or 12d. English to 13d. Irish). English inflation disturbed the exchange in the 1690's but in 1701 the same ratio was reestablished. Under the pressure of the silver drain the ratio had since slipped to £100 to £110 or even to £100 to £120.[53] Boulter made an effort to combat this situation in 1728, supplying the government with official gold and silver values for all foreign coins then legal tender to prove the necessity for reform.[54] He met with too much opposition from both English and Irish bankers, who apparently profited by buying silver coins in Ireland and selling them in London.

[51] John Loveday, *Diary of a Tour in 1732 through Parts of England, Wales, Ireland and Scotland,* 4th ed. (Edinburgh, 1890), p. 57.

[52] *Description of Dublin by a Citizen of London* (London, 1732), p. 23.

[53] L. M. Cullen, *Anglo-Irish Trade 1660–1800* (Manchester, 1968), pp. 155–157.

[54] Report compiled for Archbishop Boulter listing foreign coins current in Ireland, Eng. P.R.O., S.P. 63/391, fols. 24–25; Boulter to Newcastle, Nov. 22, 1729, *ibid.,* fol. 23.

In 1737, supported by the Irish administration, Boulter fared better. The government issued a proclamation correcting the silver values despite some demonstrations in Dublin against the measure.[55] According to L. M. Cullen, the 1737 proclamation restored and stabilized the Irish pound at the 100 to 108/6/8 ratio though it did not effectively remedy the shortage of specie.[56]

From the late 1730's to the Peace of Aix-la-Chapelle in 1748 the attention of the Irish administration turned increasingly from other questions to military matters. Although the Irish parliament was seldom called upon to deal directly with military problems, its members kept a close eye on the government's policy regarding the army. Military costs accounted for a large share of the budget while the condition and behavior of the army were of vital concern. Unlike the American colonists, the Anglo-Irish accepted a standing army as essential to their own security. In no other major part of the British dominions did the military play so important a domestic role as in Ireland. There were barracks in or near most of the key towns, and the lord lieutenant was distinctly a military as well as a civil governor. The ceremony that customarily attended his arrival bore all the trappings of a martial affair; Cary has left us a description of the event in 1735:

His Grace was received at his landing by their Excellencies the Lords Justices and by the Lord Mayor, Aldermen and Sheriffs of Dublin. The Foot-forces in Garrison with the militia of the City lined the Streets through which His Grace (attended by a regiment of Horse, the Battle Axe Guards, and other Officers attending the State) proceeded, amidst the acclamations of a vast concourse of People to the Castle, upon which the Great Guns at the Barracks were fired, and answered by Vollies from the Regiments upon duty which were drawn out upon College-Green; (and His Grace received the Com-

[55] Devonshire to Newcastle, Oct. 28, 1737, *ibid.*, S.P. 63/400, fol. 104; *Diary of Viscount Percival*, II, 341–342; Dublin *Evening Post*, Apr. 27, May 11, 1737.
[56] Cullen, *Anglo-Irish Trade 1660–1800*, pp. 157–158.

pliments of the Nobility and other Persons of distinction upon his safe arrival in this Kingdom).[57]

When a standing army was first taking shape in England at the time of the Restoration, Charles II raised a regiment known as the Irish Guards. Initially recruited in England the guards became predominantly Irish and Catholic during Tyrconnell's viceregency. When James II landed in Ireland in 1689 the guards, along with other units then stationed in Ireland, joined his forces with the exception of a part of one regiment, which threw in its lot with the Protestants. Most of the troops supporting James left Ireland for foreign service following the Treaty of Limerick. During the Williamite War, however, three new regiments were formed among the Protestants.[58]

From the time of the Treaty of Limerick the government maintained a standing army in Ireland, the size of which was fixed at 12,000 by an English statute of 1699.[59] This army might contain units with an Irish name, such as the Inniskilling Dragoons, but it did not constitute an Irish army in any national sense. Although paid for by the Irish administration largely out of taxes provided by the Irish parliament, it consisted of regular regiments of the British army. Until 1781 there was no Irish Mutiny Act, the forces in Ireland being specifically covered in the English Mutiny Act of 1701.[60]

The Army in Ireland during the early eighteenth century thus actually represented an extension of Britain's home defense force. Speaking in 1733 against a government plan to increase the size of the army stationed in Britain to 18,000, William Windham denied the need for so large a force. "Suppose," he demanded, "an invasion should happen, have we not 12,000 men in Ireland? These joined with 12,000 men proposed for England, make 24,000, a sufficient number to

[57] Cary to Mr. [Andrew ?] Stone, Sept. 24, 1735, Eng. P.R.O., S.P. 63/398, fol. 48.

[58] Clifford Walton, *History of the British Standing Army* (London, 1894), pp. 52–56.

[59] English Statute, 10 and 11 William III, c.1.

[60] English Statute, 13 William III, c. 2.

oppose invaders." [61] Since Windham was an opposition leader, his opinion may be discounted; his point was, nevertheless, well taken: the Irish regiments could be and were employed for the defense of Britain itself, as well as serving as a reserve from which troops were drawn for overseas stations such as New York or the West Indies.[62] In the light of eighteenth-century communications facilities and supposedly lax administrative machinery, the speed with which Irish troops could be mobilized for service is impressive. Early in March 1734 Dorset informed Newcastle that, in view of the unsettled state of European affairs, he was taking steps to quarter several regiments near convenient ports. On April 10 Newcastle wrote requesting the lord lieutenant to hire transports and send six regiments as soon as possible. Despite contrary winds that held up their departure, Dorset was able to report on April 25 that one regiment had sailed for Bristol and two for Scotland. One more was scheduled to leave Dublin within a day or two, and the two remaining regiments were to embark shortly from Waterford.[63] In 1744 Devonshire arranged equally rapidly to send reinforcements to Flanders, while at the same time assembling troops near the northeast Irish ports for immediate transportation to Scotland should the need arise.[64] On September 6, 1745, Newcastle asked Chesterfield to make ready two regiments of foot for embarkation "upon the first notice."

[61] *Diary of Viscount Percival*, I, 319.

[62] Irish troops were sent to New York in 1700 (*Documents Relative to the Colonial History of the State of New York*, ed. E. B. O'Callaghan, 15 vols. [Albany, 1853–1887], IV, 642, 721, 769, 882); to Jamaica in 1701 and the Leeward Islands in 1707 (*Calendar of State Papers Colonial, America and the West Indies, 1701* [London, 1910], p. 279, *Calendar of State Papers Colonial, America and the West Indies*, 1706–1708 [London, 1916], p. 465). In 1750 three regiments were sent to Nova Scotia. Eng. P.R.O., S.P. 63/412, fol. 112. General Braddock had Irish regiments with him in 1755. *The Papers of Sir William Johnson*, ed. James Sullivan, 14 vols. (New York, 1922–1965), IX, 154; see also John W. Shy, *Toward Lexington: The Role of the British Army in the Coming of the American Revolution* (Princeton, Princeton University Press, 1965), pp. 34–35.

[63] Newcastle to Dorset, Apr. 2, 10; Dorset to Newcastle, Apr. 10, 19, 25, 1734, Eng. P.R.O., S.P. 63/397, fols. 88, 97–99, 115, 129.

[64] Devonshire to Newcastle, Jan. 5, 30, 31, 1743/44, and Newcastle to Devonshire, Jan. 26, 1733/34, *ibid.*, S.P. 63/406, fols. 1–2, 24–25, 30–32.

He sent the order for their departure on September 25, and
on September 30 Chesterfield wrote back from Dublin that
some of the troops had already sailed and that the rest were
now leaving.[65]

From the standpoint of the British government the existence
of an army in Ireland, paid for out of Irish taxes, constituted
perhaps Ireland's greatest contribution to the welfare of the
empire. The Irish parliament willingly voted money for the
military establishment but it proved increasingly reluctant to
shoulder the costs of maintaining the Irish regiments when
they were called upon to serve outside of Ireland. During the
War of the Spanish Succession the Dublin Commons had
provided such funds with little objection, and by way of
compensation the English parliament stipulated that clothing
for Irish troops abroad should be purchased in Ireland.[66]
After the war pressure grew to have the British treasury pay
the expenses of any Irish regiments withdrawn from the country. Lord lieutenants and officials of the Irish administration
generally endorsed this position. They were, after all, dependent upon the Irish Commons for the military budget. It is
clear from one of the provisions of Burton's Bank Act that
as late as 1725 the Irish treasury was still supplying money
for Irish troops in England, but from the late 1720's on the
British government sometimes agreed to finance Irish regiments that served overseas for any length of time.[67] By 1745
Newcastle was ready to assure Chesterfield that the troops he
dispatched to England would "immediately" be placed on the
English instead of the Irish establishment.[68] Two respective

[65] Newcastle to Chesterfield, Sept. 6, 25, 1745, and Chesterfield to Newcastle, Sept. 30, 1745, *ibid.*, S.P. 63/408, fols. 72–73, 118, 130.

[66] *English Commons' Journal*, Apr. 13, 1707.

[67] Wogan attempted to have Irish overseas regiments placed on the
British establishment in 1711. Wogan to [Southwell ?], June 26, July 21,
31, Aug. 2, 4, Sept. 8, 1711, B.M., Add. MSS. 37673, fols. 127, 143–44;
ibid., 37674, fols. 5, 7, 9, 31. Burton's Bank received money to be sent to
England for payments of regiments there. Irish Statute, 7 George II, c. 26,
sect. 28. A report signed by R. Arnold, War Office, Feb. 25, 1730/31, states
that four regiments sent from Ireland to England in 1726 were placed on
the British establishment. Eng. P.R.O., S.P. 63/389, fols. 145–146.

[68] Chesterfield to Newcastle, Jan. 22, 1745/46, Eng. P.R.O., S.P. 63/409,
fol. 16.

secretaries of the lord lieutenants, Clutterbuck and Cary, who worked to win this concession from the military, discovered, ironically, that they had thereby lost the fees paid on commissions granted to Irish officers when on the British payroll.[69]

The question of who should pay for Irish regiments abroad reveals a basic difference in attitude between the government and the Irish parliament. The British ministry, as has been demonstrated, viewed the troops stationed in Ireland as a part of the total military force available for imperial defense. The Anglo-Irish thought of them primarily as constituting an army specifically designed to defend Ireland from invasion and to maintain domestic law and order. The composition of the army reflected its dual nature. Many of the officers were members of the Anglo-Irish aristocracy, and appointments to Irish military commissions came more and more under the influence of Irish parliamentary leaders. The lord lieutenants not only handed some of the military patronage over to recognized undertakers like Boyle; they also used their patronage to win support in the Irish Commons. Writing to secure the promotion of an officer, Chesterfield admitted: "He is an utter stranger to me and I freely owe to Your Lordship [Secretary Harrington] that my true reason for recommending his request is that he is Brother to Lord Lanesborough, is himself, and has many relatives, in the Irish Parliament." [70] Contracts for military supplies, transport ships, building and maintaining barracks, and other such expenditures also formed a part of the political patronage system.[71] Thus, in a fiscal sense as well as in its officer personnel (which included many inactive officers on half-pay), the Irish regiments represented an agency of the ruling classes in Ireland. In contrast, the rank and file of the army was an alien group; they came from England.

[69] *Ibid.*, 63/401, fols. 79–84.

[70] Chesterfield to Harrington, May 21, 1745, *ibid.*, 63/407, fol. 183.

[71] Chesterfield made Henry Brooke, author of pamphlets favorable to the Irish administration, a barrack master. Irish Public Record Office, Calendar of Departmental Correspondence, 1741–1759, p. 131. On military contracts, see *Irish Commons' Journal*, Sept. 26, 1717; Eng. P.R.O., S.P. 65/385 (1725), fol. 71; S.P. 63/407 (1744–1745), fol. 20; S.P. 63/409 (1745–1746), fol. 30.

The fact is the Anglo-Irish did not dare put arms in the hands of the Catholic Irish. To be sure, there were Protestants among the lower classes (from which the common soldiers were almost exclusively drawn in the eighteenth century) but the great majority of the population consisted of Catholics, and even among the professing Protestants many were converts whose loyalty was doubtful. Thus the Irish parliament fully endorsed the government's policy of recruiting all troops for the Irish regiments in England, a practice already well established by 1715.[72] The Irish legislature displayed, in fact, a much stronger distrust of Catholics than did the British ministry.

For the most part the lord lieutenants of the early eighteenth century respected the prejudices of the Anglo-Irish and cooperated in maintaining the system of English recruitment. When, in 1727, Archbishop Boulter suggested that, if strict steps were taken to enlist only Protestants, soldiers could safely be raised in Ireland, neither Carteret nor the Irish parliament agreed with him.[73] The next year Carteret backed the action of the Board of General Officers in suspending certain officers for enlisting Irish recruits.[74] Devonshire, though troubled with the problem of finding wartime replacements, seems fully to have shared in the Irish parliament's fear of Catholics. He approved a new bill for disarming Catholics in 1739 and helped convince the ministry to accept it. On several occasions he took steps to tighten the restrictions against Irish recruiting.[75] Chesterfield, who succeeded him in 1745, took a similar

[72] Addison to Townshend, May 31, 1715, *Letters of Addison*, ed. Graham, p. 325. Harrington explained the government's policy: "It has been a necessary Policy and Precaution in the governing of this Kingdom to keep Roman Catholics, as much as possible, from the possession and use of Arms." Harrington to Bedford, Feb. 23, 1747/48, Eng. P.R.O., S.P. 63/410, fol. 171.

[73] Boulter to Newcastle, Mar. 11, 1726/27, Eng. P.R.O., S.P. 63/388, fol. 196.

[74] Carteret to Newcastle, Mar. 27, 1738, Eng. P.R.O., S.P. 63/390, fol. 54.

[75] Devonshire to lords justices, July 10, Dec. 18, 1742, Irish Public Record Office, Calendar of Departmental Correspondence, 1741–1759, pp. 28, 43. The 1741 disarming law is Irish Statute, 13 George II, c. 6. In 1744 Devonshire wrote that, despite numerous allegations, few arms had been

position, but found himself compelled by the need for men to request a temporary modification of established policy. At his suggestion the government permitted the Irish generals to raise Protestant troops in Ulster.[76] Two years later, however, the government renewed orders for recruiting troops only in Great Britain and only among British-born subjects.[77] Aside from the temporary suspension in 1745, the only significant exception to the recruiting policy until the Seven Years' War appears to have been the practice of "impressing sea-faring men for His Majesty's Fleet,"[78] but a few popish seamen in the Royal Navy were scarcely cause for alarm.

The presence of British troops in Ireland caused some resentment, not only among Catholics but among Protestants as well. Unpleasant incidents could not be avoided. In 1711 the city officials in Limerick petitioned the lord lieutenant to discipline the officers of the garrison there for causing a riot.[79] The same year an officer shot a civilian who had been taunting his drilling troops on Oxmantown Green. Although the victim was "a recent papist and a man of very ill life," the officer was demoted and forced to pay damages to the wounded man.[80] The bishop of Limerick had an altercation with the garrison there in 1718, while in 1721 the bishop of Londonderry along with the city fathers had a dispute with the Derry garrison.[81] In Dublin in 1736 a fight broke out between soldiers and apprentices in which several people were reportedly

---

found among Catholics. Devonshire to Newcastle, Mar. 22, 1743/44, Eng. P.R.O., S.P. 63/406, fol. 143.

[76] Chesterfield to Newcastle, Sept. 7, 1745, and Newcastle to Chesterfield, Sept. 21, 1745, Eng. P.R.O., S.P. 63/408, fols. 96, 107–108.

[77] Earl of Harrington to Newcastle, Apr. 19, 1747, *ibid.*, S.P. 63/410, fol. 23. But the government did find it necessary to raise another 660 recruits in Ireland. Harrington to Newcastle, Oct. 29, 1747, *ibid.*, fol. 95.

[78] Dorset to Newcastle, Apr. 25, 1734, *ibid.*, S.P. 63/397, fol. 130.

[79] Ormond to lords justices, Jan. 10, 1710/11, Irish Public Record Office, Calendar of Departmental Correspondence, 1683–1714, p. 199.

[80] B.M., Add. MSS. 38160, fol. 13.

[81] Bolton to lords justices, Oct. 18, Nov. 18, 1718, Irish Public Record Office, Calendar of Departmental Correspondence, 1714–1740, pp. 41–43; James, *North Country Bishop*, p. 275.

killed or wounded.[82] Hoping to prevent such outbreaks, parliament had in Anne's reign passed a law laying down regulations concerning marching troops, commandeering wagons, and forbidding the quartering of soldiers on the march or in seaports except immediately before embarkation. In Dublin no troops could be billeted at any time outside of barracks.[83] The lord lieutenants seem to have done their best to subordinate the military to the civil authorities. Even during wartime Devonshire refused to disregard the billeting rules, despite instructions from London to do so.[84] There was, nonetheless, no disguising the fact that government possessed a military force to back up its authority.

A parliamentary regime dependent upon the military can only achieve real power if it exerts full control over the army. Such control remained beyond the reach of the Dublin legislature. The Irish army was responsible to the British crown. King William had brought over an army to rescue the Protestant Irish in 1690. His venture completed, the king had returned to England; the army had remained. The complete Protestant victory in 1692 made future rebellion improbable and ushered in one of the longest periods of peace in Irish history. Yet, in the last analysis, the Irish state in the early eighteenth century rested upon British military power. So long as the Anglo-Irish insisted on maintaining a monopoly of political office and economic privilege they could not dispense with the need for a standing army.

The war of 1739–1748 brought into focus the nature of the existing regime in Ireland. The system that had evolved since 1692 represented a balance between the interests of the imperial government and the Protestant ascendancy. Though

---

[82] Dublin *Evening Post*, June 15, 1736.

[83] Irish Statute, 6 Anne, c. 14.

[84] Devonshire to Newcastle, Jan. 31, 1743/44, Eng. P.R.O., S.P. 63/406, fol. 33. In January 1750 Lord Harrington requested that a soldier, accused of murdering an innkeeper in Bray fifteen years before, be returned from Scotland for trial, and the government ordered that he should be. *Ibid.*, S.P. 63/412, fols. 31, 34. For a similar incident a year later, see *Edsall's Newsletter*, Apr. 24, 1751. There is repeated evidence that the civilian administration attempted to keep the military in line.

ultimate authority lay with the British ministry, the country was normally administered by the undertakers in the privy council and parliament and by the local Anglo-Irish officials in the counties and boroughs. Despite the frustrations experienced by both sides, this modus vivendi worked so effectively that Froude could write: "For the half century intervening between the Duke of Grafton's government and the revolt of the American colonies, Ireland was without a history." [85] Froude, as usual, is more eloquent than accurate, yet for nearly a score of years after 1734 Irish history appears remarkably uneventful.

Froude follows the above quotation with the observation that the "misgovernment" of the period prepared the way for the eventual breakdown of the system in the late eighteenth century. Though exaggerating, he is in a sense correct. The very success of the compromise between the British ministry and the ruling Anglo-Irish undermined the principal reason it had come into being: the fear that Catholic Ireland would rise up, join forces with England's enemies, and overthrow British rule. The relative calm in Ireland during the second quarter of the eighteenth century made possible three changes that were to upset the balance of the existing regime. One, the firm establishment of limited representative government and orderly constitutional procedures opened the way for a popular political opposition by groups hitherto excluded from power. Two, the invulnerable position of the ascendancy turned Catholics from schemes of rebellion to hopes for concessions; as they demonstrated the peaceful nature of their aims, Protestant intransigence began to falter. Three, within the ruling groups themselves the growing influence of the undertakers inevitably gave rise to rivalries that in time ripened into open division. Each of these three changes began to manifest itself during the decade of the 1740's.

The person most clearly identified with popular discontent at the time of the Declaratory Act and Wood's halfpence is Swift. Before Swift's death in 1745 another churchman, Bishop

---

[85] Froude, *English in Ireland*, I, 657.

Berkeley, won acclaim for denouncing Britain's economic exploitation of Ireland. Other less famous pamphleteers were writing attacks on British economic policy throughout the period. Famine conditions in the late twenties and particularly in 1740–1741 aroused widespread dissatisfaction. But no effective leader of popular discontent appeared until 1747. Swift and Berkeley, though respected by all classes, were after all clergy in the established church. Furthermore Swift never held political office, and Bishop Berkeley spent much time abroad. Charles Lucas, who became the popular champion in the late 1740's, sprang from a different background.[86] Son of a Presbyterian landlord who had lost his estate, Lucas grew up in Dublin in modest circumstances. He entered the apothecary trade and thus became a member of one of the Dublin guilds. He early displayed an interest in public affairs. A kind of eighteenth-century muckraker, he published in 1735, at the age of twenty-four, *A Short Scheme for Preventing Frauds and Abuses in Pharmacy*. This pamphlet was, apparently, chiefly responsible for the 1736 act to prevent the sale of fraudulent drugs. In 1741, when the act came up for renewal, Lucas wrote a second treatise on pharmacy to enlist support for the measure. That same year he was chosen as a representative of the corporation of apothecaries to the Dublin city council. During the next few years he became an advocate for the council against what he called the usurped powers of the mayor and board of aldermen. By 1747, when he began the publication of a weekly newspaper for the discussion of national issues, *The Censor or Citizen's Journal*, Lucas was already widely known in the capital.

It proved an auspicious moment to launch a campaign against the government. A royal proclamation prohibiting trade with the enemy had seriously curtailed the vital provision trade, while the initial fears of invasion engendered by the war were evaporating, and with them the solidarity of

[86] Lucas' life is in the *DNB*, XXXIV, 231–234; see also Robbins, *Eighteenth-Century Commonwealthman*, pp. 153–154; *Gentlemen's Magazine*, XIX (1749), 523.

the Anglo-Irish.[87] Lord Chesterfield, who had spent nearly a full year in Dublin in 1745–1746 and had won considerable popularity, had just been replaced by William Stanhope, first earl of Harrington, as lord lieutenant. Harrington spent less time in Ireland and did not possess the same capacity for making friends. In 1747, too, George Stone, Dorset's former chaplain, became primate and subsequently one of the three lords justices. Stone, an open opportunist, could not command the respect enjoyed by his predecessors (Boulter, 1724–1742, Hoadly, 1742–1745). Most important of all, the lower middle class and artisan groups to whom Lucas appealed had apparently grown in both numbers and political aspirations since the days of Wood's halfpence.

At first Lucas confined himself to criticizing the unjust behavior of the landlords and other members of the privileged classes, but he soon extended his attacks to include the law courts and eventually Dublin Castle. Like Molyneux and Swift, Lucas challenged the whole system of Ireland's subordination to England. Then, in August 1748, when one of the M. P.'s for Dublin died, Lucas decided to stand for parliament. Deploring the lack of spirit in parliament, Lucas attacked the sinister influence of patronage: "The Infection came wrapped in *Ermine, Purple* and *Lawn*; and unhappily found a climate not unprepared to receive and nourish the baneful weed. *Sham-Patriots* were employed to explain away your rights: Prelates who bowed only to the *Molten Calf* expounded legal subjection into *implicit Faith* and *passive Obedience*; and mercenary, corrupt Judges refined *sacred Right* into Expediency."[88] A few months later, when he was under attack, Lucas reported a dialogue among five squires: *Num, Ranter, Kickall, Jolly*, and *Gentle*. In it *Kickall* remarked that Lucas was no gentleman: " 'Sflesh, were I a Candidate, I'd make no

[87] Petitions against the embargo are found in Eng. P.R.O., S.P. 63/406, fol. 120; S.P. 63/409, fol. 58; see also Chesterfield to Newcastle, Feb. 1, Mar. 5, 1745/46, *ibid.*, fols. 48, 50. Wartime restrictions encouraged an increase in smuggling. Harrington to Bedford, Feb. 23, Mar. 10, 1747/48, *ibid.*, S.P. 63/410, fols. 170–171, 182.
[88] *The Censor or Citizen's Journal*, July 11, 1749.

more of kicking him and all his little Mechanics, than I would of kicking my tenants." At this outburst Mr. *Gentle* objects and is backed by *Farmer*, who comments on the "very extraordinary Spirit" among the citizens of Dublin: " 'Tis not a *flash* from the Pan . . . It has been long rising, as You have seen the Sun in a foggy morning, and the higher it has gotten, the more the Mist has been dispersed, and the calmer and clearer the People begin to see everything about them. They will therefore no longer be led, they can observe and judge for themselves." [89] There are times when Charles Lucas sounds more like Tom Paine than Dean Swift.

Although Lucas had made enemies of the mayor and aldermen, the Dublin franchise was broad enough to make his election a distinct possibility. The prospect proved too much for Harrington. Rallying parliament with the help of the undertakers, the lord lieutenant succeeded in having a resolution passed condemning Lucas' writings as seditious and declaring him an enemy of the country in October 1749, just a few days before the Dublin election.[90] Threatened with arrest, Lucas fled abroad but his ally, James Digges La Touche, won one of the two vacant seats.[91] Popular clamor did not disappear with Lucas' exile. Like Wilkes, Lucas eventually returned to win a seat in the Commons a decade later. In 1760 La Touche proudly observed that "Our Dublin citizens, since that memorable year 1749, have been so wrong headed as to talk of *National Rights*, of *Liberty*, . . . *and free and uninfluenced Electors.* They now read Newspapers, and even the votes of the Commons, and have more than once been audacious enough to crowd the streets about the Parliament." [92]

The second change referred to above, the improved position

[89] *Ibid.*, Sept. 30, 1749.

[90] *Irish Commons' Journal*, Oct. 11, 12, 13, 16, 1749.

[91] When La Touche won, his opponent Burton challenged the election, and the Commons found in favor of Burton. *Ibid.*, Nov. 21, Dec. 18, 1749.

[92] [James Digges La Touche], *A Short but True History of the Rise, Progress and Happy Suppression of Several Late Insurections* (London and Dublin, 1760), p. 16.

of Catholics, came about more imperceptibly. In fact on the surface the 1740's witnessed an extension of the penal laws. It has already been mentioned that a new law disarming Catholics was enacted in 1742. The war also brought about the arming of the Protestant militia.[93] Then, in 1746, the Irish parliament revived the bill to outlaw marriages between Catholics and Protestants when solemnized by Roman priests. In 1732 a similar bill had died in London; this time, no doubt alarmed by the Jacobite threat, the British ministry approved the measure.[94] But the above steps represent a temporary wartime reaction rather than a genuine revival of active anti-Catholicism. The almost complete absence of overt Jacobite sympathy among the Irish Catholics soon quieted suspicions and led to a new spirit of tolerance on the part of many Protestants. Furthermore, despite the disabilities that prevented Catholics from acquiring land or political office, some Catholic landlords survived, and, more important, many of that religion had turned to trade and prospered. Thus there existed a class of propertied Catholics who, though they might chafe at the penal laws, had a vested interest in maintaining peace and order. Likewise some of the Catholic clergy, who now normally suffered little interference from the authorities, became advocates of accepting the legality of the Hanoverian succession and the established regime. In 1749 a number of leading Catholic laymen formed an association which, pledging loyalty to the government, sought to win some modification of the penal legislation.[95] Although this movement met with much criticism, it slowly won support from some Protestants. The tide had turned.

The third change of the period, the split of the undertakers into competing factions, was the outgrowth of rivalries that actually dated back to the beginning of the undertaking system. It will be recalled that the key move by which Dorset had established the system was his decision to cooperate with

[93] Chesterfield to Newcastle, Oct. 31, 1745, Eng. P.R.O., S.P. 63/408, fol. 196.

[94] Irish Statute, 19 George II, c. 13.

[95] Maureen Wall, *The Penal Laws* (Dundalk, 1961), pp. 65–66.

Henry Boyle, formerly a leader of the opposition, or at least of nongovernment forces. Alliance with Boyle naturally aroused the jealousy of the old Castle party, which had previously been led by Conolly, and after his death by Henry Singleton and John Ponsonby.[96] During Devonshire's administration the Ponsonby family gained considerable influence, Devonshire's two daughters having married two of John Ponsonby's sons. In 1737 John became earl of Bessborough on his father's death; two years later he took Boyle's place on the revenue board, the key body for financial businesses and patronage. Bessborough, with the support of George Stone, apparently attempted to convince Devonshire that Speaker Boyle was undermining the Castle's position in Commons. These divisions did not, however, cause an open breach among the undertakers during the 1740's.

Chesterfield, during his term as lord lieutenant, proved less pliable than Devonshire; he had no intention of delegating power to any individual or group. He kept the undertakers in line by requiring them, as McCracken puts it, "to fulfill what he considered to be their engagements," [97] while at the same time making it clear that he would cooperate with them. In ecclesiastical appointments he worked closely with the English-born Stone and with Bishop Edwin Synge of Elphin. For secular patronage he sought the advice of Robert Jocelyn, viscount Newport and lord chancellor, and of Henry Singleton, now lord chief justice of common pleas, as well as of Boyle and other parliamentary leaders. Chesterfield tightened the Castle's control of the administration of the army barracks, an important addition to his control of patronage.[98] Chesterfield also strengthened the Irish privy council, the importance of which he clearly recognized. "The Council door has not been opened for some years, I think seven or eight, and crowds are pressing at it, as it is really a board of consequence here, being part of the legislature. Some new members are really

[96] J. L. McCracken, "The Conflict between the Irish Administration and Parliament 1753–56," *Irish Historical Studies*, III (1942–1943), 160.
[97] McCracken, "Undertakers," p. 97.
[98] *Ibid.*, pp. 97–98, 100–102.

wanting, it being sometimes difficult to make up a Quorum. But the greatest difficulty of all, was where to stop. I have at last reduced the number to eight, of which I don't reckon above five effective, which is about the number wanted." [99] His additions included the earl of Kildare (because of his large holdings and insistence), a son-in-law of Boyle's, and two reliable "Castle-men." [100]

William Stanhope, first earl of Harrington, who succeeded his half brother, Lord Chesterfield, in 1746, tried to improve the government's position in several ways. He responded favorably to a parliamentary request to build a number of new barracks, both a military necessity and an economic benefit to the communities involved.[101] He recommended the elevation to the peerage of prominent landowners, complaining to London that the Irish Lords lacked resident peers "of any considerable Fortune and Figure." [102] In spite of, or perhaps because of, his efforts to broaden the base of the government in Ireland, Harrington does not appear to have been popular with the undertakers. Although he recommended that Stone be made primate on the death of Hoadly, the new archbishop, in cooperation with the Ponsonbys, accused Harrington of weakness in handling the Lucas affair and thereby brought about his replacement by Stone's old patron, the duke of Dorset.[103]

When Dorset returned to Dublin in 1751 he brought with him instructions to restore the power of the administration over parliament, that is, to reduce the influence of the undertakers he had done so much to establish seventeen years before. It is doubtful whether these instructions would have been carried through if Stone and the Ponsonbys had not convinced

[99] Chesterfield to Newcastle, Mar. 11, 1745/46, Eng. P.R.O., S.P. 63/409, fols. 92–94.

[100] *Ibid.*, fol. 90.

[101] Harrington to Newcastle, Dec. 12, 1747, Feb. 4, 1747/48, *ibid.*, S.P. 63/410, fols. 142–144, 162–164.

[102] Harrington to Bedford, Mar. 13, 1749/50, *ibid.*, S.P. 63/412, fol. 72.

[103] Harrington to Newcastle, Feb. 26, 1746/47, *ibid.*, S.P. 63/410, fol. 11; McCracken, "Conflict between the Irish Administration and Parliament," p. 16.

Dorset that the Castle could no longer trust Boyle. Although the 1751–1752 session of parliament completed its business without serious conflict, Boyle, aware of the administration's hostility, was already preparing to attack his rivals.[104] The actual break came in 1753, when Boyle decided to challenge the government's budget. The growth of Irish trade during the past decade had increased the yield of customs to a point that finally produced a treasury surplus. The parliament of 1751 had passed heads of a bill applying the surplus to the reduction of the national debt. Though approving the bill, the British ministry had inserted into it a clause noting the king's previous endorsement of the proposal. The reason for this insertion was to make explicit the crown's control over the surplus. In 1753, when the ministry again added such a clause to the Irish revenue bill, Boyle determined to oppose the measure on the grounds that the government should not alter money bills and that disposal of the Irish surplus was strictly the concern of the Irish parliament. Dorset did his best to muster the Castle's strength but, in the words of Horace Walpole, "Satires and claret were successful even against corruption! The Money Bill . . . was rejected in Ireland by a majority of five." [105] Dorset immediately retaliated by dismissing Boyle from his post as chancellor of the Exchequer and removing from office all placemen who had joined the opposition; open factional conflict once again prevailed in the Irish parliament.

[104] Dr. Edward Barry to John Boyle, earl of Orrery, Dublin, Jan. 6, 1752, and Earl of Orrery to Dr. Barry, Marston House, Mar. 18, 1752. *The Orrery Papers*, ed. the Countess of Cork and Orrery, 2 vols. (London, 1903), II, 97, 107.

[105] *Memoirs of the Reign of King George the Second by Horace Walpole*, ed. Lord Holland, 2nd ed., 3 vols. (London, 1846), I, 243; *Irish Commons' Journal*, Nov. 14, Dec. 15, 17, 1753. According to *Gentlemen's Magazine*, XXIV (1754), 151, the vote was 122 to 117. It is significant that in 1753 the Irish Commons first authorized the printing of its *Journals* and provided £7,450 to Edward Sterling to print 400 copies of the set for the members. *Irish Commons' Journal*, Nov. 8, 1753.

VIII
Economic Development

The study of Irish political history between 1692 and 1750 has revealed how the Dublin parliament asserted increasing control over the government of Ireland, without, however, succeeding in challenging the ultimate authority of Great Britain. To what extent did this limited self-government affect the economic development of Ireland during the early eighteenth century? It is now generally accepted that British mercantilism did not seriously curtail the expansion of the American colonies before 1763. A number of British trade regulations directly and intentionally fostered colonial development, while others did so unintentionally and indirectly. Furthermore, lax enforcement resulted in frequent evasion so that some regulations remained virtually inoperative.[1] While the beneficent effects of "salutary neglect" upon the American colonies have long been recognized, writers on Irish history have continued to assume that the British mercantilist system was applied to Ireland with nearly complete disregard for Irish interests and with devastating effectiveness.[2] In 1809 Thomas Newenham summarized the aims of British policy

[1] Beer, *British Colonial Policy, 1754–1765*, and *Old Colonial System, 1660–1754*; Lawrence A. Harper, "The Effect of the Navigation Act on the Thirteen Colonies," in *The Era of the American Revolution*, ed. Richard B. Morris (New York, Columbia University Press, 1939); Oliver M. Dickerson, *The Navigation Acts and the American Revolution* (Philadelphia, University of Pennsylvania Press, 1951), pp. 296–300. For a good brief discussion, see Carl Ubbelohde, *The American Colonies and the British Empire 1607–1763* (New York, Crowell, 1968), pp. 44–62.

[2] Froude, *English in Ireland*, I, 263–269; Lecky, *England in the Eighteenth Century*, II, 226–241; Ephraim Lipson, *Economic History of England*, 6th ed., 3 vols. (London, A. & C. Black, 1956), III, 197; George O'Brien, *The Economic History of Ireland in the Eighteenth Century* (Dublin, 1918), pp. 95–110, 174–175.

in what had already become, and has remained, the prevailing interpretation. "To cramp, obstruct, and render abortive the industry of the Irish, were the objects of British traders. To gratify commercial avarice, to secure Britain at the expense of Ireland, or to facilitate the government of the latter, were the varying objects of the British ministers." [3]

Is this traditional picture accurate? Or was British mercantilism in Ireland mitigated in the same ways as in the American colonies — by compensating advantages and evasion? To answer the question it is necessary to ascertain certain facts: the nature of British regulations affecting Ireland; the character of Irish economic legislation approved by the British government; and the consequences of both types of regulation, including the degree to which they were actually enforced.

During the first half of the seventeenth century, particularly during Wentworth's administration, the Irish policies of the English government appear to have been guided primarily by a concern for English political security rather than for its economic advantage. After the Restoration, with the emergence of more self-conscious English mercantilism, economic factors became more important and at times outweighed political and religious considerations. Charles II's only Irish parliament expressed criticism of English restrictions, but was dissolved before resistance became organized.[4] Meanwhile the English parliament proceeded to deal with Ireland in most respects as a foreign country outside the walls of the empire, yet at the same time as a dependent state subject to English control. The initial Navigation Acts of 1651 and 1660 had treated Ireland on a par with England, permitting Irish trade with the colonies and allowing Irish ships the same status as English vessels, but in 1663 Ireland was forbidden to export anything directly to the colonies except servants, horses, and provisions.[5] In 1667 the English parliament prohibited the importation of Irish cattle into England, thereby striking at

[3] Newenham, *View of Ireland*, p. 97.
[4] *Irish Commons' Journal*, Mar. 30, 1666.
[5] English Statute, 15 Charles II, c. 7.

one of Ireland's chief sources of earnings.[6] Next, the Navigation Act of 1671 (which lapsed in 1680, but was renewed in
1685) introduced the principle that certain enumerated articles, such as sugar, tobacco, and indigo, must be shipped
from the colonies exclusively to England. Although this act
still permitted Ireland to import unenumerated articles from
the colonies, that trade too was prohibited in 1696.[7] Perhaps
the most damaging of all English restrictions came with the
famous (or infamous) Woolens Act of 1699, which forbade
the exportation of Irish wool or woolens to the colonies or
to any foreign country and limited Irish wool exports to
England alone.[8]

The English legislation passed between 1663 and 1699 seems
to justify Alice Effie Murray's conclusion that "the Navigation
Laws and the harsh interpretation placed on them inflicted
severe injury on the colonial trade of Ireland and checked the
development of Irish shipping and commerce for ninety years
after the Revolution of 1688."[9] The Navigation Acts undoubtedly curtailed and diverted Irish trade, but Miss Murray
and others have exaggerated their adverse effects.

From 1700 onward London appeared increasingly concerned
with fostering the economic health and political harmony of
the empire, seeking where possible to offer advantages to all
the divergent interests in the imperial community. The growing political influence of the Anglo-Irish drew attention to
the needs of Ireland. The preceding chapters have made it
clear that from the late 1690's on the Irish Commons used
their control over taxation to bargain for concessions. Assisted
by what we have called the "Irish lobby" in London, the
Anglo-Irish succeeded in persuading the British ministry and

[6] English Statute, 18 Charles II, c. 2.

[7] Andrews, *Colonial Period of American History*, IV, 127–219.

[8] English Statute, 7 and 8 William III, c. 22. All of these regulatory acts
are summarized in Lawrence A. Harper, *The English Navigation Laws*
(New York, 1939), pp. 394–399.

[9] Alice Effie Murray, *A History of the Commercial and Financial Relations between England and Ireland, from the Period of the Restoration*,
rev. ed. (London, 1907), p. 75; see also O'Brien, *Economic History of
Ireland*, pp. 4–5.

parliament to modify some regulations affecting Irish trade. Although much British legislation dealing with Ireland still sought to implement previous statutes by providing for improved enforcement, only a few acts introduced any further restraints on Irish trade.[10] It is even more significant that several new laws specifically withdrew or reduced existing restrictions. The most important of these new laws have been discussed above in connection with the political history of the period, such acts as those opening colonial markets to Irish linens, permitting the direct importation into Ireland of colonial goods not on the enumerated list, reducing British duties on Irish woolen yarn, and increasing the number of British ports open to Irish wool imports. In short, instead of ushering in an era of unchecked English exploitation, as such writers as A. E. Murray and George O'Brien imply, the Woolens Act of 1699 stands out as one of the last, if the most deleterious, of the English restrictive acts. After 1705 the trend of British legislation was gradually in the direction of a cautious relaxation of controls over Ireland.

More important than the grudging modification of British mercantile legislation was the British government's acceptance of a body of Irish legislation designed to stimulate that country's economic expansion. With the winning of the virtual power of initiating legislation described above, the Dublin parliament devoted increasing attention to economic matters. Unlike the American colonies, Ireland possessed its own import and export duties and its own customs service. Thus, even before the Irish parliament exerted much effective influence, Irish tariffs and regulations were not completely synchronized with or subordinate to those of England. London, of course, enjoyed ultimate control over the Irish administration but Irish officials, including lord lieutenants like the

[10] In Anne's reign the British parliament passed a law forbidding the importation of foreign hops into Ireland, thus reserving the market for Britain. The Molasses Act of 1733 required that all sugar, molasses, and rum from any American colony (foreign or British) must first be shipped to Britain before going to Ireland. This law, however, did not apply to sugar shipped directly to Ireland from Spain or Portugal. English Statutes, 9 Anne, c. 12; 6 George II, c. 13.

two Ormonds, sought to defend Irish interests. If the Navigation Acts severely curtailed Irish trade with the English colonies they did little to limit Irish commerce with the French, Spanish, or Dutch empires. Aside from wool and woolen exports (after 1699), the Irish could export to and import from foreign countries almost any commodity they desired, with the exception of trade protected by special monopolies such as that enjoyed by the East India Company. The English government could, theoretically, have compelled the Irish parliament to enact any kind of restriction it desired; in practice London avoided direct interference. In wartime executive orders prohibited trade with the enemy; otherwise Irish commerce remained relatively uncontrolled outside of the limits prescribed by specific English statutes, as the English attorney general pointed out to the Board of Trade in 1717.[11]

Such a system resulted in anomalies. The inclusion of sugar among the enumerated articles meant that the Irish could import sugar from the British West Indies only via English ports, yet until 1733 they were free to import directly the competing and cheaper sugar produced by the French — a state of affairs that greatly annoyed the British West Indian interest.[12] As has been said of Ireland's constitutional position, its economy was at the same time in some respects more dependent upon Britain than that of the colonies and in other ways far more autonomous.

The increasing political initiative of the Anglo-Irish in the early eighteenth century led them to formulate a body of Irish legislation that may, without exaggeration, be said to constitute a form of Irish mercantilism. In 1703–1705 the Dublin parliament reduced or eliminated tariffs on materials needed for the Irish provision and linen industries: wrought iron,

[11] *Journal of the Commissioners for Trade and Plantations, 1704–1782,* 14 vols. (London, 1920–1938), III, 220–221.

[12] *Calendar of State Papers Colonial, America and the West Indies,* 44 vols. (London, 1860–1969), XXXIV, 123. Although in 1733 the Molasses Act curtailed the French sugar trade, British sugar interests continued to complain against Irish importation of Portuguese sugar. *Journal of the Commissioners for Trade and Plantations,* IX, 268, 275–276.

hoops, barrel staves, and rapeseed.[13] In 1709, to encourage
Irish salt refining, the duty on rock salt was drastically cut,
while that on brine salt remained unchanged.[14] As a consequence the Cheshire salt producers found themselves losing
the Irish market to native competitors.[15] In 1719 a high duty
of twenty shillings a hundredweight was levied on molasses,[16]
apparently to protect the grain producers from the danger of
an increase of rum manufacture at the expense of whiskey.
Relatively high duties on imported spirits already offered
some protection to domestic distillers. Many Irish efforts at
protection were opposed by various British interests, sometimes effectively. It took over a decade before the British
government would approve an Irish "tillage" or corn law,
while Irish attempts to place a quota on East Indian silks and
calicoes failed ever to win British acquiescence. Nevertheless,
the Irish parliament could usually employ its bargaining power
to effect at least a compromise with the British.

A good example of the give-and-take that could occur between Westminster and Dublin took place in 1717. In that
year the British parliament, despite several petitions against
the measure, extended the Linen Act of 1705 (legalizing the
exportation of Irish linens to the colonies) for "so long as
the merchants and other persons of Great Britain shall be
permitted to import into Ireland, free of all duties, such white
and brown linen as is or shall be manufactured in Great
Britain." [17] In return the Irish Commons passed a resolution
to end all duties on British linen "during such times as it
shall continue to be lawful to export Irish linen cloth from
this kingdom to the West Indies." [18] This combination of
concessions and threats satisfied both parliaments and soon
afterward resulted in a mutually beneficial settlement. An-

---

[13] Irish Statutes, 2 Anne, c. 2; 4 Anne, c. 4.

[14] Irish Statute, 8 Anne, c. 2.

[15] *English Commons' Journal*, Mar. 12, 1710/11.

[16] Irish Statute, 6 George I, c. 4, par. 6.

[17] English Statute, 3 George I, c. 21; see also *English Commons' Journal*, Apr. 4, 5, May 11, 1711.

[18] *Irish Commons' Journal*, Oct. 20, 1717.

other duel between the two parliaments ended in their can-
celing out each other. In 1745 the Irish parliament voted a
subsidy on exported sailcloth, which, by reducing the price
of exported Irish sailcloth, threatened the British linen industry. Five years later the British parliament retaliated by
placing a duty on Irish sailcloth equal to the Irish subsidy.[19]
Thus, in effect, the government, rather than antagonizing
either the Dublin or Westminster legislatures, approved contradictory measures by both bodies. The incident well illustrates the British administration's desire to placate conflicting
interests in the two countries.

In dealing with the British government the Irish parliament possessed a negative power the importance of which
can easily be overlooked: the right to delay or refuse government bills they disliked. For instance, London's repeated
efforts to get effective Irish legislation against smuggling never
met with complete success. It is true that the Irish parliament
did pass a series of acts to prevent the running of illegal imports but these laws met with delays and proved neither as
comprehensive nor as severe as their British counterparts. It
is more significant that the Irish parliament never enacted a
single law against wool smugglers. Furthermore, Irish courts
frequently refused to convict persons accused of violating the
English Woolens Act or to protect officials who attempted to
enforce its provisions.[20]

Irish economic legislation followed, in general, conventional
mercantilist lines: it included laws establishing high duties
on imported luxuries,[21] a tax on pensions paid to nonresi-

[19] Irish Statute, 19 George II, c. 6; English Statute, 23 George II, c. 33.
sect. 1.

[20] F. G. James, "Irish Smuggling in the Eighteenth Century," *Irish Historical Studies*, XII (1960–1961), 312; Matthew O'Conor, *History of Irish
Catholics from the Settlement of 1691* (Dublin, 1813), p. 149. Estimates of
the value of smuggled woolen exports to Portugal range from £40,000 to
£87,000 per annum. *Diary of Viscount Percival*, I, 130, II, 113.

[21] For example, Irish Statute, 6 George I, c. 14, par. 7, placed an additional duty of 12d. per pound on tea and 3d. per pound on coffee and
chocolate. Irish Statute, 3 George II, c. 3, placed duties on cards, dice,
coaches, and so forth.

dents,[22] a law to prohibit the burial of the dead in anything except domestic woolens.[23] A number of statutes laid down standards for maintaining the quality of exports.[24] There were likewise many acts designed to encourage or regulate domestic industries and agriculture. Most notable among these was legislation to foster the linen industry, but there were numerous others.[25] The Tillage Act and similar measures encouraged the draining of bogs and the increase of arable land.[26] Parliament passed several acts providing subsidies to entrepreneurs engaged in establishing new industries such as gunpowder,[27] silk manufacture,[28] and coal mining.[29] A series of laws granted government funds to improve navigation on waterways such as the Shannon and the Liffey, as well as for the improvement of harbors.[30] Under parliamentary pressure the lord lieutenants were induced to persuade the crown to give a grant to the Dublin Society for the encouragement of arts and manufactures.

In view of the predominance of the landed interests in the Dublin parliament it is not surprising that much of the regulatory legislation displays a suspicion of commercial business and a concern for consumers. In Anne's reign a series of

[22] Irish Statute, 2 George I, c. 3.

[23] Irish Statute, 7 George II, c. 13. This law was passed when criticism of foreign luxuries was at its height.

[24] Irish Statutes, 2 Anne, c. 15; 6 Anne, c. 12; 2 George I, c. 16; 4 George I, c. 12; 8 George I, c. 7; 10 George I, c. 9; 7 George II, c. 9; 12 George II, c. 5; 13 George II, c. 12; 21 George II, c. 7; 19 George II, c. 8. The *Dublin Evening Post* for Dec. 20, 1735, reported the seizure of forty carcasses of beef in Cork and their being brought before the Cork exchange. It remarked that "If our magistrates did not keep a watchful eye on some who trade to France such Beef would be shipped off as would be a scandal to the nation."

[25] Gill, *Rise of the Irish Linen Industry*, pp. 61–82.

[26] Irish Statutes, 2 George I, c. 12; 1 George II, c. 10, par. 7; 5 George II, c. 9.

[27] *Irish Commons' Journal*, Sept. 30, Oct. 1, 12, 1723.

[28] *Ibid.*, Nov. 25, Dec. 8, 1725; Irish Statute, 27 George II, c. 1, par. 14; Maxwell, *Dublin under the Georges*, p. 254.

[29] *Irish Commons' Journal*, Oct. 5, 13, 1721; Oct. 9, 12, 1723; see also O'Brien, *Economic History of Ireland*, pp. 159–161.

[30] Irish Statutes, 3 George II, c. 3; 23 George II, c. 5; 25 George II, c. 10; 29 George II, c. 10.

laws sought to prevent the establishment of monopolies for the control of coal imports [31] and during the same reign a stiff law was passed to limit the attempts of butchers to manipulate cattle prices.[32] Three successive acts in 1703, 1715, and 1731 set the legal interest rate in Ireland at 8, 7, and 6 percent, respectively.[33] When one views the legislation of the period as a whole, he finds that the Irish parliament sought to regulate the national economy in much the same fashion as did the British legislature during the early eighteenth century. Irish "mercantilism" cannot be considered either as complete or as effective as that practiced by Britain, yet its aims and methods were very similar.

The character of the British and Irish legislation that regulated the Irish economy in the early eighteenth century can be determined by reference to the statute books; the effects of the system, if such it can be called, are far more difficult to evaluate. Did Ireland prosper or not during the period, and to what degree can its growth or decline be attributed to government regulations? One body of evidence is available: the official figures for legitimate overseas trade. Although the monetary values given by customs officials to imports and exports may be questioned, they were supposedly based on actual prices; certainly the customs figures do offer a reasonably accurate index of the volume of trade.[34] The following tables illustrate the principal changes in the size and distribution of Irish trade between 1700 and 1765.[35]

Three conclusions may be drawn from the figures below: Irish trade grew rapidly; from 1710 on Ireland enjoyed a

[31] Irish Statutes, 4 Anne, c. 8; 6 Anne, c. 12; 11 Anne, c. 4.

[32] Irish Statutes, 2 Anne, c. 15; 9 Anne, c. 7.

[33] Irish Statutes, 2 Anne, c. 16; 10 George I, c. 13; 6 George II, c. 7.

[34] Thomas Prior commended the accuracy of the customs valuations, saying that the officials "made it their business to be well informed by merchants and other dealers of the current rates of commodities both at home and abroad." *A List of the Absentees of Ireland and the Yearly Value of their Income Spent Abroad*, 2nd ed. (Dublin, 1729), p. 45.

[35] These figures are from "Value of Trade of Ireland 1698–1767," examined by John Wetheral, in the Irish National Library. The figures are for the year from Dec. 25 to Dec. 25 before 1710 and for the year Mar. 25 to Mar. 25 thereafter. Similar figures for the years 1750–1751 and 1760–1761 are to be found in Newenham, *View of Ireland*, Appendix XII.

Table 1   Irish imports (in thousands of pounds) for each fifth year,
1700–1765

Year Ending	From Great Britain	From British colonies	From foreign sources	Totals
Dec. 25, 1700	428		364	792
Dec. 25, 1705	348		150	498
Mar. 25, 1711	377		294	671
Mar. 25, 1716	529		394	873
Mar. 25, 1721	404		279	683
Mar. 25, 1726	541		349	890
Mar. 25, 1731	453		326	779
Mar. 25, 1736	630	37 [a]	369	1,036
Mar. 25, 1741	583	69	252	904
Mar. 25, 1746	961	44	224	1,229
Mar. 25, 1751	1,026	86	481	1,593
Mar. 25, 1756	913	93	412	1,418
Mar. 25, 1761	1,097	69	362	1,528
Mar. 25, 1766	1,602	82	606	2,290

[a] Importation from the British colonies illegal until after 1731.

Table 2   Irish exports (in thousands of pounds) for each fifth year,
1700–1765

Year ending	To Great Britain	To British colonies	To foreign countries	Totals
Dec. 25, 1700	373	61	381	815
Dec. 25, 1705	296	42	179	517
Mar. 25, 1711	358	74	446	878
Mar. 25, 1716	509	107	452	1,068
Mar. 25, 1721	374	89	397	860
Mar. 25, 1726	478	104	445	1,027
Mar. 25, 1731	449	127	467	1,043
Mar. 25, 1736	657	116	421	1,194
Mar. 25, 1741	729	136	343	1,208
Mar. 25, 1746	901	86	391	1,278
Mar. 25, 1751	1,230	155	583	1,969
Mar. 25, 1756	1,147	174	498	1,820
Mar. 25, 1761	1,494	236	515	2,245
Mar. 25, 1766	2,083	246	465	2,794

favorable balance of trade; the relative importance of Britain to Irish trade increased significantly. To be more specific, Irish imports tripled, and Irish exports quadrupled between 1700 and 1765, with much of the increase being accounted for by the expansion of Irish-British commerce.

Undoubtedly the most outstanding of these three features of Irish trade during the period was its rate of growth, which was more rapid than that of Britain itself.[36] This remarkable increase can be attributed to several causes. First of all, however unreasonable the Cattle Act of 1667 may have been, it led not to disaster but to the development of a new industry, the processing of meat products. It will be recalled that the Navigation Act of 1663 did include one concession to the Irish: it permitted them to ship directly to the colonies servants, provisions, and horses. Within a few decades Ireland had turned from sending live cattle to England to shipping salt beef, salt pork, butter, and some cheese to the British American colonies and also in increasing amounts to continental Europe and the American colonies of the continental powers. By 1700 the provision trade had made cattle raising the most important agricultural activity of southern Ireland and meat processing, centered particularly in Cork, the key industry of the region. By 1776 Arthur Young estimated that Cork had a population of 76,000, plus 20,000 seasonal workers.[37]

Another Irish industry that grew impressively in the early eighteenth century was that of linen manufacture, concen-

---

[36] British imports jumped from £5,796,000 in 1701 to £12,419,000 in 1761; British exports from £6,241,000 to £12,873,000. B. R. Mitchell and Phyllis Deane, *Abstract of British Historical Statistics* (Cambridge, Cambridge University Press, 1962), pp. 279–280.

[37] *Arthur Young's Tour in Ireland*, ed. Arthur W. Hutton, 2 vols. (London, 1892), I, 333. Young says there were 700 coopers in Cork, which gives some indication of the size of the packing industry. Limerick, Waterford, and Dublin were also centers of the provision trade. Cullen, *Anglo-Irish Trade 1660–1800*, pp. 11–12. It is noteworthy that in 1775 neither Philadelphia nor New York had a population of much over 20,000. Stella H. Sutherland, *Population in Colonial America* (New York, Columbia University Press, 1936), p. 271.

trated largely in Dublin and the northeast. The Irish linen trade has been extensively studied but one factor contributing to its prosperity is often overlooked. As a result of the British act of 1731, permitting the Irish to import unenumerated articles from the colonies, Irish flax growers found a cheap source for flaxseed in the Middle Atlantic colonies, especially Pennsylvania. By the 1760's Ireland imported an annual average of 26,000 hogsheads of flaxseed (out of a total of 31,000) from the American colonies.[38]

Although the expansion of both the provision and linen industries, especially the latter, has been recognized by writers on Irish history, the impact of their growth has often been discounted. The figures for their expansion go far toward explaining the jump in Irish exports. Exports of Irish salt beef, salt pork, and butter nearly tripled between 1700 and 1765; those of linen yarn more than tripled; while exports of Irish linen cloth were eight times as large in 1760 as in 1710.[39] Most of the linen products went to Britain, though some were reexported. On the other hand, Irish provisions were excluded from Britain until the Seven Years' War, and even after that remained relatively unimportant for a number of years. According to customs records for the four years ending with 1768, 74,000 of an average of 193,000 barrels of beef exported from Ireland went to the British plantations and nearly 72,000 to France and its colonies. Out of an average of 43,000 barrels of pork shipped, 28,000 were destined for the British plantations while Spain and Portugal combined ran second with 4,000 barrels. The largest importers of Irish butter were the Baltic countries and Germany, which together took 74,000 hundredweight compared with 45,000 shipped to the British colonies.[40]

Probably one reason historians have concentrated on Ire-

[38] F. G. James, "Irish Colonial Trade in the Eighteenth Century," *William and Mary Quarterly*, 3rd ser., XX (1963), 581–582.

[39] O'Brien, *Economic History of Ireland*, pp. 202–203, 222.

[40] "Customs Abstract 1764–1773," National Library of Ireland, MS. 353. For figures on Irish provision trade with Great Britain after 1760, see Cullen, *Anglo-Irish Trade 1660–1800*, Table 17, p. 70.

land's exploitation rather than on its growing trade stems from their indignation over the injustice of the Woolens Act. That law was intended to eliminate Irish competition with Britain in woolens and also to stop the exportation of Irish wool to Britain's continental competitors. As regards Irish exportation of woolen cloth the act seems to have proved effective. As a result Irish woolen manufacture was undoubtedly checked; yet, as William O'Sullivan points out, loss of the export market did not mean the complete ruin of the industry since the domestic market, which had always consumed most of the product, remained and in fact expanded.[41] It was not until after 1750 that cheap English woolens could compete effectively in the Irish market.[42]

Two other factors partially reduced the harm done by the Woolens Act: Irish evasion of the law and minor British modifications of its restrictions. The prohibition against shipping Irish wool to foreign countries proved extremely difficult to enforce. Although it is impossible to estimate the extent of wool smuggling, or "owling" as it was called in both England and Ireland, there is little doubt that substantial amounts of raw wool were carried illegally over the channel from the small harbors of the south coast, chiefly to France. As in New England, respectable merchants and even officials acted in collusion with the smugglers. At least one member of the Irish Commons, a large landowner in County Cork, appears regularly to have sold his wool in France.[43] The British revisions of the Woolens Act have already been mentioned: the removal of duties on imported Irish wool yarn and the increase in the number of British ports open to Irish wool imports. Irish exports of both yarn and raw wool subsequently

[41] William O'Sullivan, *The Economic History of Cork City from the Earliest Times to the Act of Union* (Cork, 1937), p. 195; cf. Murray, *Relations between England and Ireland*, p. 70.

[42] Ralph Davis, "English Foreign Trade, 1700–1774," *Economic History Review*, 2nd ser., XV (1962), 291.

[43] James, "Irish Smuggling in the Eighteenth Century," p. 316. Cullen believes that the extent of wool smuggling to France has been exaggerated. *Anglo-Irish Trade 1600–1800*, p. 54.

increased, but only moderately.[44] Allowing for all of the above considerations it is still obvious that the Woolens Act did curtail Irish wool and woolen production. On the other hand, the effects of this check on the total Irish economy have been exaggerated. The resulting shift from sheep to cattle raising helped to facilitate the expansion of the provision trade. In Cork the weavers declined in importance, while the meat packers prospered.[45] Like the Cattle Act, the Woolens Act deflected rather than destroyed Irish economic development.

It is clear, then, that government regulation on the one hand caused the relative stagnation of the woolen industry and on the other fostered the growth of meat, dairy, and linen production. Its effects on other industries, most of which have never been carefully studied, affords a more confusing picture. The demands of the provision trade encouraged some exportation of salt herring. Meat processing also supplied two by-products that entered the export market, tallow and hides.[46] The British regulation concerning hides, in the form of export duties on English leather, stimulated another Irish processing industry, that of leather curing.[47] In contrast, a British law of 1746, forbidding the exportation of Irish glass, put a damper on the manufacture of Waterford, Cork, and Dublin glass.[48] The development or decline of a number of industries seems to have been largely determined by factors unconnected with

[44] Newenham, *View of Ireland*, Appendix IX.

[45] In 1732 and 1754 weavers in Cork demonstrated against their plight. F. H. Tuckey, *Cork Remembrancer* (Cork, 1837), pp. 128, 136. On the Cork provision and woolen industries, see O'Sullivan, *Economic History of Cork*, pp. 143–170, 192–196.

[46] O'Sullivan, *Economic History of Cork*, pp. 170–173. Cullen *Anglo-Irish Trade 1660–1800*, pp. 51, 69. Legislation to encourage fisheries was passed beginning in 1731; Irish Statutes, 7 George II, c. 11; George II, c. 4; 3 George III, c. 24.

[47] *English Commons' Journal*, Dec. 9, 16, 1718, Jan. 7, 28, Mar. 5, 1718/19. Apparently the Irish succeeded in underselling English leather, especially to Portugal. During the years 1743–1745 Cork exported an annual average of 18,000 hundredweight of tallow, 34,000 rawhides, and nearly 6,000 tanned hides, Charles Smith, *The Ancient and Present State of the County and City of Cork*, 2 vols. (Cork, 1893), II, 410.

[48] English Statute, 19 George II, c. 12, sect. 21; Maxwell, *Dublin under the Georges*, pp. 219–220.

either British or Irish governmental action. Prohibitive British duties on imported beer together with low Irish duties on beer certainly resulted in an increasing market for English beer in Ireland coupled with a decline in domestic brewing; yet the change can scarcely be considered significant since Irish brewers continued to supply 90 percent of the local demand in 1765.[49] If lack of protection had small effect on brewing, Irish protective duties appear to have done little to ensure the domestic market to Irish distillers. Production of spirits in legal Irish stills jumped threefold between 1700 and 1765 but so did the importation of foreign spirits, which provided over two-thirds of the demand throughout the period.[50] Irish silk manufacture, founded by Huguenot immigrants, though favored by the Irish parliament, declined in the face of foreign competition.[51] Growth of some luxury manufactures, such as coaches, pianos, furniture, clothing, and bookbinding, can be largely attributed to increased prosperity rather than protective tariffs. For example, the yield from a tax on coaches rose nearly 50 percent between 1748 and 1758.[52]

Whether Irish trade multiplied in spite of or because of government regulations, its growth undeniably indicates an expanding national economy, as does, on the surface, Ireland's

[49] O'Brien, *Economic History of Ireland*, pp. 210–211; Newenham, *View of Ireland*, Appendix XIII.

[50] Newenham, *View of Ireland*, Appendix XIII.

[51] O'Brien, *Economic History of Ireland*, pp. 208–209; Maxwell, *Dublin under the Georges*, p. 254.

[52] *Irish Commons' Journal* (1782 edition), VIII–IX, 23, 305; Maxwell, *Dublin under the Georges*, pp. 262–265. There is evidence of a number of other Irish industries. John Loveday mentions Dublin tapestries of "very lively" colors in *Diary of a Tour in 1732* (Edinburgh, 1890), p. 45. There were paper mills near Dublin (*Irish Commons' Journal*, July 21, Oct. 17, 1719), and some cotton manufacturing began in the early eighteenth century (O'Brien, *Economic History of Ireland*, pp. 207–208). Several Irish industries besides those mentioned above provided exports. For example, some soap was shipped to England (English P.R.O., Customs MS. 15/14, fols. 1–2); likewise some copper was exported to Liverpool (*Customs Letter-Books of the Port of Liverpool 1711–1813*, ed. Rupert C. Jarvis [Liverpool, Chetham Society, 1954], p. 32). Irish black marble was used in building St. Paul's in London. Irish P.R.O., "Calendar of Departmental Correspondence," I, 36; see also James, "Irish Colonial Trade," p. 579.

favorable balance of trade. Closer analysis, however, suggests that Ireland's trade balance may be evidence more of the nation's economic backwardness than of its advance. Great Britain's favorable balance, to be sure, represented a substantial increase in national wealth. British ships carried most of Britain's exports and imports, British merchants received the lion's share of the commissions earned in handling foreign trade transactions, while British obligations to foreign landlords and investors constituted only a fraction of the nation's balance of payments. Thus the country's surplus of exports over imports resulted in considerable capital accumulation, which in turn financed further development. In contrast, Ireland's favorable balance was consumed in large part by charges paid for shipping, by merchants' commissions, by interest on loans, and especially by rents paid to absentee landlords. As one writer put it, "What are our merchants but *French* and *Dutch* and *British* factors: unless in some little matters not worth their notice?"[53] In other words, Ireland's excess of exports over imports probably does not reflect a marked gain in capital; rather it means that the nation was paying for its invisible imports by selling its surplus products.[54]

It would be wrong, nonetheless, to conclude that Ireland's growing exports represent only an increasing tribute paid to Britain. Not all of the profits of expansion left the country. L. M. Cullen has shown that Irish merchants and bankers provided many of the services needed for foreign trade and thus received a share of commissions and shipping charges.[55] Furthermore, despite a widespread impression to the contrary, Irish shipping was far from nonexistent during the early eighteenth century. Table 3 shows that Irish tonnage accounted for a sizable portion of ships leaving Irish ports and that Irish tonnage increased during the period, though not as

[53] Daniel Webb, *An Inquiry into the Reasons for the Decay of Credit, Trade and Manufactures in Ireland* (Dublin, 1735), p. 17.

[54] British as well as Irish writers recognized this fact; see, e.g., Joshua Gee, *The Trade and Navigation of Great Britain Considered*, 2nd ed. (London, 1730), pp. 19–20.

[55] Cullen, *Anglo-Irish Trade 1660–1800*, pp. 158–170.

Table 3   Ship registry and tonnage of vessels using Irish ports
(figures to nearest 1,000)

Year	Irish	British	Foreign
1700	32,000	78,000	12,000
1710	23,000	82,000	20,000
1730	40,000	132,000	19,000
1740	34,000	117,000	41,000
1750	43,000	173,000	37,000
1770	64,000	311,000	26,000

Sources: The figures for 1700, 1730, 1750, and 1770 are from Cullen, *Anglo-Irish Trade 1660–1800*, p. 21, which, in turn, are from figures given in the Eng. P.R.O. Customs MSS. 15/4, 15/34, 15/54. The figures for 1710 and 1740 are taken directly from Customs MS. 15/14, fol. 47, and 15/44, fol. 44. Murray, *Relations between England and Ireland*, p. 78, states that after 1688 Irish tonnage decreased but she seems to be mistaken. As Sir Thomas Browne wrote in 1729, the Navigation Acts benefited Irish shipping. *Essay on Trade in General and on that of Ireland in Particular* (London, 1729), pp. 76, 81. In 1732 the Irish parliament passed an act regulating mariners and sailors in the merchant service. Irish Statute, 5 George II, c. 13. Much of the Irish trade of Glasgow was carried in Irish ships at the opening of the eighteenth century. T. C. Smout, *Scottish Trade 1660–1707* (Edinburgh, Oliver and Boyd, 1963), p. 180.

rapidly as British tonnage. Many Irish merchants prospered, and a few waxed rich through foreign trade.[56] The long-range balance of payments was favorable to Ireland; capital accumulated; Irish banks appeared and expanded, even though some failed.[57] Another indication of an increase in the amount

[56] English merchants tended to dominate Anglo-Irish trade but Irish merchants handled much of Ireland's trade with Europe and America. Cullen, *Anglo-Irish Trade 1660–1800*, pp. 97–98. Browne implies that much of Ireland's trade was in the hands of Irish merchants. *Essay on Trade*, p. 58. In 1756 several Dublin merchants quickly found the money to outfit a privateer. *Dublin Evening Post*, Nov. 3, 1756. The *New York Evening Post* for Aug. 12, 1745, lists three privateers that had been fitted out in Dublin. Irish merchants also benefited from government contracts. See note 74, below.

[57] Cullen, *Anglo-Irish Trade 1660–1800*, pp. 189–204; O'Sullivan, *Economic History of Cork*, pp. 202–203; Eoin Kelly, *The Private Banks and Banking of Munster* (Cork, 1959), pp. 15–19. As early as Mar. 10, 1705, the Dublin *Flying Post and Postmaster* advertised an assurance company; on

of actual specie in Ireland is shown by the fact that in 1787–1788 the average yearly weight of plate assayed in Dublin was over three times what it had been during the years 1694–1700.[58]

The most reliable index of Ireland's economic development is found in the increasing imports that the country was able to afford. Table 1 shows that Irish imports in general kept pace with exports. Their threefold increase between 1700 and 1765 was substantially more rapid than that of population, which certainly did not more than double in the same years.[59] Thus per capita consumption of imports must have grown by at least 50 percent. Ireland's imports consisted primarily of consumers' goods such as clothing, furniture, coal, sugar, tobacco, tea, coffee, chocolate, fruits, wines, brandy, medicines, toys, laces, and silks.[60] If some of these represented luxuries bought only by the wealthy, the large amounts imported of commodiites like coal, sugar, tobacco, and textiles point to a wide distribution. In 1735 Dublin weavers became so incensed at women, even of the "meaner sort," wearing Indian silks and calicoes that they resorted to "squirting and throwing Acqua Fortis" on their growns and petticoats.[61] Between the 1690's and the 1760's the annual average of imported legal tobacco rose from 2,577,000 to 4,927,000 pounds [62] — a probable in-

---

July 7, 1709, it contained an advertisement offering "a great many thousands of pounds to be lent on real or personal security." In 1731 the Irish government was able to float a loan of £200,000 at 5 percent with little difficulty. Dorset to [Newcastle], Dublin, Nov. 15, 1731. Eng. P.R.O., S.P. 63/394, fol. 121.

[58] Maxwell, *Dublin under the Georges*, p. 261.

[59] On population, see introduction, above.

[60] For a list of imports from Great Britain, see Eng. P.R.O., Customs MSS. 15/14, fols. 16–21, and 15/54, fols. 14–19; see also list of imports not included in the Book of Rates for the years 1752–1759, *Irish Commons' Journal* (1782 ed.), vol. X–XI, 355. Contemporary writers stressed particularly the money spent on imports that might have been produced in Ireland. Dobbs, *Essay on Trade*, p. 43 (for years 1719–1727); *A List of Commodities Imported into Ireland. Being Such as May Either [be] Raised or Manufactured therein, together with their Yearly Value . . . for the years 1734, 1735, 1736* (pub. by the Dublin Society, Dublin, 1740).

[61] *Dublin Evening Post*, May 20–24, 1735.

[62] The figures for the five years 1693–1697 (inclusive) are given in *Irish Commons' Journal*, Dec. 2, 1698; those for 1763–1768 in "Customs Abstract 1764–1773," National Library of Ireland.

crease in per capita consumption from about 1.4 to 1.8 pounds. When one remembers that there was also extensive smuggling of tobacco, tea, wines, spirits, and a number of other items, it is evident that Irish consumption of luxuries and semi-luxuries reached impressive dimensions. Swift denounced Irish women as spendthrifts, while another contemporary declared categorically that "the great Bane of Ireland is luxury. The Pleasure and Indolence which attends it, viciates our Appetites, makes us love what we ought to hate." [63] Perhaps this criticism of the extravagance of the upper classes was justified, but their very extravagance proves their prosperity.

Further evidence of the nation's increasing wealth lies in the extensive new building that took place. Both Cork and Dublin witnessed the erection of government buildings, churches (Catholic as well as Protestant), and hospitals, in addition to many substantial residences.[64] In the rural areas the Anglo-Irish landed classes enlarged or rebuilt their country houses, while a number of market towns and ports experienced considerable growth.[65]

One of the principal causes for the building of new country estates was the increase of rents. According to Sir William Petty, Irish rents had amounted to a little less than £1,000,000 in the 1670's; a century later Arthur Young estimated them at £6,000,000.[66] William McNeill suggests that there is good reason to believe that rents doubled about every twenty to thirty years in the early eighteenth century, noting that in 1764 John Irwin wrote that they were then twice as high as they had been twenty-five years before.[67] Although the benefits

[63] Jonathan Swift, *A Proposal to the Ladies of Ireland* (Dublin, 1729); *An Inquiry into some of the Causes of the Ill Situation of the Affairs of Ireland* (Dublin, 1731), p. 36.

[64] Maxwell, *Dublin under the Georges*, pp. 56–65, 73–75; Smith, *Ancient and Present State of Cork*, pp. 377, 382–389, 400–401.

[65] *A Tour through Ireland in Several Entertaining Letters* (London, 1748), pp. 55–56, 152, 160–161, 171–172; Loveday, *Diary of a Tour in 1732*, pp. 29, 33, 35–36.

[66] Sir William Petty, *The Political Anatomy of Ireland* (London, 1691), p. 17; *Arthur Young's Tour in Ireland*, ed. Hutton, I, 15–16.

[67] William McNeill, "The Influence of the Potato on Irish History," unpub. diss., Cornell University, 1947, pp. 125–126.

of rising rents went largely to the landlords, they also brought advantages to long-term leaseholders. The increase in rents reflects, further, the expansion of the export trade and the growth of towns and is additional evidence of the country's burgeoning economy. It is also noteworthy that the proportion of rents going to absentee landlords appears to have been decreasing. In 1729 Thomas Prior estimated the annual rent of absentees at £389,800. A revision of Prior's work in 1769 put the figure at £632,200 — an increase of 62 percent in forty years. Since all rents must have risen by at least 100 percent (and possibly 200 percent) during the same period, the proportion of the national wealth siphoned off by absentees was almost certainly declining. One writer put the value of Irish rents in 1727 at £2,000,000, which would mean Prior's absentee rents represented about 19 percent of the total income from rent. Young placed the total rents at approximately £6,000,000 and the absentee rent in 1779 at £732,000, or only about 12 percent.[68] The total amount of money sent to Britain in rents could not have equaled more than a fraction of that expended by resident landlords on improvements, construction, and consumers' goods.

Another manifestation of Ireland's improved economic position was the state of government finances. During the first three decades of the eighteenth century government expenditures frequently outran income, and a national debt was contracted. After 1730 the situation changed so that by the middle of the century the Irish Exchequer enjoyed a surplus. Although excise and customs duties were raised during the earlier period to meet rising costs, mostly for military expenditures, the per capita tax burden was much lower than in Britain, and after 1730 taxes remained relatively fixed.[69] The rising government income can be largely attributed to the augmentation of customs and excise duties resulting from the

[68] Thomas Prior, *A List of the Absentees of Ireland*, 2nd ed., p. 19; *List of Absentees and an Estimate of the Yearly Value of their Incomes Spent Abroad* (Dublin, 1769); *Arthur Young's Tour in Ireland*, ed. Hutton, II, 15–16; Newenham, *View of Ireland*, p. 239.
[69] O'Brien, *Economic History of Ireland*, pp. 311–313.

growth of foreign and domestic trade. Although the increasing tax yield reflects expansion, the tax structure may help to account for some of the maldistribution of wealth in Ireland. Except for quitrents, the ruling landlord class, unlike their British cousins, avoided paying a land tax except for a brief period in the seventeenth century — convincing evidence of the preponderance of the landed over the commercial influence in the Irish Commons.[70] In the late seventeenth century the introduction of both a hearth tax and a poll tax constituted a burden on the poor.[71] Since, however, the poll tax lapsed in the early eighteenth century and paupers were exempt from the hearth tax, the principal share of taxes came from those classes which consumed dutiable and excisable goods, pre-sumably the better paid workers, the middle and the upper classes. To put it another way, once an individual rose above the subsistence level and could afford semiluxuries, he was called upon to shoulder a large proportion of the costs of government. One tax fell on all rural classes, the tithes paid to the established church, though even here the landlords came off lightest since pasture lands were legally exempt from the tithe during the early years of the century and were often evaded throughout the period.[72]

The next question to consider is how government expen-ditures affected the Irish economy. One drain on the country arose from the fact that the British ministry drew on the Irish treasury to pay pensions to a number of persons not resident in Ireland. This practice aroused much contemporary criti-cism, which has since been often repeated, but the total

[70] The "Abstracts of the hereditary revenue" for the years 1731–1732 put the income from quitrents at £63,697 for the year ending Mar. 25, 1732, and £63,619 for the year ending Mar. 25, 1733. This represented about 11 percent of the total annual income for each of those two years. The proportion was roughly the same for the four years ending Mar. 25, 1734, 1735, 1736, and 1737. *Irish Commons' Journal* (2nd ed., Dublin, 1763), VI, 218, 480, 704.

[71] R. V. Clarendon, *A Sketch of the Revenue and Finances of Ireland* (London, 1791), pp. 18, 29–36; *Irish Commons' Journal*, Feb. 24, 1703/04.

[72] O'Brien, *Economic History of Ireland*, pp. 143–147; *History of the Church of Ireland*, ed. Phillips, III, 218. The relevant Irish statute is 10 William III, c. 3.

amount of the pensions paid to absentees represented less than 4 percent of the Irish budget.[73] Their political importance far outweighs their economic significance.

A more serious problem is how to evaluate the economic effects of military expenditures. In view of the English abhorrence of a standing army the British government found Ireland a most convenient spot to station troops, and the Dublin parliament proved quite willing to vote taxes to support the dozen or so regiments normally stationed in Ireland. Without the army costs the hereditary income of the crown (voted during Charles II's reign) might have sufficed to support the Irish establishment, but, as it was, Britain counted on the Irish parliament to pay a sizable portion of its regular military expenses. Ireland thus played a fiscal role in imperial defense not shared by any other overseas territory. It will be recalled, however, that the Irish Commons felt that when regiments were transferred from Ireland to Britain or abroad the Irish Exchequer should cease paying for them. The Irish administration usually backed this position so that normally the Irish treasury only financed regiments actually resident in Ireland. This meant that most of the money spent for supplies and soldiers' pay remained in the country. Furthermore, the British government often bought, out of its own budget, provisions in Ireland to supply troops in places like Gibraltar and to victual the British fleets that put in at Cork and other Irish ports, especially Kinsale which served as a rendezvous for convoys.[74] All in all, it seems likely that the economic benefits derived from the military more than compensated for the burden involved.

The third characteristic of Irish trade noted above was the increasing proportion of exports sold to and imports bought

[73] Prior, *List of the Absentees of Ireland*, p. 17, estimates that four-fifths of the pensions went to absentees and puts the figure at £30,048 for 1727. Four-fifths seems high, but to the absentees must be added absent officeholders.

[74] *A Tour through Ireland in Several Entertaining Letters*, pp. 99–100. Six Irish merchants received £4,500 for supplying the Mediterranean fleet in 1744. Eng. P.R.O., S.P. 63/406, fol. 228. On supplies for Gibraltar, see S.P. 63/407, fol. 20; for the West Indies fleet, S.P. 63/409, fol. 30.

from Great Britain. The steady growth of Britain's share in Irish trade resulted in part from the advantages Britain gained from the restrictions imposed on Irish colonial and foreign commerce; in part it simply reflects the influences of geography and the strength of the British economy. The frequency of war during the period also contributed to the relative decline of Irish trade with the Continent, especially with France and Spain. British economic growth certainly stimulated Ireland, and the relaxation of British prohibitions against such Irish imports as meat products opened up new opportunities for the Irish, but at the expense of increased reliance upon Britain. It is paradoxical that after 1760 as Ireland achieved greater political autonomy its economic dependence upon Britain was to become more pronounced.

When one reviews the evidence regarding Irish trade and general economic activity, it becomes obvious that, despite Ireland's subordination to Britain, the country enjoyed a substantial advance in wealth between 1700 and 1760. Greater prosperity did not, unfortunately, eliminate poverty. Widespread use of consumers' goods cannot hide the fact that a significant proportion of the Irish population remained at the edge of subsistence. As one eighteenth-century writer put it, "twenty poor families, who never taste fresh meat, might be comfortably supplied for a whole year, with as much Beef and Butter as has been exported to purchase a Headdress for a lady. If this be the Effect of Trade, we shall be undone by trading." [75]

Fluctuations in the basic food supply proved a chronic difficulty. Both business crises, like the South Sea Bubble,[76] and crop failures, such as occurred in the late 1720's and in 1740–1741, resulted in economic dislocation and severe want — even famine.[77] The expansion of potato growing provided

[75] *Dublin Newsletter*, Feb. 2, 1736/37.

[76] James, *North Country Bishop*, p. 248.

[77] O'Brien, *Economic History of Ireland*, pp. 102–105; George Rye, *Considerations on Agriculture* (Dublin, 1730), pp. v–viii; *The Groans of Ireland* (Dublin, 1741), pp. 3–15; Michael Drake, "The Irish Demographic Crisis of 1740–41," *Historical Studies*, VI, ed. T. W. Moody (New York, 1968), 101–124.

one answer, since the yield per acre, in terms of food, was much higher than that of grain. Several writers, such as Archbishop King and George Rye, advocated the cultivation of potatoes. Rye estimated that, although the cost of improving bog land for most crops was too high to make the venture attractive, bogs could be drained, burned, and made suitable for potatoes at relatively low cost. Writing in 1730, he stated that within the past five years new methods of potato culture had led to fairly large-scale production as contrasted with the older methods characteristic of the usual small tract or "potato garden." Rye also pointed out the advantages of certain kinds of barley over wheat for cultivation in Ireland, remarking that books on English husbandry were often misleading when used as a guide for Irish farmers.[78] In the course of the next few decades improved methods of agriculture became more common in Ireland and resulted in some increases in production. The Tillage Act and other legislation that encouraged the draining of bog land, led to an extension of arable land. By the time Young visited Ireland in the 1770's he noted several areas where crop land produced high yields, although he found animal husbandry in general far superior to other types of farming.[79]

Contemporary descriptions of conditions in Ireland during the years 1700–1760 afford a conflicting picture which covers the whole spectrum of possibilities. The majority of writers had a propaganda motive which, if usually discernible, is not easy to discount quantitatively. The most famous Irish author of the period, Dean Swift, expressed himself with such exaggeration that one should disregard virtually any statistical statement he makes. Swift alleged, for example, that Ireland imported even its ale and potatoes and that its foreign trade consisted of little except the importation of French wine [80]

---

[78] Rye, *Considerations on Agriculture*, pp. xi–xii, 49–50.

[79] *Arthur Young's Tour in Ireland*, ed. Hutton, I, 87–88, 106, 110–111; II, 104–108.

[80] *A Short View of the State of Ireland* (1728), in *The Prose Works of Jonathan Swift*, ed. Davis, XII, 9. For a new evaluation of Swift, see Thomas J. Casey, Jr., "Jonathan Swift and Political Economic Thought in Ireland," unpub. diss., Tulane University, 1971.

— this at a time when Ireland's exports exceeded imports and
the country's trade had been increasing for over a decade. It
is amazing that Swift's comments on Ireland have been accepted almost literally by many scholars who, well knowing
his gift for Gargantuan satire, would never dream of crediting
his accuracy on any other subject. Yet it would be unwise to
pay no heed to Swift's denunciation of the economic plight
of Ireland. In the first place, what he wrote was widely
believed at the time; in the second place, he was a keen if
highly prejudiced observer. At the other extreme from Swift,
the glowing account of Irish prosperity found in James Eyre
Weeks and Henry Brooke is equally suspect. Weeks, for
example, stated in 1752 that Ireland had improved in industry, arts, and science "more than any nation under Heaven"
and spoke of the draining of a "vast quantity of boggs." [81] It
is highly probable that such writers stressed the economic
expansion of Ireland during the reign of George II to curry
favor with the government. Brooke, for instance, was a place-
man.[82] Other writers, like Arthur Dobbs, who made use of
customs figures, seem to have aimed at greater objectivity.
Their observations can be treated with more respect, yet even
here special pleading (in Dobbs's case for changes in the English
Navigation Acts) may well have influenced their selection of
evidence.[83]

Most historians have likewise approached the period with
some special thesis to prove. As J. C. Beckett has commented,
both Froude and Lecky searched the early eighteenth century
chiefly to discover how its history might provide insight into
the question of home rule which dominated the thinking of

[81] James Eyre Weeks, *A New Geography of Ireland*, 2nd ed. (Dublin,
1752), p. 37.

[82] Brooke, who had held a government post since 1746, wrote that "the
Trade of Ireland, however in former Times miserably restrained and
limited, hath in this happy Reign received considerable Enlargements."
An Essay on the Antient and Modern State of Ireland (Dublin, 1760),
p. 62. It should be noted, however, that both he and Weeks supported
the patriots, not the Castle, in the 1750's.

[83] Arthur Dobbs, *An Essay on the Trade and Improvement of Ireland*
(Dublin, 1729), pp. 6–9.

their own times.[84] O'Brien's extensive study, *The Economic History of Ireland in the Eighteenth Century*, bears a similar stamp. The author admits that he has written to show that the autonomy achieved by the Irish parliament in the 1780's directly brought about a prosperity that had previously evaded Ireland.[85] In dealing with the period before 1780 he constantly stresses the different ways in which British mercantilism all but ruined the Irish economy, with almost complete disregard, it should be added, for some of the statistics so meticulously provided by his own careful scholarship. It is obvious that these historians fail to escape partisan interpretations. From the standpoint of economic history, the question is not how just or unjust were British intentions, nor how valid the principles of mercantilism, but how to reconcile the convincing evidence of Ireland's economic expansion with the equally impressive testimony of the country's continuing problem of ever-present poverty. The answer is not easy to determine but one traditional assumption can be challenged.

Like the majority of contemporary writers, most historians have assumed that Ireland's primary agricultural need in the eighteenth century was to bring more land under cultivation, not only by reclaiming bogs but also by reducing the acreage devoted to pasture. O'Brien summarizes the tenets of this orthodox creed: "The two great divisions of agricultural activity are pasture and tillage. The whole agricultural state of a country depends on which is predominant; where tillage prevails, the population of the countryside tends to increase and the industry of the people is encouraged; on the other hand, when pasture predominates, large tracts are converted to grazing, and the human inhabitants are driven to extreme poverty or emigration." [86] The Tillage Act of 1727 was based on this assumption though its provisions, that five out of every hundred acres be employed for crops, were modest

[84] J. C. Beckett, "The Irish Parliament in the 18th Century," Belfast Natural History and Philosophical Society, *Proceedings*, 2nd ser., vol. IV (1955), 17.

[85] O'Brien, *Economic History of Ireland*, pp. 2–3.

[86] *Ibid.*, p. 107.

enough. Agitation for further legislation to encourage tillage continued, especially in times of poor harvest. In 1741 the author of *The Groans of Ireland* advocated an act offering bounties on domestic grains, similar to those provided by the English corn laws, as well as a system of storage granaries.[87] Finally in 1784, after the modification of Poynings' Law, the Irish parliament passed Foster's Corn Law, which established a system of bounties and protective tariffs.[88] By that time potato culture was also rapidly expanding. Thus by the close of the eighteenth century Irish food production achieved a level that should have removed all threat of famine. In the long run the results proved just the contrary. The growth of subsistence farming appears to have encouraged earlier marriages and large families so that, in what might be called a classic example of Malthusian economics, population increase outdistanced the food supply and eventually brought on the catastrophe of the 1840's.[89]

The problem of Irish agrarian distress in the early eighteenth

[87] *The Groans of Ireland*, pp. 4–15.

[88] The Irish parliament voted a bounty on exported grain in Anne's reign (Irish Statute, 6 Anne, c. 18) but this was to be paid only when the price of grain had reached an exceptionally low level: for example 14s. per quarter for wheat as contrasted with the English Corn Law which provided bounties when the price of wheat fell below 48s. per quarter. See Williams, *Whig Supremacy*, p. 106. An Irish act of 1759 paid bounties on grain brought from the interior to Dublin which encouraged flour milling. O'Brien, *Economic History of Ireland*, pp. 112–117. For legislation affecting grain bounties and for annual average grain imports and exports, see Newenham, *View of Ireland*, Appendix IV. Ireland exported some grain most years between 1704 and 1740 and again after 1776. Between 1740 and 1776 it normally imported grain and flour. In the late seventeenth century Ireland had shipped grain to relieve famine conditions in Scotland. Smout, *Scottish Trade 1660–1707*, p. 146. In 1770 Ireland supplied 14 percent for Scotland's imports, chiefly provisions. Henry Hamilton, *An Economic History of Scotland in the Eighteenth Century* (Oxford, Clarendon Press, 1963), p. 262.

[89] K. H. Connell, "Land and Population in Ireland 1780–1840," *Economic History Review*, 2nd ser., II (1949), 284–285, and "Some Unsettled Problems in English and Irish Population History 1750–1845," *Irish Historical Studies*, VII (1950–1951), 225–234. For a criticism of Connell's thesis regarding early marriages, see M. Drake, "Marriage and Population Growth in Ireland 1750–1845," *Economic History Review*, 2nd ser., XVI (1963), 301–313.

century cannot therefore be attributed to the imbalance between pasture and tillage. If land utilization in the twentieth century by independent landowners can be taken as an index, the proportion of land devoted to pasture in the early eighteenth century seems to represent a far healthier balance between the two than that which came to prevail after the enactment of grain bounties and protection. Intensive cultivation of land best suited to extensive agriculture simply represents the spread of marginal subsistence farming — in short, a less efficient utilization of land, labor, and capital.

The poverty that plagued Ireland arose not from unexploited resources but from the inequities of economic power, intensified by the fruits of conquest and rebellion. The system of land tenure seems to be at the root of the difficulty; the absence of any organized system of poor relief further intensified it. Many of the Irish peasants outside Ulster had only yearly leases and could not easily defend themselves against rack-renting. The number of this cottier class greatly increased after 1750.[90] Herein lies one explanation for the paradox of Ireland's economic history in the eighteenth century: the increase of national wealth accompanied by the persistence of widespread destitution. To understand Ireland's economic problems one must study its social structure.

[90] O'Brien, *Economic History of Ireland*, pp. 126–127; Constantia Maxwell, *Country and Town in Ireland*, rev. ed. (Dundalk, 1949), pp. 114–119; and on Ulster, Gill, *Rise of the Irish Linen Industry*, p. 29. L. M. Cullen challenges the traditional view on tenancy, holding that before 1750 tenants at will were not numerous. "Problems in the Interpretation of Eighteenth-Century Irish Economic History," *Transactions of the Royal Historical Society*, 5th ser., XVII (1967), 1–22.

IX

The Structure
of
Irish Society

From the standpoint of social change the central theme of Irish history before the eighteenth century was immigration. From the early Middle Ages Ireland had experienced a series of incursions by Danes, Scots, Normans, and English. Some of these intruders returned from where they came; many remained. Although one can pinpoint major invasions and migrations — the Viking expeditions of the ninth century, Strongbow and his henchmen in the twelfth, the Ulster plantation under James I, Cromwell's soldiers in the 1650's — many of these foreign settlers came singly or in small groups — Anglo-Norman soldiers and adventurers, English merchants, ecclesiastics, and officials, Scottish farmers, Huguenot and Palatine refugees. Thus Ireland can be considered a British colony in the sense of a home for colonists as well as in the sense of an underdeveloped area over which England established economic and political domination.

But Ireland differed from any other English colony in a variety of ways. First of all, the English penetration of Ireland began in the feudal period. Second, the Ireland that the English invaded already possessed a fairly large population with a relatively complex culture. Strongbow and his successors, if they resemble any of the European invaders of the New World, come far closer to the Spanish conquistadors than to the founders of Virginia or New England. Like the Spanish settlers in America, the Anglo-Norman colonists in Ireland established themselves as a ruling minority, subordinating and exploiting the indigenous population rather than driving it out or destroying it. In the end both sets of conquerors succeeded in large measure in superimposing their language and culture on the native population, while at the same time unconsciously absorbing many of the attributes of the people over whom they ruled. Although one can detect similarities between the Creole-Mestizo-Indian society of Latin America and that of Elizabethan Ireland, it is obvious that the civilization of Gaelic Ireland was far closer to that of its British invaders than was that of Mexico or Peru to the Spanish. In addition, the proximity of Ireland to Great Britain made for a much more intimate relationship between the metropolitan nation and the colony. One may, indeed, just as logically consider the English conquest of Ireland as a chapter in state building (that is, the unification of the British Isles) as in colonialism. Nevertheless eighteenth-century Ireland possessed many of the features of a colonial society. Instead of being integrated politically with Great Britain it remained a separate dominion governed by a viceroy; locally, power rested in the hands of a quasi-alien class of colonists; while the descendants of the original population continued to resist assimilation.

In 1700 Ireland clearly bore the stamp of the successive invasions and settlements that had characterized its history. As a result it presents a confused pattern of internal fissures and tensions. In terms of structure its society may be viewed from three different angles. Like most contemporary European countries it contained the traditional classes: a ruling landed aristocracy, both rural and urban middle classes, and a large lower class of tenants and laborers. It may likewise be broken down into religious groups: Anglicans, other Protestants (chiefly Presbyterians), and Roman Catholics. Finally it can be divided along ethnic-historical lines: Gaelic Irish, Old English (the pre-Reformation settlers), Anglo-Irish, Ulster Scots, in addition to some Welsh, as well as Huguenots, Palatine Germans, and other non-British elements.[1] The immi-

---

[1] For an excellent discussion of Tudor colonization, see D. B. Quinn, "Ireland and Sixteenth Century European Expansion," *Historical Studies*, I, ed. T. Desmond Williams (New York, 1958), 20–32. On Palatines, see R. H. Murray, *Revolutionary Ireland and Its Settlement* (London, 1911), pp. 359–361; Maxwell, *Country and Town in Ireland*, pp. 146–147. On Huguenots, see Maxwell, *Country and Town in Ireland*, pp. 147, 230, 240;

gration of Protestant aliens was encouraged by liberal naturalization laws.[2] To a degree the three divisions — economic,
religious, and ethnic — reinforced each other. The majority
of the landlords were Anglicans in religion and Anglo-Irish
in background; the lower classes consisted mostly of Catholics
of Gaelic extraction. Yet there were numerous exceptions to
these generalizations: Catholic and Presbyterian landlords at
one extreme and impoverished English, Scottish, and other
Protestant immigrants at the other.[3] The middle classes especially present a heterogeneous picture. Although the professional groups may largely have consisted of Anglo-Irish
Episcopalians, the mercantile and artisan elements included
many Catholics and Protestant Dissenters, while the yeomen
and other independent farming groups also possessed numerous non-Anglican members, especially Scottish Presbyterians
in Ulster.

Our knowledge of the masses who composed the base of the
social pyramid is incomplete and distorted, depending as it
must upon the evidence and opinions of their superiors. The
growth of humanitarianism in the eighteenth century brought
about increasing interest in the plight of the destitute, but
before 1750 few observers concerned themselves with the living

---

O'Sullivan, *Economic History of Cork*, pp. 119–120; and Grace Lawless
Lee, *The Huguenot Settlements in Ireland* (New York, 1936).

[2] George Hansard, *A Treatise on the Law Relating to Aliens and
Denization and Naturalization* (London, 1844), pp. 62–63, 208–209. The
basic Irish naturalization law, 14 and 15 Charles II, c. 13, was revived with
a few modifications in 1704. *Irish Commons' Journal*, Feb. 28, Mar. 4,
1703/04; Irish Statute, 2 Anne, c. 14.

[3] Dublin newspapers in the early eighteenth century contain many
advertisements for the recovery of army deserters. See, e.g., *The Flying
Post*, May 4, 1708, Jan. 16, Feb. 16, 1708/09; *The Dublin Journal*, Sept.
11, Nov. 3, 1733, Feb. 19, June 8, 1734. Presumably many of these deserters
remained in Ireland. Dublin, too, received its share of adventurers and
quacks. An advertisement in the *Dublin Evening Post*, Mar. 18, 1757
announced: "there is lately arrived in this city a gentleman from London,
of many years experience, who has an *infallible* and the most speedy
method ever found for curing THE VENEREAL DISEASE in all its
stages . . . The medicines he uses are extremely safe and pleasant, and
does [sic] not require the patient to alter his way of living (*tho' ever so
irregular*) nor to be confined."

conditions among the poor. Declamations on the poverty of Ireland by propagandists such as Swift or Berkeley are based in part upon firsthand knowledge, but they do not represent any careful study of the poor. Information is available to prove, nonetheless, that a significant proportion of the lower classes in Ireland lived very close to a marginal existence. There is some indication that conditions may have been improving. John Loveday (in the 1730's) and Arthur Young (in the 1770's) both thought so.[4] On the other hand, what appeared as a higher standard of living may really represent more a shift from pastoral to agrarian economy. David Beers Quinn observes that most English and Anglo-Irish commentators had little understanding of the older pastoral life of Gaelic Ireland.[5] Herdsmen who dwelt in temporary cabins and migrated with the seasons struck them as semibarbarous. It is likely that the life of these people was actually far more highly organized and less impoverished than it appeared to witnesses whose standards of judgment were derived from a society composed of established villages, fixed property rights, and permanent farms. Still, even many of the Irish peasants who engaged in settled agriculture lived in mean cottages with few outbuildings. In 1732 a traveler remarked that the roads near Dublin itself were lined with one-room "cabins." [6]

The prevailing type of tenure in Ireland was so insecure that it discouraged any efforts by the tenant to improve the land or its buildings. A further evil arose from the widespread custom of employing middlemen as estate agents, who in turn often subcontracted their job to subordinates. This practice was not confined to absentee landlords who lived in England, but was popular with many who preferred to live in Dublin or other towns. Tithe collecting, too, was often contracted in similar fashion.[7] Since most of the landlords and middlemen

[4] Loveday, *Diary of a Tour in 1732*, p. 58; *Arthur Young's Tour in Ireland*, ed. Hutton, II, 254–258.

[5] David Beers Quinn, *The Elizabethans and the Irish* (Ithaca, N.Y., 1966), pp. 36–38.

[6] Loveday, *Diary of a Tour in 1732*, pp. 27–28.

[7] Maxwell, *Country and Town in Ireland*, pp. 114–115, 172–173; *Arthur Young's Tour in Ireland*, ed. Hutton, II, 25–28.

were of Anglo-Irish background and Protestant religion, class divisions were accentuated by ethnic and religious prejudices, and often by a language barrier as well. Today Gaelic is normally spoken only in the west and parts of the south of Ireland; in the eighteenth century it appears to have served most of the peasants outside the old Pale and parts of Ulster.[8] The combination of economic exploitation and cultural alienation imposed a bitter yoke on many of the peasantry, a degradation that cannot be measured solely in monetary terms. As one native poet put it:

> 'Tis not the poverty I most detest
> Nor being down forever,
> But the insult that follows it
> Which no leech can cure.[9]

The absence of any system of public relief also made the plight of the poor more precarious than in England and the responsibility of the propertied classes less onerous. It benefited the landlord in another way. Knowing that he faced catastrophe if he lost his holding or his job, the Irish tenant or laborer proved ready to go to desperate lengths to hold on to his farm or his position. The system meant high rents and low wages. Dean Richard Woodward alleged in 1768 that many boasted of Ireland as an ideal place to hold land because the landlord could obtain the utmost profit yet abandon the laborer to perish when he was no longer able to work. With no poor rates to pay, the landlord enjoyed a complete exemption from the consequences of his callousness. Urging the adoption of a poor law, Woodward wrote: "A wise man would not glory in such an exemption, a good man would not claim it, and he who wishes to enjoy it, doth not deserve it." [10] Like

---

[8] Daniel Corkery, *The Hidden Ireland* (Dublin, 1925), pp. 7–8; R. A. Breatnach, "The End of a Tradition: A Survey of Eighteenth-century Gaelic Literature," *Studia Hibernica* (no. 1, 1961), pp. 128–150.

[9] Quoted by Corkery, *Hidden Ireland*, p. 9; see also *Arthur Young's Tour in Ireland*, ed. Hutton, II, 53–55.

[10] Richard Woodward, *Argument in Support of the Right of the Poor in Ireland to a National Provision* (Dublin, 1768), p. 18. Another English

many commentators, Woodward lay most of the blame on the absentees, noting that the middling sort of farmers gave much to charity.

Living conditions of the urban poor may well have been worse than those in rural areas. William O'Sullivan found that the poor shared little in the prosperity of Cork, while Constantia Maxwell's account of the poor in Dublin reveals appalling overcrowding.[11] Teeming Dublin, like London, attracted thousands from the countryside in search of new jobs and excitement. It probably had some of the worst slums in Europe. In the "Liberties" of the old city several families often shared a single room. While government regulations helped to keep down the price of bread, no effective steps were taken to regulate that of fuel; the poor apparently paid dearly for coal when they could afford it at all.[12] Figures on deaths in both Dublin and London for 1708 strongly suggest that the death rate was proportionately higher in the Irish than in the English capital.[13]

It is difficult to avoid agreeing with Corkery that if the eighteenth century saw hard times for the lower classes everywhere, they were probably worse in Ireland than in most places.[14] Yet there is some evidence to the contrary. With

---

observer, John Bush, agreed in *A Letter from a Gentleman in Dublin* (London, 1769), p. 31.

[11] O'Sullivan, *Economic History of Cork*, pp. 176–177; Maxwell, *Dublin under the Georges*, pp. 138–143.

[12] *Hints Relating to Some Laws that may be for the Interest of Ireland to have Enacted, in a Letter to a Member of Parliament* (Dublin, 1749), p. 16. The assize price for bread was regularly published in the newspapers. The key law was Irish Statute, 1 George II, c. 16.

[13] The Dublin *Flying Post and Postmaster*, Apr. 7, 1708, gave the number of baptisms reported for the previous year in London as 16,066, the number of deaths 21,600. In Dublin for the same year the baptisms stood at 1,415, the deaths at 2,585. Perhaps, however, the ratio of deaths to baptisms in Dublin indicates simply a larger influx from the country. Since London was probably not more than six or seven times the size of Dublin the death rate in Dublin may have been lower. In 1743 the ratio of deaths to baptisms was lower in Dublin. In that year Dublin recorded 1,517 baptisms and 2,193 deaths; London 15,050 baptisms, 25,200 deaths. *The Dublin Journal*, Jan. 7, 1743/44.

[14] Corkery's whole approach is questioned by L. M. Cullen, "The Hidden Ireland: Re-assessment," *Studia Hibernica* (no. 9, 1969), pp. 7–47.

lower prices for food in Ireland than in England, real wages may have been roughly comparable. Young believed that the diet of the Irish laborer (potatoes and milk products) offered more nourishment than the bread and beer available to his English counterpart and was more plentiful.[15] Some of Young's comments on France also suggest that the lot of the French peasant in many regions would compare unfavorably with that of the Irish. Though the term "slave" was employed to refer to the casual laborer in Ireland, he was no bondsman like the serfs of Eastern Europe or the slaves in the colonies. Insecurity may have made freedom meaningless for many, but opportunities to improve his position did exist. The meat packing industry in Cork, it will be recalled, gave part-time work to thousands at reasonably good wages. Seasonal labor in England also offered relatively high wages, while the growing affluence of the middle and upper classes increased the demand for servants.[16] Dublin had an employment agency for domestics by 1710.[17] Service trades, too, were expanding; in 1719 parliament approved the licensing of fifty more coaches and forty more sedan chairs in Dublin to meet the growing demand.[18] However precarious the life of the lower classes appears, the increase in population in the eighteenth century is proof of a rise in the chance of subsistence and probably of at least a temporary rise in the standard of living as well.

One must also not overemphasize the disadvantages suffered by the lower classes because of their Gaelic culture and Catholic religion. William McNeill writes:

The Wild Irish driven to subsist upon the potato could work more cheaply for the new landowners than English or Scottish settlers were willing to do: hence they prevailed demographically but at the price of a miserable economic bondage to a culturally alien aristocracy. Although the legal form differed, the social pattern of eighteenth-century Ireland resembled

[15] *Arthur Young's Tour in Ireland*, ed. Hutton, II, 45.
[16] Dorothy George, *London Life in the 18th Century* (London, K. Paul, Trench, Trubner & Co., 1925), pp. 111–125.
[17] *Flying Post and Postmaster*, Dec. 13, 1710.
[18] Irish Statute, 6 George I, c. 15.

that of eastern Europe and the southern colonies of North America in being sharply polarized between a privileged body of landowners who shared in European civilization and a culturally deprived, psychologically alienated mass of agricultural laborers.[19]

While McNeill's comments on the cultural alienation of the peasant are perceptive, on two points his interpretation appears exaggerated: he discounts the European character of Gaelic culture, and he assumes that had it not been for the potato immigrant labor would have driven out the original inhabitants. It is evident that the potato, which did not come into common use before the middle of the seventeenth century, cannot account for the failure of English colonization schemes under Mary or Elizabeth, or for the slowness of British colonization in Ulster.[20] Although the English professed the hope of transforming Ireland by planting Protestant settlers, this program never seems to have had much chance except to a limited degree in Ulster. In a conquered area with a large indigenous population the dispossessed natives naturally offer a cheap labor supply. The new English and Scottish landowners in Ireland simply followed economic advantage in employing Irish labor and in renting to Irish tenants rather than to immigrants. Under the circumstances the natives generally outnumbered the invaders and usually retained their language and customs, as had many Welsh peasants under somewhat similar conditions. By 1700 the Anglo-Irish accepted the Gaelic peasant as part of the social system.

The conversion of all Ireland to Protestantism remained the official policy of the government; its fulfillment lay completely outside the realm of probability. The charity school

[19] William McNeill, *The Rise of the West* (Chicago, University of Chicago Press, 1963), p. 664; see also his "Influence of the Potato on Irish History," p. 69.

[20] McNeill, "Influence of the Potato on Irish History," p. 70. McNeill stresses the fact that in Ulster, before potato culture had become common, the native Irish were easily expelled by the settlers from Britain, but this was scarcely true. See Moody, *The Londonderry Plantation 1609–41*, pp. 185, 319–335.

movement of the 1730's and 1740's represented the only serious attempt to Anglicize the native lower classes. The objective of the schools was to provide a means whereby the children of the Catholic poor might "be instructed in the Established Religion and taught to read the Holy Scripture in the English Tongue" and "to be early inured to a laborer's way of life in the improvement of husbandry, gardening and linen manufactures." [21] The Protestant exclusiveness of the project doomed it to failure; the hold of the Catholic faith on the Irish masses was, indeed, growing stronger.[22] The penal laws were primarily aimed at the propertied classes; lower-class Catholics suffered few disabilities beyond the burden of contributing to the established church through tithes. In much of rural Ireland the "mass houses" constituted the only church available. Religious festivals offered numerous holidays; marriage celebrations and funerals provided breaks in the monotony of workaday life. The Irish peasant could, in effect, carry on most of his traditional religious and social customs without interference — provided he could eke out a living. He even discovered ways to compensate for the handicaps inherent in his position. Although low liquor taxes and widespread illicit distilling created a serious social problem, it is unlikely that cheap "usquebah" struck the peasant as an unmitigated evil. His livelihood may have been insecure, yet he did not spend all his days in drudgery. Most travelers agree that the "wild Irish" possessed many likable qualities — loyalty, courage, hospitality, cheerfulness — that not only bear testimony to their intrepid spirit but seem incompatible with a life of total exploitation.[23] The very indolence so often complained of by

[21] The Dublin *Weekly Miscellany*, Apr. 25, 1734.

[22] Mary Gwladys Jones, *The Charity School Movement, A Study of Eighteenth Century Puritanism in Action* (Cambridge, 1938), pp. 222–238, 384–385. Archbishop Boulter, writing to Newcastle, Mar. 7, 1727/28, remarked that "the descendants of many of Cromwell's officers and soldiers have been going off to popery." Eng. P.R.O., S.P. 63/390, fol. 35; see also *First Report of the Commissioners of Inquiry on Education in Ireland*, British Sessional Papers, Session 1825, XII, 5–8.

[23] Eachard, *An Exact Description of Ireland*, p. 16; Guy Miege, *The Present State of His Majesty's Dominion of Ireland* (London, 1717), p. 4.

observers shows that the Irishman had learned to take some of the reward for his labor in leisure since he could collect so little in cash. A comparison of sixteenth-century with eighteenth-century accounts also suggests that, though many of the characteristics of the Irish peasantry had changed little, the standards of sexual morality and the stability of family life had been raised markedly, testimony both to the increased influence of the Catholic Church and to a more settled way of existence.[24]

One other factor mitigating the lot of the poor was the concern and generosity of at least some of the governing class. Lord Chesterfield warned his successor of the need to be "as much upon your guard against poverty as against Popery, — take my word for it, you are more in danger of the former than the latter."[25] Others shared his view and sought to ameliorate conditions. A number of landlords attempted to improve both their lands and the life of their tenants. Among them were even some absentees such as viscount Percival and the earl of Shelburne.[26] Private charity likewise did something to alleviate want, especially in times of famine. It was, apparently, a widespread custom to collect alms regularly in parish churches.[27] Henry Brooke listed nine different hospitals in Dublin in 1760, remarking that "we may without any Risque . . . pronounce Dublin to be as charitable a metropolis as any in the known world."[28] According to the *Dublin Newsletter*, one of these institutions, the Mercers' Charitable Hospital in Stephen Street (which served primarily the poor) took in 162 patients during the year 1735–1736 and treated 1,082 out-patients.[29]

[24] Quinn, *Elizabethans and the Irish*, pp. 80–82.

[25] Thomas Campbell Foster, *Letters on the Condition of the People of Ireland*, 2nd ed. (London, 1847), p. 299.

[26] *Diary of Viscount Percival*, II, 173–174; Maxwell, *Country and Town in Ireland*, p. 192.

[27] Loveday, *Diary of a Tour in 1732*, p. 57; *A Tour through Ireland in Several Entertaining Letters*, pp. 163–164.

[28] Henry Brooke, *An Essay on the Antient and Modern State of Ireland* (Dublin and London, 1760), p. 52.

[29] *Dublin Newsletter*, Feb. 19, 1736/37. For the period Mar. 25, 1745,

Although parliament never enacted a poor law it established workhouses in Dublin and Cork and took other steps to assist the destitute.[30] It will be recalled that the very poor were exempted from the hearth tax; certain other tax laws reveal a similar discrimination in their favor. An excise act of Charles II's reign levied a tax of 25s.6d a barrel on beer and ale worth 6s. or more but only 6d. on barrels of cheaper brews,[31] a measure indicating that in the late seventeenth century some beer was available for as little as a few pennies a gallon.

Legislation regulating labor, if obviously class oriented, was not exclusively for the benefit of employers. In 1706 parliament enacted a law for the relief of poor debtors that freed all who could show they had less than 5 £ worth of property.[32] An act in Anne's reign provided a method for recovering wages withheld from a worker, and an act early in George II's time sought to help hackneymen to collect their fares.[33] It is true that a law in 1749 forbade combinations of labor but its passage arose partly from the strength of skilled labor, which appears to have been in short supply in many crafts.[34] To remedy this shortage a series of laws attempted to encourage the training of linen workers while the charity school movement, encouraged by parliament, also sought to provide skills as well as Protestant education for the lower classes.[35] It is clear that economic opportunities were made available to the underprivileged, especially to those who proved willing to

---

to July 1, 1746, the Dublin Lying-in Hospital for poor women in George's Lane reported that out of 209 women admitted, 204 had been delivered of 208 babies, of which 190 babies "all very well," and 191 mothers had been discharged. This was a very good record for the eighteenth century. *The Dublin Journal*, July 8, 1746. This was the first maternity hospital in the British Isles. Maxwell, *Dublin under the Georges*, p. 166.

[30] Irish Statutes, 2 Anne, c. 19; 1 George II, c. 27; 9 George II, c. 25. See George Nicholls, *A History of the Irish Poor Law* (London, 1856), pp. 35–49.

[31] Irish Statute, 14 Charles II, c. 8, secs. 2, 3.

[32] Irish Statute, 4 Anne, c. 13; see also 6 George 1, c. 17.

[33] Irish Statutes, 6 Anne, c. 13; 2 George I, c. 17.

[34] *Irish Commons' Journal*, Dec. 22, 1749; see also Maxwell, *Dublin under the Georges*, pp. 230–233.

[35] Gill, *Rise of the Irish Linen Industry*, pp. 75–76.

conform to the religious and social system of the ruling classes. As for the middle classes, the urban elements at least were expanding. The rapid growth of Irish trade and of such native industries as meat-packing and linen manufacturing and the increased size of towns like Dublin, Cork, and Belfast all point to this conclusion. The increase in imports attests to their rising standard of living. Some of the new bourgeoisie came from Britain, and a number were Huguenots, but most appear to have been born in Ireland. Native-born Protestants faced no barriers: men like Henry Lucas, for example, could enter guilds, hold office, and take full advantage of new economic opportunities. What of the Catholics? What chance did they have? Religious and ethnic groups which for one reason or another find themselves excluded from profitable agriculture often turn successfully to trade. The Jews in parts of Europe, the East Indians in East and South Africa, and the Chinese in the Malay Peninsula come to mind as examples, as do the Scots in Britain itself. Was there any comparable movement among the Catholic Irish?

Like the landed Anglo-Irish, the Protestant middle classes in the towns sought to stifle all competition from Catholic interlopers. They engineered acts through parliament excluding Catholics from professions like the law and passed local ordinances to keep the guilds a Protestant monopoly. Earlier writers tended to accept these prohibitions as effective and thus assumed that Catholics seldom had the opportunity to become skilled craftsmen or successful merchants. There is considerable evidence that the anti-Catholic statutes and ordinances did not prove enforceable.[36] In 1757 all but five of the numerous bakers in Dublin were reportedly Catholic. In fact, if one can believe contemporary Protestant propaganda, Catholics threatened to dominate not only commerce but even trades and professions from which they were expressly excluded. Lord Wilmington told Viscount Percival that he sup-

---

[36] *Irish Commons' Journal*, Dec. 23, 1757; Maureen Wall, "The Rise of the Catholic Middle Class in Eighteenth-Century Ireland," *Irish Historical Studies*, XI (1958–1959), 91–115. For a different view, see Robert E. Burns, "Irish Popery Laws: A Study of Eighteenth-Century Legislation and Behavior," *Review of Politics*, XXIV (1962), 500–505.

ported a revision of the legislation against Catholic land ownership and long-term leases on the grounds that "the trade of Ireland is all in the hands of the Papists, who for want of liberty to purchase land in that kingdom carry their wealth elsewhere and have no tie to keep them good subjects." [37] Wilmington exaggerated, as Percival hastened to inform him, but it is clear that Catholics played an important role in Irish business. Indeed, according to *Faulkner's Dublin Journal*, two Dublin bankers, who were secretly Protestant, for years professed to be Catholics "on account of their business." [38]

Although in most towns Catholics were compelled to pay a special quarterage fee, these fees remained small and proved no real handicap.[39] Once the fees had been paid, Catholic townsmen enjoyed full economic privileges even if still denied all political rights. In Cork the provision trade expanded so rapidly that Protestants simply could not meet the demands. They complained about the Catholic competition, but had no alternative other than to accept it.[40] Similar conditions existed elsewhere. As with so many aspects of Irish life in the early eighteenth century, Protestants denounced Catholic initiative with alarm while at the same time they condoned it in practice. The fact that Ireland traded extensively with Catholic countries tended to encourage tolerance. In Waterford for over thirty years local merchants (presumably Protestant and Catholic alike) sought bills of health for their ships and cargoes from Catholic priests rather than Protestant magistrates, since officials in Spanish and Portuguese ports gave more credence to papers drawn up by the former.[41] While Dublin Castle made an effort to stop this particular practice, the government itself had employed a Catholic merchant from Sligo to carry

[37] *Diary of Viscount Percival*, I, 356.

[38] *The Dublin Journal*, Aug. 6, 1748.

[39] Maureen Wall MacGeehin, "The Catholics of the Towns and the Quarterage Dispute in Eighteenth-century Ireland," *Irish Historical Studies*, VIII (1952–1953), 91–114.

[40] O'Sullivan, *Economic History of Cork*, pp. 135–136.

[41] Carteret to Newcastle, Feb. 28, 1725/26, and Report of the Assize Judges to Lords Justices, May 25, 1726, Eng. P.R.O., S.P. 63/387, fols. 88, 206.

on negotiations with Madrid.[42] Some idea of the wealth of
the Catholics in Anne's reign can be estimated from the outcome of the 1704 law requiring that all registered priests find
two persons each of whom must put up £50 security for their
good behavior. Following its enactment 1,089 priests registered;[43] if the terms of the law were respected the Catholic
community must have provided over a million pounds as
security.

All government appointments and certain occupations were
legally closed to Catholics. It was fairly easy to keep Catholic
sympathizers out of higher government posts, not as easy to
exclude them from lesser positions, and extremely difficult to
control the private business and professional activities of
Papists. Despite restrictions and avowed government hostility
there appears to have been a large enough contingent of Catholic printers to provide an underground Catholic press.[44]
When it came to the legal profession Protestants found legislation quite ineffective. In 1728 Archbishop Boulter alleged
that:

The practice of the law from the top to the bottom, is at
present mostly in the hands of new converts who give no
further security of the reality of their conversion on this acc't
than purchasing a certificate of their having received the
sacrament in the Church of England or Ireland, which several
of them, who were Papists in London, obtain on the road
hither and demand to be admitted, barristers in virtue of it
on their arrival; and several of them have popish wives, and
mass said in their houses and breed up their children papists.
Things are at present so bad with us, that if about 6 Protestants should be removed from the bar to the Bench, there
would not be a Barrister of note left that is not a convert.[45]

[42] Edward Southwell to ?, Apr. 23, 1712, Irish P.R.O., Calendar of
Departmental Correspondence 1683–1714, p. 245.
[43] Wall, *The Penal Laws, 1691–1760*, p. 18.
[44] George Dodington to Joshua Dawson, Dec. 7, 1708, Irish P.R.O.,
Calendar of Departmental Correspondence 1683–1714, p. 126.
[45] Boulter to Newcastle, Mar. 7, 1727/28, Eng. P.R.O., S.P. 63/390,
fol. 35.

Since Boulter's statement was written in support of a bill to prevent converts from practicing, one must discount his statement. It is possible, nevertheless, that conditions approached those he described, and there is little evidence that the new bill (which passed) proved very effective.

The one area in which the penal laws came closest to proscribing Catholics effectively was that of land ownership. The forfeitures following the wars of 1689–1691 left Catholics with only a seventh of Irish land still in their hands. Subsequent laws prohibiting long-term leases to Catholics and controlling inheritance by them further reduced the number and influence of the remaining Catholic landed classes, and every attempt by dispossessed Catholics to recover their estates raised an outcry in the Dublin parliament. At the same time, economic as well as political pressures undermined the position of the smaller Catholic farmers, such as the "sculoags" (independent yeomen engaged in diversified agriculture).[46] Although enclosures for sheepwalks fell off after the Woolens Act of 1699, the demand for pasture increased as the meat and butter trade expanded so that by the middle of the eighteenth century much of the best land in Ireland had been taken over by large landowners for grazing purposes. Even as early as 1705 the Irish parliament estimated that the country contained some 26,000 landowners with 30 or more acres, not a large figure for a population of about 2,000,000.[47] On the other hand, the shift did not always mean the exclusion of substantial Catholic farmers. There is good evidence that some Protestants regularly leased tracts to Catholics whom they protected from prosecution.[48] Collusive evasion of the

[46] McNeill, "Influence of the Potato on Irish History," pp. 86, 136; Nicholas Taafe, *Observations on the Affairs of Ireland* (London, 1766), p. 12.

[47] Irish Statute, 4 Anne, c. 9, required all persons owning thirty acres to plant ten trees and "no other person or persons." Since the act speaks of 260,600 trees to be planted, it estimates that there were 26,060 landowners of 30 or more acres.

[48] Mrs. Morgan John O'Connell, *The Last Colonel of the Irish Brigade*, 2 vols. (London, 1872), I, 5–6; Sir James Caldwell alleged that one Catholic, Justin MacCarty, "merely by the number of Protestants that were his

penal laws could not be prevented. Though reduced in numbers it is clear that the middle sort of Catholic farmer did not disappear; in Connaught he still survived in significant numbers.[49] There is no denying, nevertheless, that Ireland's primary economic activity, agriculture, was largely under the control of Protestants. In Ulster this included many small Scottish farmers who supplemented their livelihood with linen manufacturing (or vice versa). Elsewhere the large Anglo-Irish landlord dominated the scene, along with his agents, "the middlemen," and a small group of Protestant yeomen farmers.

Under the pressure of hostile laws and policy a number of Catholic peers and gentry accepted Protestantism, but not all. In 1716 a number of peers summoned to parliament refused to take any oath other than one of allegiance. In response the Lords passed resolutions that peers who refused to abjure the Stuarts and to subscribe to the oaths contained in the Act to Prevent Popery should be denied the right of bearing a coronet or of using a title. The king of arms was instructed forthwith to "deface and erase such coronets" while any peer who disregarded the resolutions was to be deemed guilty of "a breach of privilege of the Peerage of the Kingdom."[50] It is doubtful if the resolutions proved fully effective. In dealing with the Catholic upper classes, as with the middle classes, the government appeared indecisive. For example, in accordance with the Treaty of Limerick some hundred or more loyal Catholics were licensed to "bear and carry arms," then a matter of personal honor and social status as well as safety. Although in 1714 all existing licenses were revoked, a new and somewhat longer list of licenses was immediately issued.[51] Apparently the prestige and reputation of some of the Cath-

---

debtors . . . effectually prevented them from putting any of the Popish Laws in Execution." *Brief Examination of the Question whether . . . to pass an act to enable papists to take real securiteis etc.* (Dublin, 1764), p. 13.

[49] J. G. Simms, "Connacht in the Eighteenth Century," *Irish Historical Studies*, XI (1958–1959), 116–133.

[50] *Irish Lords' Journal*, June 16, 1716.

[51] *Ormonde MSS*, II, 475–480.

olic gentry assured official recognition of their social position; many more probably enjoyed unofficial recognition. In Connaught especially the Catholic landlords retained importance. This remaining Irish aristocracy enhanced its prestige by patronizing, and even on occasion producing, Gaelic bards and poets.[52]

Discussion of the penal laws brings up the question of the Roman clergy's position. Their treatment in the early eighteenth century illustrates perhaps more clearly than anything else the contradictory nature of the government's whole Catholic policy. The Irish penal laws were predicated on a mixture of reality and fiction. Recognizing the impossibility of denying any toleration to two-thirds or more of the population who adhered to the Roman faith, the 1704 law legalized the status of the secular clergy then serving in Ireland (the 1,089 registered priests mentioned above). This and other laws, however, forbade the entrance into Ireland not only of all regulars but also of any new secular priests. Since the laws also prohibited Catholic educational institutions and banished all Catholic bishops, they technically made it impossible for any of the tolerated priests to be replaced. The theory behind this legislation was that as the existing clergy died out so would the church, since it was hoped that the laity would be absorbed by the Church of Ireland.

It is doubtful if the Protestant leaders ever took this theory seriously. A few attempts to seize and banish Catholic monks and bishops caused riots and demonstrated the strength of Catholic opinion.[53] They also elicited criticism from friendly Catholic powers.[54] Likewise efforts to employ informers failed to produce convictions in the courts. Within a few years after 1704 the government already condoned the presence of a

[52] Corkery, *Hidden Ireland*, pp. 30–37, 108–113.

[53] *Ormonde MSS*, II, 473–474, tells of the rescue of a bishop. In County Derry a serious riot resulted from the seizure of a priest in 1725. Eng. P.R.O., S.P. 63/385, fols. 168–235. For an excellent treatment of position of the Catholics, see Wall, *Penal Laws*, pp. 23–33.

[54] Wall, *Penal Laws*, pp. 24–25; Carteret to lords justices, Feb. 5, 1722/23, Irish P.R.O., Calendar of Departmental Correspondence, II, 1714–1740, 133.

Catholic hierarchy. They had no alternative. When an act in 1709 stipulated that all registered priests must take a new oath only thirty-three of them obeyed.[55] The government quietly dropped the requirement rather than stir up further resistance. Under the circumstances it is not surprising that the first half of the eighteenth century witnessed an increase in the number of priests, the building of many new "mass houses," and the establishment of a fairly complete and well-organized Roman hierarchy.

One reason for the change in Protestant attitude arose from the failure of either of the Stuart rebellions of 1715 or 1745 to win active Irish support. Catholic as well as Protestant opinion was slowly shifting. Although the Papal Curia consistently refused to abandon the House of Stuart, and a number of Irish clergy took a similar position, influential Catholic laity and even some clergy showed an increasing willingness to support the government.[56] The eighteenth-century climate discouraged fanaticism and intolerance. The new outlook of the period is well expressed in a pamphlet by Henry Brooke in 1760 when he argued that it is interest, not religion, that men fight over, observing that without an interest in lands the Catholics had "little to lose by any change of estate; without a loan lodged with the Government, they had the less to lose by a change of constitution." [57] This same pragmatic approach is illustrated by the formation of the Catholic Association referred to in Chapter VII. In 1751, when the Catholic bishop of Fernes, Nicholas Sweetman, was summoned before the Irish privy council on charges of treason he ad-

[55] Dublin *Flying Post and Postmaster*, Mar. 24, 1708/09; Wall, *Penal Laws*, pp. 55–56.

[56] As early as 1728, Francis Stuart, the provincial of the Franciscans and later bishop of Down and Connor, wrote to the Pretender deploring the "disloyalty" of some of the Irish clergy. James O'Boyle, *The Irish Colleges* (Dublin, 1935), pp. 217–218.

[57] *The Farmers Case of the Roman Catholics of Ireland* (bound with Brooke, *Essay on Antient and Modern State of Ireland*), p. 71. Brooke, whose original *Farmers Letters* in 1746 had called upon Protestants to defend Ireland from Catholics, alleges here that he was never anti-Catholic, but merely fearful that persecution had made Catholics disloyal.

mitted openly that there were twenty-four Catholic bishops in Ireland, all appointed by the pope and in communication with Rome, that he ordained priests, and that there existed Catholic regulars in the country. He also acknowledged that he had raised funds to use in a peaceful manner to dissuade parliament from enacting further penal laws, but he denied in any way acting treasonably. Impressed by his frankness and his respect for law and order, the privy council dismissed all charges against him.[58] Such an incident would have been unthinkable a few decades earlier.

During the first half of the eighteenth century the Catholic Church in Ireland thus flourished. By 1731 there existed 1,445 known priests and some regulars; by 1750 Catholic clergy were actually being trained in Ireland as well as abroad.[59] Despite the disaffection of some of the upper classes the majority of the Catholics remained staunchly loyal to their faith, partly because the Roman church respected and fostered the perpetuation of Gaelic language and culture. Since the greatest increase in the population was among the masses the proportion of Catholics to Protestants inevitably increased. Naturally a church without tithes or glebelands lacked adequate financial resources, yet fees and gifts from the Catholic laity provided funds enough to support the parochial priests and the hierarchy and to finance expansion. With such strong material and moral backing the Catholic clergy enjoyed much influence in the country despite their precarious legal position.

In Ulster the Presbyterian ministers likewise played an important part in most communities. Although not empowered by law to officiate at marriages until 1782 and suffering from other disabilities, they did receive a small financial stipend from the crown and thus enjoyed a quasi-official status.[60]

---

[58] Wall, *Penal Laws*, p. 67.

[59] *Ibid.*, pp. 57–58. For the size and distribution of the Catholic and Protestant population, see Appendix. On Catholic churches in Dublin, see F. P. Carey, *Catholic Dublin* (Dublin, 1932).

[60] Irish Statute 21, 22 George III, c. 25; J. C. Beckett, *Protestant Dissent in Ireland 1687–1780* (London, 1946), pp. 29, 84, 106. In 1709 the synod of Ulster estimated there were over 130 Presbyterian congregations and

Socially their followers came chiefly from middle-class groups, the poorer tenants and laborers in Ulster often being Catholic or Church of Ireland and most of the gentry adhering to the Church of Ireland. Presbyterians could vote and thus exercised some political influence. Although barred from office by the Test Act of 1704, after the introduction of the Indemnity Acts in the 1720's they could even hold government posts.[61] In addition to Presbyterians Ireland had small groups of other Dissenters, among whom the most significant were the Quakers.[62] If Protestant nonconformists probably suspected Rome more thoroughly than the Anglicans, they shared one characteristic with the Catholics: official policy submitted both to humiliating restrictions while at the same time suffering their existence. As a result members of both religious bodies felt aggrieved and restless under the ascendancy.

It is natural to lay the blame for the prevailing system of ineffectual religious persecution primarily on the Church of Ireland. Well endowed, politically powerful, and jealous of their monopoly, the established clergy appear as an exploiting group preserving their privileges at the expense of the three-fourths of the population who looked for spiritual guidance outside the Anglican communion. This judgment is not entirely fair. A number of the established clergy, including some bishops, displayed a sense of responsibility and concern for the material and moral welfare of the entire nation. On several occasions a sizable proportion of the episcopal bench in the Irish Lords stood out for greater toleration for Roman Catholics than did the majority of their lay associates. Seven

about the same number of ministers. James S. Reid, *History of the Presbyterian Church in Ireland*, 3 vols. (Belfast, 1867), III, 2.

[61] Beckett, *Protestant Dissent in Ireland*, pp. 79–80.

[62] There appear to have been some ten Huguenot congregations in Ireland. See map in front of Lee, *Huguenot Settlements in Ireland*. The Baptist minister in Dublin in 1726–1748 was a classical scholar of some fame. *Faulkner's Dublin Journal*, Sept. 17, 1748. On the Quakers, see T. Wight and J. Rutty, *Rise and Progress of the People called Quakers in Ireland*, 4th ed. (London, 1811). Catholics appear to have burned a Quaker meetinghouse in County Kildare in 1739. Devonshire to [Newcastle ?], Jan. 12, 1739/40, Eng. P.R.O., S.P. 63/403, fols. 9–10.

bishops signed a protest against the Irish parliament's modification of the Treaty of Limerick in 1697.[63] A number likewise
resisted the most stringent of the penal laws.[64] William King,
then bishop of Derry, explained their position in an attack
on a 1697 bill to require Catholics to denounce Papal authority. "Now inasmuch as the Pope's supremacy is an article of
the Roman faith, it seems a direct intention to impose on
them an oath to renounce an article of their faith. I think it
reasonable that Papists should be debarred from all public
trust, profit, or power and kept from all such advantages as
would put them in a capacity for disturbing the public peace,
but I think it hard to take away men's estates, liberties, or
lives merely because they differ in estimate of religion." [65]

A somewhat similar spirit was manifest in the resistance of
most Irish bishops to an act outlawing marriages between
Protestants and Catholics celebrated by Catholic priests. Although aimed at an avowed abuse, the practice of some Catholic fortune hunters to abduct Protestant heiresses, traditional
Anglicans hesitated to challenge the validity of sacraments or
rites performed by ordained Catholic clergy.[66] While those
with high church inclinations showed a certain leniency
toward Papists, the more Latitudinarian among the established
clergy felt a sympathy with Presbyterians, and several bishops
were active in bringing about the Protestant Act of Toleration
in 1719.[67]

It would also be a mistake to accuse all the established

[63] Collection of the Irish Lords Protests 1634–1770 (London, 1771),
pp. 23–24.
[64] According to a list in the Southwell Papers, the Irish bishops appear
to have divided eight to six against the act in 1709, the stringent penal
act of that year. BM, Add. MSS. 34777, fol. 68.
[65] Quoted by Murray, Revolutionary Ireland and Its Settlement, p. 316.
[66] Froude, English in Ireland, I, 663–665. In 1731 the Irish bishops
finally accepted a bill to stop these marriages. Cary to [Delafaye ?], Jan. 2,
1731/32, Eng. P.R.O., S.P. 63/395. The bill, however, was rejected in
England but a similar one finally passed in 1745. 19 George II, c. 13.
[67] Beckett, Protestant Dissent in Ireland, pp. 59–61, explains the background of this act. Beckett convincingly argues that Presbyterians had
so much influence in Ulster they acted less as a tolerated minority than
as the dominant group. Ibid., pp. 35–39.

clergy of complacency and neglect when it came to their spiritual duties. In the diocese of Derry, for example, first Bishop King and a decade later Bishop William Nicolson strove to improve the standards of their clergy and to build up the church.[68] Their efforts met with considerable success. Pluralism and nonresidence, characteristic of the Church of England itself during this period, proved particularly difficult to control in Ireland. So few Anglicans lived in some dioceses that the established clergy had little motivation to live in their parishes or to care for the parsonages or churches. Bishop Henry Downes wrote of the diocese of Elphin that the Papists outnumbered Anglicans by fifty to one, "but the gentry are generally Protestants and very loyal; and the clergy are very well; and both Clergy and laity very respectful to their bishop." [69] One fears that far too many of the Irish clergy would have considered such a diocese a model. Despite serious attempts to remove abuses and to raise the standards of the established church as regards residence, regularity of services, and care of the church property, the Church of Ireland never really extended itself to convert the Gaelic Irish. Even as great a churchman and scholar as Archbishop James Ussher had opposed translating the prayer book into Gaelic in the seventeenth century. By the opening of the eighteenth century feeling had moderated, and a Gaelic prayer book appeared but it was never widely used. Few of the established clergy knew the native language or cared to learn it.[70] The greatest single effort to reach the "mere" Irish was the charity school movement, which as has been pointed out, met with limited success. In religion, as in all areas, the Anglo-Irish appeared far more anxious to preserve the status quo than to Anglicize Irish society.

One reason for the relative ineffectualness of the Church of Ireland arose from its own internal dissensions. Divisions between the high and low church factions accounted for part

[68] James, *North Country Bishop*, pp. 271–274.
[69] Downes to Nicolson, Sept. 15, 1720, quoted *ibid.*, p. 259.
[70] Norman Sykes, "Ussher as a Churchman," *Hermathena* (no. 88, 1956), pp. 59–80; Phillips, *History of the Church of Ireland*, III, 136–137, 188–189.

of the difficulties. During this period, in Ireland as in England, matters of churchmanship hinged as much on political as on doctrinal or liturgical differences. Jacobite sympathies persisted among many Irish clergy in George I's reign; the primate, Thomas Lindsay, was, in fact, a suspected Jacobite, which is one reason for his virtual eclipse by Archbishop King of Dublin.[71] Far more divisive than ideological disagreements was the inevitable rivalry between English-born and native clergy. As in all ranks of officialdom, the Anglo-Irish resented strongly the fact that the British ministry seemed to favor British over Irish appointees. No primate between 1702 and 1800 was of Irish birth, and about half of the episcopal as well as the judicial bench came from England.[72] As noted above, Hugh Boulter, when he replaced Lindsay as primate in 1726, set out to increase the proportion of English office-holders in Ireland. Carteret put some check on him, while later the inauguration of the system of undertakers recovered a degree of patronage for the Anglo-Irish. The problem, however, continued throughout the first half of the century and beyond. The established clergy, like the whole governing class during the ascendancy, suffered from their peculiar position; they were caught between the need to seek English support and the desire to manage Irish affairs without interference from London (or Canterbury).

Whether churchmen or laymen, officials or private persons, merchants or professionals, farmers or gentry, the Anglo-Irish formed a peculiar breed whose contradictory character has never been adequately delineated. From their ranks during the eighteenth century sprang many whose ability placed them among the leading figures in the English-speaking world: Swift, Berkeley, Oliver Goldsmith, Sheridan, Edward Burke, the duke of Wellington, and viscount Castlereagh, to name only the most prominent. It is generally agreed that the term Anglo-Irish, which appears to have originated about 1700, came to apply primarily to Protestants. The Anglo-Irish thus

[71] Phillips, *History of the Church of Ireland*, III, 193.
[72] *Ibid.*, 203–205, 276.

included descendants of the Old English and Gaelic Irish who had joined the Church of Ireland, a group that probably increased in numbers during the eighteenth century as many recusant families conformed to protect their estates from division or for the sake of professional advancement. Evidence of this shift is found in the frequency of Old English and even Gaelic names among Irish officials and members of parliament. But the majority of the Anglo-Irish represented descendants of post-Reformation immigrants, although not all of them were English. A few like the Molyneux family had older French origins, many others like the great banking house of La Touche represented the more recent Huguenot arrivals, some were Welsh like the Bowens, while landed Scottish families such as the Hamiltons certainly belonged to the ascendancy.[73] Intermarriage between the Anglo-Irish, Old English, Gaelic Irish, and Scots-Irish was frequent. Despite their diverse origins the Anglo-Irish can be said to form a distinct element in Irish society, and for that matter in English society as well. What were their peculiar characteristics?

The Anglo-Irish have found few defenders. It is natural that the Gaelic Irish and their sympathizers have viewed them as an arrogant ruling caste who exploited the country and prevented the fulfillment of Irish national aspirations. "The first article of an Ascendancy's creed," wrote Corkery, "is, and always has been, that the natives are a lesser breed, and that anything that is theirs (except their land and their gold!) is therefore of little value." [74] To Englishmen the Anglo-Irish have often seemed to combine some of the worst faults of the Irish with the less attractive attributes of the English ruling classes. An English visitor to Ireland in the 1760's, John Bush, reacted rather typically to the lavish entertainment he received by commenting ungratefully that "too much of their boasted hospitality in every province has a much greater right to be

[73] On the La Touche family, see Maxwell, *Dublin under the Georges,* p. 277; on the Bowens, see Elizabeth Bowen, *Bowens Court,* 2nd ed. (New York, Alfred A. Knopf, 1964); on the Hamiltons, see article on Gustavus Hamilton in the *DNB,* XXIV, 159–160.
[74] Corkery, *Hidden Ireland,* pp. x–xi.

denominated ostentation." [75] Young was kinder but still critical of the laxness of Irish landlords and farmers. The Anglo-
Irish certainly must be classified among the villains in Froude's
study, while they did not fare much better at the hands of
Lecky. By contrast, the Anglo-Irish saw themselves as representing the best of English traditions tempered by Irish
friendliness and humor. As Brooke boasted in 1760, "The
Nobility and Gentry of *Ireland* are Loyalists and Patriots
by Principle and Education; They are brave without Arro-
gance, gay, without Levity; polite, without Affectation; charitable, without Ostentation; religious, without Formality, affable,
without Meanness; generous, without View; and hospitable,
without Reserve." [76] It is not easy to reconcile such con-
tradictions.

One trait of the Anglo-Irish, which explains at once the
hostility of the Gaelic Irish and the contempt of English
critics, is that so many considered themselves fundamentally
as transplanted Englishmen. New arrivals tended to retain the
political, religious, and social prejudices of the English. The
proximity of England kept them in easy touch with English
views, fashions, and way of life. Some had relatives in England,
and many traveled there for business, for study, or for pleasure.
They likewise brought with them and preserved the aspirations of Englishmen. The vast majority had migrated with
the express intention of increasing their wealth and raising
their social status. For them Ireland represented, as did America to others, a land of opportunity where they could realize
thwarted ambitions. For most these ambitions meant achieving a higher place in a society like England's, not sharing in
some utopian dream. They aspired to become gentry with
broad acres and imposing country houses, to rise in church
or state to positions of prestige and power, or to make their
fortunes in trade. It is probable that most hoped initially to
return to England once they had made their way in the world.

[75] John Bush, *A Letter from a Gentleman in Dublin* (London, 1769),
p. 15.
[76] Brooke, *Essay on the Antient and Modern State of Ireland*, p. 66.

Those who did, of course, can scarcely be termed Anglo-Irish, but others who divided their time and interest between the two countries entered more fully into Irish life. The majority settled down and struck root in their new home, yet they and their children after them still looked to England as their hereditary homeland. Ultimate success was never just fame and fortune in Ireland but recognition and reward in England. Though a larger and more of a political and cultural center than any colonial city, Dublin never represented the real metropolis to the Anglo-Irish; that was always London.

While the tradition that they were still English persisted among many of the Anglo-Irish in the eighteenth century, the realities of the Irish environment inevitably altered their outlook. Those who acquired estates by grant or purchase might set themselves up as proper country gentry, but their relationship with tenants and laborers was seldom if ever identical with that found in England. It proved impossible to escape the consequences of the fact that they represented an alien aristocracy, holding forfeited lands and divided from the native population by religion, culture, and often language. The English village community, for all its class differences, possessed a homogeneity rarely found in Ireland. The gulf between the Anglo-Irish landlord and the Gaelic peasant, although not as great as that between the planter and slave in America, was far wider than that which separated the English squire and tenant. The Irish landlord probably enjoyed greater power but less respect, and like the planter he had cause to fear rebellion. Although many landlords displayed a kindly indulgence toward their inferiors and some a generous concern for their welfare, relatively few of the Anglo-Irish sought to understand or share the culture of the people among whom they lived.

If, as McNeill has pointed out, the Anglo-Irish felt psychologically alienated from those below them, they likewise became increasingly distrustful of those who exercised authority over their destiny — the English officials in London. Like the British colonists in America they expected to enjoy the full rights and liberties of freeborn English subjects. In theory and to a degree in practice English law, whether at home, in Ireland, or in the colonies, did guarantee these privileges. When it came to a conflict of interests between the mother country and Ireland or the colonies, nevertheless, British administrators and the British parliament showed little hesitation in asserting the paramount rights of Britain. Faced with this challenge Anglo-Irishmen like Molyneux and King had sought to maintain Ireland's autonomy as a separate and equal kingdom under the British crown. As has been seen, they failed to establish any such claim. Since the Anglo-Irish were too dependent upon British support to consider rebellion, they had to content themselves with seeking as much independence of action as could be peacefully achieved through negotiation and political pressure.

In the process of his struggles with the British government the English emigrant in Ireland transformed his ethnocentrism from that of an English nationalist, first into a loyalty to his own group, and gradually into a sense of Irish patriotism. During the early eighteenth century the Anglo-Irish preserved the myth that they were nonetheless loyal Englishmen for defending Irish interests, but their patriotism looked like something quite different to the men who governed in Westminster. When the British ministry made concessions to Dublin it did so more for the sake of expediency than from sympathy with Irish pretensions. Irishmen of any kind scarcely struck the average Briton as true Englishmen, regardless of the origin of their ancestors. The Anglo-Irish were, as the boy William Butler Yeats found out years later, already looked upon as at least half foreign. This attitude on the part of the English could not fail to antagonize the Anglo-Irish. They found themselves classified as outsiders in both Ireland and England.

The Anglo-Irish controlled the one kingdom with the aid of the other; that was the secret of their power. The price they paid for this power was that they were aliens in both. The indifference, if not resistance, they met from both Irish and English offended their pride and turned them alternately against first the one and then the other. With neither people could they feel complete identity; thus they became ambivalent toward both their adopted country and the land of their origin. Ethnic ambivalence created tension and often bitterness; it also developed sensitivity and sometimes tolerance. Among many it fostered an almost fierce individualism. No one perhaps better illustrates the discordant elements of the Anglo-Irish character than Jonathan Swift.

When he was at the high tide of his influence in London, during the ministry of Harley and St. John, Swift unconsciously identified himself with the English government. During the 1713 crisis in Ireland, when the Irish parliament refused to vote taxes, Swift, in a rather patronizing tone, warned Archbishop King that unless the Irish leaders behaved they would regret it.[77] The new dean of St. Patrick's sounded very much like an English official. Within a short time, however, he found himself back in Ireland, a virtual political exile from the Hanoverian court. During the controversies over both the Annesley case and Wood's halfpence Swift composed a series of pamphlets asserting Ireland's rights. From then on the dean became the symbol of Irish resistance to English domination. He proved particularly vehement in denouncing Anglo-Irish expatriates in London. Deploring the evils of absenteeism, he wrote:

I speak not of those *English* Peers or Gentlemen, who, beside their Estates at home, have Possessions here . . .; but I mean those Lords, and wealthy Knights, or Squires, whose Birth, and partly their Education, and *all* their Fortune (except some trifle . . .) are in this Kingdom. I knew many of them well enough during several Years, when I resided in *England*; and truly I could not discover that the *Figure* they made was, by any Means, a Subject for *Envy*; at least it gave me *two very different Passions*; for, excepting the Advantages of going now and then to an *Opera*, or sometimes appearing *behind a Crowd* at Court, or adding to the Ring of *Coaches* in *Hyde Park*, or

[77] Swift to King, Oct. 20, 1713, *Swift's Correspondence*, ed. Bell. II, 79.

losing their money at the *Chocolate House*, or getting News, Votes, and Minutes, about five Days before us in *Dublin*, I say, besides these, and a few other Privileges of *less* Importance, their Temptations to live in *London* were beyond my Knowledge or Conception.[78]

Perhaps Swift had not envied his fellow expatriates when he frequented the vestibules of power, but his comments have a nostalgic tone. When Swift visited London in 1727 it is almost certain that he attempted to arrange for his own transfer to England. Bishop William Stratford reported to Harley that "he was much disappointed when he was last here, that he was in hopes, by the interest he had in a certain lady, to have exchanged his preferment in Ireland for as good in England. Nay, that at last he would have quitted all he had in Ireland, for £400 *per annum*, but could not get it." [79]

One is tempted to conclude that the Irish patriotism of Swift and other Anglo-Irish may have been a virtue arising from necessity. Such a conclusion would not be altogether just. When influential in London, Swift, like many of his compatriots, did much to further the interests of Ireland. The informal Irish lobby consisted chiefly of Anglo-Irishmen who had achieved position and influence in England. St. James's Coffee House appears to have been their rendezvous in Anne's reign, and the Thatched House in St. James's Street two decades later.[80] To a rather remarkable degree many who lived almost exclusively in England, like some of the Southwells and viscount Percival, retained an active interest in Irish affairs. Yet, as time passed, those who seldom if ever returned to Ireland tended to shift their attention to other matters: Percival, for instance, became increasingly absorbed in the Georgia colony, and the last volume of his diary contains few references to Ireland. Of course a number of Irish

---

[78] Davis, *The Prose Writings of Jonathan Swift*, X, 130 (Drapier's Letter No. 7).

[79] Stratford to Harley, May 20, 1728, *Portland MSS*, VII, 463.

[80] "St. Jame's Coffee House is the rendezvous of our country men." E. Worth to Joshua Dawson, Mar. 6, 1707/08, Irish P.R.O., Calendar of British Correspondence, I, 1673–1714, 103. On the Thatched House see *Diary of Viscount Percival*, I, 168–169.

landowners, including many peers like the Petty family (earls of Shelburne), although they shared a concern in Irish business and often managed their estates there carefully, never really became Anglo-Irish in any but a superficial sense.[81] Many never troubled to take their seats in the Irish Lords. The term Anglo-Irish is primarily meaningful as a state of mind, not a condition of birth or inheritance.

Proof of this last statement is shown by a consideration of the English who went to Ireland during the period as office-holders. Such men represented the Anglo-Irish in the making. Some, of course, always regarded their Irish sojourn as an exile, counting the days until it would end. Judge John Wainwright, though he extolled the beauties of Dublin Bay (second to that of Naples only because of its climate!), refused to accept his appointment to the Irish bench as permanent even after serving years in the country.[82] More often, English appointees realized that they could never hope to receive positions of comparable prestige, and especially income, back home; that is, indeed, the very reason why most of them went to Ireland in the first place. Under the circumstances, the realistic attitude to take was to settle down in their adopted country. Official responsibilities, land purchases and other investments, the marriage of their children into Anglo-Irish families, their daily social contacts — all tended to engross them rapidly in Irish affairs. Even a man in his sixties, like Bishop William Nicolson, with a full set of prejudices and lifelong ties, changed his attitudes on some questions within a few years of his arrival. Less than five years after his translation to Londonderry he wrote, on his way back to Ireland after a trip to England, that he longed to be back again in Derry.[83] Archbishop Boulter, for all his efforts to have English appointees named to Irish posts, came to see the world more

[81] In the seventeenth century there were even a number of Irish peers who held no lands there. Kearney, *Strafford in Ireland*, p. 51. In 1735 Percival wrote that he knew of only two Irish peers without holdings in Ireland, *Diary of Viscount Percival*, I, 178–179.

[82] Wainwright to [Devonshire ?], June 17, 19, 1736, Eng. P.R.O., S.P. 63/400, fols. 17, 21.

[83] James, *North Country Bishop*, p. 268.

and more from an Irish viewpoint. The same was true of several of the English lawyers who were appointed to the Irish bench, such as Chancellor Richard West. After all, even temporary appointees, like the lord lieutenant, often altered their opinions after only a few months in Dublin. Although this process was repeated again and again, government officials in London continued to be surprised and chagrined by the changed attitudes of the English who moved across Saint George's Channel, just as they failed to comprehend the English who went to America. It proved difficult for those who remained at home to understand the simple fact that imperial affairs looked different from Dublin, Boston, or Philadelphia. Few men are untouched by their everyday environment.

Despite the fact that the ruling classes in Ireland lived between two worlds, it would be a mistake to conclude that most of them were acutely aware of their plight, or reacted as did a few like Swift, by becoming restless and embittered. The underlying tensions of Irish life often remained below the surface; for the upper classes particularly existence was pleasant and easygoing. The autocracy of the landlord frequently took the form of benevolent if less seldom of enlightened despotism, of a kind of arbitrary yet kindly paternalism that resembled older Celtic ways. Somewhat sentimentally, but not without justification, Sir John Barrington recalled that during his youth (in about 1750) "good landlords and attached peasantry were then spread over the face of Ireland." [84] If the deep fissures inherent in the Irish social structure defied solution, overt conflicts were slowly diminishing. Catholics and Protestants, Anglicans and Dissenters, English and native officials came more and more to accept each other. Except for the poor, times were generally good. Dublin offered theater, music (Handel's *Messiah* had its first performance there), and intellectual pursuits as well as horse racing, the Donnybrook fair, and hurling matches.[85] In the countryside the expanding

[84] Quoted by Maxwell, *Country and Town in Ireland*, p. 180.
[85] Handel was in Dublin in 1741–1742. Maxwell, *Dublin under the Georges*, pp. 122–124. The Dublin newspapers, especially from the 1730's

provision trade spelled prosperity for the gentry with a minimum of supervision and effort.

From the viewpoint of Dublin Castle the nation suffered seriously from a widespread disrespect for law and order, but the country squire, meting out unofficial justice to his tenants, enjoyed relative security until the Whiteboy outbreaks in 1759. Illegal activities, such as pillaging wrecked ships or smuggling, caused little concern to the local landlords; after all the first practice brought money into the neighborhood, and the second reduced the price of liquor and tobacco and raised the price of wool.[86] Let them worry about such matters in London. Life among the landed classes often resembled that attributed to the Tory squires in England by Thomas Babington Macaulay: a round of hunting, horse racing, and carousing. Foreign visitors often spoke critically of the gentry's excessive drinking, of its flamboyance, and of its irresponsibility, but all agreed that the Irish landed classes were hospitable. It is obvious that they were a vigorous and uninhibited lot. One inveterate old sinner, convicted by a church court in a paternity case at the age of eighty, proudly elected to stand penance in church instead of paying the customary fine — with the lamentable result that thereafter few were ashamed to accept the same punishment.[87] One cannot but feel an awesome respect for a man like Daniel McCarthy of

on, are full of notices of horse racing. A notice of a hurling match "between 30 men from each side of the Liffy for 30 shillings" is found in the *Flying Post and Postmaster,* June 28, 1708.

[86] James, "Irish Smuggling in the Eighteenth Century," pp. 314–317. On pillaging of a ship there is a long account involving a Danish vessel in 1735. Eng. P.R.O., S.P. 63/398, fols. 95–97, 63/399, fols. 17–19, 38, 40–41, 52–57, 63–69. Periodic fights in Dublin between the "Bail Boys" (or later the "Ormond Boys") and the "Liberty Boys" are reported in the Dublin press. See, e.g., *Dublin Evening Press,* May 27, June 24, July 8, 1735, *Faulkner's Dublin Journal,* Oct. 20, 27, 1748.

[87] The offender was "Old Colonel Evans," a Welshman who went to Ireland under Cromwell and "after the Restoration set up a cobbler's trade in the County of Cork, . . . but being a cunning, industrious and saving man," built up a fortune by buying army debentures. *Diary of Viscount Percival,* II, 388.

County Kerry, apparently one of the surviving Gaelic gentry, who reputedly died at the age of 112.

He buried four wives, his fifth . . . he married when he was eighty-four and she only fourteen, by whom he had about twenty children . . . : he was a very healthy man, no cold did affect him, he could not bear the warmth of a shirt at night, but put it under his Pillow; for seventy years past, when in company, he drank plentifully of Rum and Brandy, which he called the *Naked Truth*; and if in compliance with other gentlemen, he drank claret or punch, he always drank an equal amount of Rum or Brandy, to qualify those liquors, this he called a *Wedge*. No man remembers to have seen him spit; his custom was to walk eight or ten miles in a winter morning, over mountains, with greyhounds and firearms . . . and seldom failed to bring home a brace of hares; He was an honest gentleman.[88]

An upper class that produced men with the stamina of McCarthy, the integrity and intellect of Archbishop King, the political sagacity of parliamentary leaders like the Brodricks, Speaker Conolly, or Henry Boyle deserves historical recognition whatever its failings.

[88] This report was printed in the *Boston Weekly Newsletter*, May 14, 1752.

X

Ireland
and the
Imperial Crisis

The period in English history from the accession of James I to the Civil Wars has been said to represent "the crisis of the constitution"; the era between the outbreak of the Seven Years' War and the close of the American Revolution could well be called the crisis of the imperial constitution. Conflict in early Stuart England arose because, although the Tudors had created a strong state, they had failed to "clarify, to integrate and bring up to date the constitutional arrangements of the different parts of the government which served their immediate purposes." [1] When the first two Stuarts attempted to define the constitution they precipitated civil war. In similar fashion when the British government in the 1760's strove to clarify, to integrate, and to bring up to date the machinery of imperial administration it unleashed forces that led to revolution. The military and financial demands of the Seven Years' War undoubtedly constitute a primary cause for the crisis. There were also underlying and long-standing reasons why government through "salutary neglect" would, sooner or later, come to an end.

The history of England suggests that a well-established representative legislature cannot indefinitely be combined with an autonomous executive. The mixed constitution inherited from the Middle Ages eventually fell apart over the issue of divided sovereignty. By 1700 the representative bodies of Ireland and most of the British overseas colonies had become an integral part of the government. Initially advisory, they

---

[1] Margaret Atwood Judson, *The Crisis of the Constitution: An Essay in Constitutional and Political Thought in England* (New Brunswick, N.J., Rutgers University Press, 1949), p. 1.

had gained wide legislative powers and developed political self-consciousness.

Until the middle of the eighteenth century, the British administration normally managed to satisfy the demands of the dominant groups in the Irish and colonial legislatures without raising constitutional issues. Yet the question of ultimate sovereignty could not be avoided indefinitely. The arguments for Irish autonomy expressed by Molyneux, King, and Swift were revived by Lucas in 1747. Soon the colonies began to formulate similar constitutional theories as they came to recognize that British hegemony threatened their interests. Even before the French wars convinced the British government of the need to strengthen its hold on imperial administration, opposition groups in a number of colonies were beginning to challenge British control. Until 1763, however, the Irish moved more rapidly toward a confrontation with the British than did the Americans.

In 1755 William Cavendish, marquis of Hartington, replaced Dorset as lord lieutenant. He was the son of the duke of Devonshire who had served as viceroy from 1737 to 1744. In 1748 he had married Charlotte Elizabeth Boyle, heiress to the head of the Boyle family, the earl of Cork and Burlington.[2] Hartington thus had powerful Irish connections, but he faced a difficult situation. His predecessor had not only broken with Speaker Henry Boyle; he had likewise alienated the leader of one of the oldest and most influential families in Ireland, James Fitzgerald, twentieth earl of Kildare, who had been appointed to the privy council by Chesterfield. Lord Kildare had joined Speaker Boyle in the attacks on the Castle in 1752.[3] By 1754 his antagonism toward Dorset had reached a point where he threatened to beat up a Dublin newspaper editor, George Faulkner, for reporting that Dorset had been toasted at a banquet presided over by Kildare. Infuriated, the earl demanded to know by what authority Faulkner had "dared

[2] Since two of Hartington's sisters married into the Ponsonby family (see Chapter VII, above) he was related to two of the leading Anglo-Irish families.

[3] Dr. Barry to earl of Orrery, Mar. 4, 1752, *Orrery Papers*, II, 102.

to mention that man [Dorset], whose health was not drunk, nor ever would be when he was present." [4]

Hartington, who became fourth duke of Devonshire on his father's death late in 1755, carried with him instructions to make peace with the opposition. The new lord lieutenant set out to minimize the role of Archbishop Stone and the English party in the government. He thus hoped to be able to reestablish more friendly relations with the Boyle group and, if possible, encourage a rapprochement between Boyle and Ponsonby. Early in 1756 Henry Boyle accepted a peerage as earl of Shannon. When Boyle resigned as speaker to move up to the House of Lords, John Ponsonby (second son of the earl of Bessborough) was elected speaker with the assistance of the Boyle faction.[5] The system of undertakers once more seemed to be functioning. Nevertheless, the disputes of the past few years had led to the formation of patriotic societies, an opposition press, and a growing sense of national grievance among the politically articulate classes. Despite the fact there had been no general election since George II ascended the throne in 1727 the temper of the Irish Commons had altered. By-elections had become more frequently contested, more controversial, and more expensive.[6] The pressure of patriotic agitation increasingly affected parliament even if few of its members represented popular constituencies.

During the year 1755–1756 the opposition forces concentrated their efforts on one aspect of the budget: the civil list. They succeeded in passing a request that the administration present a careful accounting of all pensions granted during

[4] Faulkner to earl of Orrery, Feb. 16, 1754, *ibid.*, p. 119.
[5] Beckett, *Making of Modern Ireland*, p. 194.
[6] Lecky, *History of England*, II, 472. During George II's reign the average number of new members elected to the Commons was twenty-three per session. J. L. McCracken, "Irish Parliamentary Elections 1727–68," *Irish Historical Studies*, V (1946–1947), 212. Until the time of the Lucas affair Irish newspapers had been remarkably nonpolitical, but in the 1750's a number of them carried on the tradition of the *Censor*: James Esdall's *Newsletter*, L. Dunn's *The Universal Advertiser*, James Eyre Weeks's *The Dublin Spy*, and a journal known as *The Patriot*. Robert Munter, *The History of the Irish Newspapers 1685–1760* (Cambridge, 1967), pp. 183–187.

the preceding year.[7] They also carried a vote to draw up
heads of a bill to prevent crown officials from holding seats
in the Commons. Thanks to its understanding with Boyle
the Castle mustered sufficient votes to defeat the place bill 85
to 59.[8] On the other hand, the opposition put through a
resolution declaring that the accountant general's report on
the amount of pensions was scarcely a third as large as it
should have been. In other matters the session went fairly
well. The government got a satisfactory revenue act, and
parliament finally passed a law permitting Protestant Dissenters to hold commissions in the militia, thereby pleasing the
Ulster Presbyterians and strengthening the defense against
possible invasion.[9] It will be recalled that London had first
suggested such a measure as early as 1719.

Devonshire, upon his return to London, resigned as lord
lieutenant to form an administration with William Pitt. The
new ministry named John Russell, fourth duke of Bedford,
to succeed Devonshire in Ireland. Bedford went to Dublin in
September 1757 to open parliament. In addition to the political disagreements that had troubled Ireland for nearly a
decade, Bedford faced an economic crisis brought on partly
by the dislocation of trade caused by the war and partly by
crop failures. Bedford, unlike most of the recent lord lieutenants, had no Irish connections; his knowledge of the country
was confined largely to his experiences as secretary of state
for the southern department from 1748 to 1751, during the
Lucas affair. He seems to have resented the influence enjoyed
by the undertakers and to have envisaged governing without
any binding commitment to any of the Irish factions. He
continued Devonshire's recent policy of cultivating Lord Kildare and of remaining on friendly terms with Lord Shannon,
who had now withdrawn somewhat from active politics.[10]

[7] *Irish Commons' Journal*, May 3, 5, 1756.
[8] *Ibid.*, Mar. 6, 12, 17, 1756.
[9] Irish Statute, 29 George II, c. 24. Because of the war and of popular
demand Devonshire issued a call for the militia in 1756. Protestants,
especially in Ulster, responded in large numbers. Sir Henry McAnally,
"The Military Array of 1756 in Ireland," *Irish Sword*, I (1949–1953),
94–102.
[10] Bedford to Pitt, Dec. 5, 1757, *Correspondence of John, Fourth Duke*

Since these two earls were popular with the patriot groups, the chances of building a broad-based Castle party strong enough to control parliament appeared promising. There remained, nonetheless, much popular discontent.

The session no sooner opened than opposition groups renewed the battle against the government's power of patronage. Instead of proposing a new place bill, they pushed through the Commons resolutions deploring the size of the civil list and condemning the granting of pensions to absentees. Since Bedford had just arranged a generous pension for his sister-in-law, he viewed this move with something less than enthusiasm. He refused to forward the Commons' resolutions to England, at least not until he had time for further deliberation. The Commons replied that they would not consider the money bills until he had complied with their wishes.[11] Under the circumstances the lord lieutenant had little choice. He sent the resolutions to the ministry, complaining to Pitt that he found himself virtually powerless to control parliament: "Revenue officers, officers in the army, even — which is more extraordinary — pensioners who have enjoyed his Majesty's bounty, were so disgusted at the marks of favour which the King had been pleased to bestow on others within the two years past, that they voted to obstruct his Majesty's public service."[12] As Dr. Edward Barry explained to the earl of Orrery, "interest or resentment are the springs that actuate our political machine."[13] Devonshire's and Bedford's efforts to win support outside the ranks of the old undertakers had so alienated the Stone and Ponsonby parties that they had joined the patriots in attacking the Castle, notwithstanding the fact that many of them were placemen and pensioners.

---

of Bedford [hereafter cited as *Bedford Correspondence*], ed. Lord John Russell, 3 vols. (London, 1842–1846), II, 311. It should be noted, however, that Horace Walpole blamed Bedford and his secretary, Richard Rigby, for failing to carry out the policies of Devonshire and his secretary, Conway. *Memoirs of the Reign of George the Second by Horace Walpole*, ed. Lord Holland, 2nd ed., 3 vols. (London, 1846), III, 65–66.

[11] *Irish Commons' Journal*, Nov. 1, 11, 12, 14, 15, 1757; Bedford to Pitt, Nov. 12, 17, 1757, *Bedford Correspondence*, II, 285–292.

[12] *Bedford Correspondence*, II, 292.

[13] Barry to earl of Orrery, Dec. 15, 1757, *Orrery Papers*, II, 130.

The implications of this incident were clear enough: either the lord lieutenant must destroy the influence of the primate and the speaker, or he must make peace with them. The first alternative, though it certainly had its appeal for Bedford, was scarcely practical. It would prove too disruptive to the administration to turn out of office Ponsonby's many followers; as for Archbishop Stone, his key supporters were bishops and judges, men who were virtually immune from removal, and many of whom, like Stone himself, had friends in Westminster. For several months Bedford attempted to find some way of managing without forming an alliance with Stone or Ponsonby. He gained popularity by an enlightened policy toward the country's economic plight. He took the lead in raising £20,000 for the relief of the destitute and supported a bill to grant bounties on grain transported from country districts to Dublin, thereby both assisting to alleviate the food shortage in the capital and benefiting the landlords.[14] Meanwhile he deferred beyond the usual time (January) the selection of the lords justices who would serve as regents upon his return to England at the close of parliament.[15]

By February Bedford recognized that he must seek an alliance with the two key factions. During January a bill to liberalize the rules for registering Catholic clergy (which included a provision to recognize bishops) passed both houses only to be thrown out by the privy council on January 21. In the vote there (13 to 11) Stone and the three other archbishops, the lord chancellor, the chief justice of King's Bench, and the lord chief baron joined the earl of Shannon and others in defeating the measure, even after the lord lieutenant had spoken at length in its favor.[16] Of the key Irish leaders only

[14] Richard Rigby to Bedford, Feb. 3, 1757, *Bedford Correspondence*, II, 232; Bedford to Kildare, June 16, 1757, *ibid.*, 247-248; *Irish Commons' Journal*, Oct. 11, 12, 25, 27, 1757; Irish Statute, 31 George II, c. 3.

[15] Barry to Lord Cork (formerly earl of Orrery), Feb. 4, 1758, *Orrery Papers*, II, 132-133.

[16] Barry to earl of Orrery, Jan. 24, 1758, *ibid.*, pp. 130-131. James Hamilton, earl of Clanbrassil, was the author of the bill in the Lords. He argued that if the Catholic parish priests were given official status they would become as "good subjects to the King of Great Britain, as the

Kildare voted with the lord lieutenant and secretary Richard
Rigby. If Stone could override the combined influence of the
Castle and Fitzgerald in the council, while Speaker Ponsonby
could threaten his control of the Commons, it was clearly time
to come to terms. Bedford now turned to Lord Shannon.[17]
Stone had already been making overtures to the Boyle faction
so that a reconciliation between the three old undertakers was
rapidly effected. Bedford thus finally exercised those "softening and healing arts of Government" and achieved the "comprehension and harmony" Pitt had recommended to him the
previous November.[18]

The events of the 1757–1758 session reveal the degree to
which Irish politics were then determined by the interplay
of rival factions, primarily the four led respectively by Stone,
Ponsonby, Shannon, and Kildare. That, as lord lieutenant,
Bedford should have been provoked by party maneuvering
is understandable, but his experience in England might have
made him more tolerant. Factions, as Lewis Namier has
demonstrated, dominated London as well as Dublin, and
Bedford, with his "Bloomsbury Gang," was soon to play the
same game in Westminster.[19] Archibald Foord notes that one
of the chief aims of the English opposition leaders in the early
eighteenth century was to make such a nuisance of themselves
that the ministry would seek their alliance.[20] On this score
there seems to be little difference between Ireland and England. Horace Walpole described the Irish patriots as a "flying
squad," composed "as is usual, of the discontented — that is
those who had been too insignificant to be bought off, or

German priests in the Electorate are to the Elector of Hanover." Clanbrassil to Bedford, July 17, 1757, *Bedford Correspondence*, II, 264.
[17] Barry to Lord Cork, Feb. 18, 1758, *Orrery Papers*, II, 133–134; Bedford to Pitt, Feb. 13, 1758, *Bedford Correspondence*, II, 328.
[18] Pitt to Bedford, Nov. 26, 1757, *Correspondence of William Pitt, Earl
of Chatham*, ed. William Stanhope Taylor and John Henry Pringle, 4 vols.
(London, 1840), I, 287.
[19] Sir Lewis Namier, *England in the Age of the American Revolution*,
2nd ed. (London, Macmillan & Co., 1961), pp. 206–215; G. Grant Robertson,
England under the Hanoverians, 3rd ed. (London, 1917), p. 244.
[20] Foord, *His Majesty's Opposition*, pp. 33–34.

whose demands had been too high — and a few well meaning men." [21] Yet there are differences. The emerging system of ministerial responsibility in England compelled factional leaders, once they accepted office, to commit themselves at least temporarily to government policies. This was much less true in Ireland where their only commitment was to expediency or to their own sense of honor or public interest. On the other hand, while Irish political leaders displayed less administrative responsibility when in power, they came closer to representing popular interests when they were in opposition.

Although in Ireland as in England "party" meant merely "faction" at this time, the formation of a genuine patriot party can be clearly discerned during the 1750's.[22] The Irish counterpart of the English country party did not constitute simply an independent group desiring more honest, efficient, and inexpensive government; it also expressed a growing resentment of English rule. During the 1757–1758 session the patriot movement gained momentum. Carteret (now Lord Granville) advised Bedford that all he had to do was remain "quietly and coolly at the Castle," while the factions in the Irish parliament "dash their loggerheads together, and to transmit whatever nonsense they may cook up to England to be rejected." [23] As a veteran of Wood's halfpence, Carteret might have proved more sympathetic; it was no easy matter to remain cool while the patriots stirred up the Dublin parliament. In November the Commons unanimously ordered the drawing up of heads of a bill "to limit the sitting of parliament . . . and for more frequent calling of new parliaments." In December they established a special committee to review the management of the revenue for the past twenty years and only defeated a

[21] *Memoirs of the Reign of George the Second*, III, 69.

[22] Beckett, *Making of Modern Ireland*, p. 195. In its origins, of course, the Patriot party goes back to the 1720's. See Chapters V and VI. In 1732 Archbishop Boulter advised London against amending Irish heads of bills, "since they call such an addition tacking and most that set up for patriots will on that very account reject it." Boulter to Newcastle, Jan. 15, 1731/32, Eng. P.R.O., S.P. 63/395, fol. 3.

[23] Fox to Bedford, Jan. 7, 1758, *Bedford Correspondence*, II, 316.

proposal for a bill to reinterpret Poynings' Law by a vote of 102 to 75. In January 1758 they endorsed a resolution declaring the government's wartime embargo on Irish beef, pork, and butter as "highly prejudicial to this Kingdom." [24]

However opportunist some opposition leaders may have been, the unifying force underlying all resistance to the Castle became more and more a desire for greater Irish autonomy. In his memoirs the earl of Charlemont later commented that the struggles of the 1750's showed "that the government might be opposed with success" and taught the people to think, "a lesson which is the first and most necessary step to the acquirement of liberty." [25] As has been remarked, agitation outside parliament was becoming more pronounced. In 1759 Bedford's chief secretary, Richard Rigby, alleged that: "For many years past, the mob in this kingdom has been wickedly and infamously made use of by differing parties as an engine to carry questions in parliament." [26] The last session of parliament in George II's reign, which convened in October 1759, was to prove just how volatile the situation had become.

When the Irish parliament assembled in 1759 the country was full of rumors of an impending French invasion. Among the measures backed by the government was one to provide for emergency meetings should an invasion occur when parliament was not in session. The proposal may scarcely seem controversial, but the circumstances surrounding its origin made it extremely suspect to the opposition. A similar law regarding the British parliament had been affixed to a recent British militia act. In its initial form the British bill had been designed to apply to Ireland as well as Great Britain. During the debates on the bill Rigby, member for Tavistock in the British Commons, had objected to the inclusion of Ireland on the grounds that this would antagonize the Irish. Promising to bring up a similar bill in the Dublin Commons, Rigby

---

[24] *Irish Commons' Journal*, Nov. 11, Dec. 5, 12, 1757, Jan. 17, 1758.
[25] Historical Manuscripts Commission, *Charlemont Manuscripts* [hereafter cited as *Charlemont MSS*], 2 vols. (London, 1891–1894), I, 7.
[26] Rigby to Pitt, Dec. 23, 1759, *Correspondence of William Pitt*, ed. Taylor and Pringle, I, 476.

won his point.[27] When he now sought to fulfill his promise, opposition leaders raised a clamor in Dublin, asserting that such an act would violate custom and would give the administration undue control. What was more important, its passage would, in their eyes, represent evidence that the Irish parliament took orders from Westminster. Somehow, perhaps because of remarks by Viscount Hillsborough (who was attending the Dublin Lords), the patriots came to suspect that the whole business was part of a plot to effect a union with Britain and to abolish the Irish parliament.[28] Whoever fomented these ideas — it is possible French agents may have had a hand in it — the fears they engendered resulted in the most dangerous riot Dublin had witnessed for decades.

On December 3, 1759, as parliament was reconvening after a brief recess, several thousand demonstrators converged on College Green. They stopped both burgesses and lords on their way to the Parliament House and forced them to take an oath never to consent to union. In the course of the disturbances a number of members were threatened, some handled roughly, one peer was stripped of his robes, and the attorney general was injured. The mob entered the Lords' chamber and installed an old lady in the lord chancellor's chair; in the Commons' chamber they threatened to burn the journals of the House. The mayor and city officials failed to intervene to restore order; the rioting continued until the arrival of a contingent of soldiers from the Castle.[29]

Following the riot, parliament passed resolutions thanking the lord lieutenant for restoring peace, condemning violent demonstrations, and rebuking the mayor for his inaction.[30] Both the Commons and the city administration offered rewards for information about the ringleaders. It is apparent, nevertheless, that there was considerable sympathy for the demonstrators. Dubliners had come to accept political agitation as

[27] *Gentlemen's Magazine*, XXIX (1759), 638.
[28] Walpole, *Memoirs of the Reign of George the Second*, III, 239.
[29] On the riot see *ibid.*, p. 243; *Gentlemen's Magazine*, XXIX (1759), 638–639; *Universal Magazine*, XXV (1759), 324–326.
[30] *Irish Commons' Journal*, Dec. 4, 1759.

normal and were loath to take any drastic steps. Rigby wrote in alarm to Pitt of the "restive almost rebellious disposition of the people here," remarking that there existed widespread admiration for anyone who dared "fly in the face of the English government." It would, he added, "Amaze you, Sir, to see the reluctance I have met with to probe this flagrant evil to the bottom, and the impossibility to get a ringleader by ever so lucrative an offer, which I have made to those who I am certain are capable, if they were willing, to inform." [31] When the government eventually made some arrests the accused rioters were acquitted by the jury, on the grounds that their identity could not be proven.[32]

The immediate results of the December riot were less disruptive than Rigby anticipated. News of Edward Hawke's great victory at Quiberon Bay minimized the danger of a major invasion even though the daring French admiral, François Thurot, briefly captured Carrickfergus early in 1760. The almost certain prospect of victory over the French did much to restore calm. Meanwhile the Castle strengthened the position of the undertakers by wooing several of the opposition leaders in parliament.[33] Although the Commons refused to pass Rigby's bill for emergency meetings and resisted the administration's efforts to put through an Irish riot act, the revenue bills met with no difficulties, and the 1759–1760 session closed with the customary exchange of compliments between the lord lieutenant and parliament.[34] As he had two years before, Bedford named Archbishop Stone, Speaker Ponsonby, and Lord Shannon as lords justices. In the autumn of 1760, when George III ascended the throne, Ireland appeared to be enjoying both relative political peace and limited economic recovery.

Appearances proved deceptive; the reign of George III was to be one of momentous change. Since the Treaty of Limerick the Irish political system had remained outwardly unaltered.

[31] Rigby to Pitt, Dec. 23, 1759, *Correspondence of William Pitt*, I, 478.
[32] *Gentlemen's Magazine*, XXX (1760), 344.
[33] Walpole, *Memoirs of the Reign of George the Second*, III, 245.
[34] *Irish Commons' Journal*, May 15, 17, 1760.

Despite periods of tension, relations between the British government and Ireland had never become critical enough to require more than the passing attention of the British parliament. Like colonial affairs, Irish business had been handled by a few officials with some consultation with the cabinet. After 1760 events moved at a different pace. By 1782 the American colonies had overthrown British rule, and Ireland had come close to realizing the kind of political and economic autonomy advocated by the Irish opposition. The ultimate success of the Irish patriots owed much to the impact of the American revolt, but during the first decade of George III's reign changes in Ireland represented the culmination of older developments. The 1760's thus constitute an epilogue to the period 1688–1760 as well as a link with the more revolutionary era that was to follow.

In 1760 three political aims, inherited from the 1750's, remained major objectives of the patriot groups: fuller budgetary control by the Irish Commons, more frequent parliamentary elections, and the reduction of Castle patronage and crown pensions. The first two of these became issues even before the meeting of George III's first Irish parliament. The accession of a new king necessitated a new election in 1761. Patriot propaganda had now become sufficiently influential to convince a number of parliamentary candidates of the advisability of pledging their support for an Irish septennial act.[35] The question of the Commons' control of money bills likewise came up for discussion before parliament met. In response to the growth of patriot sentiment, the lords justices decided to depart from a long-standing practice regarding supplies. Almost all Irish legislation now began as heads of a bill in either the Irish Commons or Lords. Nevertheless, the British government still submitted bills at the beginning of each session in order to conform to Poynings' Law, which stipulated that the Irish parliament only be convened to pass on legislation presented by the crown. To facilitate the procedure the

[35] Froude, *English in Ireland*, II, 7–8; Beckett, *Making of Modern Ireland*, p. 197.

Irish privy council drew up some bills prior to each session and sent them to London for endorsement, one of them normally being a supply bill. In 1761 the lords justices notified the ministry that they intended to omit any supply bill. The move would appeal to the sensibilities of the Commons, which periodically since 1692 had sought complete initiative on money bills. In the British cabinet Pitt spoke in favor of this suggestion but his colleagues voted it down. After some argument the lords justices agreed to follow the customary practice.[36]

When George III's first Irish parliament assembled in October 1761 it still contained a majority of members who owed allegiance either to the crown or to the undertakers. But the patriot movement had made gains and had found new leadership. In the Lords James Caulfield, viscount Charlemont (earl of Charlemont after 1763), advocated the popular cause and associated himself with the patriots in the Commons. These patriots included Dr. Charles Lucas, who had returned and had successfully stood for reelection in Dublin. Among others was the country gentleman, Sir William Osborne, and a number of young lawyers, such as John Fitzgibbon, Sexton Perry, and the eloquent Henry Flood. Even government officials, like Hely Hutchinson, showed sympathy with the patriot program. Although the opposition won only limited concessions during the next three sessions of parliament, a patriot party was now emerging that would continue to agitate for reforms until they finally achieved their objectives. Charlemont explained their position:

If in Great Britain, the seat of empire, where the constitution has been long settled upon the most apparently secure and firm basis, and where there exists an internal strength, which appears sufficient at all times to check the encroachments of the crown, opposition has, by the wisest politicians, been ever deemed necessary to public safety, how much more so must it be in a country comparatively feeble, fluctuating in its constitution, and which has not only to struggle with the crown,

[36] Lecky, *History of England in the Eighteenth Century*, IV, 388.

but with a powerful neighbour, always willing and ready to encroach . . .[37]

The new lord lieutenant in 1761 was George Montagu Dunk, second earl of Halifax. President of the Board of Trade from 1748 to 1761, Halifax was experienced largely in colonial affairs, and he brought with him as chief secretary another member of the Board of Trade, William Gerard Hamilton, who was elected to the Irish Commons from the borough of Killebegs. Halifax saw in Ireland an opportunity to solve one of the empire's most pressing problems: financing an expanded standing army without burdening either the British or the colonial taxpayer. He proposed increasing the size of the Irish establishment from 12,000 to 18,000. Whether the plan would have won endorsement by the Irish is extremely doubtful. In any event, it proved unacceptable to the English "Tories," as Rigby described them, and was abandoned.[38] The government also met defeat when Hamilton proposed a bill to permit Irish Catholics to provide six regiments for England's ally, the king of Portugal.[39]

Hamilton's proposal was more than a war measure; it represented an appreciation on the part of the government of growing Catholic support. At the opening of the Seven Years' War several Roman Catholic bishops had expressed their loyalty to the Hanoverian succession despite the Papacy's continued recognition of the Stuarts.[40] At the succession of George III several hundred Catholic merchants and gentry drew up a loyal address to the new king.[41] Soon afterward Lord Trimleston and other leading Catholics petitioned that Catholics be permitted to enlist in the service of King George or of his allies. The government naturally welcomed these

[37] *Charlemont MSS*, I, 7.
[38] Rigby to Bedford, Feb. 23, 1763, *Bedford Correspondence*, III, 209; Shy, *Toward Lexington*, pp. 74–75.
[39] T. H. D. Mahoney, *Edmund Burke and Ireland* (Oxford, 1960), pp. 14–15.
[40] Wall, *Penal Laws*, pp. 68–69.
[41] Matthew O'Conor, *The History of the Irish Catholics* (Dublin, 1813), pp. 269–270.

moves and responded with Hamilton's bill, but the patriots joined with the country members and the "Protestant bashaws of the south" to defeat it.[42] While a few Anglo-Irish, like Henry Brooke, had by now come to accept the good faith of men like Trimleston, the majority could not yet envisage cooperation with Catholics. The patriot movement still remained almost exclusively Protestant.[43]

In dealing with other issues Halifax and Hamilton were more successful. They got a generous supply bill to assist with the war effort, and they headed off a critical resolution regarding pensions. On the other hand, the Castle deemed it wise to remain officially neutral while, under much popular pressure, a rather unwilling Commons passed heads of a bill for septennial elections, a measure London quietly shelved.

Lecky observes that the first seven years of George III's reign "were singularly uneventful in Ireland," remarking that the undertakers "cooperated cordially with the Castle, and public affairs . . . moved on very smoothly." [44] Although it is true that the opposition was frustrated in its objectives during these years, its leaders continued to agitate for reform, and with increasing popular support. Furthermore, the relations between the undertakers and the Castle became more and more strained and were near the breaking point by 1767. Undismayed by their lack of success in 1761–1762, the patriots attacked the government on a number of fronts during the parliamentary session of 1763–1764 with a logic and eloquence that Lecky himself admits compared favorably with English parliamentary debates of the same period.[45] Lucas, with

---

[42] *Charlemont MSS*, I, 19.

[43] Brooke expressed the hope that they would soon enjoy full rights since they had been so peaceful since the Treaty of Limerick. *Essay on the Antient and Modern State of Ireland*, p. 68. The Catholic apologist, Viscount Nicholas Taafe, took much the same position, *Observations on Affairs in Ireland from the Settlement of 1691* (Dublin, 1766), pp. 27–28. Archbishop Stone likewise voiced his confidence in the loyalty of the majority of the Catholics. Stone to Bedford, May 28, 1759, *Bedford Correspondence*, II, 380.

[44] Lecky, *History of England in the Eighteenth Century*, IV, 392.

[45] *Ibid.*, 389.

Flood's backing, reintroduced the septennial bill, stressing the need for more representative government.[46] The Commons again passed the measure, and likewise heads of bills for an Irish habeas corpus act and an act to ensure Irish judges the same security of tenure granted to English judges in 1701. Aligning the patriots with the English opposition, Perry and Flood attempted to register disapproval of the Peace of Paris.[47] The most controversial issues were as usual financial. "The greatest Distinction and highest Privilege, of this House," declared Sir Robert Deane, "is to be the Purse-bearer of the Nation: To have the power of determining what Proportion of National Wealth, consisting of the aggregate Property of Individuals, shall be applied to Public purposes." [48]

Early in November 1763 Flood denounced the growing deficit, attributing it primarily to poor management rather than to the war, especially to the increase in pensions.[49] The opposition passed a resolution condemning the increase (69 to 68) and then attempted to push through an address to the crown "suggesting the absolute illegality of His Majesty's Prerogative to grant pensions on the Irish establishment." [50] Although the Castle mustered sufficient strength to kill the proposal 112 to 75, the opposition continued to harass the administration. Hugh Percy, second earl of Northumberland, the new lord lieutenant, wrote to Halifax on November 17 that the opposition vote was growing; a little later he expressed his dismay with "the mixed and equivocal proceedings" of the undertakers.[51] As in the previous session, the Castle managed in the end to check all the patriots' efforts,

[46] [Sir James Caldwell,] *Debates Relative to the Affairs of Ireland in the Years 1763 and 1764. Taken by a Military Officer*, 2nd ed., 2 vols. (London, 1766), I, 47. The first edition of Caldwell's *Debates* was published in London in 1765. The appearance of two editions of these Irish debates, edited anonymously by a member of the Irish Commons, indicates the increased interest in Irish politics.

[47] *Ibid.*, II, 607, 643–646.

[48] *Ibid.*, I, 184.

[49] *Ibid.*, 188–199.

[50] Northumberland to Halifax, Nov. 10, 1763, Great Britain, *The Calendar of Home Office Papers 1760–75*, 3 vols. (London, 1878–1899), I, 323.

[51] Northumberland to Halifax, Nov. 17, 26, 1763, *ibid.*, 327, 330.

but only by extensive use of what amounted to the veto power. The habeas corpus bill was stopped in the Irish privy council, while the English privy council so amended the tenure bill that it proved unacceptable to the Irish Commons. The popular septennial bill (on which the lord lieutenant maintained at least official neutrality) was left, as in 1762, for London to reject.[52] The Irish opposition seemed to have gained little ground, aside from a rather vague commitment from Northumberland that there would be no immediate increase in the number of pensions. But the old order was cracking. It was becoming apparent that the government must soon devise a more effective method for controlling the Irish parliament or make a number of concessions to the patriots.

In December 1764 both Archbishop Stone and the earl of Shannon died, thus removing two of the triumvirate who had served as lords justices since 1758 and had acted as the chief undertakers in the Irish parliament. Faced with the task of seeking a new alliance on which to base Castle support, the Grenville ministry met on February 11, 1765, to consider a course of action. Present were the lord lieutenant (Northumberland) and his two immediate predecessors Bedford (now lord president of the council) and Halifax, who had been secretary of state for the southern department since shortly after his return from Ireland. Another of the nine men attending also knew much of Irish affairs, John Perceval, second earl of Egmont, who had sat in the Irish Commons from 1731 to 1748 and had served as secretary of state for the southern department between 1761 and 1763. The brief cabinet minutes for the day read as follows:

The affairs of Ireland taken into consideration by His Majesty's order:

The Lords were all of opinion that after the death of the Lord Primate and Lord Shannon it was advisable to appoint one Lord Justice instead of those two in conjunction with Mr. Ponsonby till the return of the Lord Lieutenant. That the Ld. Chancellor of Ireland should be appointed be a Lord Jus-

---

[52] Northumberland to Halifax, Feb. 8, 1764, *ibid.*, 387–388.

tice accordingly and as my Lord Northumberland expressed great doubts whether his health would permit him to go again to Ireland as Lord Lieutenant it was the opinion of all the Lords that there was a necessity as well as propriety at this conjuncture to advise the King that whenever a new Lord Lieutenant should be appointed by His Majesty he should be directed to reside [almost] constantly and in case of necessity that there should be a short leave of absence given to him and a Lord Deputy appointed to the government during that absence.[53]

The plan to have a resident lord lieutenant meant that the government would no longer depend primarily on the undertakers. It would instead keep the lord lieutenant on the spot to build up a strong Castle party, as Ormond had attempted to do under Queen Anne. The plan fitted in with Grenville's general imperial policy of increasing administrative efficiency and revenue. Unfortunately Grenville's efforts in regard to the American colonies — the Proclamation Line of 1763, the Sugar and Currency Acts of 1764, and especially the Stamp Act of March 1765 — met with so unfavorable a response that they helped to precipitate the fall of the ministry in July 1765. Rockingham, who succeeded Grenville, remained in power scarcely a year. The ministerial crisis created a hiatus in Irish affairs: three different lord lieutenants were named within two years. Rockingham's nominee, Francis Seymour Conway, soon to become earl of Hertford, who served during the parliamentary session of 1765–1766, was the only one of the three to visit Ireland. Like the two previous sessions, that of 1765–1766 produced no significant legislation, but witnessed the continued growth of the opposition.

After the fall of Rockingham in 1766, George III finally convinced Pitt to take over the leadership of the government. Despite Pitt's great abilities, his ministry proved unstable. Removed to the Lords as earl of Chatham, plagued by illness, and jealous of his colleagues, Pitt failed to direct affairs effec-

---

[53] *Additional Grenville Papers, 1763–1765*, ed. John R. G. Tomlinson (Manchester, Manchester University Press, 1962), p. 336.

tively, although he remained in nominal control until 1768, and most of his coalition cabinet continued for another two years under Grafton. While these years of vacillating policies contributed to the further deterioration of colonial relations, the Chatham ministry acted with more decision toward Ireland. In August 1767, just before the convening of the Irish parliament, it carried out the recommendation of Grenville's cabinet by appointing George Townshend as lord lieutenant with specific instructions to remain in Ireland during his term of office.[54]

Townshend's administration (1767–1772) brought significant changes. The new lord lieutenant had orders to approve the septennial bill. This time when the heads of the bill reached London the ministry accepted it with only one modification. Since the Irish parliament met only every other year, and in order to avoid a simultaneous election in both Ireland and Britain, the government altered its terms to provide for an Irish election every eight instead of seven years. The Dublin parliament endorsed the revision. The Octennial Act of 1768 represented the fulfillment of one of the patriots' principal aims, and it made the Irish Commons more responsive to popular opinion. More important, however, was Townshend's policy toward the undertakers. In the spring of 1768 Townshend introduced a proposal to increase the size of the army in Ireland. Although he apparently would have preferred to postpone the measure until the next session, the ministry was anxious to push through the augmentation as part of its general program for financing imperial defense.[55] In order to minimize Irish objections, the bill stipulated that, except in emergencies, the strength of the resident forces in Ireland would remain at approximately its traditional level (about 12,000). In other words, the number of troops on the Irish establishment stationed abroad would normally equal the size of the proposed addition to the army (approximately 3,000).[56]

[54] Beckett, *Making of Modern Ireland*, p. 199.
[55] John Lees to Townshend, Apr. 23, 1768, "Townshend Letters 1768–1800," National Library of Ireland, Dublin, letter 3.
[56] *Irish Commons' Journal*, Apr. 19, 1768.

The Castle won a postponement of debate on the question to give it time to gain support, but a fortnight later the opposition passed a resolution (105 to 101) against any increase in government expenditures, thus eliminating any plan for expanding the military budget.[57] The failure of the new earl of Shannon and Ponsonby to support the augmentation provoked Townshend, but he decided to wait until after the election of a new parliament (as provided by the Octennial Act) before taking steps against them.

The parliamentary session of 1768–1769 saw a showdown between the administration and the undertakers. Their power threatened by a resident lord lieutenant, and probably influenced by the popularity of the patriots, Shannon and Ponsonby openly lined up with the opposition. The key issue was no longer the army augmentation. The Anglo-Irish landlord class felt a genuine concern for British defense needs, and the Castle won wide support for the army increase despite the cost; early in the session the Commons approved the measure. The patriots attacked the government from another quarter: they had the Commons throw out the government's supply bill on the grounds that it had originated in the English privy council. The opposition resolution (carried by a vote of 94 to 71) explicitly stated that all Irish revenue measures must come from the Irish Commons, an allegation, George III noted with displeasure, almost identical with that made by the Irish parliament of 1692.[58] Like Lord Sydney on that previous occasion, Townshend entered an official protest in the Journal of the Lords. He determined, unofficially, to oust the undertakers, for he held them clearly responsible for the government's humiliation: "The Duke of Leinster, Lord Shannon and the Speaker [Ponsonby], who all supported the Government upon this question in 1761, by a majority of 147 to 37, deserted it on the present occasion." [59]

<hr/>

[57] *Ibid.*, Apr. 19, May 3, 1768.

[58] George III to the duke of Grafton, Nov. 29, 1769, *The Correspondence of George III*, ed. Sir John Fortescue, 6 vols. (London, Macmillan & Co., 1927–1928), II, 60.

[59] Townshend to Lord Weymouth, Nov. 21, 1769, *Calendar of Home Office Papers*, II, 521.

Townshend had no easy time achieving his aims. In the first place, the Grafton ministry, which was faltering toward collapse, wished to avoid any radical steps. It took time and persuasion to win their consent to remove Shannon and Ponsonby from the offices they held and to prorogue parliament. Meanwhile Townshend had to fight off opposition maneuvers. Suspecting his plans, the patriots in the Commons passed a resolution (107 to 69) calling for an address to the lord lieutenant asking him to inform the House whether or not he had any instruction or intention to prorogue parliament. Townshend, although furious, replied politely if evasively: he feared that if he did otherwise the Commons might paralyze business by deciding to adjourn from day to day, as they had in their contest with the duke of Bedford. Townshend's answer placated the House, which defeated a motion to adjourn by 114 to 99.[60] By the spring of 1769 the lord lieutenant was finally in a position to carry out his policy "of establishing a stable government under the direct control and immediate guidance of the Castle." [61]

Thus by 1770 the system of government prevailing in Ireland for decades appeared radically altered. Two of the patriots' objectives had been realized: the Irish parliament was now subject to periodic elections, and the right of the Irish Commons to initiate money bills had been recognized in practice if not in theory. The government had, on the other hand, taken two steps to strengthen its control of Irish affairs: the lord lieutenant had been made a resident viceroy, and the undertakers were no longer permitted to manage the Irish Commons for the Castle. These changes did not actually resolve the fundamental problems of the country, and neither the patriots nor the government was satisfied with their results.

Despite a series of victorious encounters with the Castle, the patriots remained incapable of wresting power from the government. They suffered from two interrelated weaknesses: lack of unity and the inability to coerce the executive. Al-

[60] Townshend to Lord Weymouth, Dec. 23, 1769, *ibid.*, 549.
[61] Edith Johnston, "The Career and Correspondence of Thomas Allan c. 1725–1798," *Irish Historical Studies*, X (1956–1957), 301.

though the opposition counted among its numbers most of the effective orators in the Commons and enjoyed strong popular support, the patriots constituted a party only in the amorphous eighteenth-century sense of a coalition of individual leaders and their clients. They shared a general objective — to win for the Irish parliament what amounted to legislative autonomy — but they lacked consistency, organization, and discipline. The leaders of the movement seldom pooled their political resources; when they did, their influence over their followers proved unreliable. Some members who owed their election to the patronage of opposition leaders refused to display the obedience expected. Even when united and controlling a majority, the patriots found it impossible to exert control over an administration under the direction of the British cabinet.

On its part the government had difficulty in constituting a Castle party. The insubordination of placemen had troubled the Castle at least since the 1720's. Like the opposition grandees, the lord lieutenant enjoyed only limited influence over many members whose offices, pensions, or election obligations should have bound them to strict discipline.[62] An even more endemic difficulty facing the government was that any policy the government espoused was suspected of being designed to benefit English rather than Irish interests. Nevertheless, backed by George III and the new North ministry, Townshend and his successor Simon Harcourt, first earl of Harcourt (lord lieutenant, 1772–1777), judiciously employed the power of patronage to build up a strong following in parliament. To be sure of a majority, they found it wise to form an alliance

[62] David Large, "The Irish House of Commons in 1769," *Irish Historical Studies*, XI (1958–1959), 27. Large estimates the strength of the Castle in the Commons at some 112 supporters of whom only about a half were tied to the government by open patronage. In 1771 Townshend recommended that the government openly denounce the pretentions of the Irish Commons to control money bills, but the secretary of state told him that since the Irish parliament had provided the kind of supply bill desired, the ministry saw no point in making an issue of the question. Townshend to the earl of Rochford, Dec. 22, 1771, and Rochford to Townshend, Dec. 28, 1771, *Calendar of Home Office Papers*, II, 352–353, 365.

with at least one of the former undertakers and to do their best to seduce opposition spokesmen by offers of office. The Castle's relative freedom from the undertakers after 1769 permitted it to deal with the opposition with a surer hand. One way or another, the government succeeded in avoiding any major concessions to the patriots during the early 1700's. When, in 1773–1774, the opposition advocated a tax on absentee landlords, the administration officially backed the measure, but indirectly maneuvered to defeat it by convincing a majority of the Commons that such a bill would open the way to a general land tax on all landlords.[63] By 1774 the Castle's strength had apparently persuaded Flood that further opposition was fruitless; he joined the administration as a vice-treasurer to the disgust of his colleagues. What changed the more or less static situation of 1769–1775 was the outbreak of the American Revolution.

The culmination of the imperial crisis in the American war ushered in a new chapter in Anglo-Irish relations, a chapter that lies beyond the scope of this study. The course of events in America gave the opposition in both Great Britain and Ireland cause to attack the North ministry. It is significant that opposition leaders in the two countries began to cooperate. As early as 1773 Pitt expressed a respect for the position of the Irish patriots comparable to that he showed toward the American opponents of the government. When his colleague Lord Shelburne wrote for advice regarding an Irish bill to tax absentees, Pitt defended the constitutional rights of the Irish Commons with the kind of traditional Whig argument that had long been accepted in England and that the American as well as the Irish patriots employed to justify legislative autonomy in levying taxes. Shelburne, a large landowner in Ireland, admitting his bias, indicated that he thought the absentee tax harmful and believed the British government should reject it. Pitt replied as follows:

[63] Lecky, *History of England in the Eighteenth Century*, IV, 446–447. The Boyle and Ponsonby factions decided to vote against the bill, for which Flood criticized Ponsonby in a scathing attack. The incident illustrates the divisions among the opposition.

The fitness or justice of the tax in question, I shall not consider, if the Commons of Ireland send it here; I can only ask myself this single question in that case, What ought I to advise the Crown to do with it? The line of the constitution — a line written in the broadest letter, through every page of parliament and people — tells me that the Commons are to judge of the propriety and expediency of supplies. All opposition to be made to them is in its place, during the pendency of any such bill, by petition, or by members in the House; or for repeal, if inconvenience be found to result from a tax: but to advise the Crown to substitute, in the first instance, the opinion of the taxed in place of the judgment of the representative body, repugns to every principle I have been able to form myself, concerning the wise distribution of powers lodged by the constitution in various parts respectively of the legislature. This power of the purse in the Commons is fundamental, and inherent; to translate it from them to the King in Council, is to annihilate it.[64]

When two months later Shelburne suggested that he and Rockingham, another large Irish landholder, were considering some kind of parliamentary resolution against the threatened tax, Pitt answered sharply that "any proposition, resolution, or declaration in parliament here, censuring, branding or forbidding in future, a tax laid in a committee of supply, upon Ireland, in the Irish House of Commons, appears to me to be fatal." [65]

Within the next few years most of the opposition leaders in Britain had come to join the cause of the Irish and the American patriots in their attacks on the government. In 1779 Shelburne himself argued convincingly that Irish grievances must be remedied, pointing out that Ireland's provocations were greater than those suffered by the Americans in 1775.[66]

In Ireland itself the patriots naturally turned the American crisis to their advantage. Although Harcourt adroitly man-

[64] Pitt to Shelburne, Nov. 4, 1773, *Correspondence of William Pitt*, ed. Taylor and Pringle, IV, 306.
[65] *Ibid.*, IV, 320.
[66] *Parliamentary History of England from the Earliest Times to the Year 1803*, ed. William Cobbett, 36 vols. (London, 1806–1820), XX, 666.

aged to win expressions of loyalty from the Irish parliament,[67] the British administration could do little to prevent the growing strength of the Irish patriot movement. The outbreak of hostilities in America led to the creation of an unofficial volunteer military force. Similar volunteers had been raised in Ulster during the Seven Years' War.[68] Attempts by the Irish Commons to institute a regular civilian force by passing a militia act had been thwarted by London. Faced with the existence of thousands of volunteers, drawn chiefly from the Protestant middle classes, the government hastened to pass an act establishing a regular Irish militia over which it could exert control.[69] The political power of the volunteer movement, whose membership embraced a large proportion of the electorate, remained, however. The demands of the Irish patriots could no longer be ignored. Opposition criticism, American reverses, and Irish pressure finally compelled the North ministry to make some concessions [70] by removing restrictions on Irish trade. In 1782, after North's fall, the Whig ministry of Rockingham and the subsequent Fox-North coalition worked to repeal the British Declaratory Act of 1720 and approved of Yelverton's Act in Ireland, which drastically revised Poynings' Law. In that year "the 'Irish nation' of the Protestant ascendancy," as Beckett puts it, finally achieved the kind of constitution it had sought since 1692.[71]

The success of the American and Irish patriots represented a repudiation of the old imperial system by which Britain had governed its overseas dependencies since the seventeenth century. One alternative to that system was complete colonial independence, which the thirteen colonies had now achieved. Another alternative, which would take shape in the next

---

[67] O'Connell, *Irish Politics*, pp. 26–27.

[68] Stone to Bedford, May 28, 1759, *Bedford Correspondence*, II, 280–282.

[69] O'Connell, *Irish Politics*, pp. 72–74. Flood and the patriots had backed a militia bill in 1765 and almost convinced Pitt to endorse it. *Correspondence of William Pitt*, ed. Taylor and Pringle, III, 1–4.

[70] The drive for trade concessions was launched in the British Commons by an Anglo-Irish member of the opposition, Lord Nugent. O'Connell, *Irish Politics*, pp. 129–130.

[71] Beckett, *Making of Modern Ireland*, p. 205.

century, was that of responsible government for the colonies. In 1782 Ireland had taken a decisive step in the direction of becoming what would later be known as a dominion. The essential characteristic of dominion status — the accountability of the executive to an independent legislature — did not, however, exist in Ireland at this time. Indeed, the concept of responsible colonial government was probably beyond the comprehension of eighteenth-century politicians. Furthermore, the unrepresentative character of the Irish parliament — still exclusively Protestant and dominated by a small group of aristocrats — lessened the chances for additional reform. Under different circumstances, nevertheless, the problem of reconciling Irish parliamentary power with allegiance to Britain might have resulted in a united Ireland becoming the first self-governing dominion. Whatever chances such a solution might have had, the crises precipitated by the French Revolution and subsequent wars led to a totally different outcome: the attempt to integrate Ireland into the United Kingdom.

The Act of Union, which disregarded the nascent Irish nationalism of the eighteenth century, deflected for over a century Ireland's evolution as an emerging nation. In the nineteenth century Ireland formed a part, however dissident, of metropolitan Britain rather than a part of the empire. By contrast, before the American Revolution, Ireland had been essentially a colonial dependency, aspiring as the American colonies to greater self-government. At a number of points in previous chapters comparisons have been drawn between Ireland and the American colonies. It is appropriate to close this study with a chapter devoted to an analysis of the differences and similarities between Ireland and the other British colonies of European settlement and to the influence of Ireland upon the American colonies.

XI

Ireland's Place
in the
Old Empire

The English revolution of 1688 had immediate repercussions in England's overseas dependencies: in America it ended the attempt to create the Dominion of New England and precipitated an abortive revolution in New York; in Ireland it led to the Williamite War and the Treaty of Limerick. In addition to these initial results, the revolution caused a basic shift in the general character of imperial government. In 1709 a British official urged Irish acceptance of a government supply bill on the grounds that "it is an undoubted truth that the crown is the best, perhaps the only shelter against any hardship the parliament of England may at any time lay on Ireland." [1] Though historically sound, his argument was already obsolete. Before 1688 the position of the crown in both Ireland and America remained relatively independent of the English parliament. After the Glorious Revolution the crown's authority over Ireland, as over the colonies, became increasingly subordinate to the British parliament as that body gained influence over the different agencies of royal administration. The growth of cabinet government in Britain must be considered one of the factors that contributed to the imperial crisis of the 1760's and 1770's. The emergence of the cabinet as the key administrative body of the empire affected Ireland more pervasively than it did the American colonies. The chief difference between Ireland and the colonies would appear, technically, to arise from Ireland's unique status as a separate kingdom with its own apparatus of royal courts, privy council, Lords, and Commons. Ireland's proximity and long history of troubled relations with England were, actually, more significant than

[1] J[ohn] Pulteney to Joshua Dawson, Aug. 9, 1709, Dublin P.R.O., Calendar of Departmental Correspondence, I, 142.

its peculiar constitutional position. Spanish and French intervention in Ireland had convinced English statesmen that control of Ireland was essential to English security. British ministers concerned themselves more directly with Irish than with American affairs. At the beginning of each session of the Irish parliament the British cabinet appointed a special committee to review Irish legislation. This committee weighed the recommendations of the English attorney general and solicitor general, to whom interested groups presented their petitions and arguments. Between Irish parliamentary sessions the secretary of state for the southern department kept in close touch with the viceroy (usually himself in London during these periods), the lords justices, and certain other important Irish leaders.[2] This whole arrangement represents a much more tightly knit system than that practiced in dealing with the colonies. Colonial business was largely relegated to the Board of Trade; Irish decisions were made at the ministerial level. In fact, the lord lieutenant frequently served as a member of the cabinet.

In addition to the lord lieutenant there were often other ministers who had had experience in the Irish administration or who had economic interests or family connections in Ireland. It will be recalled that at the cabinet meeting in February 1765, which decided in favor of a resident lord lieutenant, four of the nine men present had been connected with the Irish government. That was an exception, but between the resignation of Walpole in 1742 and 1782 there were usually two or three high government officials in London who had a firsthand knowledge of Irish affairs. Following Devonshire's resignation in 1745, five of the next six lord lieutenants who served in Ireland subsequently held important posts in London.[3] The same is true of three of the Irish chief secretaries

---

[2] J. C. Beckett, "Anglo-Irish Constitutional Relations in the Later Eighteenth Century," *Irish Historical Studies*, XIV (1964–1965), 21–23. Apparently all papers relating to Ireland were abstracted in the secretary of state's office for the use of the ministers. R. Powys to [Joshua Dawson], May 20, 1708, Calendar of Departmental Correspondence, I, 107.

[3] Chesterfield (lord lieutenant, 1745–1746) was secretary of state for the northern department, 1746–1748; Dorset (lord lieutenant, 1730–1737, 1750–

from the same period: General Henry Seymour Conway, Lord George Sackville Germain, and Richard Rigby.⁴ Four Irish peers — Egmont, Hillsborough, Nugent, and Shelburne — held ministerial posts in the 1760's and 1770's. These men did not, of course, view matters identically. Hillsborough, despite a concern for Irish poverty, opposed concessions to the Irish as well as to the American patriots. On the other hand, Conway, and eventually Shelburne, tended to support both groups.⁵ Regardless of their political sympathies, most of them had an intimate knowledge of Irish problems. In contrast, almost none of the British leaders possessed a comparable understanding of America. Although some ministers had economic interests involving America, including investments in colonial land companies, none had ever lived there.⁶

1755) was lord president of the council in 1745 and master of the horse, 1755–1757; Devonshire (lord lieutenant, 1755–1756) was chief minister with Newcastle, 1756–1757, and lord chamberlain, 1757–1762; Bedford (lord lieutenant, 1757–1760) was lord privy seal, 1761–1763, and lord president of the council, 1763–1765; Halifax (lord lieutenant, 1761–1763) was secretary of state for the northern department, 1762–1763, and for the southern department, 1763–1765.

⁴ General Henry Seymour Conway, a nephew of Sir Robert Walpole's, sat in the Irish Commons in 1741 and, after military service abroad, served as chief secretary to Devonshire when he was lord lieutenant in 1755–1756. He was secretary of state for the southern department, 1765–1766, and for the northern department, 1766–1768. Germain (first viscount Sackville after 1782) was the son of Dorset and attended Trinity College during his father's first term as lord lieutenant; during Dorset's second term he served as chief secretary. He was secretary of state for the colonies, 1775–1782. Rigby was Bedford's chief secretary, 1758–1760, and vice-treasurer of Ireland in 1765. He was paymaster of the forces, 1768–1782.

⁵ Sir John Percival (or Perceval), second earl of Egmont, sat in the Irish Commons from 1731 until 1748, when he inherited his father's title. He was first lord of the admiralty, 1763–1766. Wills Hill, viscount Hillsborough in 1742 and earl of Hillsborough in 1751, served as president of the board of trade, 1763–1765, and in 1766, and as secretary of state for the colonies, 1768–1772. Robert, earl of Nugent, vice-treasurer of Ireland, 1760–1765 and 1768–1782, served as president of the Board of Trade, 1766–1768. Sir William Petty, second earl of Shelburne, was secretary of state for the southern department, 1766–1768. These four Irish peers sat for some years in the British Commons and were more active in England than Ireland, although both Egmont and Hillsborough attended the Irish Lords periodically.

⁶ One American did serve as undersecretary of state for the colonies between 1770 and 1782, William Knox of Georgia. On the question of

Because of the British government's close attention to Irish business there existed important differences between the position of the lord lieutenant and that of the colonial governor. The former was more definitely a British official. Until 1767 he spent two-thirds of his time in England, leaving the day-to-day administration of Ireland during his absence in the hands of the lords justices. The problems confronting the Irish viceroy and the colonial governor arose, nevertheless, from the same cause: both served as an intermediary between central and local government and came under attack from both quarters. Several viceroys, such as Shrewsbury, Grafton, and Dorset, received rebukes from London for succumbing to Irish pressures. More often, like Townshend in the case of the army augmentation proposal, they followed their instructions, but at the price of strengthening the Irish opposition. One way out of their dilemma was to leave to London the onus of rejecting popular measures. Ormond tried this in 1705, when he approved a penal law to win support for supplies, meanwhile suggesting to London that he would not be disappointed should the bill not be returned.[7] Halifax and Northumberland remained ostensibly neutral toward the septennial bills of the early 1760's, knowing full well that London would stop them. By its very nature the viceroy's role was essentially negative. Even more than the colonial governor, the lord lieutenant found it difficult to offer positive leadership: the British ministry counted upon him to preserve the status quo; the Irish distrusted any initiative he might take. Chesterfield observed that "Lord lieutenants are suspected persons, their proposals have *foenum in cornu,* and the answer to any scheme that takes rise from them, though singly meant for the public good would be *timeo Danaos et dona ferentes.*"[8] And Arch-

---

colonial lands and British politics, see Bernard Donoughue, *British Politics and the American Revolution, The Path to War, 1773–75* (London, Macmillan & Co., 1964), pp. 113–117.

[7] *Ormonde MSS,* n. s., VIII, xliv.

[8] *Chesterfield's Letters,* ed. Dobrée, III, 650. *Foenum in cornu* [hay on the horn] refers to the Roman custom of putting a sprig of hay on the horn of a dangerous bull; *timeo Danaos et dona ferentes* [I fear the Greeks even when they offer gifts] is a quote from Vergil.

bishop King remarked that the best Ireland could expect from a lord lieutenant was that he would do no harm.[9]

Historians have generally joined earlier writers in criticizing the lord lieutenants of the period, except for Carteret and Chesterfield. These two displayed sympathy for Irish difficulties, but their good reputation probably owes something to their gift for witty expression. Chesterfield, in particular, has left a satirical picture of his colleagues that stresses their shortcomings — in contrast to his own high aims. "I am sensible I shall be reckoned a very shallow Politician from my attention to such trifling Objects, as the Improvement of your lands, the Extension of your Manufactures and the Increase of your Trade . . . Whereas an able Lord-Lieutenant ought to employ his thoughts in greater Matters. We should think of jobs for Favourites, Sops for Enemies, managing Parties, and engaging Parliament to vote away their own and their Fellow Subjects' Liberties and Properties." [10]

Actually, when one reviews the record of the viceroys from Ormond through Townshend it is only fair to observe that most of them showed concern for Irish welfare as they saw it, although of course all of them had to play politics, including Chesterfield. It is often said that the lord lieutenants spent a scant six months out of every two years in Dublin, arriving in Ireland in time to open parliament and leaving immediately after each session. In reality, the majority arrived several weeks in advance of the opening of parliament and sometimes remained following the close of the session. The average stay was eight months in every two years.[11] Several viceroys besides Carteret and Chesterfield, notably Ormond, Dorset, the third duke of Devonshire, Bedford, and Halifax, recognized the social as well as political importance of their office.[12] Lord

[9] For a discussion of the caliber of colonial governors in New York, see Stanley N. Katz, *Newcastle's New York: Anglo-American Politics 1732–1753* (Cambridge, Harvard University Press, Mass., 1968), pp. 21–38.

[10] Chesterfield to Mr. Prior, n. d., *Orrery Papers*, II, 41.

[11] McCracken, "Undertakers in Ireland," p. 347.

[12] Chesterfield opened the grounds of the viceroy's suburban residence at Chapel Izod to the public and thus provided Dublin with its great Phoenix Park. During Halifax's administration parliament raised the lord lieutenant's stipend from £12,000 to £16,000. Halifax declined the increase

lieutenants who served for longer terms, such as Ormond, Carteret, Dorset, the third duke of Devonshire, and Bedford, devoted considerable time to Irish affairs when they were in London, striving to explain the Irish point of view to the British ministers. Townshend, as the first resident lord lieutenant, kept a personal representative, Thomas Allan, in London and through him brought effective pressure on the government.[13] Not one of the viceroys in the eighteenth century fully identified himself with Irish interests or ever settled there permanently, while a few of the colonial governors were American born, and some settled in America. Yet, the lord lieutenant, because of his close English connections, often proved a more effective advocate for Ireland than did the colonial governor for his colony.

In both the colonies and Ireland the chief executive had an advisory council with extensive influence. The colonial council and Irish privy council were similar in many respects, even though the functions of the colonial council appear more sweeping because it exercised legislative and judicial as well as administrative powers. The Irish council, too, was more than just an executive agency: it served as a kind of third legislative chamber. According to Poynings' Law, as amended under Mary, the Irish privy council was responsible for drawing up Irish legislation. By the middle of the eighteenth century it initiated only a few bills, but it retained the task of reviewing and approving all heads of bills passed by either the Irish Commons or Lords. Irish efforts to have heads of bills pass both houses of parliament before going to the Castle were, as mentioned, stopped by the government. Instead, each house sent its proposed bills directly to the lord lieutenant who placed them before the council. Only after being forwarded by the Irish council to London and approved

---

for himself, although he spent £20,000 per annum while in Ireland. *Memoirs of Richard Cumberland by Himself*, ed. Henry Flanders (Philadelphia, 1856), p. 118. In the mid-eighteenth century the governor of New York received about £4,000, half of which he spent on entertainment. Katz, *Newcastle's New York*, p. 31.

[13] Johnston, "Career and Correspondence of Thomas Allan," 298–324.

there was a bill returned to be voted upon by both houses of the Irish parliament, at which time it could only be passed without amendment or rejected. The accusation, made by opposition leaders, that the privy council regularly altered bills is certainly an exaggeration. On the other hand, its role was far from perfunctory; it changed some bills and blocked others. During each session it spent considerable time going over legislation and apparently had borrowed from parliament the practice of reading bills three times.[14] The British government gave weight to its recommendations and held it resposible for checking the factual information in all private bills.[15] Since the Irish privy council contained several high court justices and the chancellor it also had a quasi-judicial character and was specifically granted certain judicial functions by several statutes.[16]

In composition the colonial councils and the Irish privy council likewise resembled each other. Both were made up of prominent men appointed by the executive with the approval of the crown, and both American and Irish councillors frequently displayed independence in spite of the fact that they

[14] J. T. Ball, *Historical Review of the Legislative Systems Operative in Ireland from the Invasion of Henry II to the Union*, new ed. (London and Dublin, 1889), p. 269. William Cary writing to Delafaye Jan. 5, 1733/34 spoke of having "frequent councils to form into Acts the Heads of Bills sent from each House of Parliament." Eng. P.R.O., S.P. 63/397, fol. 3. Harrington writing to Bedford, Feb. 10, 1749/50 likewise spoke of the heavy business sent to the privy council by parliament. Eng. P.R.O., S.P. 63/412, fol. 46.

[15] Lords of council of Great Britain to Lord Lieutenant and Council of Ireland, Sept. 24, 1719, Calendar of Departmental Correspondence, I, 55.

[16] By Irish Statute, 2 Anne, c. 8, it was to hear Catholic claims to certain kinds of land; by Irish Statute, 4 Anne, c. 8, sect. 10, it was to hear appeals regarding prices set for Dublin coach fares; by 6 George I, c. 1, it was to issue warrants to the lord chancellor instructing him to make out writs to empower judges to postpone the Michaelmas term until Nov. 2; by 17 George II, c. 11, sect. 2, it was to hear appeals for adjustment of salvage awards. The council also had an important part in choosing local magistrates. Boulter to Newcastle, Jan. 10, 1729/30, Eng. P.R.O., S.P. 63/392, fol. 65. The council's judicial role was, however, limited. When it ventured to hear an appeal from a judgment of the Court of Queen's Bench it was challenged by the Irish Commons. *Irish Commons' Journal*, Oct. 13, 17, 1707; see also *ibid.*, Dec. 17, 1713.

owed their appointment to the government. The Irish body was more formal and technically much larger. Like its English prototype, the Irish privy council had a number of ex officio members: the lord lieutenant's chief secretary, the primate and several other bishops, the chancellor and several justices, and the Speaker of the Commons. These officials plus a selected number of prominent peers and influential members of the Commons brought its nominal size up to fifty or more.[17] In practice its effective membership was much smaller. Several statutes specify that it might take action upon a vote of a majority of six, which suggests that its operating size was about a dozen, much the same as the average colonial council.[18] There were, nevertheless, two definite differences between the Irish council and its colonial counterpart. First, the lord lieutenant could vote at its meetings, a right denied colonial governors after the 1720's.[19] Second, its members, almost without exception, sat in either the Irish Lords or Commons, making it really a kind of select committee of parliament rather than a separate body. The colonial councils, in contrast, constituted the upper house of the legislature.

The most obvious distinction between the colonial and the Irish governmental structure was the existence in the latter of a House of Lords. Colonial councillors had no such exalted rank; nor were they hereditary. Since the crown appointed the Irish bishops (who made up a sizable portion of the active members of the upper house) and could create new peers as well as raise others in rank, the Irish lords should have been easily dominated by the Castle. Such was rarely the case. Like the English House of Lords in the eighteenth century, the ties of family, patronage, and social connection between the peers

---

[17] Petty says the council had fifty members in the late seventeenth century. *Economic Writings of Sir William Petty*, I, 163. There were officially seventy members in 1771. Johnston, *Great Britain and Ireland*, p. 95.

[18] Irish Statutes, 2 Anne, c. 8; 2 George I, c. 14; 8 George I, c. 11, sect. 2. Some important meetings were certainly larger; there were, for example, twenty-three at the meeting on Jan. 21, 1758.

[19] Greene, *The Provincial Governor*, pp. 43-44; Labaree, *Royal Government in America*, p. 162.

and the Commons proved stronger than those which bound them to the crown. In struggles between the Irish parliament and the government the Lords often lined up with the Commons. Furthermore, as was seen in the dispute over the Annesley case in 1719, the Irish Lords were jealous of their prerogatives. That house adopted most of the standing orders of the British Lords and viewed itself as a comparable body.[20]

The relative strength and importance of the Irish Commons and the colonial assemblies are difficult to determine. Both history and geography created marked variations between them. Ireland was much more populous than any of the individual colonies, and its Commons had 300 members. Many of the assemblies had only thirty or forty.[21] Ireland also had much older traditions and the prestige that went with them. On the other hand, the recent origin of the colonial assemblies, combined with the fluid conditions of a frontier society, provided advantages as well as drawbacks. For example, while it took considerable effort for colonial legislatures to win recognition of such parliamentary privileges for their members as freedom from arrest,[22] the rapid growth of settlements in America helped assemblies to establish control over the creation of new constituencies, clearly a prerogative of the crown in Ireland.[23] Despite the differences between the Dublin Commons and the colonial assemblies one can readily detect parallel developments.

[20] *Irish Lords' Journal*, July 30, 1707.

[21] William Douglass said that the assembly in New York had twenty-seven, New Jersey twenty-four, Pennsylvania thirty-four, Maryland forty-four, Connecticut ninety-six, and Rhode Island fifty-eight, which means that all six together would have fewer members than the Irish Commons. William Douglass, *A Summary Historical and Political of the First Planting, Progressive Improvements, and Present State of the British Settlements in North America*, 2 vols. (Boston, 1749–1752), I, 497.

[22] Judging from the requests by speakers of the assembly for parliamentary privileges for members, the colonies seem to have won these rights as follows: Jamaica, 1677; Maryland, 1682; Virginia, 1684; New York, 1691; South Carolina, 1702; New Jersey, 1703; Pennsylvania, 1707; Georgia, 1755; Nova Scotia, 1759; North Carolina, 1760. Mary Patterson Clarke, *Parliamentary Privileges in the American Colonies* (New Haven, Yale University Press, 1943), p. 70.

[23] Greene, *Quest for Power*, p. 8.

Like the colonial assemblies, the Irish Commons assumed
increasing control over finances. The insufficiency of the
crown's hereditary income compelled the government to seek
additional taxes and thus provided the Commons with sufficient leverage to achieve many of the same gains won by
colonial legislatures: the right to audit accounts, to designate
by specific statute both the character of new taxes and new
expenditures, and after 1753 to dispose of the surplus by the
simple device of spending it on internal improvements.[24] In
the area of parliamentary privileges, except for establishing
new constituencies, the Irish parliament remained in advance
of most colonial bodies. It passed election laws, determined
its own disputed elections, and jealously guarded the immunities enjoyed by its members. It also exercised, if with mixed
results, the right to arrest persons for contempt of either house.
Its efforts to influence executive policy met with both rebuffs
and successes. For instance, the sensitiveness of the Irish parliament to religious questions forced the lord lieutenants to
accept and to a degree implement the penal laws after they
were no longer favored by the British ministry. It is obvious,
on the other hand, that the Castle refused to enforce anti-
Catholic legislation with any consistency. It is equally clear,
conversely, that the Irish administration, under pressure from
parliament and popular opinion, was normally lax in its efforts to carry out such British regulations as the Woolens Act.

The one area in which colonial legislatures appear to have
enjoyed a distinct advantage over the Irish parliament is in
their influence over the appointment and actions of royal
officials. With virtually the entire revenue of the colonies
coming from nonpermanent taxes, appropriations for the civil
list depended directly on legislative approval. But the lord
lieutenant's need for parliamentary cooperation compelled
him to share patronage with the undertakers until the 1750's,

---

[24] Commenting on this practice, Bedford wrote to Pitt, Nov. 17, 1757:
"the method by which of late years has been exorbitantly used by the
House of Commons in loading the money bills by resolutions of their own,
without previous consent or address to his Majesty, ought undoubtedly to
put a stop to." *Bedford Correspondence*, II, 297.

and after that the Irish Commons regularly made an issue of the government's expenditures on pensions and administrative positions. The differences on this score are more apparent than real. If the Irish Commons failed in its efforts to pass a place bill, colonial attempts to exclude placemen from membership in the assemblies met with only limited success.[25]

The most striking contrast between the Irish Commons and the colonial assemblies is that the latter were more representative of popular opinion. In the first place, until the Octennial Act of 1768 the Irish Commons could go without a general election throughout an entire reign, as it did between 1727 and 1760. Colonial assemblies seldom went more than six or seven years without new elections, and, although London vetoed proposals for biennial and triennial elections, it approved a septennial act for New York in the 1740's and one for Virginia in 1762.[26] It is even more important that the colonies had more liberal voting qualifications. Although the colonies suffered from unequal election districts and required property ownership for the franchise, their assemblies were far more representative than the Irish Commons, except perhaps in the West Indies.[27] The disparity in the size of county electorates in Ireland had its counterpart in the colonies, but the latter had no rotten or pocket boroughs, while about half of the Irish M.P.'s came from boroughs controlled by individuals or small corporate bodies. Furthermore, the disfranchisement of the Catholics excluded from direct participation over two-thirds of the Irish population.

The narrow electoral base of the Irish Commons did not, however, prevent it from taking a lead in the struggle against executive power. The Castle could never on its own muster a permanent majority; it always needed support from either the country party or the undertakers. Even when the undertaking system was operating at its smoothest, some Irish lead-

[25] Greene, *Quest for Power*, pp. 188–189.
[26] Greene, *Provincial Governor*, pp. 155–156.
[27] For a convenient summary of colonial voting requirements, see Oscar T. Barck, Jr., and Hugh T. Lefler, *Colonial America* (New York, Macmillan & Co., 1958), pp. 259–260.

ers and independent members periodically formed an opposition. From 1750 on the Castle had to contend with the fact
that influential aristocrats, like Lord Kildare, Lord Shannon,
and later Lord Charlemont, with their bloc of pocket boroughs,
were willing to ally themselves with the patriot party. The
growing political consciousness of the Irish Commons led to
an increased attendance and participation which are reflected
in the recorded divisions. Earlier in the century the number
voting was sometimes less than a hundred and seldom much
more. Right after the excitement over Wood's "brass farthings," a vote in the Commons on the government debt ran
as high as 207, and some hotly contested elections in 1727 were
decided by from 143 to 170 members.[28] In 1735, 194 members
voted on a resolution attacking customs officials, and the La
Touche election, following the Lucas affair in 1749, was determined by 171.[29] Before 1750 divisions involving over 50 percent (150) were relatively rare; after 1750 they were common.
The series of votes between 1757 and 1769 ranged from 165
to 213. Divisions in 1771 concerning the question of the Irish
Commons' control of finances ran between 211 and 240.[30] The
other high votes during the period came in connection with
the dispute over the budget surplus in 1753. Several divisions
that year involved 239 voters and one 240, or 80 percent of the
total membership.[31] These figures compare quite favorably
with those for the British Commons; its high point was also
80 percent, at the time of the Dunning resolution in 1780.[32]

The emerging nationalism manifested by the Dublin parliament, though exclusive both from the standpoint of class
and religion, posed a definite threat to British rule. After all,

---

[28] *Irish Commons' Journal*, Nov. 15, 1725, Dec. 20, 1727, Feb. 2, 15, 19,
1727/28.

[29] *Ibid.*, Nov. 25, 1735, Dec. 18, 1749.

[30] *Ibid.*, Feb. 28, Mar. 2, 7, 1771. Thomas St. George unofficially reported
votes of from 211 to 245 during the following autumn. St. George to
Hardwicke, Nov. 7, 16, 28, Dec. 2, 12, 28, 1771, British Museum, Additional
Manuscripts 35610 (Hardwicke Papers), fols. 71–72, 82, 86, 92, 96, 107–108.

[31] *Irish Commons' Journal*, Nov. 25, Dec. 17, 1753.

[32] John Brooke, *The House of Commons 1754–1790* (New York, Oxford
University Press, 1968), p. 287.

it was the "economic and social elite" who led the movement to increase the power of the colonial legislatures.[33] As Beckett observes, the eighteenth-century Irish parliament did represent "fairly accurately the outlook of the whole landlord class."[34] The number of Protestant freeholders eligible to vote in county elections appears to have been about 50,000; the total number of voters in the boroughs approached 20,000.[35] An electorate of 70,000 out of a total of 2,500,000 to 3,000,000 can scarcely be called democratic. On the other hand, counting five to a family, it constituted from 10 to 15 percent of the population. It is quite possible that a larger percentage of the Protestant middle classes could vote in Ireland than in Great Britain, and even the electorate in some colonies, such as Rhode Island, may not have been proportionately larger.[36]

The most significant difference between the Irish and colonial governments did not arise from the dissimilarities between their outward structure; it resulted from the manner in which British rule had been established in Ireland. In a far more fundamental sense than in conquered colonies like Jamaica

[33] Greene, *Quest for Power*, p. 11.

[34] J. C. Beckett, "The Irish Parliament in the 18th Century," Belfast Natural History and Philosophical Society, *Proceedings*, 2nd ser., IV (1955), 18.

[35] These figures are based on Appendix B in Johnston, *Great Britain and Ireland*, pp. 321-330.

[36] One contemporary estimate puts the number of voters in Rhode Island in 1749 as under 1,000 out of a total population of over 28,000 whites, 3,000 Negroes, and 1,000 Indians. Douglass, *Summary Historical and Political*, II, 89. A recent study maintains that from 14 to 19 percent of the total population could have qualified to vote although only between 4 and 9 percent actually voted. David S. Lovejoy, *Rhode Island Politics and the American Revolution* (Providence, Brown University Press, 1958), pp. 16-17. There were apparently only 1,515 voters in New York City in 1769. Cortland F. Bishop, *History of Elections in the American Colonies* (New York, 1893), p. 164. According to a report in the *Pennsylvania Gazette*, May 18, 1769, only 508 voted in the election of that year that elected James Otis, Thomas Cushing, Samuel Adams, and John Hancock to the Massachusetts General Court. Even Robert and Katherine Brown, who argue that the colonial franchise was quite democratic, admit that frequently only a small proportion of those qualified actually voted. See figures in *Virginia 1705-1786, Democracy or Aristocracy* (East Lansing, Mich., 1964), pp. 141-143.

or New York, the Irish government rested on conquest and could not readily escape its military origins. Yet even this distinction, on which colonists like Daniel Dulany and James Otis laid great stress, must not be exaggerated.[37]

Despite the warlike heritage of the seventeenth century, the presence of a standing army, and the restrictive legislation concerning Catholics, Ireland in the early eighteenth century constituted neither an occupied territory nor a police state. Although the government occasionally employed troops to effect arrests and to quell disorders, it did not rule through martial law. The lord lieutenants were careful to keep the movement and stationing of troops within the limits prescribed by Irish laws; other actions on the part of the administration reveal the same concern for legality. When attempts to stifle a free press by patronage and influence failed, the Castle normally prosecuted for libel rather than resorting to arbitrary suppression. The Dublin authorities even held royal warrants (to exempt pensioners from the absentee tax) invalid when not in accordance with Irish statute.[38] Although Ireland had no habeas corpus act, long imprisonment without trial appears rare.[39] Judges, while they might harangue juries and require acquitted defendants to post security to assure good behavior, followed English procedures and were bound to accept jury verdicts. Speaking of several offenders arrested for illegal recruiting, Boulter remarked: "I rather fancy, it will happen, as it happened in most of the like occasions, that, though there was evidence enough to commit them, yet upon the tryal there will not be evidence enough to convict them." [40] When

---

[37] [Daniel Dulany,] *The Late Occurrences in North America and Policy of Great Britain Considered* (London, 1766), p. 5; James Otis, *The Rights of British Colonies Asserted and Proved* (Boston, 1764), note p. 33.

[38] W. Lingen to James Payzart, Apr. 1, 1731, Eng. P.R.O., S.P. 63/394, fol. 37.

[39] A John Casey was held, "on suspicion of being a Torey," without any indictment, but his release is ordered "seeing nothing is proved against him." British Museum, Additional Manuscripts 38173, Irish Petitions and Country Letters, fol. 5.

[40] Boulter to Newcastle, Mar. 1, 1730/31, Eng. P.R.O., S.P. 63/394, fol. 25.

a dispute developed between the crown and the chapter of St. Patrick's Cathedral, the lord lieutenant advised London to drop the case because any Dublin jury would side with the chapter.[41] Most of the Irish judges, in the opinion of McCracken, refused to kowtow to the undertakers.[42] Though technically Irish judges could be removed at royal pleasure, in practice they enjoyed tenure.[43]

The government's restraint and respect for law were both the cause and effect of more peaceful conditions. Armed resistance, especially after Anne's reign, became confined to the activities of a few outlaw bands of tories or rapparees. Legislation making local inhabitants responsible for the restitution of damages done by raiders probably helped to reduce the support given them by native tenants.[44] The restoration of order and at least partial economic recovery after 1700 diminished the incentives for rebellion. The most restless and dissatisfied element in the population left Ireland to enlist in foreign armies. To be sure, violence never disappeared. In 1735 the lords justices felt compelled to issue two proclamations: one to set a reward for the capture of the murderer of the sheriff of Tipperary; another to warn several "Tories, Robbers and Rapparees" indicted by the grand juries of Kerry, Meath, Cork, and Londonderry that, unless they surrendered within six weeks, they would be judged guilty of high treason.[45] Ill feeling between civilians and the military did, occasionally, erupt in violence, and other types of crime and disorder did exist. In the 1760's a new wave of agrarian violence, the Whiteboy movement, directed chiefly against tithes, arose among embittered tenants. It is far from clear, nevertheless, that the Irish countryside was any less safe than that in many parts of contemporary Europe. According to figures given by Newenham, only fifty-four persons were sen-

---

[41] Harrington to Bedford, Mar. 3, 1747/48, Eng. P.R.O., S.P. 63/410, fol. 178.
[42] McCracken, "Undertakers in Ireland," pp. 24–25.
[43] Ball, *Judges in Ireland,* I, 93.
[44] Irish Statute, 7 William, c. 21.
[45] *Dublin Evening Post,* June 14, 1735.

tenced to hang in County Cork during the period 1767–1786: two for Whiteboy outrages, twelve for murder, and forty for stealing — a relatively low number for a populous area in the eighteenth century. An English visitor to Ireland in 1779 wrote that "the most perfect security attends travelling throughout this kingdom; for excepting the environs of Dublin, it is very unusual to hear of any highwayman or footpad." [46]

If, on the one hand, the processes of civilian law, including the jury system, remained in force, there can be little doubt that the justice administered reflected both class and religious prejudice. In theory all native-born Irish, like all freeborn colonists, enjoyed the legal rights of Englishmen — a principle set down as early as Calvin's case in 1608.[47] Equality before the law did not, however, mean equal rights for everyone, since the laws themselves specifically restricted the privileges of certain religious groups. Although the fact that the penal laws were frequently evaded may have lightened their burden, evasion created an atmosphere of arbitrary enforcement that did much to foster disrespect for law. The eccentricities of law enforcement in Ireland arose not only from the discrepancies between official policy and popular opinion, but also because the central administration sometimes sought to set aside the penal laws while local Anglo-Irish officials strove to apply them. At the beginning of George I's reign, when Anglo-French relations were friendly, London favored granting permission to the French to recruit troops in Ireland to fill the depleted ranks of the Irish regiments in French service. A recent Irish statute had, unfortunately, made it a felony to recruit for foreign service without an explicit royal license.[48]

[46] Philip Luckombe, *A Tour Through Ireland wherein the Present State of That Kingdom is Considered* (London, 1780), p. 17; Newenham, *View of Ireland*, Appendix XXX. On the Whiteboy movement, see Lecky, *History of England in the Eighteenth Century*, IV, 351–370.

[47] Coke maintained that "any that was born in Ireland was no alien to the realm of England"; he held the Irish to be "natural-born subjects." *Reports of Sir Edward Coke*, rev. George Wilson (London, 1777), pp. 18, 23.

[48] Opinion on recruiting signed by P[hilip] Yorke, Mar. 8, 1727/28, Eng. P.R.O., S.P. 63/390, fols. 37–39.

While Walpole's ministry hesitated to arouse anti-Catholic feeling, they wished to oblige the French ambassador, Count Broglie. As Newcastle explained it to the Irish lords justices, "The King did not think fit to give an authority in form for it, yet His Majesty was pleased to promise that, provided the officers behaved themselves well, they should be suffered to raise Recruits . . . The King has that dependence upon your Grace's prudent management of this affair, that His Majesty leaves it to you to take such measures as you shall think proper." Boulter wrote back bluntly that if the Irish government did as instructed local justices of the peace, acting upon the law, would promptly arrest the French officers, who could not then be released "but by due process of law, or by granting them a pardon." [49] Shortly after Boulter's reply the cabinet, at a special meeting, decided it would be too dangerous politically to grant licenses. Instead they successfully appealed to Cardinal Fleury to release them from their commitment.[50]

The widespread evasion of the excise and customs acts, especially the English regulations against the wool trade, likewise undermined respect for the law. Nullification, as a colonial heritage and product of the frontier environment, is recognized as a long-standing American tradition. A similar attitude toward unpopular legislation, particularly British legislation, developed in Ireland. In 1729, for example, when the Irish parliament was seeking to impress the British government with its willingness to curtail wool smuggling in return for British concessions, it still never explicitly outlawed the exportation of wool to foreign countries. It confined itself instead to passing an act to remove export duties on raw wool and woolen yarn exported to Great Britain.[51] In one instance an Irish jury refused to convict a defendant accused of wool running on the grounds that he had broken no Irish law.[52]

In short, Anglo-Irishmen, like colonials, were convinced that

[49] Newcastle to Boulter, Sept. 26, 1730, and Boulter to Newcastle, Oct. 14, 1730, Eng. P.R.O., S.P. 63/393, fols. 4, 6.
[50] *Ibid.*, fols. 8–10, 14, 30, 32.
[51] Irish Statute, 3 George II, c. 3, sect. 45.
[52] James, "Irish Smuggling in the Eighteenth Century," p. 317.

they possessed certain fundamental rights. They recognized in principle the authority of the government while at the same time they developed a highly individualistic interpretation of the limitations of that authority. Resistance to British domination through parliamentary opposition, through disregard for unpopular laws, through freedom of speech and press, and through popular demonstrations did not, in their minds, constitute illegal behavior. The Irish patriot movement, limited though it still was to Protestants, stood for more popular government, and, in common with the colonial patriots, those of Ireland identified popular government with national self-determination. Though it would be an anachronism to describe them as either nationalists or democrats in the modern sense, the Irish patriots of the 1750's and 1760's can rightfully be considered harbingers of what R. R. Palmer calls "the Age of Democratic Revolution." [53]

Several historians have treated Ireland's relationship to the revolutionary movements of the 1790's.[54] The effect of the American Revolution upon Ireland has also been treated, by R. Coupland, Michael Kraus, R. B. McDowell, and most recently and thoroughly by Maurice R. O'Connell.[55] What has

[53] Robert R. Palmer, *The Age of Democratic Revolution, A Political History of Europe and America*, 2 vols. (Princeton, Princeton University Press, 1958–1964), I, 287–294, II, 491–504.

[54] Jules Albert Deschamps, *Les isles britanniques et la révolution française, 1789–1803; entre la guerre et la paix* (Brussels, 1949), esp. pp. 85–102; H. L. Calkin, "La propagation en Irlande des idées de la révolution française," *Annales historiques de la révolution française*, XXXII (Paris, Société des études robespierristes, 1953), 142–160; Philip A. Brown, *The French Revolution in English History* (London, Lockwood & Son, 1918), pp. 157–158; J. Holland Rose, *William Pitt and the Great War* (London, G. Bell & Sons, 1914), pp. 350–358; Richard Hayes, *Ireland and Irishmen in the French Revolution* (London, Ernest Benn, 1932).

[55] R. Coupland, *The American Revolution and the British Empire* (London, Longmans, Green, 1930); Michael Kraus, "America and the Irish Revolutionary Movement in the Eighteenth Century," in *The Era of the American Revolution, Studies Inscribed to Evarts Boutwell Greene*, ed. Richard Morris (New York, Columbia University Press, 1935), pp. 332–348; R. B. McDowell, *Irish Public Opinion 1750–1800* (London, Faber and Faber, 1949), pp. 39–50; Maurice R. O'Connell, *Irish Politics and Social Conflict in the Age of the American Revolution* (Philadelphia, University of Pennsylvania Press, 1965). See also Vincent T. Harlow, *The Founding of the Second British Empire 1763–1793*, 2 vols. (London, Longmans,

received much less attention is Ireland's role in precipitating the imperial crisis of the 1760's. It is evident that in the first half of the eighteenth century events in both the American colonies and Ireland were moving toward a point when the challenge to British control would result in some kind of confrontation. To what degree did developments in Ireland affect those in America?

There appear to be three principal ways in which Ireland influenced the American colonies. First, the extensive experience of British officials in dealing with Ireland conditioned some of their attitudes and policies toward American problems. Second, internal tensions, combined with economic pressures, caused emigration of a large number of people from Ireland to America. Third, the political ideas and prejudices engendered by Irish conflicts were transmitted to the colonies, partly through these immigrants, partly through trade contacts, and partly through Irish writers.

The first of the three kinds of influence is the most difficult to detect. As has been demonstrated, Irish business received close attention in London, and many men in the British government, at virtually all levels, had at one time or another been involved in Irish affairs. Ireland was governed as an overseas dependency and was, to a degree, still considered a "plantation." William Blackstone wrote that its inhabitants were descended mostly from British colonists.[56] It was thus only natural that British administrators, members of parliament, and merchants should keep Ireland in mind when they considered imperial questions. Not only did an Anglo-Irishman like Sir John Browne view colonial and Irish problems as parallel and interrelated; so did the Bristol merchant John Cary.[57]

Green, 1952–1964), I, 508–557; and Theresa M. O'Connor, "The More Immediate Effects of the American Revolution on Ireland 1775–1785," Queen's University, master's thesis, 1938.

[56] William Blackstone, *Commentaries on the Laws of England*, 4 vols. (Oxford, 1765–1769), I, 99.

[57] John Cary, *Discourse concerning the Trade of Ireland and Scotland* (London, 1696); on Browne, see Chapter VIII, above.

The clearest example of the effect of Irish affairs on American policy was the decision of the Rockingham ministry in 1766 to accompany the repeal of the Stamp Act with a Declaratory Act modeled almost word for word on the Irish act of 1720, with which both British and colonial leaders were familiar.[58] There are other and earlier examples. Lord Bellamont, an Irish peer, recommended the levying of a quitrent on land grants in New York similar to that collected in Ireland, and he also felt that the lands forfeited by participants in the recent rebellion in New York could best be disposed of by the English parliament in the same manner that it had dealt with the Irish forfeited estates.[59] Advisers to General James Oglethorpe recommended that Georgia adopt a law modeled after the Irish act for the relief of small debtors.[60] The Board of Trade sometimes drew on Irish experience in giving advice to colonial officials: they suggested the Irish form of warrants for certain colonial appointees;[61] they maintained that a person could sit as an "assembly man" in Nevis "whilst a councillor at St. Christopher" since "it was common to have a member of the House of Lords in Ireland in the House of Commons in England."[62] The board assured Lord Cornbury that, like the lord lieutenant of Ireland, he had clear authority to issue orders as the governor of New Jersey when absent from that colony.[63] It informed Governor William Burnet that he could continue the colonial assembly elected under his predecessor on the grounds that the situation was "exactly conformable to that in Ireland where one Parliament has subsisted under different governors."[64] Both radicals and con-

---

[58] Edward S. Morgan and Helen M. Morgan, *The Stamp Act Crisis, Prelude to Revolution* (Chapel Hill, University of North Carolina Press, 1953), pp. 277, 285–286.

[59] Lord Bellamont to lords of trade, Aug. 24, 1699, Jan. 2, 1701/02, *Documents Relative to the Colonial History of the State of New York*, ed. E. B. O'Callaghan, 14 vols. (Albany, 1854–1883), IV, 555, 823.

[60] *Calendar of State Papers Colonial, America and the West Indies*, XLIV, 190.

[61] *Ibid.*, XVIII, 376, 381.

[62] *Journal of the Commissioners for Trade and Plantations*, XIII, 323.

[63] *Documents Relative to the Colonial History of New York*, V, 47.

[64] *Ibid.*, 583.

servatives appealed to Irish precedents. When the governor of South Carolina objected to the speaker of the assembly "demanding" parliamentary privileges, the assembly justified his language on the grounds of Irish precedent.[65] On the conservative side, former Governor Thomas Pownall of Massachusetts argued that the Americans should have no fear of a standing army since, as in Ireland, the troops would be subordinate to the civil authority.[66]

The most obvious Irish influence upon the colonies is that of the numerous Irish emigrants who settled in America. Before 1700 immigration had been one of the central themes of Irish history; after that date emigration replaced it as a comparable force in Irish life. In the eighteenth century officeholders and adventurers still arrived from Britain, as did a few Huguenots and Palatines, but the demographic tide had turned. Even in the seventeenth century the Cromwellian and Williamite wars had resulted in the exodus of thousands of Catholics, mostly soldiers who enlisted in the service of Catholic princes abroad, particularly in the French army.[67] The Irish parliament, which saw a possible Jacobite invader in every Irish soldier abroad,[68] enacted legislation forbidding foreign enlistments, but the flight of the "Wild Geese" continued, many leaving Ireland on "the pretense of going to England to work." [69] Not all Catholic émigrés entered military

[65] Mary Paterson Clarke, *Parliamentary Privileges in the American Colonies*, pp. 80–81.

[66] Thomas Pownall, *The Administration of the Colonies* (London, 1764), p. 70.

[67] J. P. Prendergast, *The Cromwellian Settlement of Ireland* (New York, 1868), pp. 73, 78.

[68] Lords justices to Carteret, Aug. 1, 1726, Eng. P.R.O., S.P. 63/388, fol. 29.

[69] Boulter to Newcastle, May 19, 1726, Eng. P.R.O., S.P. 63/387, fol. 197. Recruiting of Catholics continued; a report in 1768 stated that "there are agents at all times in this city [Dublin] and the Southwest parts of Ireland." Townshend Letters, letter 51. The government did on occasion grant licenses. In 1720 it provided a license to an officer of the emperor's and the same year permitted the raising of twenty or thirty men of "extraordinary size, either Protestants or Papists," as a present to King Frederick William of Prussia for his famous guards. Calendar of Departmental Correspondence, II, 69–70, 75.

service; some were artisans and merchants. A number of the artisans employed their skill in the French and Flemish woolen and linen industries; [70] others turned to trade like the family of "la petite Morfi," who became mistress of Louis XV.[71] Irish merchants, especially a group settled in Nantes, handled much of the Irish provision trade with the French colonies.[72] Britain, as well as the Continent, received an influx of Irish seeking employment and other opportunities. The competition offered by Irish laborers led to ill feeling and sometimes to violence on the part of English workers. Several Irish were killed in a riot in London in 1736.[73] Many of the Irish came to Britain on a seasonal basis; others settled permanently, including representatives of the Irish middle classes and of the Anglo-Irish aristocracy. No area, however, received more Irish immigrants in the eighteenth century than the British American colonies.

The largest group to migrate, and the one that has been most carefully studied, were the Ulster Scots, or as they were called in America, the Scotch Irish. A sizable number left Ulster in the second and third decades of the eighteenth century, partly because of the failure to repeal the Irish Test Act, but principally because of economic conditions.[74] The devastation and uncertainties of the Williamite War reduced Ulster rents, making it possible for tenants to acquire favorable leases (usually for twenty-one to thirty years) and attracting back to Ireland many Scots who had left the country. When the leases ran out, about 1720, rents climbed steeply. At the same time,

[70] Conrad Gill, *Merchants and Mariners of the 18th Century* (London, E. Arnold, 1961), p. 14; *Diary of Viscount Percival*, I, 48. There were also Irish Catholic merchants in Spain. Eng. P.R.O., S.P. 63/402, fols. 12–13.

[71] *Journal et Mémoires du Marquis d'Argenson*, Société de l'Histoire de France, ed. E. J. B. Rathery, VII (Paris, 1865), 440–441.

[72] Jules Mathorez, *Notes sur la colonie irlandaise de Nantes du XVI au XVIII siècles* (Nantes, 1913), p. 21.

[73] *Diary of Viscount Percival*, II, 292; Dorothy George, *London Life in the Eighteenth Century* (new ed., New York, 1965), pp. 111–125.

[74] Beckett, *Protestant Dissent in Ireland*, p. 75; Boulter to Newcastle, Nov. 23, 1728, Eng. P.R.O., S.P. 63/390, fol. 175; the report of the Justices of the assize of the northwest circuit of Ulster on emigration, 1729, Eng. P.R.O., S.P. 63/391, fols. 77–79.

the prices of provisions and linen advanced only slowly and unevenly. When provision prices were low, real wages rose, thus benefiting farm laborers but putting the squeeze on farmers and tempting them to pull out for the colonies. In periods of scarcity provision prices increased, helping the farmers, but causing unemployment and low wages among the workers, who then turned to emigration.[75] These fluctuating forces led to a fairly continuous, if uneven, flow of Ulster emigrants to America throughout the eighteenth century.[76] Ulster, itself a kind of frontier society of colonists, produced men and women willing to seek their fortunes in a new environment, just as their descendants pushed westward from Pennsylvania and the Carolinas.[77] The Presbyterian emigrants from Ulster brought with them a sense of dissatisfaction with British rule because of the religious disabilities and economic hardships they had suffered, but their contribution to the revolutionary spirit in America has probably been exaggerated. Most of them, in the opinion of James Leyburn, were not initially politically minded, and when they turned to politics local issues attracted their attention. In two of the four colonies in which they became active, Pennsylvania and Virginia, they supported the Revolution, but in the two Carolinas many sided, in a rather negative way, with the British because of their opposition to the local oligarchies.[78]

Aside from the Ulster Scots, it is difficult to assess either the numerical strength or importance of the Irish in colonial America. During the reigns of Charles II and James II many

[75] R. J. Dickson, *Ulster Emigration to Colonial America 1718–1775* (London, Routledge & Kegan Paul, 1966), pp. 10–31.

[76] For example, the *Pennsylvania Gazette* for July 23, 1772, reports the landing in Newcastle, Delaware, of 340 emigrants from Londonderry and 350 from Belfast. See also Henry James Ford, *The Scotch Irish in America* (Princeton, Princeton University Press, 1945); and E. R. R. Green, "The Scotch Irish and the Coming of the Revolution in North Carolina," *Irish Historical Studies*, VII (1950–1951), 77–86.

[77] E. Estyn Evans, "The Scotch-Irish: Their Cultural Adaption and Heritage in the American Old West," in *Essays in Scotch-Irish History*, ed. E. R. R. Green (New York, Humanities Press, 1969), p. 74.

[78] James C. Leyburn, *The Scotch Irish, a Social History* (Chapel Hill, University of North Carolina Press, 1962), pp. 297–308.

Irish went to the British West Indies, some of them undoubtedly from the middle or upper classes.[79] After the accession of William III the Protestants in Barbados, Montserrat, and St. Kitts took steps to prevent a Catholic take-over.[80] After the Treaty of Limerick Catholics leaving Ireland preferred Catholic countries or colonies to the British colonies, providing they had the money or connections to permit choice of their destination. Between 1691 and 1770 the vast majority of the Irish Catholics who migrated to British America came from necessity rather than preference. A few paid their way; most came as indentured servants. Ship captains advertised for indentured emigrants in Irish newspapers.[81] Some appear to have been kidnapped; in 1749 the Irish parliament considered but failed to pass a bill to protect persons from forcible abduction.[82] Finally, several thousand convicted felons were transported to the colonies.[83] Transportation was the regular punishment for some offenses and was also used as an alternative to the death sentence: "Last Week two women were found guilty of Cow-stealing which is Death by Law, but on account of their great poverty the Jury recommended them an object of Distress and they are to be transported." [84] A few months later the same paper noted that "three coaches full of Transports were sent from Newgate to Waterside to be shipped for the Plantations in America." [85]

The reception awaiting the poor Irish immigrant was often far from cordial. The planters of Nevis agreed not to accept Catholic servants, and authorities in Virginia and Maryland

[79] During the 1650's several thousand Irish had been shipped to the West Indies as servants. Prendergast, *Cromwellian Settlement*, pp. 245–246. After 1660 the emigration there was largely voluntary.

[80] G. H. Guttridge, *The Colonial Policy of William III in America and the West Indies* (reprinted, Hamden, Conn., Shoestring Press, 1966), pp. 69–70.

[81] For example, the *Dublin Daily Advertiser*, Jan. 19, Feb. 23, 1736/37.

[82] *Irish Commons' Journal*, Nov. 15, 21, 24, 1749.

[83] Newenham says that 1,890 felons were transported between 1736 and 1743, but he does not give the source for his figures. *View of Ireland*, Appendix XXX.

[84] *Faulkner's Dublin Journal*, July 9–12, 1748.

[85] *Ibid.*, Oct. 1, 1748.

expressed concern over their increasing numbers.[86] The plantation colonies were, generally, too anxious for laborers to
turn any away, but in the eighteenth century the Negro slave
was replacing the indentured European. The New England
colonies showed considerable reluctance to accept Irish servants. Boston required bonds for those who stayed and compelled some shipmasters to take servants to other colonies.[87]
During the mid-eighteenth century the middle colonies probably received the largest number of Catholic Irish, in part
because of the extensive shipping connections between Ireland
and Pennsylvania and New York. A number of Irish arrivals
were craftsmen who found employment in Philadelphia and
other towns as well as among the farmers of the area.[88]

Though the life of indentured servants in the middle colonies may not have been as difficult as on the plantations of
the southern and West Indian colonies, it still presented many
hardships. The frequency of advertisements for runaway servants of both sexes suggests that working conditions must have
left much to be desired, or possibly that the opportunities of
an expanding economy tempted many to seek escape. In any
event, the advertisements reveal much prejudice against the
Irish Catholic. One rhymed notice for a runaway Irish woman
describes her with something less than Christian charity:

> Her age I know not, but appears
> To be at least full twenty years;
> The same religion with the Pope,
> Short neck, scarce room for a rope . . .

[86] *Calendar of State Papers Colonial, America and the West Indies*,
XVII, 261; XVIII, 504; XIX, 574; XX, 769; XXIII, 67, 195, 384, 760.

[87] City of Boston, *A Report of the Record Commission, Records of
Boston Selectmen 1736–1742* (Boston, 1886), pp. 71, 72, 74, 279, 312, 316–318.
Yet servants did come to Boston: there is an advertisement for "a parcel
of hearty likely servants" just arrived from Cork in *The Massachusetts
Gazette and Boston Newsletter*, Oct. 22, 1767. Many Irish apparently
settled in Halifax, Nova Scotia. Gipson, *British Empire before the American Revolution*, IX, 144.

[88] An advertisement in the *Pennsylvania Gazette*, Apr. 30, May 7, 14,
21, 1772, mentions smiths, nail makers, shoemakers, tailors, skinners, car-
penters, gardiners, grooms, and farmers.

> Upon her tongue she wears a brogue
> And was she man, would be a rogue.[89]

The Catholic Irish had little love for the British government, and many sided with the American patriots, but their
part in the American Revolution has been exaggerated even
more than that of the Ulster Scots. T. W. Moody observed
twenty-five years ago that most studies of the early Irish-
Americans owed more to "filio-pietistic" enthusiasm than to
exacting scholarship.[90] Except for the Scotch-Irish the criticism
still remains valid. One of the most recent books on the
subject, Michael J. O'Brien's *The Irish at Bunker Hill*, though
based on extensive research, gives the impression that the Irish
overwhelmingly supported the American cause. Because the
immigrants were economically exploited and submitted to so
much anti-Catholic prejudice, it must have been difficult for
many to identify with colonial leaders. Certainly some remained indifferent to the struggle. Others joined the British
forces; General Henry Clinton organized a company of loyal
Irish.[91]

One of the weaknesses of O'Brien's book, and of other similar studies, arises from the failure to distinguish between the
Catholic Irish and the Anglo-Irish. The latter were affiliated
with the Church of Ireland and prided themselves on their
English ancestry, while at the same time they displayed an
increasing feeling of Irish nationality. Although most of the
Anglo-Irish probably possessed a sense of group consciousness,
it is difficult for a historian to identify them. The majority
had English surnames (some of which had become more common in Ireland than in England), but others had Irish names —

[89] *Ibid.*, June 22, 1769. In that paper of Sept. 21, 1769, there is an
advertisement for a runaway Irish artisan. See also *New York Evening
Post*, Oct. 19, 1747.

[90] T. W. Moody, "The Ulster Scots in Colonial and Revolutionary
America," *Studies, An Irish Quarterly Review*, XXXIV (1945), 85.

[91] *The American Rebellion: Sir Henry Clinton's Narrative of His Cam-
paigns, 1775–1782, with an Appendix of Original Documents*, ed. William
B. Willcox (New Haven, Yale University Press, 1954), pp. 110–111; Michael
J. O'Brien, *The Irish at Bunker Hill* (Shannon, Irish University Press,
1969).

like the Dulanys of Maryland — or even Scottish names. Thus one cannot distinguish them by name. Where the name fails to help, there is little to go on except when specific evidence of Irish origin exists. The Anglo-Irish immigrant came from all classes, from the landed gentry to the indentured servant. According to one estimate they outnumbered the Catholics among the emigrants from Ulster,[92] though not of course the Scotch-Irish. Some were officials, like Governor Arthur Dobbs of Carolina and Governor William Cosby of New York and Sir William Johnson, superintendent for Indian affairs.[93] Such men tended to be conservative; the majority, however, must have brought over from Ireland a distrust of British rule similar to that shared by most Irish Catholics and the Ulster Scots. The Reverend James MacSparran, an Irish-born Anglican clergyman in Rhode Island, expressed a point of view no doubt common among many of his countrymen whatever their religion. On hearing rumors of efforts to unite Ireland and England, he wrote to a friend in Ireland: "I pray God they may never take effect; for if they do, farewell Liberty. You are greater Slaves already than our Negroes; and an Union of that kind would make you more Underlings than you are now . . . Corruption will increase, Pedlars be promoted to power, but the clergy and landed Interest will sink into Disesteem." [94] Elsewhere MacSparran commented that the American colonies might be made "greatly serviceable" to Britain by proper management; instead "false, I had almost said fatal Policy, has

[92] *Surnames in the United States Census of 1790, An Analysis of National Origins of the Population* (new ed., Baltimore, Genealogical Publication Co., 1969), pp. 267–268.
[93] Johnson, whose deputy superintendent, George Groghan, was an Irish trader, was instrumental in encouraging the immigration of schoolteachers from Ireland. *The Papers of Sir William Johnson*, 14 vols. (Albany, 1921–1965), I, 35, 257–258, II, 343, VIII, 18, 20, 26–27, 31–32. There is a biography of Dobbs: Desmond Clarke, *Arthur Dobbs, Esquire 1689–1765, Surveyor General of Ireland, Proprietor and Governor of North Carolina* (Chapel Hill, 1957).
[94] James MacSparran, "America Dissected" in *A History of the Episcopal Church in Narragansett Rhode Island*, ed. William Updike, 2nd ed., 3 vols. (Boston, 1907), III, Appendix, 50.

overlooked both the civil and religious interests of English America." [95]

MacSparran's remarks serve to illustrate the way in which Irishmen brought to America ideas and prejudices that must have helped to mold colonial attitudes. The regular trade between Ireland and particularly the middle colonies must also have contributed to colonial awareness of Irish developments.[96] Ships bound for Ireland almost invariably advertised passenger accommodations, which suggests that merchants and other colonials besides seamen visited Ireland. Americans became familiar with Ireland's conflict with British interests in other ways as well, through the press and through pamphlets and books.

Until 1760 Irish newspapers displayed almost no interest in the colonies and colonial newspapers little in Ireland. Aside from war and shipping news, the colonies seldom received mention in the Irish press. Irish news in colonial papers occurred more frequently, but most of it consisted of small items of human interest: obituaries, notices of murders and trials, oddities. International affairs and English politics drew far more attention in both Ireland and the colonies than news of each other. Yet there was some awareness of significant events. An account of the Zenger trial in New York was reprinted in Dublin in 1738.[97] News of Dublin elections, demonstrations over currency reform, "liberty rioters" in 1752, and of the bigger 1759 riot all reached colonial readers.[98] With the mounting tension that followed the passage of the Sugar and Stamp Acts colonial interest in Ireland became more pronounced.

---

[95] *Ibid.*, 43.

[96] A false rumor in Philadelphia in 1766 that an English act banned the shipment of flaxseed to Ireland caused something of a business crisis. Theodore Thayer, *Pennsylvania Politics and the Growth of Democracy 1740–1776* (Harrisburg, Pennsylvania Historical and Museum Commission, 1953), pp. 139–140.

[97] *The tryal of J. P. Zenger of New York, Printer, who was lately try'd for printing and publishing a libel against the government with the pleadings and arguments on both sides* (Dublin, 1738).

[98] See, e.g., *Pennsylvania Gazette*, Aug. 5, 1731; May 4, 11, 1732; Jan. 14, 1752; *Boston News Letter*, Feb. 28, 1760.

From the mid-1760's colonial newspapers devoted some attention to Irish parliamentary affairs (including occasional summaries of speeches), Whiteboy outrages, popular demonstrations, and patriot leaders, although Irish news never received the space allotted to Wilkes or to the growing political conflict in other colonies.[99] A more important source of information — and misinformation — about Ireland were the writings of British and Irish publicists.

The ideological background of the American Revolution has been explored from many angles; it is among the most controversial topics in American historiography. Some historians have stressed the importance of the American environment in determining colonial opinion; others the influence of British traditions and political thought.[100] Since these and other forces interacted, it would seem almost impossible to isolate any of them. It is clear, however, that the articulate political leaders in the colonies both consciously and unconsciously derived many of their ideas from the Old World. Caroline Robbins has shown that the "Old Whig" tradition in England survived into the early eighteenth century and formed a link with the later radicalism of the age of George III. This English opposition group had connections with the nascent patriot movements in both Ireland and America. Several of the leaders of the English movement, notably Molyneux, Viscount Molesworth, and John Trenchard, were Anglo-Irishmen who championed constitutional reform partly because their Irish background made them apprehensive of arbitrary government. Their writings, such as Molyneux's *Case of Ireland,* Moles-

[99] See, e.g., *Pennsylvania Gazette,* Feb. 16, Apr. 5, 1764, July 18, 1765, Jan. 9, Mar. 27, 1766, Jan. 4, 11, Mar. 1, 1770, Apr. 9, May 28, June 11, 1772; *Virginia Gazette,* Apr. 2, 28, 1767, May 9, 1771, Feb. 27, Apr. 2, 30, 1772. George Wythe wrote to London in August 1769 ordering a book of "Debates of the Parliament of Ireland." *John Norton and Sons, Merchants of London and Virginia,* ed. Frances Norton Mason (Richmond, Va., Dietz Press, 1937), p. 101.

[100] There is also a division between those who stress political ideology and those who view the struggle as primarily an economic or class struggle. For a brief review of the varying interpretations, see *The American Revolution, The Critical Issues,* ed. Robert F. Berkhofer (Boston, Little, Brown, 1971), pp. vii–xiv, 175–183.

worth's *An Account of Denmark*, and especially *Cato's Letters*
by Trenchard were influential in the colonies.[101] Undoubtedly
still better known were the works of a Tory critic of the
government, Dean Swift; colonial newspapers carried many
references to both him and his books.[102] It is difficult to know
to what degree his political writings on Ireland circulated in
America. Did the colonists read, for example, his pamphlet
recommending an Irish nonimportation agreement against
England (in 1720), or his *Drapier's Letters?* In any event,
there can be no doubt that the ideas expressed by a number of
Anglo-Irishmen, including Dobbs and Bishop George Berkeley
(both of whom came to America),[103] as well as those just
mentioned, entered into the formation of colonial opinion.

In *The Origins of American Politics* Bernard Bailyn develops
further Caroline Robbins' emphasis on the early eighteenth-
century opposition writers, explaining that because of certain
characteristics of the colonial system of government Americans
found their attacks on Walpole's ministry especially convincing. The contradiction between the wide legal authority of
the colonial governor and his actual weakness in dealing with
colonial leaders created an impatience with what they con-
ceived of as an arbitrary executive: "the rise of arbitrary
power in the midst of deepening corruption was an only too
reasonable, and too familiar story, told a hundred times over
in the pages of Bolingbroke, Trenchard, Gordon, Molesworth,

[101] Robbins, *Eighteenth-Century Commonwealthman*, pp. 93, 100–104,
112, 115, 134–176.

[102] There are a dozen references to Swift in the *Virginia Gazette* between
1736 and 1752, but none specifically to his political ideas or writings.
Lester J. Cappon and Stella F. Duff, *Virginia Gazette Index*, 2 vols.
(Williamsburg, Institute of Early American History and Culture, 1950),
II, 1155. J. F. Ross argues that Franklin derived "Poor Richard" from
Swift's character Bickerstaff, "Character of Poor Richard: Its Sources and
Alteration," *Publications of the Modern Language Association*, LV (1940),
785–794.

[103] One of the few Irish works actually reprinted in the American
colonies was George Berkeley's *A Word to the Wise*, 4th ed. (Boston, 1750).
In it Berkeley stressed the poverty of the Irish, remarking (p. 4), "the
negroes in our Plantations have a saying, 'If Negro was not Negro, an
Irishman would be Negro.' "

Rapin and Sidney." [104] Colonial polemicists developed a rhetoric of protest that, drawing on the British and Anglo-Irish opposition writers, denounced the imperial government for subverting their rights and liberties as Englishmen. Bailyn criticizes previous historians for discounting this revolutionary rhetoric, maintaining that the colonists came to believe quite seriously their own propaganda.[105] Jack P. Greene takes Bailyn to task for depending too heavily on the colonial pamphlets and press while neglecting such political records as the journals of the colonial assemblies. The colonial political leaders, Greene argues, derived their fear of arbitrary government from an older English tradition: the parliamentary heritage of distrust of royal power handed down from Stuart times.[106]

As far as Ireland is concerned, the colonists' interpretation of its position in the empire and its relevance to colonial problems was based primarily on three sources: English legal authorities like Coke and Blackstone, opposition critics of the early eighteenth century like Trenchard and Swift, and, after 1760, the Irish patriots like Lucas and Flood. Colonial propagandists, such as John Dickinson, Daniel Dulany, Benjamin Franklin, James Otis, and James Wilson, referred specifically to Ireland in order to make a number of points regarding colonial-British relations. Taking the allegations of the Irish patriots at face value (as have most American historians ever since) they depicted conditions in Ireland as almost universally wretched, not only for Catholics but for Protestants as well; they thus attributed Ireland's plight to British exploitation and misrule.[107] They emphasized three constitutional argu-

[104] Bailyn, *Origins of American Politics*, pp. 11–23. This attitude is well illustrated by a quotation from an obituary of Charles Lucas reprinted in the *Pennsylvania Gazette*, Feb. 13, 1772: "In the midst of venality and corruption, unplaced, unbribed and unpensioned, he stemmed the torrent of abuse, the opposition of party, and the frowns of power."

[105] Bailyn, *Origins of American Politics*, pp. 148–149.

[106] Jack P. Greene, "Political Mimesis: A Consideration of the Historical and Cultural Roots of Legislative Behavior in the British Colonies in the Eighteenth Century," *American Historical Review*, LXXV (1969), 341.

[107] John C. Miller, *Origins of the American Revolution*, rev. ed. (Stanford, Calif., Stanford University Press, 1959), p. 292; *The Privileges of the Island of Jamaica Vindicated with an Impartial Narrative of the Late*

ments that bore directly on the colonies. First, that, although England could enact laws binding the dependent kingdom of Ireland, no English statute applied to Ireland unless it was specifically stated in the statute.[108] Second, that Ireland's internal affairs were governed exclusively by Irish statutes; that, in other words, the Irish parliament had what Blackstone called full "municipal" jurisdiction.[109] In this regard, they pointed out that the British parliament had never levied an internal tax upon Ireland.[110] Third, that all native-born persons in any of the king's dominions, even a conquered territory like Ireland, enjoyed individually the full legal rights of Englishmen,[111] which was another argument that could be used against internal taxes, since taxation without representation resulted in the loss of property without due process.[112]

While the eighteenth-century colonial was anxious to justify himself on the grounds of constitutionality and political theo-

---

Dispute between the Governor and the House of Representatives upon the Case of Mr. Olyphant a Member of that House (printed in Jamaica, reprinted in London, 1766), p. 64.

[108] *Selected Political Essays of James Wilson*, ed. Randolph G. Adams (New York, Alfred A. Knopf, 1930), pp. 68–70.

[109] Blackstone, *Commentaries on the Laws of England*, I, 93, 98–99. In an essay in the *Pennsylvania Gazette* (Apr. 10, 1766), "Aequus" admitted Britain's superior jurisdiction over Ireland as set forth in the Declaratory Act: "But this sovereign jurisdiction, thus exerted over Ireland, related only to that Kingdom and People in their aggregate or collective capacity, and as a dependent or subordinate whole; and widely differs from the act of making local laws for the individuals of it, or from levying any internal taxes upon them."

[110] John Dickinson, *Farmer's Letters*, Letter X, in *Sources and Documents Illustrating the American Revolution*, ed. Samuel Eliot Morison (Oxford, Clarendon Press, 1929), p. 53; Daniel Dulany, *Considerations on the Propriety of Imposing Taxes in the British Colonies for the Purpose of Raising a Revenue, by Act of Parliament* (London, 1766), p. 58.

[111] James Otis, *The Rights of British Colonies Asserted and Proved*, 3rd ed. (London, 1766), pp. 65–70, 93.

[112] Supplement of *Pennsylvania Gazette*, Feb. 2, 1769, argued that an Englishman "in every part of the King's dominions" had the right to be "heard for himself or his representative, concerning taxation of his property." The writer called for a federal parliament with representatives from Britain, America, and Ireland. The West Indian, Joshua Steele, advocating a similar system, wrote: "We are all fellow subjects, whether our properties lie in Britain, Ireland or America." *An Account of the Late Conference on the Occurrences in America in a Letter to a Friend* (London, 1766), p. 6.

ry, he did not overlook practical and economic considerations. The British Empire contained a number of competing pressure groups that sought to shape government policies, and contemporaries recognized the importance and legitimacy of these different "interests." In Cato's letter on colonies Trenchard bluntly explained the position of colonies. "Every Man's first thought will be for himself and his own Interest, and he will not be long to seek Arguments to justify his being so when he knows how to attain what he proposes. Men will think it hard to work, toil, and run Hazards, for the Advantage of others, any longer than they can find their own Interest in it, and especially for those who use them ill; All Nature points out that course; No Creatures suck the Teats of their Dams longer than they can draw Milk from thence, or provide themselves with better Food." [113] When principle clashes with interest, the former must bend.

Michael Kammen's recently published *Empire and Interest* approaches the imperial crisis of the eighteenth century from this viewpoint, suggesting that one of the chief causes of the American Revolution was the ineffectiveness of the American interest in London after 1760 in contrast to other pressure groups such as the East Indian interest and even the Irish interest.[114] His argument makes sense, and yet, no matter how well organized, individual lobbies, especially those representing overseas constituencies, enjoyed a precarious influence.

[113] *Cato's Letters or Essays on Liberty Civil and Religious*, 3rd ed., 4 vols. (London, 1733), IV, 7.
[114] Michael Kammen, *Empire and Interest, the American Colonies and the Politics of Mercantilism* (Philadelphia, Lippincott, 1970), pp. 98–106, 125–135. In the 1740's the West Indian interest made a logrolling agreement with the Scottish and the Irish linen interests. Lillian M. Penson, *The Colonial Agents of the British West Indies* (London, 1924), pp. 95, 113. Namier and Brooke assert that there was no Irish party in the English parliament in the latter half of the eighteenth century although there were usually twenty to thirty or more Irish members at Westminster. They added, however, that the Irish members in the British Commons "were far more concerned to help Ireland economically than to promote the cause of Irish nationalism," which implies that there was an Irish interest. Sir Lewis Namier and John Brooke, *The House of Commons 1754–1790*, 3 vols. (London, 1964), I, 161–162. The debates on proposals to help Irish trade certainly bear this out. See Cobbett, *Parliamentary History*, XX, 111–112, 135–138, 248–250, 661–662, 663–669, 673.

The British constitution, despite its theoretical separation of powers so dear to the opponents of arbitrary government, offered no guarantee to ensure the colonists and the Irish the balance of interests that had prevailed earlier in the century. The ordinary member of the British Commons naturally subordinated imperial interests to those of England when he thought the two conflicted. Viscount Percival discovered this in 1731 when he attempted to stop an English bill to compel the registry of Irish wool. "I spoke to several members about the injustice of taxing Ireland by an English law: That it is the essential mark of a free people, that no taxes should be laid but by the nation's own representatives . . . Some agreed with me, and others though they allowed what I said to be true, yet they added that it must be so when the preservation of England is concerned in it." [115]

In the decades leading up to the American Revolution it is clear that many colonials recognized that their struggle for greater autonomy ran parallel to Ireland's and that some Americans were directly influenced by the Irish patriots. Beginning about 1760 the advocates of Irish liberty derived inspiration in turn from the American patriots. In Britain itself, radicals like the Irish-born Isaac Barré, and opposition leaders like Burke, Fox, and Shelburne gave support to both the American and Irish patriots. There is little wonder that Dr. Johnson remarked in 1775 that "patriotism is the last refuge of a scoundrel," by which Boswell assures us, "he did not mean a genuine love of our country, but that pretended patriotism which so many, in all ages and countries, have made a cloak of self interest." [116] Boulter had complained forty years earlier that the Irish House of Commons was full of "giddy young members . . . full of false Patriotism, who are too likely to throw out a thing they liked, merely for its coming from England." [117]

Three quotations from the 1760's illustrate Ireland's close

[115] *Diary of Viscount Percival*, I, 162.
[116] G. B. Hill, *Boswell's Life of Johnson*, rev. and enlarged L. F. Powell, 6 vols. (Oxford, Clarendon Press, 1934), II, 348.
[117] Boulter to Delafaye, Jan. 4, 1731, Eng. P.R.O., S.P. 63/395, fol. 18.

relations with America. The *Pennsylvania Gazette* of March 27, 1766, stated: "On Monday last we received the following most agreeable intelligence, viz. that a vessel arrived from Cork at Oxford in Maryland, in forty days passage: the Captain of which brought a Cork News Paper, in which was a paragraph taken from one printed in Dublin, containing a letter from a Member of Parliament in London, to his Friend in Ireland, . . . the substance of which was; 'that everything relating to the affairs of America was settled; that the Stamp-Act was repealed.' " [118] Isaac Barré said in a speech in the English Commons, attacking the declaratory bill, on February 3, 1766: "All colonies have their date of independence. The wisdom or folly of our Conduct may make it sooner or later. If we act injudiciously this point may be reached in the life of many members of this house." [119] Henry Flood addressed a letter to the American colonies on January 16, 1768, in which he wrote: "You are happily, at too great a distance from ministerial tyranny, to fall an immediate sacrifice to the policies of despotism, though the essay has been commenced nearer home. We have been treated, of late, not as the children but the bastards of our mother country . . . Your circumstances and ours then, being exactly the same, the difference of our situation can possibly gain you but the poor respite of Ulysses' petition to Polyphemes, of being devoured the later." [120]

The impact of Ireland and the American colonies upon each other cannot be assessed precisely; nor should it be exaggerated. Both the Irish and the American struggles for political independence resulted from forces inherent in their respective relationships with Britain and would have occurred in any

[118] *Pennsylvania Gazette*, Mar. 27, 1766. Word of the exact vote on repeal also arrived via a Dublin dispatch. *Ibid.*, Apr. 17, 1766.

[119] Quoted by Namier and Brooke, *House of Commons*, II, 52. Barré's father was a Huguenot refugee who became a prominent Dublin merchant. Isaac was born in 1726 and was graduated from Trinity College, Dublin, in 1745. He served with General James Wolfe and was associated with Shelburne in the English Commons.

[120] *Baratariana, A Select Collection of Fugitive Political Pieces Published during the Administration of Lord Townshend in Ireland*, rev. ed. (Dublin, 1773), p. 2.

case. The fact remains, nevertheless, that both movements took place more or less simultaneously at a time when Ireland and America formed part of the same empire and were linked by personal and commercial ties. Inevitably developments in one interacted upon the other. Ireland's place in the "Atlantic Civilization" of the eighteenth century, while in no way predominant, must be recognized. Any study of the British Empire before the American Revolution that neglects close attention to Ireland is bound to be incomplete.

Appendix,
Bibliography,
and
Index

Appendix

Note on the Maps

Among the best estimates of the distribution of population in Ireland is a survey compiled from hearth tax data in 1732–1733, which gives the number of Catholic and Protestant families in each county with separate figures for the cities of Cork and Dublin.[1] The two maps in this book show the distribution of Catholics and Protestants according to this survey, representing a total 386,902 families in Ireland. The number agrees closely with Arthur Dobbs's estimates for the total number of houses in Ireland in 1725 (386,229) and in 1726 (384,851), also based on hearth tax returns.[2] Dobbs attributes the difference between the two years to the fact that tax collectors varied in their estimates of the number of houses of poor families exempt from the tax because they were certified as living upon alms. "The collectors," he explains, "being frequently moved from one district to another, occasions the poor in some years to be returned, in others not, according to the care or negligence of the several collectors." It would also seem that the number of poor families so certified must have fluctuated with economic conditions. Dobbs gives, in addition to figures by county, specific estimates of the number of houses in the following towns for 1725:[3]

Dublin	11,466	Waterford	2,044
Cork	7,536	Galway	1,567

[1] The families listed do not include those of soldiers or those living in colleges, hospitals, or poorhouses; nor does it include all of the families in "certificate houses" (houses exempt from the hearth tax because of poverty). *An Abstract of the Number of Protestant and Popish Families in the Several Counties and Provinces of Ireland Made by the Hearth-money Collectors to the Hearthmoney Office in Dublin, in the Years 1732 and 1733* (Dublin, 1736), pp. 5–7.

[2] Arthur Dobbs, *An Essay upon the Trade of Ireland* (Dublin, 1729), pp. 90–91. Dobbs also gives the figures for 1712 (349,849 houses) and for 1718 (361,508 houses).

[3] The largest English colonial town in America, Philadelphia, had only 2,079 houses in 1749, 2,969 in 1760, and 3,318 in 1769. *Pennsylvania Gazette*, Jan. 18, 1770.

Limerick	3,169	Drogheda	1,212
Kilkenny	2,138	Newry	1,031
Belfast	2,093		

Michael Drake believes that the hearth tax estimates probably exaggerate the proportion of Protestants, since collectors wished to make a good impression on the authorities.[4] That some of the Protestants reported in many areas were only outward conformists at least seems probable. On the other hand, the proportion of Protestants reported for Ulster and for the cities of Cork and Dublin appears to be substantiated by the size of the exclusively Protestant militia enrolled in 1756. Out of a total of approximately 150,000 men reported in the militia array of that year 106,000 were raised in Ulster, nearly 12,000 in the city of Dublin, and 3,000 in Cork city — leaving only 29,000 for the rest of the country.[5]

Incidentally, the four Irish provinces, Connaught, Leinster, Munster, and Ulster, though historical divisions with a few nominal officials, had no real political significance in the eighteenth century, being little more than geographical terms.[6] The key administrative unit of the period was the county, not the province.

[4] Michael Drake, "The Irish Demographic Crisis of 1740–41," *Historical Studies*, VI, 120, n. 2.

[5] Sir Henry McNally, "The Militia Array of 1756 in Ireland," *The Irish Sword*, I (1949–1953), 100–101.

[6] M. W. Heslinga, *The Irish Border as a Cultural Divide: A Contribution to the Study of Regionalism in the British Isles* (Assen, Netherlands, 1962), p. 38.

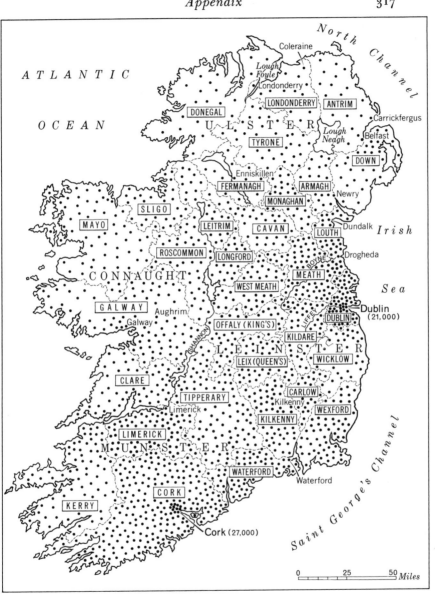

Estimated Catholic population in 1732–1733, 281,401 families or probably about 1,407,000. Each dot represents 200 Catholic families or about 1,000 people. The dots are distributed by county according to the estimate, but the distribution within the county has no significance except for the larger towns.

Estimated Protestant population in 1732–1733, 105,501 families or probably about 527,000. Each dot represents 200 Protestant families or about 1,000 people.

Bibliography

Manuscript Sources

British Museum
    Additional Manuscripts 34777, 34778, 37637, 37674 (Southwell
        Papers).
    Additional Manuscripts 35609, 35610, 35933 (Hardwicke Papers).
    Additional Manuscripts 38160, 38173 (Irish Petitions and Country
        Letters).
English Public Record Office
    State Papers, 63 (Ireland), vols. 385–412.
    Customs Manuscript 15.
Irish Public Record Office
    Calendar of Departmental Correspondence, vol. I, 1683–1714,
        vol. II, 1714–1740, vol. III, 1741–1759.
    Calendar of Miscellaneous Papers Prior to 1760.
National Library of Ireland
    Value of the Trade of Ireland 1698–1767, examined by James
        Wetheral.
    Customs Abstract 1764–1773.
    Townshend Letters 1768–1800.
Oxford, Christ Church College Library
    Wake Manuscripts, vols. XIII and XIV.

Printed Sources

OFFICIAL PAPERS

Journals of the House of Commons (England), vols. XVII–XXXIII.
    London, 1742–1772.
Journals of the House of Lords (England), vols. XVI–XXXI. Lon-
    don, 1777.
Journals of the House of Commons of the Kingdom of Ireland.
    8 vols., Dublin, 1753; 2nd ed., 23 vols., Dublin, 1763–1786, 3rd
    ed., 20 vols., Dublin, 1796–1800.

Journals of the House of Lords of the Kingdom of Ireland, 1634–1800. 8 vols., Dublin, 1779–1800.

A Collection of the Protests of the Lords of Ireland, 1634–1770. London, 1771.

Stock, Leon Francis, ed. *Proceedings and Debates of the British Parliaments Respecting North America.* 5 vols., Washington, Carnegie Institution, 1924–1941.

Pickering, Danby, ed. *The Statutes at Large, Magna Carta to 1761.* 26 vols., Cambridge, 1762–1807.

The Statutes at Large Passed in the Parliaments Held in Ireland . . . 1310–1800. 20 vols., Dublin, 1786–1801.

Inventaire Analytiques des Procès-Verbaux du Conseil du Commerce 1700–1791. Paris, 1900.

Calendar of State Papers Colonial, America and the West Indies, vols. XII–XLIV. London, H. M. Stationery Office, 1899–1969 (for the years 1685–1737).

Journal of the Commissioners for Trade and Plantations, 1704–1782. 14 vols., London, H. M. Stationery Office, 1920–1938.

Calendar of Home Office Papers 1760–1775. 3 vols., London, 1878–1899.

Historical Manuscripts Commission. 10th Report (Eglinton, Maxwell, Moray, Underwood, and Digby Manuscripts). London, 1885.

—— *14th Report,* Pt. 9, Appendix (Trevor Papers). London, 1896.

—— *Bath Manuscripts,* 3 vols. London, 1904–1908.

—— *Charlemont Manuscripts,* 2 vols. London, 1891–1894.

—— *Egmont Manuscripts,* 2 vols. London, 1905–1909.

—— *Egmont Manuscripts, Diary of the First Earl of Egmont* (Viscount Percival), 3 vols. London, 1920–1923.

—— *Finch Manuscripts,* 4 vols. London, 1913–1965.

—— *House of Lords Manuscripts,* 4 vols. London, 1887–1894.

—— *House of Lords Manuscripts,* n.s., 8 vols. London, 1908–1923.

—— *Ormonde Manuscripts,* n.s., 8 vols. London, 1902–1920.

—— *Portland Manuscripts,* 10 vols. London, 1891–1931.

—— *Various Collections,* VI London, 1905.

NEWSPAPERS AND PERIODICALS

Colonial
Massachusetts Gazette and Boston Newsletter
New York Evening Post
New York Gazette

Pennsylvania Gazette
Virginia Gazette

English
Gentlemen's Magazine
The Universal Magazine

Irish
Dublin Evening Post
Dublin Newsletter
Faulkner's Dublin Journal
Flying Post and Postmaster
The Weekly Miscellany

ANONYMOUS (chronologically arranged)

A Discourse on the Woollen Manufacture of Ireland and the Consequences of Prohibiting Its Exportation. Dublin, 1698.
The Interest of England as it Stands with Relation to the Trade of Ireland Considered. London, 1698.
Some Thoughts on the Bill . . . for Prohibiting the Exportation of the Woolen Manufactures of Ireland to Foreign Parts. London, 1698.
The Substance of the Arguments for and against the Bill for Prohibiting the Exportation of Woollen Manufacture from Ireland to Forreign Parts. London, 1698.
An Essay upon the Union of Ireland with England. Dublin, 1704.
A Defence of the Constitution or an Answer to an Argument in the Case of Mr. Moore. Dublin, 1714.
A Dialogue between Mr. Freeport a Merchant and Tom Handy a Tradesman concerning the Bank. Dublin, 1721.
Last Speech and Dying Words of the Bank of Ireland. Dublin, 1721.
Subscribers to the Bank Plac'd according to their Order and Quality with Notes and Queries. Dublin, 1721.
A Collection of Tracts concerning the Present State of Ireland. Dublin, 1729.
An Inquiry into Some of the Causes of the Ill Situation of the Affairs of Ireland. Dublin, 1731.
Annoque Domini 1732. The Irish Bishops, a Satyr. By an Honest Whig Curate. London, 1732.
Description of Dublin by a Citizen of London. London, 1732.
Four Letters Originally Written in French, Relating to the Kingdom of Ireland. Dublin, 1739.

*A List of Commodities Imported into Ireland Being Such as May
    Either [be] Raised or Manufactured therein, together with their
    Yearly Value . . . for the Years 1734, 1735, 1736.* Dublin, 1740.
The Groans of Ireland, in a Letter to a Member of Parliament.
    Dublin, 1741.
Hints concerning the Present State of Ireland 1745. Dublin, 1745.
*A Tour through Ireland in Several Entertaining Letters. Wherein
    the Present State of that Kingdom is Considered . . .* (possibly
    by W. R. Chetwood). London, 1748.
*Considerations on the Woollen Manufactory of Ireland in a Letter
    Addressed to His Grace Charles Duke of Rutland.* Dublin, 1749.
The Gentlemen's and Citizen's Almanack (printed by S. Powell).
    Dublin, 1749.
*Hints Relating to Some Laws that may be for the Interest of Ireland
    to have Enacted, in a Letter to a Member of Parliament.*
    Dublin, 1749.
*An Attempt to Prove that Free and Open Trade between the King-
    dom of Ireland and all Ports of the Southern Coast of England
    would be Highly Advantageous to Both Kingdoms.* Exeter,
    1753.

COLLECTIONS OF PAMPHLETS

*A Collection of the Most Interesting Tracts, Lately Published in
    England and America.* London (J. Alman, printer), 1766.
Bailyn, Bernard, ed., *Pamphlets of the American Revolution 1750–
    1776.* Vol. I, 1750–1765. Cambridge, Mass., Harvard University
    Press, 1965.
*Baratariana, A Selection of Fugitive Political Pieces Published dur-
    ing the Administration of Lord Townshend in Ireland,* rev. ed.,
    Dublin, 1773.
*Irish Tracts and Treatises: A Collection of Tracts and Treatises
    Illustrative of the Natural History, Antiquities, and the Political
    and Social State of Ireland.* 2 vols., Dublin, 1740.

OTHER CONTEMPORARY SOURCES

Addison, Joseph. *The Letters of Joseph Addison,* ed. Walter
    Graham. Oxford, Clarendon Press, 1941.
Alexander the Coppersmith. *Remarks on the Religion, Trade,
    Government, Police, Customs, Manners and Maladys of the
    City of Cork.* Cork, 1737.
Atwood, William. *The History and Reasons of the Dependency of*

Ireland upon the Imperial Crown of the Kingdom of England, Rectifying Mr. Molineux's . . . "Case of Ireland." London, 1698.

Bedford, Duke of. *Correspondence of John, Fourth Duke of Bedford, 1742–1770,* ed. Lord John Russell. 3 vols., London, 1842–1846.

Berkeley, George. *The Querist, Containing Several Queries Proposed to the Consideration of the Public.* 3 pts., Dublin, 1735–1737.

Boate, Gerard. *Ireland's Naturell History.* London, 1652.

Boulter, Hugh. *Letters Written by His Excellency Hugh Boulter D. D., Lord Primate of All Ireland, to Several Ministers of State in England and Some Others.* 2 vols., Dublin, 1770.

Brett, Jasper. *The Sin of With-holding Tribute by Running of Goods, Concealing Excise etc.* Dublin, 1721.

Bridges, George. *Plain Dealing, or the Whole Method of Wool Smuggling Clearly Discovered.* London, 1744.

Brooke, Henry. *An Essay on the Antient and Modern State of Ireland.* Dublin and London, 1760.

——— *The Farmer's Six Letters to the Protestants of Ireland.* Dublin, 1745.

——— *The Farmer's Case of the Roman-Catholics of Ireland: In a Letter from a Member of the Protestant Church.* Dublin, 1760.

——— *The Tryal of the Roman Catholicks.* Dublin, 1762.

Browne, Sir John. *An Essay on Trade in General; and on that of Ireland in Particular.* Dublin, 1728.

——— *Seasonable Remarks on Trade.* Dublin, 1729.

Burnet, Gilbert. *History of His Own Times.* 4 vols., London, 1818.

Bush, John. *Hibernia Curiosa: a Letter from a Gentleman in Dublin to His Friend at Dover, Giving a General View of the Manners, Customs, Dispositions, etc. of the Inhabitants of Ireland.* London, 1769.

Caldwell, Sir James. *Debates in the Irish Parliament in the Years 1763 and 1764. To which is Added an Enquiry How Far the Restrictions Laid on the Trade of Ireland . . . are a Benefit or Advantage to the British Dominions . . . .* 2nd ed., 2 vols., London, 1779.

Carte, T. *Life of James, First Duke of Ormonde.* 2nd ed., 6 vols., Oxford, 1851.

Cary, John. *Discourse concerning the Trade of Ireland and Scotland as They Stand in Competition with the Trade of England.* London, 1696.

Chesterfield, Earl of. *The Letters of Philip Dormer Stanhope, Fourth Earl of Chesterfield*, ed., Bonamy Dobrée. 6 vols., London, Eyre and Spottiswoode, 1932.

——— *Miscellaneous Works and Memoirs of Lord Chesterfield*, ed. M. Maty. 3 vols., Dublin, 1787.

Clarendon, Earl of. *The State Papers of Henry Hyde, Second Earl of Clarendon*, ed., 2 vols., London, 1828.

Clarendon, R. V. *A Sketch of the Revenue and Finances of Ireland.* London, 1791.

Colson, Nathaniel. *The Mariner's New Calendar . . . to this Edition is Added the Compleat Irish Coastes.* Dublin, 1764.

Cox, Sir Richard. *The Cork Surgeon's Antitode against the Dublin Apothecary's Poyson*, Dublin, 1749.

——— *A Letter from Sir Richard Cox. Bart., to Thomas Prior, 1749.* Dublin, 1749.

——— *Some Observations on the Present State of Ireland Particularly in Relation to the Woollen Manufacture.* Dublin, 1731.

Coxe, William. *Memoirs of the Life and Administration of Sir Robert Walpole, Earl of Orford.* 2 vols. London, 1798.

Crocker, T. Crofton, ed. *Historical Songs of Ireland.* Percy Society, *Early English Poetry*, vol. 1, London, 1841.

Delany, Mrs. Mary. *The Autobiography and Correspondence of Mary Granville, Mrs. Delany* (1st and 2nd ser.), ed. Lady Llanover. 6 vols., London, 1861–1862.

Dickinson, John. *The Late Regulations Respecting the British Colonies.* Philadelphia, 1765.

Dobbs, Arthur. *An Essay on the Trade and Improvement of Ireland.* 2 pts., Dublin, 1729–1731.

Eachard, Lawrence. *An Exact Description of Ireland.* London, 1691.

Foster, Thomas Campbell. *Letters on the Condition of the People of Ireland.* 2nd ed., London, 1847.

Gilbert, Sir Geoffrey. *Report of Cases in Equity to which is Added Some Select Cases . . . in Ireland.* London, 1734.

Gilbert, Sir J., ed. *A Jacobite Narrative of the War in Ireland 1688–1691.* Dublin, 1892.

Harris, Walter, ed. *Hibernica; or Some Antient Pieces Relating to Ireland, Never hitherto Made Publick.* 2 vols., Dublin, 1747–1750.

Hely-Hutchinson, John. *Commercial Restraints of Ireland Considered.* Dublin, 1779.

Hervey, John, Lord. *Memoirs of the Reign of George II.* 3 vols., London, 1884.

Howard, Martin. *A Letter from a Gentleman at Halifax to his Friend in Rhode-Island containing Remarks upon a Pamphlet Entitled the Rights of Colonies Examined.* Newport, 1765.

Jarvis, Rupert C. *Customs Letter-Books of the Port of Liverpool 1711–1813.* Liverpool, Chetham Society, 1954.

Johnson, Sir William. *The Papers of Sir William Johnson,* ed. James Sullivan, Milton Hamilton, *et al.* 14 vols., Albany, University of the State of New York, 1921–1965.

King, William. *A Great Archbishop of Dublin, William King D.D. 1650–1729, Autobiography, Family, and a Selection from his Correspondence,* ed. Charles Simeon King. London, Longmans, Green and Co., 1906.

Labaree, Leonard W., ed. *Royal Instructions to British Colonial Governors, 1670–1776.* 2 vols., New York, D. Appleton-Century Co., 1935.

La Touche, James Digges (pseudonym, the Cheshire Weaver). *Anglia Restauranta, or the Advantage That Must Accrue to the Nation by Effectually Putting a Stop to the Detestable and Ruinous Practice of Smuggling Wool.* London, 1727.

——— *A Short but True History of the Rise, Progress and Happy Suppression of Several Late Insurrections.* London and Dublin, 1760.

Loveday, John Edward Taylor. *Diary of a Tour in 1732 through Parts of England, Wales, Ireland, and Scotland.* 4th ed., Edinburgh, 1890.

Lucas, Charles. *Divelina Libera: an Apology for the Civil Rights and Liberties of the Commons and Citizens of Dublin.* Dublin, 1744.

——— *The Political Constitutions of Great Britain and Ireland Asserted and Vindicated . . . Set Forth in Several Addresses and Letters to the Free-Citizens of Dublin . . . to Which is Added the Censor, or the Citizens Journal.* 2 vols., London, 1751.

——— *A Remonstrance against Certain Infringements on the Rights and Liberties of the Commons and Citizens of Dublin.* Dublin, 1743 (bound with Proceedings of the Sheriffs etc. 1742–1743).

Luckombe, Philip. *A Tour Through Ireland wherein the Present State of That Kingdom is Considered.* London, 1780.

Luttrell, Narcissus. *A Brief Historical Relation of State Affairs.* 6 vols., Oxford, 1857.

Lynch, William. *The Law of Election in the Antient Cities and Towns of Ireland.* London, 1731.

MacSparran, James. *America Dissected.* Dublin, 1753. [Reprinted in Appendix to Wilkins Updike, *A History of the Episcopal Church in Narragansett, Rhode Island.* 2nd ed., 3 vols., Boston, D. B. Updike, 1907.]

Madden, Samuel. *Reflections and Resolutions Proper for the Gentlemen of Ireland, as to their Conduct for the Service of their Country.* Dublin, 1738.

Mayhew, Jonathan. *Discourse Concerning Unlimited Submission.* Boston, 1750.

Miege, Guy. *The Present State of His Majesty's Dominion in Ireland.* London, 1717.

Molesworth, Robert, 1st Viscount. *An Account of Denmark, as it was in the Year 1692.* London, 1694.

—— *Franco-Gallia; or, An Account of the Ancient Free State of France and Most Other Parts of Europe,* by Francois Hotman, trans. by Robert Molesworth with preface. 2nd ed., London, 1738.

—— *Mr. Molesworth's Preface, with Historical and Political Remarks. To which is Added a True State of His Case with Respect to the Irish Convocation.* London, 1713.

Molyneux, William. *The Case of Ireland's Being Bound by Acts of Parliament in England Stated.* Dublin, 1698.

Murray, Sir Alexander. *The True Interest of Great Britain, Ireland and our Plantations.* London, 1740.

Nicolson, William. *Letters on Various Subjects, Literary, Political and Ecclesiastical to and from William Nicolson D.D.,* ed. John Nichols. 2 vols., London, 1809.

O'Callaghan, E. B., ed., *Documents Relative to the Colonial History of the State of New York.* 15 vols., Albany, 1853–1887.

Orrery, John, Fifth Earl of. *The Orrery Papers,* ed. the Countess of Cork and Orrery. 2 vols., London, Duckworth and Co., 1903.

Otis, James. *The Rights of the British Colonies Asserted and Proved.* Boston, 1764.

—— *A Vindication of the British Colonies against the Aspersion of the Halifax Gentleman in the Letter to a Rhode-Island Friend.* Boston, 1765.

Perceval, John, after 1748 2nd Earl of Egmont. *Some Observations on the Present State Of Ireland, particularly with Relation to the Woollen Manufacture.* London, 1731.

Petty, Sir William. *The Economic Writings of Sir William Petty,* ed. Charles Henry Hull. 2 vols. Cambridge, 1899.

Pierson, Samuel. *The Present State of Tillage in Ireland Considered and Some Methods Offered for its Improvement.* Dublin, 1730.

Pococke, Dr. Richard. *Tour in Ireland in 1752,* ed. G. T. Stokes. Dublin and London, 1891.

Pownall, Thomas. *The Administration of the Colonies.* London, 1765.

Prior, Thomas. *A List of the Absentees of Ireland,* Dublin, 1729.

Rocque, Jean. *Rocque's Traveller's Assistant: Being the Most General and Compact Director Extant to all Post, Principal and Cross Roads in England, Wales, Scotland and Ireland.* London, 1763.

Rye, George. *Considerations on Agriculture.* Dublin, 1730.

Sheffield, John, Lord. *Observations on the Commerce of the American States 1700–1783.* London, 1784.

—— *Letters Concerning the Trade and Manufactures of Ireland.* London, 1785.

Stone, George. "Correspondence of Primate Stone and the Duke of Newcastle," ed. D. L. Falkiner, *English Historical Review,* XX (1905), 508–542, 735–763.

Swift, Jonathan. *Correspondence of Jonathan Swift,* ed. F. E. Ball. 6 vols., London, G. Bell and Sons, Ltd., 1910–1914.

—— *Correspondence of Jonathan Swift,* ed. Harold Williams. 5 vols., Oxford, Oxford University Press, 1963–1965.

—— *The Prose Works of Jonathan Swift,* ed. Herbert Davis. 14 vols., Oxford, Basil Blackwell, 1939–1968.

Taaffe, Nicholas, Viscount. *Observations on Affairs in Ireland from the Settlement in 1691 to the Present Time.* London, 1766.

—— *Lord Taafe's Observations upon the Affairs of Ireland Examined and Confuted.* Dublin (printed by W. Sleater), 1767.

Twiss, R. *A Tour in Ireland 1775.* Dublin, 1776.

Walpole, Horace. *Memoirs of the Reign of George the Second,* ed. Lord Holland. 2nd ed., 3 vols., London, 1846.

Webb, Daniel. *An Inquiry into the Reasons of the Decay of Credit, Trade and Manufacturies in Ireland.* 2 pts., Dublin, 1735.

Weeks, James Eyre. *A New Geography of Ireland.* 3rd ed., Dublin, 1752.

Whitworth, Sir C. *State of the Trade of Great Britain from the Year 1697.* London, 1776.

Wilson, James. *Considerations on the Nature and Extent of the Legislative Authority of the British Parliament.* Philadelphia, 1774.

Woodward, Richard. *An Argument in Support of the Right of the Poor in the Kingdom of Ireland to a National Provision.* Dublin, 1768.

Young, Arthur. *A Tour in Ireland with General Observations on the Present State of the Kingdom made in the Years 1776, 1777, 1778 and Brought down to the End of 1779,* ed., A. W. Hutton. 2 vols., London, 1892.

SECONDARY WORKS ON IRELAND

Arensberg, Conrad M. *The Irish Countreyman, An Anthropological Study.* New York, Macmillan Co., 1937.

Bagwell, Richard. *Ireland under the Stuarts.* 3 vols., London, Longmans, Green, 1909–1916.

Ball, F. Elrington. *The Judges in Ireland 1221–1921.* 2 vols., London, J. Murray, 1926.

Ball, John Thomas. *Historical Review of the Legislative Systems Operative in Ireland from the Invasion of Henry II to the Union.* New ed., London and Dublin, 1889.

Barnes, G. *A Statistical Account of Ireland, Founded on Historical Facts, Chronologically Arranged.* Dublin, 1811.

Beckett, J. C. *Protestant Dissent in Ireland 1685–1780.* London, Faber & Faber, 1948.

—— *The Making of Modern Ireland.* New York, Alfred A. Knopf, 1966.

—— "The Government of the Church of Ireland in the Eighteenth Century," *Irish Historical Studies,* II (1940–1941), 280–302.

—— "Swift as an Ecclesiastical Statesman," in *Essays in British and Irish History in Honour of James Eadie Todd,* ed. H. A. Cronne, T. W. Moody, and D. B. Quinn. London, Frederick Muller, Ltd., 1949.

—— "The Irish Parliament in the Eighteenth Century," Belfast Natural History and Philosophical Society, *Proceedings,* 2nd ser., IV (1955), 17–37.

—— "Anglo-Irish Constitutional Relations in the Late Eighteenth Century," *Irish Historical Studies,* XIV (1964–1965), 20–38.

Blake, John W. "Transportation from Ireland to America, 1653–60," *Irish Historical Studies,* III (1942–1943), 267–281.

Bolton, F. R. *The Caroline Tradition of the Church of Ireland.* London, S.P.C.K., 1958.

Breatnach, R. A. "The End of a Tradition: A Survey of Eighteenth-century Gaelic Literature," *Studia Hibernica* (no. 1, 1961), 128–150.

Burns, Robert E. "The Irish Penal Code and Some of Its Historians," *Review of Politics*, XXI (1959), 276–299.

—— "The Irish Popery Laws: A Study of Eighteenth Century Legislation," *Review of Politics*, XXIV (1962), 485–508.

Butterfield, Herbert. "Eighteenth-century Ireland" [third section of an article entitled "Thirty Years' Work in Irish History"], *Irish Historical Studies*, XV (1966–1967), 376–390.

Carré, A. *L'influence des Huguenots français en Irlande aux XVII et XVIII siècles.* Paris, Presses Universitaires de France, 1937.

Casey, Thomas J., Jr. "Jonathan Swift and Political Economic Thought in Ireland," unpub. diss., Tulane University, 1971.

Chillingworth, H. R. "William Molyneux, A Herald of Democracy," *Hermathena*, no. 67 (May 1946), 60–67.

Clark, William Smith. *The Early Irish Stage.* Oxford, Clarendon Press, 1955.

—— *The Irish Stage in the Country Towns.* Oxford, Clarendon Press, 1965.

Clarke, Aidan. *The Old English in Ireland 1625–1642.* Ithaca, N.Y. Cornell University Press, 1966.

Clarke, Desmond. *Arthur Dobbs, Esquire, 1689–1765, Surveyor-General of Ireland, Prospector and Governor of North Carolina.* Chapel Hill, University of North Carolina Press, 1957.

Cokayne, G. E., *The Complete Peerage of England, Scotland, Ireland, Great Britain and the United Kingdom,* rev. Vicary Gibbs, Geoffrey White, and R. S. Lea. 12 vols. London, St. Catherine's Press, 1910–1959.

Connell, K. H. *The Population of Ireland 1750–1845.* Oxford, Clarendon Press, 1950.

—— "The Population of Ireland 1750–1840," *Economic History Review,* 2nd ser., 2 (1949), 278–289.

—— "Some Unsettled Problems of English and Irish Population History, 1750–1845," *Irish Historical Studies,* VII (1950–1951), 225–234.

Coonan, Thomas L. *The Irish Confederacy and the Puritan Revolution.* Dublin, Clonmore and Reynolds, 1954.

Corkery, Daniel. *The Hidden Ireland.* Dublin, W. H. Gill & Son, 1925.

Craig, Maurice. *Dublin 1660–1860.* London, Cresset Press, 1952.

Cullen, Lewis Michael. *Anglo-Irish Trade 1660–1800*. Manchester, Manchester University Press, 1968.

—— "The Value of Contemporary Printed Sources for Irish Economic History in the Eighteenth Century," *Irish Historical Studies*, XIV (1964–1965), 142–155.

—— "Problems in the Interpretation and Revision of Eighteenth-Century Irish Economic History," Royal Historical Society, *Transactions*, 5th ser., XVII (1967), 1–22.

—— "The Hidden Ireland: Reassessment," *Studia Hibernica* (no. 9, 1969), 7–47.

Davis, Thomas, *The Patriot Parliament of 1689*. 3rd ed., London, 1893.

Dickson, R. J. *Ulster Emigration to Colonial America, 1718–1755*. London, Routledge and Kegan Paul, 1966.

Dillon, Malcolm. *The History and Development of Banking in Ireland*. Dublin and London, 1889.

Donaldson, Alfred Gaston. *Some Comparative Aspects of Irish Law*. Durham, N.C., Duke University Press, 1957, Chaps. I and II.

Drake, Michael. "The Irish Demographic Crisis of 1740–41," *Historical Studies*, VI, ed. T. W. Moody. New York, Barnes and Noble, 1968, pp. 101–124.

—— "Marriage and Population Growth in Ireland 1750–1845," *Economic History Review*, 2nd ser., XVI (1963), 301–313.

Edwards, Robert Dudley. *Church and State in Tudor Ireland, A History of Penal Laws against Irish Catholics 1534–1603*. London, Longmans & Co., 1935.

—— and T. W. Moody. "The History of Poynings' Law, Part I, 1494–1615," *Irish Historical Studies*, II (1940–1941), 414–424.

Falkiner, Caesay Litton. *Studies in Irish History and Biography, Mainly in the Eighteenth Century*. London, Longmans & Co., 1902.

—— "Some Illustrations of the Commercial History of Dublin in the Eighteenth Century," Royal Irish Academy, *Proceedings*, XXIV (1903), 133–152.

Ferguson, O. W. *Jonathan Swift and Ireland*. Urbana, University of Illinois Press, 1962.

Freeman, T. W. *Ireland, Its Physical, Historical, Social and Economic Geography*. London, Methuen & Co., 1950.

Froude, James A. *The English in Ireland in the Eighteenth Century*. 3 vols., London, 1872–1874.

Gilbart, J. W. *The History of Banking in Ireland*. London, 1836.

Gilbert, J. T. *A History of the City of Dublin.* 3 vols., Dublin, 1861.

Gilbert, Sir Thomas. *An Account of the Parliament House Dublin with Notices of Parliaments held there 1661-1800.* Dublin, 1896.

Gill, Conrad. *The Rise of the Irish Linen Trade.* Oxford, Clarendon Press, 1925.

Gipson, Lawrence Henry. *The British Empire before the American Revolution.* 9 vols., I–III, Caldwell, Idaho, Caxton Printers, 1936. IV–IX, New York, A. A. Knopf, 1939–1956.

Goodwin, A. "Wood's Halfpence," *English Historical Review,* LI (1936), 647–674.

Hansard, George. *A Treatise on the Laws Relating to Aliens and Denization and Naturalization.* London, 1844.

Hanson, L. W. *Contemporary Printed Sources for British and Irish Economic History 1701-1750.* Cambridge, Cambridge University Press, 1936.

Hayes-McCoy, G. A. "Gaelic Society in Ireland in the Late Sixteenth Century," *Historical Studies,* IV, ed. G. A. Hayes-McCoy. London, Bowes & Bowes, 1963, pp. 45–61.

Heslinga, Marcus Willem. *The Irish Border as a Cultural Divide: A Contribution to the Study of Regionalism in the British Isles.* Assen, Netherlands, Van Gorcum, 1962.

Horner, J. *The Linen Trade of Europe during the Spinning Wheel Period.* Belfast, McCaw, Stevenson & Orr, 1920.

Hughes, J. L. J. "The Chief Secretaries in Ireland 1556–1921," *Irish Historical Studies,* VIII (1952–1953), 59–72.

James, Francis Godwin. *North Country Bishop.* New Haven, Yale University Press, 1956.

——— "Irish Smuggling in the Eighteenth Century," *Irish Historical Studies,* XII (1960–1961), 299–317.

——— "Irish Colonial Trade in the Eighteenth Century," *William and Mary Quarterly,* 3rd ser., II (1963), 274–284.

——— "The Irish Lobby in the Early Eighteenth Century," *English Historical Review,* LXXXI (1966), 543–557.

Johnston, Edith M. *Great Britain and Ireland 1760-1800.* Edinburgh, Oliver & Boyd for the University Court of the University of St. Andrew's, XXXX, 1963.

Jones, Mary Gwladys. *The Charity School Movement, A Study of Eighteenth Century Puritanism in Action.* Cambridge, Cambridge University Press, 1938.

Kearney, Hugh F. *Strafford in Ireland 1633-41.* Manchester, Manchester University Press, 1959.

———— "Mercantilism and Ireland 1620–40," in *Historical Studies*, I, ed. T. Desmond Williams. London, Bowes & Bowes, 1958, pp. 59–68.

———— "The Political Background to English Mercantilism 1695–1700," *Economic History Review*, 2nd ser., IX (1959), 484–496.

Kiernan, Thomas Joseph. *History of the Financial Administration of Ireland to 1817*. London, P. S. King and Son, 1930.

Large, David. "The Irish House of Commons 1769," *Irish Historical Studies*, XI (1958–1959), 18–45.

Lecky, W. E. H. *Ireland in the Eighteenth Century*. 5 vols., London, 1892. [These volumes are composed of the sections dealing with Ireland from his *History of England in the Eighteenth Century*. 8 vols., New York, 1891.]

Lee, Grace Lawless. *The Huguenot Settlements in Ireland*. London, Longmans and Co., 1936.

Leyburn, James G. *The Scotch-Irish: A Social History*. Chapel Hill, University of North Carolina Press, 1962.

McCracken, J. L. "The Undertakers in Ireland and their Relations with the Lord Lieutenant 1724–1771," unpub. M.A. thesis, Queen's University, Belfast, 1941.

———— "The Conflict between the Irish Administration and Parliament 1735–56," *Irish Historical Studies*, III (1942–1943), 159–179.

———— "Irish Parliamentary Elections 1727–68," *Irish Historical Studies*, V (1946–1947), 209–230.

———— "The Irish Viceroyalty, 1760–73," in *Essays in British and Irish History in Honour of James Eadie Todd*, ed. H. A. Cronne, T. W. Moody, and D. B. Quinn. London, Frederick Muller, Ltd., 1949.

McDowell, Robert Brendan. *Irish Public Opinion, 1750–1800*. London, Faber & Faber, 1944.

MacGeehin, Maureen [for other writings by her, see Maureen Wall]. "The Catholics of the Towns and the Quarterage Dispute in Eighteenth-Century Ireland," *Irish Historical Studies*, VIII (1952–1953), 91–114.

McNally, Sir Henry. "The Militia Array of 1756 in Ireland," *The Irish Sword*, I (1949–1953), 94–104.

MacNeill, John Gordon Swift. *The Constitutional and Parliamentary History of Ireland till the Union*. Dublin, Talbot Press, 1917.

McNeill, William. "The Influence of the Potato on Irish History," unpub. diss., Cornell University, 1947.

Macpherson, Davis. *Annals of Commerce, Manufactures, and Commercial Circumstances of Ireland.* London, 1809.

McSwiney, P. "Eighteenth Century Kinsale," Cork Historical and Archaeological Society, *Journal,* 2nd ser., XLIII (1938), 75–95.

Mahoney, Thomas H. D. *Edmund Burke and Ireland.* Cambridge, Mass., Harvard University Press, 1960.

Malcolmson, A. P. W. "Election Politics in the Borough of Antrim 1750–1800," *Irish Historical Studies,* XVII (1970–1971), 32–57.

Maxwell, Constantia. *Dublin under the Georges, 1714–1830.* Rev. ed., London, Faber and Faber, 1956.

—— *Country and Town in Ireland.* Rev. ed., Dundalk, W. Tempest, 1949.

—— *The Stranger in Ireland.* London, Jonathan Cape, 1954.

Mayes, C. R. "The Early Stuarts and the Irish Peerage," *English Historical Review,* LXXIII (1958), 227–251.

Moody, T. W. *The Londonderry Plantation 1609–1641.* Belfast, W. Mullen & Son, 1939.

—— "The Irish Parliament under Elizabeth and James I," Royal Irish Academy, *Proceedings,* XLV (1939), 41–81.

Mulvey, Helen F. "Modern Irish History since 1940: A Bibliographical Survey (1600–1922)," *Historian,* XXVII (1965), 516–559, reprinted in *Changing Views on British History, Essays on Historical Writing since 1939,* ed. Elizabeth Chapin Furber. Cambridge, Mass., Harvard University Press, 1966.

Munter, Robert. *The Irish Newspapers 1685–1760.* Cambridge, Cambridge University Press, 1967.

Murray, Alice E. *History of Commercial and Financial Relations between England and Ireland from the Period of the Restoration.* London, London School of Economics and Political Science, 1903.

Murray, R. H. *Revolutionary Ireland and Its Settlement.* London, Macmillan & Co., 1911.

Newenham, Thomas. *View of the Natural, Political, and Commercial Circumstances of Ireland.* London, 1809.

Nicholls, George. *A History of the Irish Poor Law.* London, 1856.

O'Boyle, James Canon. *The Irish Colleges on the Continent, Their Origin and History.* Dublin, Browne and Nolan, 1935.

O'Brien, George. *Economic History of Ireland in the Eighteenth Century.* Dublin, Maunsel & Co., 1918.

O'Brien, R. Barry, ed. *Studies in Irish History 1649–1775.* Dublin, Irish Literary Society, 1903.

O'Connell, Maurice R. *Irish Politics and Social Conflict in the Age of the American Revolution*. Philadelphia, University of Pennsylvania Press, 1965.

O'Connell, Mrs. Morgan John. *The Last Colonel of the Irish Brigade*. 2 vols., London, 1872.

O'Conor, Matthew. *The History of the Irish Catholics*. Dublin, 1813.

O'Sullivan, William. *The Economic History of Cork City from the Earliest Times to the Act of Union*. Cork, Cork University Press, 1937.

Phillips, Walter Alison, ed. *History of the Church of Ireland from the Earliest Times to the Present Day*. 3 vols., London, Oxford University Press, 1933.

Plowden, Francis. *Historical Review of the State of Ireland from the Invasion of that Country under Henry II, to its Union with Great Britain*. London, 1803.

Porritt, Edward. *The Unreformed House of Commons*. 2 vols., Cambridge, Cambridge University Press, 1909.

Prendergast, John Patrick. *The Cromwellian Settlement in Ireland*. New York, 1868.

—— *Ireland from the Restoration to the Revolution 1660 to 1690*. London, 1887.

Quinn, David Beers. *The Elizabethans and the Irish*. Ithaca, N.Y., Cornell University Press, 1966.

—— "Ireland and Sixteenth Century European Expansion," *Historical Studies*, I, ed. T. Desmond Williams. London, Bowes & Bowes, 1958.

Reid, J. S. *History of the Presbyterian Church of Ireland*, ed. W. D. Killen. 3 vols., Belfast, 1867.

Richardson, H. G., and G. O. Sayles. *The Irish Parliament in the Middle Ages*. Philadelphia, University of Pennsylvania Press, 1952.

Sadlier, Thomas V., and Page L. Dickinson, *Georgian Mansions in Ireland with some Account of the Evolution of Georgian Architecture and Decoration*. Dublin, Dublin University Press, 1915.

Simms, J. G. *The Williamite Confiscation in Ireland 1690–1703*. London, Faber & Faber, 1956.

—— *The Treaty of Limerick*. Dundalk, Dublin Historical Association, 1961.

—— *Jacobite Ireland 1685–91*. London, Routledge and Kegan Paul, 1969.

—— "Connacht in the Eighteenth Century," *Irish Historical Studies*, XI (1958–1959), 116–133.

—— "The Making of a Penal Law, 1703–04," *Irish Historical Studies*, XII (1960–1961), 105–118.

—— "Irish Catholics and the Parliamentary Franchise, 1692–1728," *Irish Historical Studies*, XII (1960–1961), 28–37.

—— "The Irish Parliament of 1713," *Historical Studies*, IV, ed. G. A. Hayes-McCoy. London, Bowes and Bowes, 1963.

—— "The Seventeenth Century (1603–1702)," [first section of an article entitled "Thirty Years' Work in Irish History"], *Irish Historical Studies*, XV (1966–1967), 366–375.

—— "The Bishops' Banishment Act of 1697 (9 Will. III, c. i)," *Irish Historical Studies*, XVII (1970–1971), 185–199.

Smiles, S. *The Huguenots, their Settlements, Churches, Industries in England and Ireland.* London, 1867.

Smither, Peter. *The Life of Joseph Addison.* Oxford, Clarendon Press, 1954.

Sykes, Norman. "Ussher as a Churchman," *Hermathena* (no. 88, 1956), pp. 59–80.

Taylor, Aline Mackensie. *The Patrimony of James Quin: The Legend and the Facts*, Tulane Studies in English, VIII, 55–106, New Orleans, Tulane University, 1958.

Tuckey, Francis H. *Remembrancer or Annals of the County and City of Cork.* Cork, 1837.

Wall, Maureen. *The Penal Laws, 1691–1760.* Dundalk, Dublin Historical Association, 1961.

—— "The Rise of a Catholic Middle Class in Eighteenth-Century Ireland," *Irish Historical Studies*, XI (1958–1959), 91–115.

Webb, J. J. *Industrial Dublin since 1698 and the Silk Industry in Dublin.* Dublin, Maunsel and Co., 1913.

—— *The Guilds of Dublin.* Dublin, 1929.

Went, Arthur E. J. "The Irish Hake Fishery, 1504–1824," Cork Historical and Archaeological Society, *Journal*, LI (1946), 41–51.

Wight, T., and J. Rutty. *Rise and Progress of the People Called Quakers in Ireland.* 4th ed., London, 1811.

Zook, G. F. "Economic Relations of England and Ireland, 1660–1750, *Historical Outlook*, XIII (1922), 235–245.

Index

261; ministerial responsibility of, 258. *See also* Cabinet

Molasses, Irish duty on, 195

Molasses Act, 159, 171, 193n10

Molesworth, Robert, viscount, 104n 46, 107n55, 109; writings of, 305–306

Molyneux, Samuel (?), 107n55

Molyneux, Sir Thomas, 38

Molyneux, William, 94, 108, 110, 139, 244, 251; background and career of, 38–39; arguments of, for Irish autonomy, 39–42; influence of, 305–306

Molyneux family, 241

Monks, Catholic, 234, 236

Montgomerie, Governor John, 137

Montgomery, Hugh, *see* Mount Alexander, earl of

Montserrat, 300

Moody, T. W., 302

Moore, Edward, 5th earl of Drogheda, 98n35

Morfi, La Petite, 298

Moryson, Fynes, 7

Mount Alexander, Hugh Montgomery, earl of, 61–62

Murray, Alice Effie, 192, 193

Mutiny Act, English, 175

Mutiny Act, Irish, proposed and defeated, 32, 175

Namier, Sir Lewis, 257, 309n114

Nantes, Irish emigration to, 298

Naples, 247

Nationalism, Irish, 94, 108–109, 288, 302. *See also* Patriotism

Naturalization laws, 220 and n2

Navigation Acts, 55; changes in favoring Ireland, 62, 154, 156–158, 214; effect of, upon Ireland, 191, 194, 200

Navy, British, 180, 211 and n74

Negroes, 289n36, 301, 303, 306n103

Nepotism, 166. *See also* Patronage

Netherlands, 94

Neville, Henry, 132

Nevis, 296, 300

New England, 202, 218, 301; Dominion of, 27, 277

New Hampshire, 137

New Jersey, 82n100, 296

New York, 27, 137, 138, 176 and n62, 277, 287, 290, 296, 304; governor's stipend in, 282n12; Irish emigration to, 301, 303; party divisions in, 49

New York City, 146, 200n37, 289

Newcastle, Thomas Pelham-Hollis, duke of, 122, 127, 142, 176, 177, 279n3; and Irish policy, 133, 170–171

Newcastle, Delaware, 299n76

Newenham, Thomas, 190, 291

Newgate (Irish), 300

Newmarket, 64

Newport, Robert Jocelyn, viscount, 187

Newry, population of, 316

Newspapers, colonial, 304–305

Newspapers, Irish, 220n3, 248n85, 300; and politics, 253n6, 290; concern with America, 304

Nicolson, William, bishop of Derry, 91–92nn20, 23, 104, 105, 106, 107, 113, 117, 239, 247

Nobility, Irish, 242. *See also* Peers, Irish

Nonconformists, *see* Dissenters

Normans, 218

North, Frederick, lord, 272, 273, 275

Northey, Sir Edward, 58, 64

Northumberland, Hugh Percy, 2nd duke of, 268; as lord lieutenant, 266–267, 280

Nottingham, Daniel Finch, 2nd earl of, 29, 30, 58, 65; supports Irish Test Act, 57

Nugent, Robert, earl of, 279 and n5

Nullification in colonies and Ireland, 293

O'Brien, George, 193, 215

O'Brien, Henry, viscount Tadcaster,

Harvard Historical Monographs

16. The Huancavelica Mercury Mine: A Contribution to the History of the Bourbon Renaissance in the Spanish Empire. By A. P. Whitaker. 1941.*

17. The Palace School of Muhammad the Conqueror. By Barnette Miller. 1941.*

18. A Cistercian Nunnery in Mediaeval Italy: The Story of Rifreddo in Saluzzo, 1220–1300. By Catherine E. Boyd. 1943.*

19. Vassi and Fideles in the Carolingian Empire. By C. E. Odegaard. 1945.*

20. Judgment by Peers. By Barnaby C. Keeney. 1949.

21. The Election to the Russian Constituent Assembly of 1917. By O. H. Radkey. 1950.

22. Conversion and the Poll Tax in Early Islam. By Daniel C. Dennett. 1950.*

23. Albert Gallatin and the Oregon Problem. By Frederick Merk. 1950.*

24. The Incidence of the Emigration during the French Revolution. By Donald Greer. 1951.*

25. Alterations of the Words of Jesus as Quoted in the Literature of the Second Century. By Leon E. Wright. 1952.*

26. Liang Ch'i-ch'ao and the Mind of Modern China. By Joseph R. Levenson. 1953.*

27. The Japanese and Sun Yat-sen. By Marius B. Jansen. 1954.

28. English Politics in the Early Eighteenth Century. By Robert Walcott, Jr. 1956.*

29. The Founding of the French Socialist Party (1893–1905). By Aaron Noland. 1956.*

30. British Labour and the Russian Revolution, 1917–1924. By Stephen Richards Graubard. 1956.*

31. RKFDV: German Resettlement and Population Policy, 1939–1945. By Robert L. Koehl. 1957.

32. Disarmament and Peace in British Politics, 1914–1919. By Gerda Richards Crosby. 1957.

33. Concordia Mundi: The Career and Thought of Guillaume Postel (1510–1581). By W. J. Bouwsma. 1957.

34. Bureaucracy, Aristocracy, and Autocracy: The Prussian Experience, 1660–1815. By Hans Rosenberg. 1958.

35. Exeter, 1540–1640: The Growth of an English County Town. By Wallace T. MacCaffrey. 1958. 2nd ed., 1973.

36. Historical Pessimism in the French Enlightenment. By Henry Vyverberg. 1958.

58. The Fall of Stein. By R. C. Raack. 1965.
59. The French Apanages and the Capetian Monarchy, 1224–1328. By Charles T. Wood. 1966.
60. Congressional Insurgents and the Party System, 1909–1916. By James Holt. 1967.
61. The Rumanian National Movement in Transylvania, 1780–1849. By Keith Hitchins. 1969.
62. Sisters of Liberty: Marseille, Lyon, Paris and the Reaction to a Centralized State, 1868–1871. By Louis M. Greenberg. 1971.
63. Old Hatreds and Young Hopes: The French Carbonari against the Bourbon Restoration. By Alan B. Spitzer. 1971.
64. To the Maginot Line: The Politics of French Military Preparation in the 1920's. By Judith M. Hughes. 1971.
65. Florentine Public Finances in the Early Renaissance, 1400–1433. By Anthony Molho. 1971.
66. Provincial Magistrates and Revolutionary Politics in France, 1789–1795. By Philip Dawson. 1972.
67. The East India Company and Army Reform, 1783–1798. By Raymond Callahan. 1972.
68. Ireland in the Empire, 1688–1770: A History of Ireland from the Williamite Wars to the Eve of the American Revolution. By Francis Godwin James. 1973.